European Studies in Social Psychology

Social representations

European studies in social psychology

Editorial Board: J. M. F. JASPARS, University of Oxford; WILLEM DOISE, Université de Genève; COLIN FRASER, University of Cambridge; SERGE MOSCOVICI, Ecole des Hautes Etudes en Sciences Sociales; KLAUS R. SCHERER, Justus-Liebig-Universität Giessen; MARIO VON CRANACH, Universität Bern.

The series is jointly published by the Cambridge University Press and the Editions de la Maison des Sciences de l'Homme, in close collaboration with the Laboratoire Européen de Psychologie Sociale of the Maison, as part of the joint publishing agreement established in 1977 between the Fondation de la Maison des Sciences de l'Homme and the Syndics of the Cambridge University Press.

It consists mainly of specially commissioned volumes on specific themes, particularly those linking work in social psychology with other disciplines. It will also include occasional volumes on Current issues'.

Cette collection est publiée en co-édition par Cambridge University Press et les Editions de la Maison des Sciences de l'Homme en collaboration étroite avec le Laboratoire Européen de Psychologie Sociale de la Maison. Elle s'intègre dans le programme de co-édition établi en 1977 par la Fondation de la Maison des Sciences de l'Homme et les Syndics de Cambridge University Press.

Elle comprend essentiellement des ouvrages sur des thèmes spécifiques permettant de mettre en rapport la psychologie sociale et d'autres disciplines, avec à l'occasion des volumes consacrés à des 'recherches en cours'.

Already published:

The analysis of action: recent theoretical and empirical advances, edited by Mario von Cranach and Rom Harré
Current issues in European social psychology, volume I, edited by Willem Doise and Serge Moscovici
Social interaction in individual development, edited by Willem Doise and Augusto Palmonari
Advances in the social psychology of language, edited by Colin Fraser and Klaus R. Scherer
Social markers in speech, edited by Klaus R. Scherer and Howard Giles
Social identity and intergroup relations, edited by Henri Tajfel

Social representations

Edited by
Robert M. Farr
and
Serge Moscovici

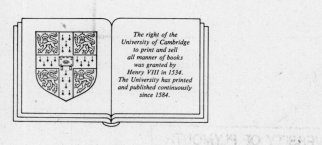

*The right of the
University of Cambridge
to print and sell
all manner of books
was granted by
Henry VIII in 1534.
The University has printed
and published continuously
since 1584.*

Cambridge University Press

Cambridge
London   New York   New Rochelle
Melbourne   Sydney

Editions de la Maison des Sciences de l'Homme

Paris

Published by the Press Syndicate of the University of Cambridge
The Pitt Building, Trumpington Street, Cambridge CB2 1RP
32 East 57th Street, New York, NY 10022, USA
296 Beaconsfield Parade, Middle Park, Melbourne 3206, Australia
and Editions de la Maison des Sciences de l'Homme
54 Boulevard Raspail, 75270 Paris Cedex 06

First published 1984

Printed in Great Britain by
Redwood Burn Limited, Trowbridge, Wiltshire

Library of Congress catalogue card number: 83–18823

British Library Cataloguing in Publication Data
Social representations.—European studies in social psychology)
1. Social groups 2. Interpersonal relations
3. Social psychology
I. Farr, Robert M. 2. Moscovici, S.
III. Series
3023   HM132

ISBN 0 521 24800 0
ISBN 2 7351 0066 9 hard covers (France only)

R. B.

Contents

Contributors

JEAN-CLAUDE ABRIC
Laboratoire de Psychologie Sociale, Université de Provence

MARIE-JOSÉ CHOMBART DE LAUWE
Centre d'Ethnologie Sociale et de Psychosociologie, Montrouge

JEAN PAUL CODOL
Laboratoire de Psychologie Sociale, Université de Provence

IRWIN DEUTSCHER
Department of Sociology, The University of Akron

WILLEM DOISE
Faculté de Psychologie, Université de Genève

ROBERT FARR
Department of Social Psychology, The London School of Economics and Political Science

CLAUDE FLAMENT
Département de Psychologie, Université de Provence

FAY FRANSELLA
Centre for Personal Construct Psychology, London

COLIN FRASER
Churchill College, University of Cambridge

JOS JASPARS
Department of Experimental Psychology, University of Oxford

DENISE JODELET
Laboratoire de Psychologie Sociale, Ecole des Hautes Etudes en Sciences Sociales, Paris

RENÉ KAËS
Institut de Formation aux Pratiques Psychologiques, Sociologiques et Educatives, Université Lyon 2

STANLEY MILGRAM
The Graduate School and University Center of the City University of New York

SERGE MOSCOVICI
Laboratoire de Psychologie Sociale, Ecole des Hautes Etudes en Sciences Sociales, Paris

JEAN PAILHOUS
Laboratoire de Psychologie de l'Apprentissage, Institut de Biométrie Humaine et d'Orientation Professionnelle, Marseille

RAGNAR ROMMETVEIT
Institute of Psychology, University of Oslo

Preface

The order in which our names appear on this volume is alphabetical. We first started working together on the topic of social representations in 1977 when one of us (RMF) was a CNRS/SSRC Professorial Fellow at the Ecole des Hautes Etudes en Sciences Sociales in Paris. At Moscovici's suggestion I used my period of study leave there to become better acquainted with the French literature on social representations. Our continuing collaboration over the intervening years has been greatly facilitated by this CNRS/SSRC programme of cultural exchange between our two countries.

Prior to 1977, my own acquaintance with the literature on social representations was confined to a reading of Herzlich's refreshing little volume *Health and Illness*, which Douglas Graham had translated into English in 1973. I was delighted to discover, on reading the French literature, an impressively rich and highly varied tradition of research dating from the late 1950s. Little, as yet, of this literature has been translated into other languages. We decided to convene an international colloquium on Social Representations. This took place from 8 to 10 January 1979 at the Maison des Sciences de l'Homme in Paris within the context of the Laboratoire Européen de Psychologie Sociale. It was Clemens Heller, Administrateur Adjoint at the Maison, who made this meeting possible and Adriana Touraine, his assistant, who helped to ensure that the occasion was a social, as well as a scientific, success.

This volume is a direct outcome of that meeting. The majority of the participants were French. Their papers reflect their own empirical studies of a variety of social representations. A minority of the participants came from outside of this tradition. They sought, in their contribution, to locate this peculiarly French tradition of research in some sort of wider international setting. The theory of social representations, as set out here by Moscovici, explains how the strange

ix

and the unfamiliar become, in time, the familiar. It follows from the theory that those who approach this French tradition of research from the outside will assimilate it to traditions of research with which they are more likely to be familiar (e.g. their knowledge of G. H. Mead; or of the symbolic interactionist tradition of social psychology within American sociology; or of cognitive psychology etc.). This is, more or less, what happened at the colloquium. All the participants subsequently re-wrote their contributions in the light of the discussions which took place there; some more than once. The present volume is based on those re-written contributions.

Our aim in publishing the volume in English is to facilitate the diffusion of a knowledge of this tradition of research throughout the English-speaking world. The present work was made possible thanks to the close links which have developed, in recent years, between the Maison des Sciences de l'Homme in Paris and Cambridge University Press. The Maison provided some of the funds for the translation of the various articles from French into English. We are indebted to the very able and experienced team of translators who have assisted us. We are particularly grateful to Professor Kenneth Varty of the Department of French Literature and Language at the University of Glasgow for his assistance in recruiting colleagues and acquaintances who were both able and willing to undertake the translation of particular chapters. We have used our editorial discretion to alter translations where we believe this might help the reader to better comprehend the original.

We decided to include as comprehensive a list as possible of research on social representations. This includes a listing of theses presented for higher degrees at French universities. The list is up to date at the time of going to press. We have done this in the hope and expectation that readers may wish to consult the original French sources of much of the work commented on in this volume. We anticipate that many Canadian social scientists will wish to read the French originals.

I am particularly indebted to my secretary at the University of Glasgow, Mrs Anna Taylor, for her cheerfulness and efficiency in preparing the successive drafts of many of the chapters. I wish to thank my wife Ann-Marie for redrawing some of the artwork for this volume, and my children Angus and Fiona for their patience while this volume was in preparation. I am also grateful to the Maison des Sciences de l'Homme where I was a guest for a month whilst preparing the manuscript for publication. We wish to acknowledge the skilful way in which Kate Owen, of Cambridge University Press, has handled the managerial aspects of the publication of this volume and the meticulous attention to detail which Chris Lyall Grant, our subeditor, has given to the complexities of a text that was originally written in more than one language.

April 1983   R. M. F.

S. M.

Foreword

IRWIN DEUTSCHER

My immediate reaction to the colloquium invitation extended by Serge Moscovici and Robert Farr was one of disbelief: a group of European psychologists gathering to discuss their work on 'Durkheimian psychology?' A contradition of terms I scoffed, for Emile Durkheim was surely the purest disciplinary chauvinist of them all and reductionism the greatest sociological sin. It was well that I kept my smug thoughts to myself. The process of doing my homework for the colloquium and being attentive to what other members were doing revealed a new Emile Durkheim to me. More important, it revealed a vibrant new social psychology grounded in everyday human processes. This novel and lively enterprise is reflected in the creative contributions to this volume. But what do these diverse articles share in common?

I was asked to prepare a paper relating the key concept of this contemporary French social psychology with the American tradition of symbolic interactionist social psychology. That central concept, I was informed, is 'social representations' – a term which became the title of this volume. In the papers which follow, that concept will be encountered more than any other. It is indeed the cement that binds this set of studies together. Yet, I could nowhere recall Durkheim employing such a concept until I encountered Moscovici's explanation that he preferred the word 'social' to the more familiar 'collective representations.' It was some comfort to learn, as Jaspars and Fraser admit in their chapter, that I was not the only Anglo-Saxon to be bemused by Moscovici's use of this concept. But now I had my clue and I could begin to try to fathom this mystery.

In this manner I was led to discover the Durkheim who reminded us in *The Elementary Forms of the Religious Life* that 'Surely, the soldier who falls while defending his flag does not believe that he sacrifices himself for a bit of cloth.' This is the Durkheim who, after commenting in *Suicide* that religion 'is the system of symbols by means of which society becomes conscious of itself,' proceeds to observe that this applies 'not only to religion, but to law, morals, customs, political institutions, pedagogical practices, etc., in a word to all forms of collective life.' There emerges in Durkheim the centrality of the shared symbol to all of human social life. Symbols stand for something other than their objective selves; they are more than 'a bit of cloth.' It is this subjective, interpretive idea of social representations on which the social psychology found in this volume rests. Moscovici, in his definitive chapter, both extends and limits the concept. In fact, picking up where Durkheim left off, he deliberately converts the concept into a phenomenon subject to analysis.

The papers in this volume suggest a movement which seeks an alternative to dominant patterns of thought (and thoughtlessness) regarding human behavior and social processes. In this sense, these neo-Durkheimians are reminiscent of the Frankfurt School of critical sociology, of the radical psychology and sociology of the sixties, of ethnomethodology, of humanistic sociology and psychology, of symbolic interactionism and, generally, of the phenomenological movement in the social sciences. It seems to me they are distinguished not only by their commitment to the concept of social representations, but also by their methodological style and their critique and rejection of contemporary fashions in theory and methodology.

Although this French School may be a social psychology, it seems more akin methodologically and theoretically to cognitive psychology. The chapters in this book suggest a (sometimes reluctant) rejection of the scientism which came to define modern social science in behaviorist terms and an equal rejection of the positivism which came to define it as natural (i.e. 'real') science. Farr has serious reservations about the appropriateness of laboratory experimentation for the study of social representations and Moscovici urges the collection of data which illuminate the transmission of the social images we all carry. To achieve this Moscovici sees the need for observations in natural settings. Chombart de Lauwe is openly anti-experimental, employing media imagery as her basic data and analyzing novels and films qualitatively through time to determine their influence on children's self-images. Jodelet's work on body images and self-concept is based on depth interviews; and in his studies of mental maps of cities Milgram has abandoned the laboratory.

Yet many of the contributors to this volume are laboratory experimenters and their chapters report experiments concerned with social representations. Experiments reported here by Abric, Codol, and Flament document the manner in which different definitions of what is really happening lead to different kinds of relationship and have different consequences for the parties involved. We find explicit in the experiments of Abric and Flament an awareness reminiscent of American social psychologists, such as Robert Rosenthal, that the experiment itself is a social situation worthy of study in its own right. Reactivity, experimental effects, experimenter effects, interviewer effects, observer effects, can all come to be recognized not as undesirable methodological artifacts, but as normal parts of the process of social interaction and the definition of the situation. Under these conditions, the experiment becomes a social representation which itself demands understanding. In fact, Farr urges such research on psychological experiments as social representations.

The empirical documentation of this symbolic imagery – these social representations – is only part of what Moscovici and his colleagues envision as their research program. He urges us to consider how such imagery is generated and how it evolves and is maintained as a shared representation. There is a heavy emphasis in this volume on social process in the smaller sense and history in the larger sense – not as context or framework, but as an integral ongoing part of the phenomenon the investigator is attempting to grasp. Thus Kaës' research on group psychotherapy becomes the study of the ongoing social production of groups as social realities; the fifteen years which separate Jodelet's two samples enable her to demonstrate dramatic shifts in sex differences, and Chombart de Lauwe traces her analysis of representations of children through three eras from pre-1914 to the contemporary period.

What we have then is an emerging self-conscious perspective in search of shape and form. It has leadership and it has a central concept. It shares a view of society as a symbolic enterprise and, although it remains for the time hospitable to experimental evidence, it scorns the behaviorist assumption of human beings as automatic responders to objective stimuli. Many of the contributors to this volume share a conception of human beings as autonomous creative interactors rather than as passive reactors buffeted by external forces over which they have no control. A commitment to Durkheim's image of social representations as guidelines to social actions makes it difficult to retain not only a behaviorist position but also the positivist position which is said to have created an authentic social *science*. For science assumes a real objective world with real components which can be examined piece by piece in an effort to grasp the whole. To reject all of this and to assume in its stead that what needs studying is Durkheim's subjective phenomena of social representations is a risky business. It is risky not because it is unreasonable, but because in the recent past such heresy has resulted in disciplinary banishment by the true scientific believers in both psychology and sociology.

It is indeed a dangerous heresy to pretend that what is real and worthy of study is what members of society define as real, since that is what they act upon. To expose the sources and evolution of such definitions it is necessary to study realities other than those created by scientists; one must explore what members of society define as real. My characterization is idealized and certainly is not shared by all contributors to this volume. They may agree that society needs to be viewed as a symbolic enterprise, but there are vast differences in the degree to which this assumption is held. At the extreme we find Rommetveit's ethnomethodological treatment of language which is explicitly in the phenomenological stream, leaning as it does on Schutz, Wittgenstein, Garfinkel and Berger and Luckmann. Rommetveit does not treat kindly those mainstream social scientists who have, in his words, yielded to the 'devil's seductive monism.'

If the rigorous laboratory experimenters included in this volume are at the other extreme – perhaps among those who have yielded to the devil – then there is also a large middle ground of those scholars who are in the process of wrestling with a departure from the comfortable traditional scientific mode which nurtured them. Milgram and Jodelet examine maps of Paris formed by people peculiarly located in and functioning in the city. They see their subjects as creating a reality which facilitates dealing with everyday life and work and mobility in a complex physical and social environment. But Milgram's discussion in this volume clearly views these mental maps as a distortion of an objective city (presumably the reality created by cartographers). The job of the social scientist according to Milgram is to contrast conventional wisdom about the city with its 'deeper reality.' Pailhous, in his studies of social space, makes the same positivist assumption when he studies 'distortions' between the real geographic configuration and the image his subjects form of it.

We have, then, a wide range of perspectives from which the contributors of this volume view their joint undertaking. There are similarities and there are differences; there are agreements and there are disagreements, yet collectively the contributors to this volume have provided social science with something of value – the seeds of a new social representation – a new collective imagery of what human behavior and social processes are all about. It is perhaps unique primarily in that, rather than a new generation of young turks rebelling against the foolishness of their elders, we have a reputable set of mature scholars, reconsidering the foolishness of their own youth.

I have been inclined toward concern for disciplinary integrity in the social sciences and somewhat skeptical about those watered-down enterprises referred to as 'inter-disciplinary' or even 'multi-disciplinary.' Like Durkheim I believed in the importance of both individual representations and social representations and felt it necessary for psychologists to do psychology and sociologists to do sociology, for if they did not, then who would? Yet it is troublesome that the traditional disciplines tend to become entrenched political entities which demand loyalty to dominant ideologies. They are ritualistic in their methods, unconcerned about either the theoretical or practical relevance of their research and intolerant of innovation. This new Durkheimian school may presage a realignment of the traditional social science disciplines. Sharp ideological, methodological, and theoretical cleavages exist in all of the social sciences – and they are the same cleavages. Perhaps it is time that traditional academic departments were shaken up and re-cast into more homogeneous entities. Surely, for example, behaviorists have more in common with each other, whether they be psychologists or sociologists, than with current colleagues who see the world differently?

It is little wonder then, that many of the contributors to this volume feel uncertain that they 'belong.' Jaspars and Fraser, for example, suggest that this French School finds in Durkheim a rallying-point for distinguishing their Gallic selves from Anglo-Saxon colleagues. Abric openly rejects the urging of some of the most prominent investigators of social representations – Moscovici, Kaës, Herzlich, Chombart de Lauwe – for naturalistic settings of research. He insists on the validity of the laboratory studies of social representations undertaken by himself and others. Rommetveit draws on a body of literature in his work which has practically no overlap with the references found in other chapters; can he feel comfortably that he 'belongs?' Pailhous admits to feeling out of place because he is a cognitive psychologist rather than a social psychologist. And I am a sociologist! What am I doing in this company of psychologists of whatever kind?

Yet, with all this strangeness there is a great affinity. I, for example, find this a uniquely appropriate book for teaching sociologists what some of us call social psychology. It is rich not only in theory and method, but in example. We find here a mixture of reasoned polemics, rigorous experiments and creative field studies. Above all, it is a distinctly sociological social psychology. Not only is the central thrust peculiarly Durkheimian, but some contributors lean heavily on Thomas and Znaniecki (Jaspars and Fraser, Deutscher) while still others view this enterprise as a sociology of knowledge (Farr, Milgram, Fransella).

Regardless of discipline, the scholar will find here a refreshing rejection of the institutionalized holiness of much contemporary psychology and sociology. There is no trace here of that banal formalism – that worship of design and technique over substance and content which began to plague the social sciences soon after the second world war. We find here no love of design for its own sake, no mystification of findings with obscure statistics, no obsession with the computer as if somehow it replaced rather than facilitated the work of the thoughtful scholar. Throughout the studies of these Durkheimian psychologists, this French School, there is an unusual concern for the validity of conclusions rather than stopping with the standard statement of reliability of measurement. Finally, it is a pleasure to discover a social psychology which takes its subjects seriously. It is among groups such as this that a valid, searching social science can be maintained during these trying dark ages when the driving force of our disciplines is toward scientific respectability and prestige. It is among groups such as this that true scholarship and the quest for knowledge and utility are maintained. In this volume there are no blind repetitions of other people's clever experiments or re-analyses of other people's data sets. This book is different.

Part 1
Perspectives on social representations

1. The phenomenon of social representations*

SERGE MOSCOVICI

I Thinking considered as environment

(1) Primitive thought, science, and everyday understanding

The belief on which primitive thought – if such a term is still acceptable – is based is a belief in the 'mind's unlimited power' to *shape* reality, to penetrate and activate it and to determine the course of events. The belief on which modern scientific thought is based is the exact opposite, that is, a belief in the 'limitless power of objects' to *shape* thought, to wholly determine its evolution and to be interiorised in and by the mind. In the first case, thought is seen as acting on reality; in the second, as reaction to reality; in the one, the object emerges as a replica of thought; in the other, thought is a replica of the object; and if, for the former, our wishes become reality – or wishful thinking – then, for the latter, to think amounts to turning reality into our wishes, to depersonalising them. But since the two attitudes are symmetrical, they can only have the same cause, and one with which we have long been familiar: man's instinctive dread of powers he cannot subdue and his endeavour to compensate for this impotence imaginatively. The one difference being that, whereas the primitive mind dreads the forces of nature, the scientific mind dreads the power of thought. Insofar as the first has enabled us to survive for millions of years, and the second to achieve so much in a few centuries, we must assume that each, in its way, represents a true aspect of the relation between our inner and outer worlds; an aspect, moreover, which is well worth investigating.

Social psychology is obviously a manifestation of scientific thought and, therefore, when studying the cognitive system it postulates that:

(i) normal individuals react to phenomena, people or events in the same way as scientists or statisticians do and

*Translated by Sacha Rabinovitch

(ii) understanding consists in information processing.

In other words, we perceive the world, such as it is, and all our perceptions, ideas and attributions are responses to stimuli from the physical or quasi-physical environment in which we live. What distinguishes us is the need to assess beings and objects correctly, to grasp reality fully; and what distinguishes the environment is its autonomy, its independence of us or even, might one say, its indifference to us and to our needs and desires. What are known as cognitive biases, subjective distortions, affective tendencies obviously do exist, as we are all aware, but they are precisely biases, distortions and tendencies in relation to a model, to rules, seen as the norm.

Yet it seems to me that some ordinary facts contradict these two postulates:

(a) *First*, the familiar observation that we are unaware of some of the most obvious things; that we fail to see what is before our very eyes. It is as though our sight or our perception were dimmed, so that a given class of persons, either because of their age – e.g. the old for the young and the young for the old – or because of their race – e.g. blacks for some whites, etc. – become invisible when, in fact, they are 'staring us in the face'. This is how a gifted black writer describes such a phenomenon:

I am an invisible man. No, I am not a spook like those who haunted Edgar Allan Poe; nor am I one of your Hollywood-movie ectoplasms. I am a man of substance, of flesh and bones, fibre and liquids – and I might even be said to possess a mind. I am invisible, understand, simply because people refuse to see me. Like the 'bodiless' head you see sometimes in circus sideshows, it is as though I have been surrounded by mirrors of hard, distorting glass. When they approach me they see only my surroundings, themselves, or figments of their imagination – indeed anything except me.   (Ellison, 1965, p. 7)

This invisibility is not due to any lack of information conveyed to the eyeball, but to a pre-established fragmentation of reality, a classification of the people and things which comprise it, which makes some of them visible and the rest invisible.

(b) *Secondly*, we often notice that some facts we had taken for granted, that were basic to our understanding and behaviour, suddenly turn out to be mere illusions. For thousands of years men were convinced that the sun circled round a stationary earth. Since Copernicus we bear in our minds the image of a planetary system where the sun remains stationary while the earth circles around it; yet we still see what our forefathers saw. Thus we distinguish the appearance from the reality of things, but we distinguish them precisely because we can switch from appearance to reality by means of some notion or image.

(*c*) *Thirdly*, our reactions to events, our responses to stimuli, are related to a given definition, common to all the members of the community to which we belong. If, while driving along a road, we see an overturned car, a wounded person and a policeman making a report, we assume that there has been an accident. We read daily about collisions and crashes in the papers under such a heading. Yet these are only 'accidents' because we define as such any involuntary interruption in the progress of a motor car which has more or less tragic consequences. In all other respects there is nothing accidental about a motor car accident. Since statistical calculations enable us to assess the number of victims, according to the day of the week and the locality, motor car accidents are no more due to chance than the disintegration of atoms in an acceleration at high pressure; they are directly related to a given society's degree of urbanisation, the speed and number of its private vehicles and the inadequacy of its public transport.

In each of these cases we note the intervention of representations which either direct us towards that which is visible and to which we have to respond; or which relate appearance and reality; or again which define this reality. I do not wish to imply that such representations don't correspond to something we call the outside world. I simply note that, where reality is concerned, these representations are all we have, that to which our perceptual, as well as our cognitive, systems are adjusted. Bower writes:

We usually use our perceptual system to interpret representations of worlds we can never see. In the man-made world we live in, the perception of representations is as important as the perception of real objects. By a representation I mean a man-made stimulus array intended to serve as a substitute for a sight or sound that could occur naturally. Some representations are meant to be stimulus surrogates; to produce the same experience as the natural world would have done. (Bower, 1977, p. 58)

In fact, we only experience and perceive a world in which, at one extreme, we are acquainted with man-made things representing other man-made things and, at the other extreme, with substitutes for stimuli of which we shall never see the originals, their natural equivalents, such as elementary particles or genes. So that we find ourselves, at times, in a predicament where we require some sign or other which will help us to distinguish one representation from another or a representation from that which it represents, that is, a sign that will tell us: 'This is a representation', or: 'This is not a representation.' The painter René Magritte has illustrated such a predicament to perfection in a painting where a picture of a pipe is contained in a picture that also represents a pipe. On this picture within a picture we can read the message: 'This is a pipe' which indicates the difference between the two pipes. We then turn to the 'real' pipe floating in the air and notice that it is real while the other is only a representation. However, such an interpretation is incorrect since both are painted on the same canvas in front of our eyes. The idea that one of them is a picture which is itself within a picture, and thus a little 'less real' than the other, is totally illusory. Once you have agreed to 'enter the frame' you are already caught: you accept the image as reality. There remains nonetheless the reality of a painting which, hung in a museum and defined as an art object, provides food for thought, provokes an aesthetic reaction and adds to our understanding of painting.

As ordinary people, without the benefit of scientific instruments, we tend to consider and analyse the world in a very similar way; especially as the world with which we deal is social through and through. Which means that we are never provided with any information which has not been distorted by representations 'superimposed' on objects and on persons which give them a certain vagueness and make them partially inaccessible. When we contemplate these individuals and objects, our inherited genetic predisposition, the images and habits we have learnt, the memories of them which we have preserved and our cultural categories all combine to make them such as we see them. So, in the last analysis, they are only one element in a chain-reaction of perceptions, opinions, notions and even lives, organised in a given sequence. It is essential to recall such commonplaces when approaching the domain of mental life in social psychology. My aim is to re-introduce them here in a manner which, I hope, will be fruitful.

(2)   *The conventional and prescriptive nature of representations*

In what way can thought be considered as an environment? Impressionistically, each of us is obviously surrounded, both individually and collectively, by words, ideas and images which penetrate his eyes, his ears and his mind, whether he likes it or not, and which solicit him without his knowing it, just as the thousands of messages conveyed by electro-magnetic waves circulate in the air without our seeing them and are turned into words in a telephone receiver or into images on a television screen. However, such a metaphor is not really adequate. Let's see if we can find a better way of describing how representations intervene in our cognitive activity and to what extent they are independent of it or can be said to determine it. If we accept that there is always a certain amount of both autonomy and constraint in every environment, whether natural or social – and in the present case it is both – let us say that representations have precisely two roles.

(*a*) First they *conventionalise* the objects, persons and events we encounter. They give them a definite form, locate them in a given category and gradually establish them as a model of a certain type, distinct and shared by a group of people. All new elements adhere to this model and merge into it. Thus we assert that the earth is round, we associate communism with the colour red, inflation with the decreasing value of money. Even when a person or an object doesn't conform precisely to the model, we constrain it to assume a given form, to enter a given category, in fact to become identical to the others, at the risk of its being neither understood, nor decoded.

Bartlett concludes from his studies of perception that:

When a common and already conventional form of representation is in use before the sign is introduced, there is a strong tendency for peculiar characteristics to disappear, and for the whole sign to be assimilated to the more familiar form. Thus 'lightning flash' practically always fell into a common, regular zig-zag form, and 'chin' lost its very sharp angle, becoming much more like ordinary conventional representations of this feature..

(Bartlett, 1961, p. 106)

These conventions enable us to know what stands for what: a change of direction or of colour indicates motion or temperature, a given symptom does or does not derive from a disease; they help us to solve the general problem of knowing when to interpret a message as significant in relation to others and when to see it as a fortuitous or chance event. And this meaning in relation to others further depends on a number of preliminary conventions, by means of which we can distinguish whether an arm is raised to attract attention, to hail a friend or to convey impatience. Sometimes it is sufficient simply to transfer an object, or person, from one context to another, in order for us to see it or him in a new light and for us to wonder whether or not they are, indeed, the same. The most striking instance has been provided by Marcel Duchamp who, from 1912 on, has restricted his artistic output to signing ready-made objects and who, by this single gesture, has promoted factory produced objects to the status of art objects. A no less striking example is that of war criminals who are responsible for atrocities that will not easily be forgotten. Yet those who knew them, and were familiar with them both during and after the war, have praised their humanity and their kindness, as well as their routine efficiency, as being comparable to that of thousands of individuals peacefully employed in office jobs.

These examples show how each experience is added to a reality predetermined by conventions, which clearly define its frontiers, distinguish significant from non-significant messages and which link each part with the whole, and assign each individual to a distinct category. Nobody's mind is free from the effects of the prior conditioning which is imposed by his representations, language and culture. We think, by means of a language; we organise our thoughts, in accordance with a system which is conditioned, both by our representations and by our culture. We see only that which underlying conventions allow us to see, and we remain unaware of these conventions. In this respect, our position is very similar to that of the ethnic African tribe, of which Evans-Pritchard wrote:

In this web of belief every strand depends upon every other strand, and a Zande cannot get out of its meshes because it is the only world he knows. The web is not an external structure in which he is enclosed. It is the texture of his thought and he cannot think that his thought is wrong.

(Evans-Pritchard, 1937, p. 194)

We may, with an effort, become aware of the conventional aspect of reality, and thus evade some of the constraints which it imposes on our perceptions and thoughts. But we should not imagine that we could ever be free of all convention, or could eliminate every prejudice. Rather than seeking to avoid all convention, a better strategy would be to discover and make explicit a single representation. Thus, instead of denying conventions and prejudices, this strategy would enable us to recognise that representations constitute, for us, a type of reality. We should seek to isolate which representations are inherent in the persons and objects we encounter and exactly what it is they represent. Among these are the cities we inhabit, the gadgets we use, the passers-by in the street and even the pure, unpolluted, nature which we seek out in the country, or enclose in our gardens.

I know that some account is taken of representations in actual research practice so as to describe more clearly the context within which the individual is called upon to react to a particular stimulus and to explain, more accurately, his subsequent responses. After all, the laboratory is one such reality which represents another, just like Magritte's picture within a picture. It is a reality in which it is necessary to indicate 'this is a stimulus', and not simply a colour or a sound, and 'this is a subject', and not a left- or right-wing student who wants to earn some money to pay for his studies. But we must take account of this in our theory. Hence, we must introduce to centre stage that which we had sought to keep in the wings. This might well be what Lewin had in mind when he wrote: 'Reality for the individual is, to a high degree, determined by what is socially accepted as reality' (Lewin, 1948, p. 57).

(b) Secondly, representations are *prescriptive*, that is they impose themselves upon us with an irresistible force. This force is a combination of a structure which is present before we have even begun to think, and of a tradition which decrees *what* we should think. A child born today in any Western country will encounter that of psychoanalysis, for example in his mother's or the doctor's gestures, in the affection with which he is surrounded to help him through the trials and tribulations of the Oedipal conflict, in the comics he reads and later, in schoolbooks, conversations with classmates or even in a psychoanalytic cure, should he have recourse to one if social or educational problems arise. This is to say nothing of the papers he will read, the political speeches he will hear, the films he will see, etc. He will find a ready-made answer, in psychoanalytic jargon, to all his questions and, to each of his abortive, or successful, actions an explanation will be available which relates back to his earliest childhood or to his sexual desires. We have mentioned psychoanalysis as a representation. We could as easily have mentioned mechanistic psychology, or man-as-machine or the scientific paradigm of a particular community.

Whilst these representations, which are shared by many, enter into and influence the mind of each they are not thought by them; rather, to be more precise, they are re-thought, re-cited and re-presented.

If someone exclaims: 'He's a fool!', stops, and then corrects himself, saying: 'No, I mean he's a genius', we immediately conclude that he has made a Freudian slip. But this conclusion isn't the result of reasoning, neither does it prove that we have a capacity for abstract reasoning, since we have simply recalled, without thinking, and whilst thinking of something else, the representation or definition of what a Freudian slip is. We might, indeed, have such a capacity, and ask ourselves why the speaker in question used one word in place of another, without arriving at any answer. Thus, it is easy to see why the representation which we have of something is not directly related to our manner of thinking but, conversely, why our manner of thinking, and what we think, depend on such representations, that is on the fact that we have, or have not, a given representation. I mean that they are forced upon us, transmitted, and are the product of a whole sequence of elaborations and of changes which occur in the course of time, and are the achievement of successive generations. All the systems of classification, all the images and all the descriptions which circulate within a society, even the scientific ones, imply a link with previous systems and images, a stratification in the collective memory and a reproduction in the language, which invariably reflects past knowledge, and which breaks the bounds of current information.

Social and intellectual activity is, after all, a rehearsal or recital, yet most socio-psychologists mistakenly treat it as if it were amnesic. Our past experiences and ideas are not dead experiences or dead ideas, but continue to be active, to change and to infiltrate our present experience and ideas. In many respects, the past is more real than the present. The peculiar power and clarity of representations – that is of social representations – derives from the success with which they control the reality of today through that of yesterday and the continuity which this presupposes. Indeed, Jahoda himself has recognised them as autonomous properties which are 'not necessarily identifiable in the thinking of particular individuals' (Jahoda, 1970, p. 42); a remark to which his compatriot McDougall subscribed, half a century earlier, in the terminology of his day: 'Thinking, by aid of the collective representations, is said to have its own laws quite distinct from the laws of logic' (McDougall, 1920, p. 74). Laws which, obviously, modify those of logic, both in practice and outcome. In the light of history, and of anthropology, we can affirm that these representations are social entities, with a life of their own, communicating between themselves, opposing each other and changing in harmony with the course of life; vanishing, only to re-emerge under new guises. Generally, in civilisations as divided and mobile as our own, they co-exist and circulate through various spheres of activity, where one of them will take precedence in response to our need for a certain coherence in accounting for persons and things. However, should a change occur in their hierarchy, or a given idea–image be threatened with extinction, our whole universe will be upset. A recent event, and the comment to which it gave rise, may serve to illustrate this point.

The *American Psychiatric Association* recently announced its intention to discard the terms 'neurosis' and 'neurotic' to define specific disorders. A journalist's comments on the decision, in an article entitled 'Goodbye Neurosis' (*International Herald Tribune*, 11 September 1978), are highly significant:

> If the dictionary of mental disorders will no longer accept 'neurotics', we laymen can only do the same.
> But consider the cultural loss: whenever someone is called 'neurotic' or 'a neurotic', it involves an implicit act of forgiveness and understanding; 'Oh, So-and-So is just neurotic' means 'Oh, So-and-So is excessively nervous. He didn't really want to toss the china at your head. It's just his way.' Or 'So-and-So is just neurotic' – meaning 'He can't help himself. He doesn't mean it every time he tosses china at your head.'
> By calling someone neurotic we place the burden of adjustment not on the someone, but rather on ourselves. It's sort of a call to kindness, to a sense of social generosity.
> Would the same be true if the 'disordered' were tossing the china? We do not think so. To excuse So-and-So by citing his disorder – the specific category of his disorder to boot – is like excusing a car for faulty brake-lining – it damn well ought to be repaired and quick. The burden of adjustment would sit squarely on the disorderee. No compassion would be asked of society at large, and naturally none would be forthcoming.
> Think too of the self-esteem of the neurotic himself, who has long been comforted by the knowledge that he is 'just a neurotic' – quite a few pegs safely below a psychotic, but quite a few above the common run of men. A neurotic is an eccentric touched by Freud. Society gives him an honorable, often a lovable, place. Would the same niche be given the sufferers of 'somatoform disorders' or 'major depressive disorders' or 'dissociative disorders'? Not bloody likely.

Such cultural gains, and losses, are obviously related to fragments of social representations. A word, and the dictionary's definition of this word, contains a means of classifying individuals, as well as implicit theories concerning their constitution, or the reasons for their behaving in one way rather than another – an almost physical image of each individual, which corresponds to such theories. Once this content has diffused, and become accepted, it constitutes an integral part of ourselves, of our intercourse with others, of our way of judging them, and of interacting with them; it even defines our place in the social hierarchy, and our values. If the word 'neurosis' were to disappear, and to be replaced by the word 'disorder', such an event would have consequences far beyond its mere significance in a sentence, or in psychiatry. It is our inter-relations, and our collective thought, which are involved and transformed.

I hope that I have amply demonstrated how, by setting a conventional sign on reality on the one hand, and, on the other, by prescribing, through tradition and age-old structures, *what* we perceive and imagine, these creatures of thought, which are representations, end up by constituting an actual environment. Through their autonomy, and the constraints they exert (even though we are perfectly aware that they are 'nothing but ideas') it is, in fact, as unquestionable realities that we are led to envisage them. The weight of their history, custom and cumulative content confronts us with all the resistance of a material object. Perhaps it is an even greater resistance, since what is invisible is inevitably harder to overcome than what is visible.

(3) *The era of representation*

All human interactions, whether they arise between two individuals, or between two groups, presuppose such representations. Indeed this is what characterises them. 'The paramount fact about human interactions', wrote Asch, 'is that they are happenings, that they are psychologically *represented* in each of the participants!' (Asch, 1952, p. 142). Once this fact is overlooked, all that remains are exchanges, that is actions and reactions, which are non-specific and, moreover, impoverished into the bargain. Always, and everywhere, when we encounter persons or things, and become acquainted with them, such representations are involved. The information we receive, and to which we try to give a meaning, is under their control and has no other significance for us than what they give it.

To enlarge the framework a little, we could maintain that what is important is the nature of change, whereby social representations become capable of influencing the behaviour of the individual participant in a collectivity. This is how they are created inwardly, for it is in this form that the collective process itself penetrates, as the determining factor, into individual thought. Such representations, thus, appear to us almost as material objects, insofar as they are the product of our actions and communications. They are, in fact, of a professional activity: I am referring to those pedagogues, ideologues, popularisers of science or priests, that is the representatives of science, cultures and religion, whose task it is to create and transmit them, often, alas, without either knowing or wishing it. In the general evolution of society, these professions are destined to multiply, and their work will become more systematic and more explicit. Partly for that reason, and in view of all that this entails, this era will become known as the era of representation, in every sense of that term.

This does not undermine the autonomy of representations in relation, either to the consciousness of the individual, or even to that of the group. Individuals and groups create representations in the course of communication and co-operation. Representations, obviously, are not created by individuals in isolation. Once created, however, they lead a life of their own, circulate, merge, attract and repel each other, and give birth to new representations, while old ones die out. As a consequence, in order to understand and to explain a representation, it is necessary to start with that, or those, from which it was born. It is not enough to start directly from such-and-such an aspect, either of behaviour, or of the social structure. Far from reflecting either behaviour or the social structure, a representation often conditions and even responds to them. This is so, not because it has a collective origin, or because it refers to a collective object, but because, as such, being shared by all and strengthened by tradition, it constitutes a social reality *sui generis*. The more its origin is forgotten, and its conventional nature ignored, the more *fossilised* it becomes. That which is ideal gradually becomes materialised. It ceases to be ephemeral, changing and mortal and becomes, instead, lasting, permanent, almost immortal. In creating representations, we are like the artist, who bows down before the statue he has sculpted and worships it as a god.

In my opinion, the main task of social psychology is to study such representations, their properties, their origins and their impact. No other discipline is dedicated to this task, and none is better equipped for it. It was, indeed, to social psychology that Durkheim entrusted the task:

As to the laws of collective thought, they are totally unknown. Social psychology, whose task it was to define them, is nothing but a word describing all kinds of varied, vague generalisations with no definite object as focus. What is required is to find out, by comparing myths, legends, popular traditions, and languages, how social representations attract and exclude each other, merge together or separate, etc. (Durkheim, 1963)

Despite numerous further studies, fragmentary ideas and experiments, we are now no more advanced than we were nearly a century ago. Our knowledge is like a mayonnaise which has curdled. But one thing is certain: the principal forms of our physical and social environment are fixed in representations of this kind and we, ourselves, are fashioned in relation to them. I would, even, go so far as to say that, the less we think about them, and the less we are aware of them, then the greater their influence becomes. This is so much the case that the collective mind transforms everything it touches. Therein lies the truth of the primitive belief which has dominated our mentality for millions of years.

II   What is a thinking society?

'We think through our mouths.' Tristan Tzara

(1)   Behaviourism and the study of social representations

We live in a behaviourist world, practice a behaviourist science and use behaviourist metaphors. I say this without pride or shame. For I am not going to embark on a critique of what must, perforce, be called *one* view of contemporary man, since its defence, or refutation, is not, as far as I can see, the concern of science, but rather of culture. One neither defends nor refutes a culture. This said, it is obvious that the study of social representations must go beyond such a view, and must do so for a specific reason. It considers man insofar as he tries to know and to understand the things that surround him, and tries to solve the commonplace enigmas of his own birth, his bodily existence, his humiliations, of the sky above him, of the states of mind of his neighbours and of the powers that dominate him: enigmas that occupy and pre-occupy him from the cradle, and of which he never ceases to speak. For him, thoughts and words are real – they are not mere epiphenomena of behaviour. He concurs with Frege who wrote:

The influence of one person on another is brought about for the most part by thought. One communicates a thought. How does it happen? One brings about changes in the common outside world which, perceived by another person, are supposed to induce him to apprehend a thought and take it to be true. Could the great events of world history have come about without the communication of thought? And yet, we are inclined to regard thoughts as unreal because they appear to be without influence on events, while thinking, judging, stating, understanding are facts of human life. How much more real a hammer appears compared with a thought. How different the process of handing over a hammer is from communication of a thought.   (Frege, 1977, p. 38)

This is what books and articles are always hammering into our heads: hammers are more real than thoughts; attend to hammers, rather than to thoughts. Everything, in the last analysis, is behaviour, a matter of driving stimuli into the walls of our organism, like nails. When we study social representations we study man, insofar as he asks questions and seeks answers or thinks, and not insofar as he processes information, or behaves. More precisely, insofar as his aim is not to behave, but to understand.

What is a 'thinking' society? That is our question, and that is what we would like to observe and to understand, by studying (*a*) the circumstances in which groups communicate, make decisions and seek either to reveal or to conceal something, and (*b*) their achievements and their beliefs, that is their ideologies, sciences and social representations. It could not be otherwise; the mystery is profound, yet understanding is the most common human faculty. It was at one time believed that this faculty was stimulated, first and foremost, by contact with the external world. But we have come increasingly to realise that it actually arises from social communication. Recent studies of very young children have shown that the origins and development of meaning and thought depend on social intercourse; as though a baby came into the world primarily equipped for a relationship with others; with its mother, its father and with all those who await it and care for it. The world of objects constitutes but a backdrop for persons and their social interactions.

When asking the question: what is a thinking society? we refute at the same time the conception which, I believe, prevails in the human sciences, that is that a society does not think, or, if it does, that this is not an essential attribute. The denial that society 'thinks' can assume two different forms: (*a*) by declaring that our minds are little black boxes, contained within a vast black box, which simply receives information, words and thoughts which are conditioned from the outside in order to turn them into gestures, judgements, opinions and so forth. In fact, we know perfectly well that our minds are not black boxes but, at best, are black holes, possessing a life and activity of their own, even when this is not obvious, and when individuals exchange neither energy, nor information with the outside world. Madness, that black hole in rationality, irrefutably proves that this is how things are. (*b*) by maintaining that groups and individuals are always and completely under the sway of a dominant ideology which is produced and imposed by their social class, the State, the Church or the school, and that what they think and say only reflects such an ideology. In other words, it is maintained that they don't as a rule think, or produce anything original, on their own: they reproduce and, in turn, are reproduced. Despite its progressive nature, this conception is essentially in accordance with that of Le Bon, who asserts that the masses neither think nor create; but that it is only individuals, the organised elite, who do so. Here we discover, whether we like it or not, the metaphor of the black box, except that now it is invested with ready-made ideas, and no longer with objects. Such may be the case, but we cannot tell, for even if ideologies and their impact have been widely discussed, they have not been extensively researched. That much has been acknowledged by Marx and Wood: 'Yet in comparison with other areas, the study of ideology has been relatively neglected by sociologists, who generally feel more comfortable studying social structure and behaviour than studying belief and symbols' (Marx and Wood, 1975, p. 382).

So what we are suggesting is that individuals and groups, far from being passive receptors, think for themselves, produce and ceaselessly communicate their own specific representations and solutions to the questions they set themselves. In the streets, in cafes, offices, hospitals, laboratories, etc., people analyse, comment, concoct spontaneous, unofficial, 'philosophies' which have a decisive impact on their social relations, their choices, the way they bring up their children, plan ahead and so forth. Events, sciences and ideologies simply provide them with 'food for thought'.

(2) Social representations

It is obvious that the concept of social representations has come to us from Durkheim. But we have a different view of it – or, at any rate, social psychology must consider it from a different angle – than does sociology. Sociology sees or, rather, has seen, social representations as explanatory devices, irreducible by any further analysis. Their theoretical function was similar to that of the atom in traditional mechanics, or of the gene in traditional genetics, that is atoms and genes were known to exist, but nobody bothered about what they did, or what they were like. Similarly, one knew that social representations occurred in societies, but nobody worried about their structure, or about their inner dynamics. Social psychology, on the other hand, is and must be pre-occupied solely with both the structure and the dynamics of representations. For us, it is summed up in the difficulty of penetrating the interior to discover the inner mechanisms and vitality of social representations in the greatest possible detail; that is in 'splitting representations', just as atoms and genes have been split. The first step in this direction was taken by Piaget when he studied the child's representation of the world and his enquiry remains, to this day, exemplary. So what I propose to do is to consider as a *phenomenon* what was previously seen as a *concept*.

Moreover, from Durkheim's point of view, collective representations described a whole range of intellectual forms which included science, religion, myth, modalities of time and space, etc. Indeed, any kind of idea, emotion or belief which occurred within a community was included. This presents a serious problem for, by attempting to include too much, one grasps little: grasp all, lose all. Intuition, as well as experience, suggests that it is impossible to cover such a wide range of knowledge and beliefs. They are too heterogeneous in the first place and, moreover, they cannot be defined by a few general characteristics. As a consequence, we are obliged to add two significant qualifications: (a) *Social representations should be seen as a specific way of understanding, and communicating, what we know already*. They occupy in effect a curious position, somewhere between concepts, which have as their goal abstracting meaning from the world, and introducing order into it, and percepts, which reproduce the world in a meaningful way. They always have two facets, which are as interdependent as the two faces of a sheet of paper: the iconic, and the symbolic, facets. We know that: Representation = image/meaning; in other words, that it equates every image to an idea, and every idea to an image. Thus, in our society, a 'neurotic' is an idea associated with psychoanalysis, with Freud, with the Oedipus Complex and, at the same time, we see the neurotic as an egocentric, pathological individual, whose parental conflicts have not yet been resolved. So, on the one hand, the word evokes a science, even the name of a classical hero, and a concept and, on the other, it evokes a definite type, characterised by certain features, and a readily imagined biography. The mental mechanisms set in motion in this instance, and which carve out this figure in our universe and give it a significance, an interpretation, obviously differ from those whose function it is to isolate a precise perception of a person or of a thing, and to conceive a system of concepts that explains them. Language itself, when it conveys representations, is located half-way between what is called the language of observation and the language of logic; the first, expressing pure facts – if such things exist – and the second, abstract symbols. This is, perhaps, one of the most remarkable phenomena of our time – this welding of language and of representation. Let me explain.

Until the dawn of the century, ordinary verbal language was a means both of communication and of knowledge; of collective ideas and of abstract research, since it was common to both common sense and science. Nowadays, non-verbal language – mathematics and logic – which has appropriated the sphere of science, has substituted signs for words, and equations for propositions. The world of our experience and of our reality has split in two, and the laws which govern our everyday world have, now, no obvious relation to those which govern the world of science. If we are much interested today in linguistic phenomena this is partly because language is on the decline, just as we worry about plants, and nature and animals because they are threatened with extinction. Language, excluded from the sphere of material reality, re-emerges in that of historical and conventional reality; and, if it has lost its relation to theory, it maintains its relation to representation, which is all that it has left. Thus, if the study of language is increasingly the concern of social psychology, this is not because the latter wants to imitate what has been happening in other disciplines or wishes to add a social dimension to its individual abstractions or for any other philanthropic motives. It is, simply, connected with the change which we have just mentioned and which links it so exclusively to our common, everyday, method of understanding and of exchanging our ways of seeing things.

(b) *Durkheim – true to the Aristotelian and Kantian tradition – has a rather static conception of these representations – somewhat akin to that of the Stoics.* As a consequence, representations, in his theory, are like a thickening of the fog, or else they act as stabilisers for many words or ideas – like layers of stagnant air in a society's atmosphere, of which it is said that one could cut them with a knife. Whilst this is not entirely false, what is most striking to the contemporary observer is their mobile and circulating character; in short, their plasticity. We see them, more, as dynamic structures, operating on an assembly of relations and of behaviours which appear, and disappear, together with the representations. Just as the disappearance from our dictionaries of the word 'neurotic' would also banish some feelings, a certain type of relationship towards a particular person, a way of judging him and, consequently, of judging ourselves.

I stress these differences for a purpose. The social representations with which I am concerned are neither those of primitive societies, nor are they survivals, in the subsoil of our culture, from prehistoric times. They are those of our current society, of our political, scientific, human soil, which have not always enough time to allow the proper sedimentation to become immutable traditions. And their importance continues to increase, in direct proportion to the heterogeneity and the fluctuation of the unifying systems – official sciences, religions, ideologies – and to the changes which these must undergo in order to penetrate everyday life and become part of common reality. The mass media have accelerated this tendency, multiplied such changes and increased the need of a link between, on the one hand, our purely abstract sciences and beliefs in general and, on the other, our concrete activities as social individuals. In other words, there is a continual need to re-constitute 'common sense' or the form of understanding that creates the substratum of images and meanings, without which no collectivity can operate. Similarly, our collectivities could not function today if social representations were not formed that are based on the stock of theories and ideologies which they transform into shared realities, relating to the interactions between people which, thus, constitute a separate category of phenomena. And the specific feature of these representations is precisely that they 'embody ideas' in collective experiences and interactions in behaviour which can, more profitably, be compared to works of art than to mechanical reactions. The biblical writer was already aware of this when he asserted that the word became flesh; and Marxism confirms it when it states that ideas, once released amongst the masses, are, and behave like, material forces.

We know almost nothing of this alchemy which transmutes the base metal of our ideas into the gold of our reality. How to change concepts into objects, or into people, is the enigma which has pre-occupied us for centuries and which is the true purpose of our science as distinct from other sciences which, in fact, enquire into the reverse process. I am well aware that an almost insuperable distance separates the problem from its solution, a distance very few are prepared to bridge. But neither shall I cease to repeat that if social psychology does not try to bridge this gap, it fails in its task and, thus, will not only fail to progress but will even cease to exist.

To sum up: if, in the classic sense, collective representations are an explanatory device, and refer to a general class of ideas and beliefs (science, myth, religion, etc.), for us, they are phenomena which need to be described, and to be explained. They are specific phenomena which are related to a particular mode of understanding and of communicating – a mode which creates both reality and common sense. It is in order to stress such a distinction that I use the term 'social' instead of 'collective'.

(3) *Sacred and profane sciences; consensual and reified universes*

The place which representations occupy in a thinking society is what concerns us here. Formerly, this place would have been – and up to a

point was – determined by the distinction between a sacred sphere –
worthy of respect and veneration and so kept quite apart from all
purposeful, human, activities – and a profane sphere in which trivial,
utilitarian activities were performed. These separate and opposed
worlds which, in varying degrees, determine within each culture and
each individual the spheres of their own and foreign forces; that which
we can alter and that which alters us; the *opus proprium* and *opus alienum*.
All knowledge presupposed such a division of reality, and a discipline
which was concerned with one of the spheres was totally different from a
discipline which was concerned with the other; sacred sciences having
nothing whatever in common with profane sciences. Doubtless, it was
possible to switch from the one to the other, but this only occurred when
the contents were blurred.

This distinction has now been abandoned. It has been replaced by
another, more basic, distinction between consensual and reified
universes. In the consensual universe, society is a visible, continuous
creation, permeated with meaning and purpose, possessing a human
voice, in accord with human existence and both acting and reacting like a
human being. In other words, man is, here, the measure of all things. In
the reified universe, society is transformed into a system of solid, basic,
unvarying entities, which are indifferent to individuality and lack
identity. This society ignores itself and its creations which it sees only as
isolated objects, such as persons, ideas, environments and activities. The
various sciences which are concerned with such objects can, as it were,
impose their authority on the thought and experience of each individual
and decide, in each particular case, what is true and what is not. All
things, whatever the circumstances, are, here, the measure of man.

Even our use of the pronouns 'we' and 'they' can express this contrast,
where 'we' stands for the group of individuals to whom we relate and
'they' – the French, scholars, State systems, etc. – to a different group, to
which we do not, but may be forced to, belong. The distance between the
first and the third person plural expresses the distance which separates a
social place where we feel included from a given, indeterminate or, at
any rate, impersonal place. This lack of identity, which is at the root of
modern man's psychic distress, is a symptom of this necessity to see
oneself in terms of 'we' and 'they'; to oppose 'we' to 'they'; and thus of
one's inability to connect the one with the other. Groups and individuals
try to overcome this necessity either by identifying with 'we', and thus
enclosing themselves in a world apart, or by identifying with 'they', and
becoming the robots of bureaucracy and the administration.

Such categories as consensual and reified universes are unique to our culture. In a *consensual universe* society is seen as a group of individuals who are equal and free, each entitled to speak in the name of the group and under its aegis. Thus, no one member is assumed to possess an exclusive competence, but each can acquire any competence which may be required by the circumstances. In this respect, everybody acts as a responsible 'amateur' or 'curious observer', in the catchphrase of the last century. In most public meeting-places these amateur politicians, doctors, educators, sociologists, astronomers, etc. can be found expressing their opinions, airing their views and laying down the law. Such a state of affairs requires a certain complicity, that is linguistic conventions, questions that must not be asked, topics that can or cannot be ignored. These worlds are institutionalised in the clubs, associations and cafés of today as they were in the 'salons' and academies of the past. The waning art of conversation is what they thrive on. This is what keeps them going and encourages social relations which, otherwise, would dwindle. In the long run, conversation creates nodes of stability and recurrence, a communality of significance between its practitioners. The rules of this art maintain a whole complex of ambiguities and conventions without which social life could not exist. They enable individuals to share an implicit stock of images and of ideas which are taken for granted and mutually accepted. Thinking is done out loud. It becomes a noisy, public activity which satisfies the need for communication and thus maintains and consolidates the group whilst conveying the character each member requires of it. If we think before speaking and speak to help ourselves think, we also speak to provide a sonorous reality to the inner pressure of those conversations through which, and in which, we bind ourselves to others. Beckett has summed up the situation in *Endgame*:

> Clov: What is there to keep me here?
> Hamm: Conversation.

And the motive is profound. Whoever keeps his ears pinned back in those places where people converse, whoever reads interviews with some attention, will realise that most conversations are about highly 'metaphysical' problems – birth, death, injustice, etc. – and about society's ethical laws. Thus, they provide a permanent commentary on major national, scientific or urban events and features and are, therefore, the modern equivalent to the Greek chorus which, though no longer on the historical stage, remains in the wings.

In a reified universe society is seen as a system of different roles and classes whose members are unequal. Only acquired competence determines their degree of participation according to merit, their right to function 'as physician', 'as psychologist', 'as trade unionist' or to abstain, insofar as 'they have no competence in the matter'. Permutations of roles, the ability to take somebody else's place, are so many ways of acquiring competence or of isolating oneself, of being different. Thus we confront each other, within the system, as pre-established organisations, each with its rules and regulations. Whence the compulsions we experience and the feeling that we cannot alter them at will. There is a proper behaviour for every circumstance, a linguistic formula for every confrontation and, needless to say, the appropriate information for a given context. We are bound by that which binds the organisation and which corresponds to a sort of general acceptance and not to any reciprocal understanding, to a sequence of prescriptions and not to a sequence of agreements. History, nature, all those things which are responsible for the system are equally responsible for the hierarchy of roles and classes, for their solidarity. Every situation contains a potential ambiguity, a vagueness, two possible interpretations, but their connotations are negative, they are obstacles we must overcome before everything becomes clear, precise, totally unambiguous. This is achieved by processing information, by the processors' lack of involvement and the existence of appropriate channels. The computer serves as the model for the type of relations which are thus established, and its rationality, we can but hope, is the rationality of that which is computed.

The contrast between the two universes has a psychological impact. The boundary between them splits collective and, indeed, physical reality in two. It is readily apparent that the sciences are the means by which we understand the reified universe, while social representations deal with the consensual. The purpose of the first is to establish a chart of the forces, objects and events which are independent of our desires and outside of our awareness and to which we must react impartially and submissively. By concealing values and advantages they aim at encouraging intellectual precision and empirical evidence. Representations, on the other hand, restore collective awareness and give it shape, explaining objects and events so that they become accessible to everyone and coincide with our immediate interests. They are, according to William James, concerned with: 'practical reality, reality for ourselves; and to have that, an object must not only appear, but it must appear both *interesting* and *important*. The world whose objects are neither interesting nor important we treat simply negatively, we brand them as unreal' (W. James, 1980, p. 295).

The use of a language of images and of words that have become common property through the diffusion of reported ideas enlivens and fertilises those aspects of society and nature with which we are here concerned. Doubtless – and this is what I set out to demonstrate – the specific nature of such representations expresses the specific nature of the consensual universe of which they are the product and to which they pertain exclusively. It thus ensues that social psychology is the science of such universes. At the same time, we see more clearly the true nature of ideologies which is to facilitate the transition from the one world to the other, that is to cast consensual into reified categories and to subordinate the former to the latter. Hence they have no specific structure and can be perceived either as representations, or as sciences. This is how they come to concern both sociology and history.

III The familiar and the unfamiliar

To understand the phenomenon of social representations, however, we must begin at the beginning and advance step by step. Up to this point, I have done no more than suggest certain reforms and tried to vindicate them. I couldn't avoid stressing specific ideas if I wanted to defend the point of view I was upholding. But, in so doing, I have demonstrated the fact that:

(*a*) social representations must be seen as an 'environment' in relation to the individual or the group; and

(*b*) they are, in certain respects, specific to our society.

Why do we create these representations? What, in our motives for creating them, explains their cognitive properties? These are the questions we shall tackle first. We could respond by recourse to three traditional hypotheses: (i) the hypothesis of desirability, that is an individual or a group seeks to create images, to make up sentences that will either express or conceal his or their intentions, these images and sentences being subjective distortions of an objective reality; (ii) the hypothesis of imbalance, that is all ideologies, all concepts of the world, are means of solving psychic or emotional tensions due to a failure or a lack of social integration. Thus they are imaginary compensations which are aimed at restoring a degree of inner stability; and (iii) the hypothesis of control, that is groups create representations so as to filter information derived from the environment and thus to control individual behaviour.

They function, therefore, as a kind of manipulation of thought and of the structure of reality, similar to those methods of 'behavioural' control and of propaganda that exert a compulsive coercion on all those to whom they are directed.

Such hypotheses are not entirely devoid of truth. Social representations may indeed answer a given need; respond to a state of imbalance; and further the unpopular but ineradicable domination of one section of society over another. But these hypotheses have, nonetheless, the common failing of being too general; they do not explain why such functions should be fulfilled by this method of understanding and communicating, rather than by some other, such as science or religion, for instance. Thus, we must seek a different hypothesis, less general and more in keeping with what researchers in the field have observed. Moreover, for want of space, I can neither elaborate my reservations nor justify my theory any further. I shall have to expose, without more ado, an intuition and a fact I believe to be true, that is that *the purpose of all representations is to make something unfamiliar, or unfamiliarity itself, familiar.*

What I mean is, that consensual universes are places where everybody wants to feel at home, secure from any risk of friction or strife. All that is said and done there only confirms acquired beliefs and interpretations, corroborates rather than contradicts tradition. The same situations, gestures, ideas are always expected to recur, over and over again. Change as such is only perceived and accepted insofar as it provides a kind of liveliness and avoids the stifling of dialogue under the weight of repetition. On the whole, the dynamic of relationships is a dynamic of familiarisation, where objects, individuals and events are perceived and understood in relation to previous encounters or paradigms. As a result, memory prevails over deduction, the past over the present, response over stimuli and images over 'reality'. To accept and understand what is familiar, to grow accustomed to it and make a habit of it, is one thing; but it is quite another to prefer it as the standard of reference and to measure all that happens, and is perceived, against it. For, in this case, we don't simply register what typifies a Parisian, a 'respectable' person, a mother, an Oedipus Complex etc., but this awareness is also used as a criterion to evaluate what is unusual, abnormal and so on. Or, in other words, what is unfamiliar.

In fact, for our friend the 'man in the street' (now threatened with extinction, along with strolls in the streets, and soon to be replaced by the man in front of the TV set), most of the opinions derived from science, art and economics which relate to reified universes differ, in many ways, from the familiar, handy, opinions he has constructed out of bits and pieces of scientific, artistic and economic traditions and from personal experience and hearsay. Because they differ, he tends to think of them as invisible, unreal – for the world's reality, like realism in painting, is largely a matter of limitations and/or convention. Thus he may experience this sense of non-familiarity when frontiers and/or conventions disappear; when distinctions between the abstract and the concrete become blurred; or when an object, which he had always thought of as abstract, suddenly emerges in all its concreteness, etc. This may occur when he is presented with a picture of the physical reconstruction of such purely notional entities as atoms or robots or, indeed, with any atypical behaviour, person or relation which might prevent him from reacting as he would before the usual type. He doesn't find what he expected to find, and is left with a sense of incompleteness and randomness. It is in this way that the mentally handicapped, or people belonging to other cultures, are disturbing, because they are like us, and yet not like us; so we say they are 'un-cultured', 'barbarian', 'irrational' and so on. In fact, all banned or remote things, topics or persons, those which have been exiled to the very frontiers of our universe, are always endowed with imaginary characteristics; and they pre-occupy and disturb precisely because they are there without being there; perceived without being perceived; their unreality becomes apparent when we are in their presence; when their reality is forced upon us – it is like coming face to face with a ghost or with a fictional character in real life; or like the first occasion when we see a computer playing chess. Then, something we had thought of as a fancy becomes reality before our very eyes; we can see and touch something we were precluded from seeing and touching.

The actuality of something absent, the 'not quite rightness' of an object, are what characterise unfamiliarity. Something seems to be visible, without being so; similar, while being different; accessible, yet inaccessible. The unfamiliar attracts and intrigues individuals and communities while, at the same time, it alarms them, compels them to make explicit the implicit assumptions that are basic to consensus. This 'not quite rightness' worries and threatens, as when a robot that behaves exactly like a living creature, although it lacks life itself, suddenly becomes the Frankenstein monster, something both fascinating and terrifying. The fear of what is strange (and of strangers) is deep-rooted. It has been observed in young children during the third quarter of their first year, and a number of children's games are really a means of overcoming this fear, of controlling its object. Phenomena of mass panic frequently stem from the same cause and are expressed in the same dramatic movements of flight and distress. This is because the dread of losing customary landmarks, of losing touch with what provides a sense of continuity, of mutual understanding is an unbearable dread. And when other-ness is thrust upon us in the form of something 'not quite' as it should be, we instinctively reject it, because it threatens the established order.

The act of re-presentation is a means of transferring what disturbs us, what threatens our universe, from the outside to the inside, from far off to near by. The transfer is effected by separating normally linked concepts and perceptions and setting them in a context where the unusual becomes usual, where the unknown can be included in an acknowledged category. Thus when trying to define and make more accessible the psychoanalyst's dealings with his patient – that 'medical treatment without medicine' which seems eminently paradoxical to our culture – some people will compare it to a 'confession'. The concept is thus detached from its analytical context and transposed to one of priests and penitents, of father confessors and contrite sinners. Then the method of free association is likened to the rules of confession. In this way, what had first seemed offensive and paradoxical becomes an ordinary, normal process. Psychoanalysis is no more than a form of confession. And later, when psychoanalysis has been accepted and is a social representation in its own right confession is seen, more or less, as a form of psychoanalysis. Once the method of free association has been separated from its theoretical context and given religious connotations it ceases to be surprising and disturbing and assumes instead a very ordinary character. And this is not, as we might be tempted to believe, a simple matter of analogy but an actual, socially significant merging, a shifting of values and feelings.

In this case, as well as in others we observed, the images, ideas and language shared by a given group always seem to dictate the initial direction and expedient by which the group tries to come to terms with the unfamiliar. Social thinking owes more to convention and memory than to reason; to traditional structures rather than to current intellectual or perceptive structures. Denise Jodelet has analysed – in a work as yet, unfortunately, unpublished – the reactions of the inhabitants of various villages to the mentally handicapped people who were placed in their midst. These patients, because of their almost normal appearance, and notwithstanding the instructions the villagers had received, continued to be seen as alien, despite the fact that their presence had been accepted for many, many years and that they shared the villagers' daily life and even their homes. Thus it became apparent that the representations to which they gave rise derived from traditional views and notions and that it was these that determined the villagers' relations with them.

However, though we are able to perceive such a discrepancy, no one can do away with it. The basic tension between the familiar and the unfamiliar is always settled, in our consensual universes, in favour of the former. In social thinking, the conclusion has priority over the premise and in social relations, according to Nelly Stephane's apt formula, the verdict has priority over the trial. Before seeing and hearing a person we have already judged him; classified him and created an image of him. So that all the enquiries we make and our efforts to obtain information only serve to confirm this image. Moreover, laboratory experiments corroborate this observation:

The common errors which subjects make suggest that there is a general factor governing the order in which such checks are carried out. Subjects seem to be biased toward attempts to *verify* a conclusion, whether it is their own initial answer, or they are given them by the experimenter to evaluate. They seek to determine whether the premises could be combined in such a way as to render the conclusion true. Of course, this merely shows that conclusion and premises are consistent, not that the conclusion follows from the premises.

(Wason and Johnson-Laird, 1972, p. 157)

When all is said and done, the representations we fabricate – of a scientific theory, a nation, an artefact, etc. – are always the result of a constant effort to make usual and actual something which is unfamiliar or which gives us a feeling of unfamiliarity. And through them we overcome it and integrate it into our mental and physical world which is thus enriched and transformed. After a series of adjustments, that which was far away seems close at hand; that which seemed abstract becomes concrete and almost normal. However, while creating them we are always, more or less, aware of our intentions, since the images and ideas by means of which we grasp the unusual only bring us back to what we already knew and had long been familiar with and which, therefore, gives a reassuring impression of *déjà vu* and *déjà connu*. Bartlett writes: 'As has been pointed out before, whenever material visually presented purports to be representative of some common object, but contains certain features which are unfamiliar in the community to which the material is introduced, these features invariably suffer transformation in the direction of the familiar' (Bartlett, 1961, p. 178).

It is as though, whenever a breach or split occurred in what is usually perceived as normal, our minds healed up the wound and refashioned from within that which had been without. Such a process reassures and comforts us; restores a sense of continuity in the group or individual threatened with discontinuity and meaninglessness. That is why, when studying a representation, we should always try to discover the unfamiliar feature which motivated it and which it has absorbed. But it is particularly important that the development of such a feature be observed from the very moment it emerges in the social sphere.

The contrast with science is striking. Science proceeds in the opposite way; from premise to conclusion, especially in the field of logic, just as the aim of the law is to ensure the trial's priority over the verdict. But it has to rely on a complete system of logic and proof in order to proceed in a manner that is quite foreign to the natural process and function of thought in an ordinary consensual universe. It must, furthermore, lay down certain laws – uninvolvement, repetition of experiments, distance from the object, independence from authority and tradition – which are never fully applied. To make the permutation of both terms of the argument possible, it creates a wholly artificial milieu by resorting to what is known as the rational reconstruction of facts and ideas. Then, to overcome our tendency to confirm what is familiar, to prove what is already known – a tendency which hampers research and the avoidance of error – the scientist is required to falsify, to try to invalidate his own theories and to confront evidence with counter-evidence. But that is not the whole story. Since it has become modern and has broken off with common sense, science is successfully occupied in constantly demolishing most of our current perceptions and opinions, in proving that impossible results are possible and in giving the lie to the bulk of our customary ideas and experiences. In other words, its object is to *make the familiar unfamiliar* in its mathematical equations as well as in its laboratories. And in this way it proves, by contrast, that the purpose of social representations is precisely that which I have already indicated.

IV   Anchoring and objectifying or the two processes that generate social representations

Science, common sense and social representations

Science and social representations are so different from each other and yet so complementary that we have to think and speak in both registers.

The French philosopher Bachelard observed that the world in which we live and the world of thought are not one and the same world. Yet we cannot help yearning for a single, identical world and striving to achieve it. Contrary to what was believed last century, far from being the antidote to representations and ideologies the sciences now actually generate such representations. Our reified worlds increase with the proliferation of the sciences. As theories, information and events multiply, they have to be duplicated and reproduced at a more immediate and accessible level by acquiring a form and energy of their own. In other words, they are transferred to a consensual universe, circumscribed and re-presented. Science was formerly based on common sense and made common sense less common; but now common sense is science made common. Unquestionably, every fact, every commonplace conceals within its very platitude a world of knowledge, a digest of culture and a mystery that make it both compulsive and fascinating. 'Can anything be more appealing', asked Baudelaire, 'more fruitful and more positively *exciting* than a commonplace?' And, we might add, more collectively effective? It isn't easy to make unfamiliar words, ideas or beings usual, close and actual. To give them a familiar face, it is necessary to set in motion the two mechanisms of a thought process based on memory and foregone conclusions.

The first mechanism strives to *anchor* strange ideas, to reduce them to ordinary categories and images, to set them in a familiar context. Thus, for instance, a religious person tries to relate a new theory or the behaviour of a stranger to a religious scale of values. The purpose of the second mechanism is to *objectify* them, that is to turn something abstract into something almost concrete, to transfer what is in the mind to something existing in the physical world. The things the mind's eye perceives seem to be before our physical eyes and an imagined being begins to assume the reality of something seen, something tangible. These mechanisms make the un-familiar familiar, the first by transferring it to our own particular sphere where we are able to compare and interpret it, the second by reproducing it among the things we can see and touch and thus control. Since representations are created by these two mechanisms it is essential that we understand how they function.

Anchoring. This is a process which draws something foreign and disturbing that intrigues us into our particular system of categories and compares it to the paradigm of a category which we think to be suitable. It is rather like anchoring a stray boat to one of the buoys in our social space. Thus, for the villagers in Denise Jodelet's study, the mental patients placed in their midst by the medical association were immediately judged by conventional standards and compared to idiots, tramps, spastics or to what in the local dialect was known as 'rogues'. Insofar as a given object or idea is compared to the paradigm of a category it acquires characteristics of that category and is re-adjusted to fit within it. If the classification thus obtained is generally accepted then any opinion that refers to the category will also refer to the object or idea. For instance, the aforementioned villagers' opinion of idiots, tramps and spastics is transferred, unmodified, to the mental patients. Even when we are aware of a certain discrepancy, of the approximation of our assessment, we cling to it if only to preserve a minimum of coherence between the unknown and the known.

To anchor is, thus, to classify and to name something. Things that are unclassified and unnamed are alien, non-existent and at the same time threatening. We experience a resistance, a distancing when we are unable to evaluate something, to describe it to ourselves or to other people. The first step towards overcoming such resistance, towards conciliating an object or person, is taken when we are able to place it or him in a given category, to label it or him with a familiar name. Once we can speak about something, assess it and thus communicate it – even vaguely, as when we say of someone that he is 'inhibited' – then we can represent the unusual in our usual world, reproduce it as the replica of a familiar model. By classifying what is unclassifiable, naming what is unnamable, we are able to imagine it, to represent it. Indeed, representation is, basically, a system of classification and denotation, of alloting categories and names. Neutrality is forbidden by the very logic of the system where each object and being must have a positive or a negative value and assume a given place in a clearly graded hierarchy. When we classify a person among the neurotics, the Jews or the poor, we are obviously not simply stating a fact but assessing and labelling him. And, in so doing, we reveal our 'theory' of society and of human nature.

In my opinion, this is a vital factor in social psychology which has not received all the attention it deserves; indeed, existing studies of the phenomena of evaluation, classification, categorisation (Eiser and Stroebe, 1972) and so forth, fail to take into account the substrata of such phenomena or to realise that they presuppose a representation of beings, objects and events. Yet, the process of representation involves the coding of even physical stimuli into a specific category, as an enquiry into the perception of colours in various cultures has revealed. Thus scholars admit that individuals, when shown different colours, perceive them in relation to a paradigm – though such a paradigm may be totally unknown to them – and classify them by means of a mental image (Rosch, 1977). In fact, one of the lessons contemporary epistemology has taught us is that any system of categories presupposes a theory which defines and specifies it and specifies its use. When such a system disappears, we are entitled to assume that the theory too has disappeared.

However, let us proceed systematically. To classify something means that we confine it to a set of behaviours and of rules stipulating what is, and is not, permissible in relation to all the individuals included in this class. When we classify a person as Marxist, angler or reader of *The Times*, we confine him to a set of linguistic, spatial and behavioural constraints and to certain habits. If we then go so far as to let him know what we have done we will bring our influence to bear on him by formulating specific demands related to our expectations. The main virtue of a class, that which makes it so easy to handle, is that it provides a suitable model or prototype to represent the class and a sort of photo-kit of all the individuals supposed to belong to it. This photo-kit represents a sort of test case that sums up the features common to a number of related cases, that is it is, on the one hand, an idealised conflation of salient points and, on the other, an iconic matrix of readily identifiable points. Thus, most of us, as our visual representation of a Frenchman, have an image of an undersized person wearing a beret and carrying a long loaf of French bread.

To categorise someone or something amounts to choosing a paradigm from those stored in our memory and establishing a positive or a negative relation with it. When we switch on the radio in the middle of a programme without knowing what it is, we assume it is a 'play' if it is sufficiently similar to P, when P stands for the paradigm of a play, that is dialogue, plot, etc. Experience shows that it is much easier to agree on what constitutes a paradigm than on the degree of an individual's resemblance to it. From Denise Jodelet's enquiry it emerges that, although the villagers were of one mind as to the general classification of the mental patients living with them, they were much less united in their opinion as to each patient's resemblance to the generally accepted 'test case'. When any attempt was made to define this test case, innumerable discrepancies came to light which were not usually obvious, thanks to the complicity of all concerned.

By and large, however, it can be said that classifications are made by comparing individuals to a prototype generally considered to represent a class, and that the former is defined by his approximation to, or coincidence with, the latter. Thus we say of certain personalities – de Gaulle, Maurice Chevalier, Churchill, Einstein, etc. – that they are representative of a nation, of politicians or of scientists and we classify other politicians or scientists in relation to them. If it is true that we classify and judge people and things by comparing them to a prototype, then we will inevitably tend to notice and select those features which are most representative of this prototype, just as Denise Jodelet's villagers were more clearly aware of the mental patients' speech and behavioural 'oddities', during the ten or twenty years of their stay, than of the general pleasantness, diligence and humanity of these unfortunate people.

Indeed, anyone who has been a journalist, sociologist or clinical psychologist knows how the representation of such and such a gesture, occurrence or word, can clinch a news item or a diagnosis. The ascendency of the test case is due, I believe, to its concreteness, to a kind of vividness which leaves such a deep imprint in our memory that we are able to use it thereafter as a 'model' against which we measure individual cases and any image that even remotely resembles it. Thus, every test case, and every typical image, contains the abstract in the concrete, which further enables them to achieve society's main purpose: to create classes from individuals. Thus, we can never say that we know an individual, nor that we try to understand him, but only that we try to recognise him, that is to find out what sort of person he is, to what category he belongs and so forth. Which really means that anchoring, too, involves the priority of the verdict over the trial and of the predicate over the subject. The prototype is the quintessence of such priority, since it fosters ready-made opinions and usually leads to over-hasty decisions.

Such decisions are generally reached in one of two ways: by generalising or by particularising. At times, a ready-made opinion comes to mind straight away and we try to find the information or 'particular' that fits it; at others, we have a given particular in mind and try to get a precise image of it. By generalising, we reduce distances. We select a feature at random and use it as a category: Jew, mental patient, play, aggressive nation, etc. The feature becomes, as it were, co-extensive with all the members of this category. When it is positive, we register our acceptance, when negative, our rejection. By particularising, we maintain the distance and consider the object under scrutiny as a divergence from the prototype. At the same time, we try to detect what feature, motivation or attitude makes it distinct. While studying the social representations of psychoanalysis, I was able to observe how the basic image of the psychoanalyst could, by the exaggeration of a specific feature – wealth, status, relentlessness – be modified and particularised to produce that of 'the American psychoanalyst', and that sometimes all these features were stressed at the same time. In fact, the tendency to classify either by generalisation or by particularisation is not, by any means, a purely intellectual choice but reflects a given attitude towards the object, a desire to define it as normal or aberrant. That is what is mainly at stake in all classifications of unfamiliar things – the need to define them as conforming to, or diverging from, the norm. Besides, when we talk about similarity or dissimilarity, identity or difference, we are really saying precisely that, but in a detached form which is devoid of social consequences.

There is a tendency, among social psychologists, to see classification as an analytic operation involving a sort of catalogue of separate features – colour of skin, texture of hair, shape of skull and nose and so on, if it is a question of race – to which the individual is compared and then included in the category with which he has most features in common. In other words, we would adjudicate his specificity or non-specificity, his similarity or difference according to one feature or another. And little wonder that such an analytic operation should have been envisaged, since only laboratory examples have been considered to date, and systems of classification which bear no relation to the substratum of social representations, for example the collective view of what is thus classified. It is because of this tendency that I feel I should say something more about my own observations concerning social representations which have revealed that when we classify we always compare to a prototype, always ask ourselves whether the object compared is normal or abnormal in relation to it and try to answer the question: 'Is it or not as it should be?'

This discrepancy has practical consequences. For, if my observations are correct, then all our 'prejudices', whether national, racial, generational or what have you, can only be overcome by altering our social representations of culture, of 'human nature' and so on. If, on the other hand, it is the prevailing view that is correct, then all we need do is persuade antagonistic groups or individuals that they have a great many features in common, that they are, in fact, amazingly similar, and we will have done away with hard and fast classifications and mutual stereotypes. However, the very limited success of this project to date might suggest that the other is worth trying.

On the other hand, it is impossible to classify without, at the same time, naming. Yet, these are two distinct activities. In our society, to name, to bestow a name on something or someone, has a very special, almost a solemn significance. In so naming something, we extricate it from a disturbing anonymity to endow it with a genealogy and to include it in a complex of specific words, to locate it, in fact, in the *identity matrix* of our culture.

Indeed, that which is anonymous, unnamable, cannot become a communicable image or be readily linked to other images. It is relegated to the world of confusion, uncertainty and inarticulateness, even when we are able to classify it approximately as normal or abnormal. Claudine Herzlich (Herzlich, 1973), in a study on the social representations of health and illness, has admirably analysed this elusive aspect of symptoms, the often abortive attempts we all make to contain them in speech, and the way they evade our grasp as a fish slips through the wide meshes of a net. To name, to say that something is this or that – if need be, to invent words for the purpose – enables us to fabricate a mesh that will be fine enough to keep the fish from escaping, and thus enables us to represent this thing. The result is always somewhat arbitrary but, insofar as a consensus is established, the word's association with the thing becomes customary and necessary.

By and large, my observations prove that to name a person or thing is to precipitate it (as a chemical solution is precipitated) and that the consequences of this are threefold: (*a*) once named, the person or thing can be described and acquires certain characteristics, tendencies, etc.; (*b*) he or it becomes distinct from other persons or things through these characteristics and tendencies; and (*c*) he or it becomes the object of a convention between those who adopt and share the same convention. Claudine Herzlich's study reveals that the conventional label 'fatigue' relates a complex of vague symptoms to certain social and individual patterns, distinguishes them from those of illness and health and makes them seem acceptable, almost justifiable to our society. It is, thus, permissible to talk about our fatigue, to say we are suffering from fatigue and to claim certain rights which, normally, in a society based on labour and welfare, would be forbidden. In other words, something which was formerly denied is now admitted.

I was able to make a very similar observation myself. I noticed that psychoanalytical terms such as 'neurosis' or 'complex' give consistency, and even reality, to states of tension, maladjustment, indeed of alienation which used to be seen as half-way between 'madness' and 'sanity' but were never taken very seriously. It was obvious that once they had been given a name they ceased to be disturbing. Psychoanalysis is also responsible for the proliferation of terms derived from a single model, so that we see a psychic symptom labelled 'timidity complex', 'sibling complex', 'power complex', 'Sardanapalus complex' which, of course, are not psychoanalytic terms but words coined to imitate them. Simultaneously the psychoanalytic vocabulary becomes anchored in the vocabulary of everyday life and thus becomes socialised. All that had been disturbing and enigmatic about these theories is related to symptoms or to persons who had seemed disturbed and disturbing, to constitute stable images in an organised context that has nothing in the least disturbing about it.

In the end, that which was unidentified is given a social identity – the scientific concept becomes part of common speech and individuals or symptoms are no more than familiar technical and scientific terms. A meaning is given to that which previously had none in the consensual world. We might almost say that this duplication and proliferation of names corresponds to a *nominalistic* tendency, a need to identify beings and things by fitting them into a prevalent social representation. We noted earlier the multiplication of 'complexes' that accompanied the popularisation of psychoanalysis and took the place of current expressions, such as 'shyness', 'authority', 'brothers', etc. By this means, those who speak and those who are spoken of are forced into an identity matrix they have not chosen and over which they have no control.

We might even go so far as to suggest that this is how all normal and deviant manifestations of social existence are labelled – individuals and groups are stigmatised, either psychologically or politically. For instance, when we call a person whose opinions do not conform to the current ideology an 'enemy of the people', this term, which according to that ideology evokes a definite image, excludes that person from the society to which he belongs. Thus it is obvious that naming is not a purely intellectual operation aiming at a clarity or logical coherence. It is an operation related to a social attitude. Such an observation is dictated by common sense and should never be ignored, for it is valid in every case and not simply in the exceptional cases I have given as examples.

In short, classifying and naming are two aspects of this anchoring of representations. Categories and names partake of what the art historian Gombrich has called a 'society of concepts'. And not simply in their content but also in their relations. I do not, in any way, deny the fact that they are naturally logical and tend towards stability and consistency as Heider and others maintain. Nor that such order is probably compelling. However, I can't help observing that these relations of stability and consistency are highly rarified and rigorous abstractions that partake neither directly nor operationally in the creation of representations. On the other hand, different relations can be seen at work which are induced by social patterns and produce a kaleidoscope of images or emotions. Friendship seems to play an important part in Fritz Heider's psychology when he analyses personal relationships (see the chapter by Flament in this volume). Doubtless he calls it by the general name of stability, but it must be obvious to all that, among every conceivable example of stability, he has chosen this one as the prototype for all the others.

The family is another very popular image for relationships in general. Thus intellectuals or workers are described as brothers; complexes as fathers; and neurotics as sons ('the complex is the neurotic's father' as someone recently stated in an interview); and so on and so forth. Conflict stands for another type of relationship and is always implicit in any description of contrasting pairs: what the term 'normal' implies and what it excludes; the conscious and the unconscious part of an individual; what we call health and what we call illness. Hostility is also in the background whenever we compare races, nations or classes. And relations of strength and weakness frequently define preferences where hierarchy enters the various categories of names. I quote at random, but it would be worthwhile to explore, in detail, the ways in which the logic of language expresses the relation between the elements of a system of classification and the process of naming. More suggestive patterns might emerge than those with which we are presently acquainted. Our present patterns are, anyhow, too artificial from a psychological point of view, and socially devoid of meaning. The fact is that if we visualise stability as a kind of friendship or conflict as outright hostility, it is simply because they are more accessible and concrete in such forms and can be correlated with our thoughts and emotions; we are thus better able to express them or to include them in a description which will be readily intelligible to anyone. This is the result of routinisation – a process which enables us to pronounce, read or write down a familiar word or notion in the place of, or in preference to, a less familiar word or notion.

At this point, the theory of representations entails two consequences. *First of all*, it excludes the idea of thought or perception which is without anchor. This excludes the idea of so-called bias in thought or perception. Every system of classifications and of the relations between systems presupposes a specific position, a point of view based on consensus. It's impossible to have a general, unbiased system any more than there exists a primary meaning for any particular object. The biases that are often described do not express, as they say, a social or cognitive deficit or limitation on the part of the individual but a normal difference in perspective between heterogeneous individuals or groups within a society. And they cannot be expressed for the simple reason that their opposite – the absence of a deficit or of a social or cognitive limitation – does not make sense. This is equivalent to admitting the impossibility of a social psychology from the point of view of Sirius, as those of yesteryear wanted it to be who pretended, at one and the same time, both to be in society and to observe it from the outside; who affirmed that *one* of the positions within society was normal and all the others deviations from it. This is a totally untenable position.

Secondly, systems of classification and naming are not, simply, means of grading and labelling persons or objects considered as discrete entities. Their main object is to facilitate the interpretation of characteristics, the understanding of intentions and motives behind people's actions, in fact, to form opinions. Indeed, this is a major pre-occupation and groups, as well as individuals, are prone, under certain conditions such as over-excitement or bewilderment, to what we might call interpretation mania. For we must not forget that to interpret an unfamiliar idea or being always requires categories, names, references in order that it may be integrated into Gombrich's 'society of concepts'. We fabricate them for this purpose, as meanings emerge, make them tangible and visible and similar to the ideas and beings we have already integrated and with which we are familiar. In this way, pre-existing representations are somewhat modified and those things about to be represented are modified even more, so that they acquire a new existence.

Objectifying. The English physicist Maxwell once said that what seemed abstract to one generation becomes concrete to the next. Amazing, incredible theories which nobody takes seriously turn out to be normal, credible and brimful of reality at a later date. How such an improbable fact as a physical body producing a reaction at a distance, in a place where it is not actually present, could become, in less than a century, a common, unquestionable fact, is at least as mysterious as its discovery – and of far greater practical consequence. We might indeed improve on Maxwell's statement by adding that what is unfamiliar and unperceived in one generation becomes familiar and obvious in the next.

This is not simply due to the passage of time or to habit, though both are probably necessary. This domestication is the result of objectification, which is a far more active process than anchoring, and one which we will now discuss.

Objectification saturates the idea of unfamiliarity with reality, turns it into the very essence of reality. Perceived at first in a purely intellectual, remote universe, it then appears before our eyes, physical and accessible. In this respect we are justified in asserting, with Lewin, that every representation realises – in the proper sense of the term – a different level of reality. These levels are created and maintained by a collectivity and vanish with it, having no reality of their own; for instance, the supernatural level, which was once all-pervasive and is now practically non-existent. Between total illusion and total reality there is an infinity of gradations which must be taken into account, for we created them, but illusion and reality are achieved in exactly the same way. The materialisation of an abstraction is one of the more mysterious features of thought and speech. Political and intellectual authorities, of every kind, exploit it to subdue the masses. In other words, such authority is based on the art of turning a representation into the reality of a representation, the word for a thing into a thing for the word.

To begin with, to objectify is to discover the iconic quality of an imprecise idea or being, to reproduce a concept in an image. To compare is already to picture, to fill what is naturally empty with substance. We have only to compare God to a father and what was invisible instantly becomes visible in our minds as a person to whom we can respond as such. A tremendous stock of words is in circulation in every society referring to specific objects, and we are under constant compulsion to provide their equivalent concrete meanings. Since we assume that words do not speak about 'nothing', we are compelled to link them to something, to find non-verbal equivalents for them. Just as most rumours are believed by virtue of the saying: 'There is no smoke without a fire', so a collection of images is created by virtue of the saying: 'Nobody speaks about nothing.'

Yet not all the words that constitute this stock can be linked to images, either because there are not enough images readily available, or because those they call to mind are taboo. Those which, owing to their ability to be represented, have been selected, merge with, or rather are integrated into, what I have called a pattern of *figurative nucleus*, a complex of images that visibly reproduces a complex of ideas. For example, the popular pattern of the psyche inherited from psychoanalysis is divided in two, the unconscious and the conscious – reminiscent of more common dualities such as involuntary–voluntary, soul–mind, inner–outer – located in space one above the other. It so happens that the higher brings pressure to bear on the lower and this 'repression' is what gives rise to the complexes. It is also noteworthy that the terms represented are those that are best known and most commonly employed. Yet, the absence of sexuality or *libido* is perhaps surprising since it plays such a significant part in the theory and is liable to be heavily charged with imagery. However, being the object of a taboo, it remains abstract. I have, indeed, been able to establish that not all psychoanalytic concepts undergo a similar transformation, not all are equally favoured. Thus, it seems that a society makes a selection of those to which it concedes figurative powers, according to its beliefs and to the pre-existing stock of images. Thus I noted some time ago: 'Though a paradigm is accepted because it has a strong framework, its acceptance is also due to its affinity with more current paradigms. The concreteness of the elements of this "psychic system" derives from their ability to translate ordinary situations' (Moscovici, 1976).

This does not, by any means, imply that changes do not occur subsequently. But such changes take place during the transmission of familiar outlines that gradually respond to the recent intake, just as a river bed is gradually modified by the waters flowing between its banks.

Once a society has adopted such a paradigm or figurative nucleus it finds it easier to talk about whatever the paradigm stands for, and because of this facility the words referring to it are used more often. Then formulae and clichés emerge that sum it up and join together images that were formerly distinct. It is not simply talked about but exploited in various social situations as a means of understanding others and one-self, of choosing and deciding. I showed (Moscovici, 1976) how psychoanalysis, once popularised, became a key that opened all the locks of private, public and political existence. Its figurative paradigm was detached from its original milieu by continuous use and acquired a sort of independence, just as a well-worn saying is gradually detached from the person who first said it and becomes an un-mediated fact. Thus, when the image linked to a word or idea becomes detached and is let loose in a society it is accepted as a reality, a conventional one, of course, but nonetheless a reality.

Although we all know that a 'complex' is a notion whose objective equivalent is highly vague, we still think and behave as though it were something that really existed when we assess a person and relate to him.

It doesn't simply symbolise his personality or his way of behaving, but actually represents him, *is* his 'complexed' personality and way of behaving. Indeed, it can be said unequivocally that in all cases, once the transfiguration has been achieved, then collective idolatry is a possibility. All images can be endowed with reality and efficiency to start with and end up by being worshipped. In our day, the psychoanalyst's couch or 'progress' are ready examples of this fact. This occurs to the extent that the distinction between image and reality is obliterated. The image of the concept ceases to be a sign and becomes a replica of reality, a simulacrum in the true sense of the word. Then the notion or entity from which it had proceeded loses its abstract, arbitrary character and acquires an almost physical, independent existence. It has the authority of a natural phenomenon for those who use it. Such is precisely the complex, to which as much reality is generally conceded as to an atom or a wave of the hand. This is an example of the word creating the means.

The second stage, in which the image is wholly assimilated and what is *perceived* replaces what is *conceived*, is the logical outcome of this state of affairs. If images exist, if they are essential for social communication and understanding, this is because they are not (and cannot remain) without reality any more than there can be smoke without a fire. Since they *must* have a reality we *find* one for them, no matter what. Thus, by a sort of logical imperative, images become elements of reality rather than elements of thought. The gap between the representation and what it represents is bridged, the peculiarities of the replica of the concept become peculiarities of the phenomena or of the environment to which they refer, become the actual referent of the concept. Thus everyone, nowadays, can perceive and distinguish a person's 'repressions' or his 'complexes' as if they were his physical features.

Our environment is largely composed of such images, and we are forever adding to it and modifying it by discarding some images and adopting others. Mead writes: 'We have just seen that imagery which goes into the structure of objects, and which represents the adjustment of the organism to environments which are not there, may serve toward the reconstruction of the objective field' (Mead, 1934).

When this takes place, images no longer occupy that peculiar position somewhere between words which are supposed to have a significance and real objects to which only we can give a significance, but exist as objects, are what is signified.

Culture – though not science – incites us, nowadays, to make reality out of generally significant ideas. There are obvious reasons for this, of which the most obvious, from society's point of view, is to appropriate and make common property of what originally pertained to a specific field or sphere. Philosophers have spent a lot of time trying to understand the process of transfer from one sphere to another. Without representations, without the metamorphosis of words into objects, there can clearly be no transfer at all. What I said about psychoanalysis is confirmed by painstaking research:

By objectifying the scientific content of psychoanalysis society no longer confronts psychoanalysis or the psychoanalyst, but a set of phenomena which it is free to treat as it pleases. The evidence of particular men has become the evidence of our own senses, an unknown universe is now familiar territory. The individual, in direct contact with this universe without the mediation of experts or their science, has progressed from a secondary to a primary relationship with the object, and this indirect assumption of power is a culturally fruitful action.

(Moscovici, 1976, p. 109)

Indeed, we thus find incorporated, in an anonymous manner, in our speech, our senses and our environment elements that are preserved and established as ordinary everyday material, the origins of which are obscure or forgotten. Their reality is a blank in our memory – but isn't all reality one? Don't we objectify precisely so as to forget that a creation, a material construct is the product of our own activity, that something is also someone? As I said: 'In the last analysis, psychoanalysis could be dead and buried, yet still, like Aristotle's physics, it would permeate our view of the world and its jargon would be used to describe psychological behaviour' (Moscovici, 1976).

The model for all learning in our society is the science of mathematical physics or the science of quantifiable, measurable objects. Insofar as the scientific content, even of a science of man or of life, presupposes this sort of reality all the beings to which it refers are conceived according to such a model. Since science refers to physical organs and since psychoanalysis is a science, then the unconscious, for example, or a complex will be seen as organs of the psychic system. Therefore, a complex can be amputated, grafted and perceived. As you can see, the living is assimilated to the inert, the subjective to the objective and the psychological to the biological. Every culture has its basic device for turning its representations into reality. Sometimes people and sometimes animals have served this purpose. Since the beginning of the mechanical age, objects have taken over and we are obsessed with a *reverse animism* that peoples the world with machines instead of living creatures. Thus we could say that where complexes, atoms or genes are concerned we don't so much imagine *an* object as create an image with *the help of the* object in general, with which we identify them.

However, no culture has a single, exclusive device. Because ours is partial to objects, it encourages us to objectify everything we come across. We personify, indiscriminately, feelings, social classes, the great powers, and when we write, we personify culture, since it is language itself that enables us to do so. Gombrich writes:

It so happens that Indo-European languages tend to this particular figure which we call personification, because so many of them endowed nouns with a gender which makes them indistinguishable from names for living species. Abstract nouns in Greek, in Latin, almost regularly take on the feminine gender and so the way is open for the world of ideas being peopled by personified abstractions such as *Victoria, Fortuna* or *Justitia*.   (Gombrich, 1972)

But chance alone cannot account for the extensive use we make of the peculiarities of grammar nor can it explain their efficiency.

This can best be done by trying to objectify grammar itself, which is achieved very simply by putting substantives – which, by definition refer to substances, to beings – in the place of adjectives, adverbs, etc. Thus attributes or relationships are turned into things. In fact, there is no such thing as *a* repression, since it refers to an action (to repress a memory), or *an* unconscious, since this is an attribute *of* something else (the thoughts and desires of a person). When we say that someone is dominated by his unconscious or suffers from repression as if he had a goitre or a sore throat, what we really mean is that he is not conscious of what he does and thinks; likewise when we say that he suffers from anxiety we mean that he is anxious or behaves anxiously.

However, once we have chosen to use a noun to describe a person's state, to say that he is dominated by his unconscious or suffers from anxiety rather than that his behaviour betrays a given particularity (that he is unconscious or anxious), we add to the number of beings by adding to the number of nouns. Thus a tendency to turn verbs into nouns, or a partiality for these among grammatical categories of words with similar meanings, is a sure sign that grammar is being objectified, that words don't merely represent things, but create them and invest them with their own properties. In these circumstances language is like a mirror that can separate appearance from reality, separate what is seen from what is and represent it immediately in the form of an object's or a person's visible appearance, while enabling us to assess this object or person as if they were not distinct from reality, as if they were real – and particularly one's own self to which one has no other way of relating. Thus the nouns we invent and create to give an abstract form to complex substances or phenomena *become* the substance or the phenomenon, and that is what we never cease to do. Every self-evident truth, every taxonomy, every reference in the world represents a crystallised set of significances and tacitly acknowledged names; their tacitness is precisely what ensures their chief representative function: to express first the image and then the concept as reality.

To have a clearer understanding of the consequences of our tendency to objectify, we might consider such dissimilar social phenomena as hero-worship, the personification of nations, races and classes, etc. Each case involves a social representation that transmutes words into flesh, ideas into natural powers, nations or human languages into a language of things. Recent events have shown that the outcome of such transmutations can be sinister and disheartening in the extreme for those of us who would like all the world's tragedies to have a happy ending and to see right prevail. The defeat of rationality and the fact that history is so sparing with its happy endings should not deter us from examining these significant phenomena and especially from the conviction that the principles involved are simple and not dissimilar to those we have considered above.

Thus our representations make the unfamiliar familiar. Which is another way of saying that they depend on memory. Memory's density prevents them from undergoing sudden modifications on the one hand and, on the other, allows them a certain amount of independence from present events – just as accumulated wealth protects us from a hand-to-mouth existence. It is from this padding of common experiences and memories that we draw the images, language and gestures required to overcome the unfamiliar with its attendant anxieties. Experiences and memories are neither inert nor dead. They are dynamic and immortal. Anchoring and objectifying are therefore ways of handling memory. The former keeps it in motion; since it is inner-directed it is always putting in and taking out objects, persons and events which it classifies according to type and labels with a name. The second, being more or less other-directed, draws concepts and images from it to mingle and reproduce them with the outside world, to make things-to-be-known out of what is already known. It would be appropriate to quote Mead again here: 'The peculiar intelligence of the human form lies in this elaborate control gained through the past' (Mead, 1934).

V   Right-wing causalities and left-wing causalities

(1) Attributions and social representations

Farr (1977) has rightly pointed out that there is a relation between the way we picture a thing to ourselves and the way we describe it to others. Let us therefore accept this relation while noting that the problem of causality has always been crucial for those concerned with social representations, such as Fauconnet, Piaget and, more modestly, myself. However, we consider the problem from a very different angle to that of our American colleagues – American being used here in a purely geographical sense. The transatlantic social psychologist bases his enquiries on the theory of attribution and is mainly concerned with how we attribute causes to the people and things that surround us. It would hardly be an overstatement to say that his theories are based on a single principle – man thinks like a statistician – and that there is only one rule to his method – to establish the coherence of the information we receive from the environment. In these circumstances a lot of ideas and images – indeed, all those society provides – either do not tally with statistical thinking and so are seen as negligible since they cannot be fitted in, or else *blur* our perception of reality such as it is. They are, therefore, purely and simply ignored.

The theory of social representations, on the other hand, takes as its point of departure the diversity of individuals, attitudes and phenomena, in all their strangeness and unpredictability. Its aim is to discover how individuals and groups can construct a stable, predictable world out of such diversity. The scientist who studies the universe is convinced that there exists a hidden order under the apparent chaos, and the child who never stops asking 'Why?' is no less sure of it. This is a fact: if, then, we seek an answer to the eternal 'Why?' it isn't on the strength of the information we have received, but because we are convinced that every being and every object in the world is other than it seems. The ultimate aim of science is to eliminate this 'Why?', whereas social representations can hardly do without it.

Representations are based on the saying: 'No smoke without fire.' When we hear or see something we instinctively assume it is not fortuitious but that it must have a cause and an effect. When we see smoke we know that a fire has been lit somewhere and, to find out where the smoke comes from, we go in search of this fire. Thus the saying is not a mere image but expresses a thought process, an imperative – the need to decode all the signs that occur in our social environment and which we cannot leave alone so long as their significance, the 'hidden fire', has not been located. Thus, social thought makes extensive use of suspicions which set us on the track of causality.

I could give any number of examples. The most notable are those trials where the accused are presented as culprits, wrongdoers and criminals, and the proceedings only serve to confirm a pre-established verdict. The German or Russian citizens who saw their Jewish or subversive compatriots sent to concentration camps or shipped to the Gulag Islands certainly didn't think they were innocent. They had to be guilty since they were imprisoned. Good reasons for putting them in prison were attributed (the word is apt) to them because it was impossible to believe that they were accused, ill-treated and tortured for no reason at all.

Such examples of manipulation, not to say of the distortion of causality, prove that the smokescreen is not always intended cunningly to conceal repressive measures, but may indeed even draw our attention to them so that onlookers will be led to assume that there were undoubtedly very good reasons for lighting the fire. Tyrants are usually masters in psychology and know that people will automatically proceed from the punishment to the criminal and the crime so as to make these strange and horrible occurrences tally with their idea of trial and justice.

(2) Bi-causal and mono-causal explanations

The theory of social representations makes the assumption, based on innumerable observations, that we generally act on *two* different sets of motivations. In other words, that thought is *bi-causal* rather than *mono-causal* and establishes simultaneously a relation of cause to effect and a relation of ends to means. This is where the theory differs from attribution theory and where, in this duality, social representations differ from science.

When a phenomenon recurs we establish a correlation between ourselves and it and then find some meaningful explanation that suggests the existence of a rule or law yet to be discovered. In this case the transition from correlation to explanation is not stimulated by our perception of the correlation or by the recurrence of the events, but by our awareness of a discrepancy between this correlation and some others, between the phenomenon we perceived and the one we had anticipated, between a specific case and a prototype, between the exception and the rule; in fact, to use the terms I have previously employed, between the familiar and the unfamiliar. This is indeed the decisive factor. To quote MacIver: 'It is the exception, the deviation, the interference, the abnormality that stimulates our curiosity and seems to call for an explanation. And we often attribute to some one "cause" all the happening that characterizes the new or unanticipated or altered situation' (MacIver, 1943).

We see a person or a thing that does not tally with our representations, does not coincide with its prototype (a woman prime minister), or a void, an absence (a city with no hoardings), or we find a Muslim in a Catholic community, a physician without physics (a psychoanalyst), etc. In each case we feel challenged to find an explanation. On the one hand, there is a lack of recognition, on the other a lack of cognition; on the one hand, a lack of identity, on the other, a statement of non-identity. In these circumstances we are always obliged to stop and think and finally to admit that we don't understand why this person behaves as he does or that object has such-and-such an effect.

How can we answer this challenge? This *primary causality* to which we spontaneously turn depends on finalities. Since most of our relationships are with live human beings we are confronted with the intentions and purposes of others which, for practical reasons, we cannot understand. Even when our car breaks down or the apparatus we are using in the laboratory doesn't work we can't help thinking that the car 'refuses' to go, the hostile apparatus 'refuses to collaborate' and so prevents us from pursuing our experiment. Everything people do or say, every natural disturbance, seems to have a hidden significance, intention or purpose which we try to discover. Likewise, we tend to interpret intellectual polemics or controversies as personal conflicts and to wonder what reason there can be for the protagonists' animosity, what private motives are at the bottom of such antagonisms.

Instead of saying: 'For what reason does he behave like that?' we say: 'For what purpose does he behave like that?' and the quest for a cause becomes a quest for motives and intentions. In other words we interpret, look for hidden animosities and obscure motives such as hatred, envy or ambition. We are always convinced that people don't act by chance, that everything they do corresponds to a plan. Whence the general tendency to personify motives and incentives, to represent a cause imagistically as when we say of a political dissident that he is a 'traitor', an 'enemy of the people', or when we use the term 'Oedipus Complex' to describe a certain type of behaviour, etc. The notion becomes an almost physical 'agent', a performer who, in certain circumstances, carries out a precise intention. And this notion comes to embody the thing itself rather than being seen as a representation of our particular perception of this thing.

Secondary causality, which is not spontaneous, is an efficient causality. It is dictated by our education, our language, our scientific view of the world, all of which tend to make us divest the actions, conversations and phenomena of the outside world of their share of intention and responsibility and to see them only as experimental data to be studied impartially. Therefore, we tend to gather all the information we can about them so as to classify them in a given category and thus identify their cause, explain them. Such is the historian's attitude, the psychologist's or indeed any scientist's. For instance, we infer from a person's behaviour that he is middle class or lower class, schizophrenic or paranoid; thus we explain his present behaviour. Proceeding from effect to cause, on the basis of information we have gleaned, we relate one to the other, ascribe effects to specific causes. Heider had already shown, long ago, that a person's behaviour derives from two different sets of motivations, inner and outer, and that the latter derive not from the person but from his environment, his social status and from the compulsions other people exert over him. Thus, the person who votes for a political party does so by personal conviction; but in some countries such a vote may be compulsory and to vote for a different party or to abstain from voting entails expulsion or imprisonment.

So, to sum up the way in which the process of attribution operates, we might say that, first and foremost, there exists a prototype which serves as a measuring-rod for events or behaviours that are considered as effects. If the effect conforms to the prototype it is assumed that it has an exterior cause; if not, if the effect does not conform, the cause is assumed to be specific and inner. A man wearing a beret and carrying a long loaf of French bread under his arm is a Frenchman, since such is our representation of the type. But if the person turns out to be an American he no longer conforms to this model and we assume that his behaviour is singular or even aberrant since it is not true to type.

Obviously all this is grossly over-simplified; what actually takes place in the mind is not so easily inferred. But I wanted to make the following fact clear: in social representations the two causalities act in concert, they merge to produce specific characteristics and we constantly switch from one to the other. On the one hand, by seeking a subjective order behind apparently objective phenomena, the result will be an inference; on the other, by seeking an objective order behind apparently subjective phenomena, the result will be an attribution. On the one hand, we reconstruct hidden intentions to account for a person's behaviour: this is a first-person causality. On the other hand, we seek invisible factors to account for visible behaviour: this is a third-person causality.

The contrast between these two kinds of causality should be stressed, since the circumstances of social existence are often manipulated for the purpose of showing up either the one or the other, for example to pass off an end as an effect. Thus when the Nazis set fire to the Reichstag they did so to make their persecutions look, not like the execution of a plan, but like a result whose cause was the fire supposedly lit by their opponents and whose smoke concealed a very different 'fire'. Nor is it uncommon for a person to provoke, on a minor scale, a fire of this kind to obtain promotion, for instance, or even a divorce. Moreover, these examples enable us to see that attributions always involve a relation between ends, or intentions, and means. As MacIver says: 'The why of the motivation lies, often obscurely, behind the why of objective' (MacIver, 1943).

The biological and social sciences try to reverse the psychological order of the two questions and to present motivations as causes. When they examine a phenomenon they ask to what purpose does it correspond? What function does it fulfil? Once the purpose or function has been established they present the former as an impersonal cause and the latter as the mechanism it triggers off. Such was Darwin's procedure when he discovered natural selection. The term *causalisation* would be apt in this case, suggesting, as it does, that ends are disguised as causes, means as effects and intentions as results. Relations between individuals, as well as those between political parties or groups of any kind, make extensive use of this procedure whenever the behaviour of other people has to be interpreted. Whenever, in fact, the question 'Why?' has to be answered. And the answer given often suffices to set minds at rest to preserve a representation or to convince an audience that was only too ready to be convinced.

(3) Social causality

To sum up, a theory of social causality is a theory of the attributions and inferences individuals make and also of the transition from the one to the other. Clearly, such a transition is inseparable from a scientific theory that deals with this phenomenon. However, psychologists are in the habit of studying either attributions or inferences and of ignoring the transition between them. Thus they ascribe causes to an environment or to an individual each seen independently, which is just as ridiculous as studying the relation of an effect to its cause without first formulating a theory or defining a paradigm to account for this relation. This very peculiar attitude has its limitations as I hope to prove with the following example.

Attribution theory gives a number of reasons to account for why an individual attributes certain behaviours to another person and other behaviours to the environment – to the fact that Peter is good at games or else that he lives in the suburbs, for example. But, as we noted earlier, these are based on a single principle: man is a statistician and his brain works like an infallible computer.[1] Psychoanalysis, on the other hand, would see such behaviours as the simple rationalisation of hostile or kindred feelings since, for the psychoanalyst, all our assessments are based on emotions. This trivial example clearly illustrates the fact that any explanation depends primarily on the idea we have of reality. It is this idea that governs our perceptions and the inferences we draw from them. And it governs our social relations as well. Thus we can assert that when we answer the question 'Why?' we start from a social representation or from the general context in which we have been led to give this specific answer.

Here is a concrete example: unemployment at the moment is widespread and each of us has at least one unemployed man or woman among his personal acquaintances. Why doesn't this man or woman have a job? The answer to this question will vary according to the speaker. For some, the unemployed just don't bother to find a job, are too choosy or, at best, unlucky. For others they are the victims of an economic recession, of unjustified redundancies or, more commonly, of the inherent injustice of a capitalist economy. Thus the former ascribe the cause of unemployment to the individual, to his social attitude, while the latter ascribe it to the economic and political situation, to his social status, to an environment that makes such a situation inevitable. The two explanations are utterly opposed to each other and obviously stem from distinct social representations. The first representation stresses the individual's responsibility and personal energy – social problems can only be solved by each individual. The second representation stresses social responsibility, denounces social injustice and advocates collective solutions for individual problems. Shaver has noted such reactions even in the United States:

Personal attributions about the reason for welfare lead to speeches about 'welfare chiselers', appeals for a return to simpler days or the Protestant ethic, and laws designed to make needed financial assistance more difficult to obtain. Situational attributions, on the other hand, are likely to suggest that expanded government-supported employment, better job training, and increased educational opportunity for all will provide more lasting reductions in public assistance.   (Shaver, 1975, p. 133)

However, I do not entirely agree with my American colleague. I myself would reverse the order of the factors involved, stressing the primacy of representations and saying that it is these, in each case, that dictate the attribution either to the individual or to the society. By so doing, I obviously do not deny the idea of rationality and a correct manipulation of received information, but simply maintain that what is taken into account, the experiences we have, that is the causes we select, is dictated, in each case, by a system of social representations.

Thus I come to the following proposition: in the societies we inhabit today, personal causality is a right-wing explanation and situational causality is a left-wing explanation. Social psychology can't ignore the fact that the world is structured and organised according to such a division and that there is a permanent one. Indeed, each of us is necessarily compelled to adopt one of these two kinds of causality together with the view of the other which it entails. The consequences which derive from such a proposition could not be more precise: the motives for our actions are dictated by, and related to, social reality, a reality whose contrasting categories divide human thought as neatly as do dualities like high and low, male and female, etc. It had seemed that motivation could be ascribed to a simple thought process and now it turns out to be determined by environmental influences, social status, one person's relation to other people, his pre-conceived opinions, all of which play their part. This is highly significant and, once it has been accepted, it precludes the existence of supposedly neutral categories of personal and situational attribution and replaces them by definitely right- or left-wing categories of motivation. Even if the substitution does not hold in all cases it is generally observable.

Experiments carried out by certain psychologists (Hewstone and Jaspars, 1982) confirm the notion of such a substitution. Here, for instance, is a typical example: the American psychologist Lerner has suggested that we explain someone's behaviour on the premise that 'People only get what they deserve.' This has come to be known as 'the just world hypothesis'. He sees this as an almost innate way of thinking. The Canadian psychologists Guimond and Simard tried to substantiate this theory, and were not surprised to find that such an attitude was mainly that of people belonging to a majority or a ruling class. On the other hand, there was no trace of it among those who belonged to minorities or under-privileged classes. To be precise, they were able to establish that English-speaking Canadians tended to see the French Canadians as responsible for their status and provided individualistic explanations. French Canadians, however, held the English Canadians responsible and their explanations involved the structure of society itself.

If a laboratory experiment can be taken as an example of what occurs in society we might improve somewhat on these findings. Dominating and dominated classes do not have a similar representation of the world they share but see it with different eyes, judge it according to specific criteria and each does so according to their own categories. For the former, it is the individual who is responsible for all that befalls him and especially his failures. For the latter, failures are always due to the circumstances which society creates for the individual. It is in this precise sense that the expression: right-wing/left-wing causality (an expression which is as objective and scientific as the dualities high/low, person/environment, etc.) can be applied to concrete cases.

(4) Conclusions

By restricting itself to an individual and an inductive frame of reference, attribution theory has proved less fruitful than it might otherwise have been. This state of affairs could be remedied by: (*a*) switching from the individual to the collective sphere; (*b*) abandoning the idea of man as statistician and of a mechanistic relation between man and the world; (*c*) re-instating social representations as necessary mediators.

Suggestions have already been made to improve the theory (Hewstone and Jaspars, 1982). However, we must bear in mind that causality does not exist on its own, but only within a representation that vindicates it. Nor should we forget that when we consider two causalities we have also to consider the relation between them. In other words, we should always seek those super-causes that have a dual action, both as agents and as efficient causes, which constitute this relation. Each of our beliefs, thought processes and conceptions of the world has a cause of this kind to which we have recourse as a last resort. It is in this we put our trust and it is this we invoke in all circumstances. What I have in mind are words such as 'God', 'Progress', 'Justice',

'History': they refer to an entity or a being gifted with social status and acting both as cause and as end. They are notable in that they account for all that happens in every possible sphere of reality. There is no difficulty in identifying them but I think we would be hard put to explain the part they play and their extraordinary power.

I am convinced that, sooner or later, we shall achieve a clearer idea of causality. And I shall consider our present enquiries concluded, even if their final aim is not achieved, when psychologists have at their command a common language which will enable them to establish a concordance between the forms of thought of individuals and the social content of those thoughts.

VI   A survey of the enquiries undertaken to date

(1) Some common methodological themes and links with other social sciences

The body of research on which these theories are based and from which they evolved is somewhat restricted. But it is all we have to date. Whatever the specific objective of these enquiries has been they have, however, always shared the following four methodological principles:

(a) *to obtain material from samples of conversations normally exchanged in a society*. Some of these exchanges deal with important topics, whilst others concern topics that may be foreign to the group – some action, event or personality, about which or whom they wonder 'What's it all about?', 'Why did it happen?', 'Why did he do it?', 'What was the purpose of that action?' – but all tending towards mutual agreement. Tarde (1910) was the first to maintain that opinions and representations are created in the course of conversations as elementary ways of relating and of communicating. He demonstrated how they emerge in specially reserved places (such as salons, cafés, etc.); how they are determined by the physical and psychological dimensions of those encounters between individuals (Moscovici, 1967) and how they change with the passage of time. He even elaborated a plan for a social science of the future which would be a comparative study of conversations. Indeed, the interactions that naturally occur in the course of conversations enable individuals and groups to become more familiar with incongruous objects or ideas and thus to master them (Moscovici, 1976). Such infra-communications and thought, based on rumour, constitute a kind of intermediate layer between private and public life and facilitate the passage from the one to the other. In other words, conversation is at the hub of our consensual universes because it shapes and animates social representations and thus gives them a life of their own.

(*b*) *to consider social representations as a means of re-creating reality*. Through communication individuals and groups give a physical reality to ideas and images, to systems of classification and naming. The phenomena and people with whom we deal in everyday life are not usually raw data but are the products or embodiments of a collectivity, an institution, etc. All reality is the reality of someone or is reality *for* someone else, even if it be that of the laboratories where we carry out our experiments. It would not be logical to think of them otherwise by taking them out of context. Most of the problems we face in the course of our social and intellectual pursuits are not derived from the difficulty of representing things or people, but from the fact that they are representations, that is substitutes for other things or other people. Thus before embarking on a specific study we must enquire into the origins of the object, and consider it as a work of art and not as raw material. Though, to be precise, it is something re-made, re-constructed rather than something constructed anew since, on the one hand the only reality available is that which has been structured by past generations or by another group, and on the other, we re-produce it in the outside world and thus cannot avoid distorting our inner images and models. What we create, in fact, is a referent, an entity to which we refer which is distinct from any other and corresponds to our representation of it. And its recurrence – either during a conversation or in the environment (for instance a 'complex', a symptom, etc.) – ensures its autonomy, rather as a saying becomes independent from the person who first said it when it has been repeated often enough. The most remarkable result of this reconstruction of abstractions as realities is that they become detached from the group's subjectivity, from the vicissitudes of its interactions and therefore from time, and thus they acquire permanence and stability. Isolated from the flow of communications that produced them they become as independent from these as a building is independent from the architect's plan or the scaffoldings employed in its construction.

It might be opportune to point out a few distinctions that should be taken into account. Some representations concern facts and others ideas. The first displace their object from an abstract to a concrete cognitive level; the second, through a change of perspective, either compose or decompose their object – they may, for instance, present billiard balls as an illustration of the atom, or consider a person psychoanalytically as divided into a conscious and an unconscious. Yet both create pre-established and immediate frames of reference for opinions and perceptions within which objective reconstructions of both persons and situations occur automatically and which underlie individual experience and thought. It is not so much the fact that such reconstructions are social and influence everybody that is surprising and has to be explained, but rather that sociability requires them, expresses in them its tendency to pose as non-sociability and as part of the natural world.

(c) *that the character of social representations is revealed especially in times of crisis and upheaval*, when a group or its images are undergoing a change. People are then more willing to talk, images and expressions are livelier, collective memories are stirred and behaviour becomes more spontaneous. Individuals are motivated by their desire to understand an increasingly unfamiliar and perturbed world. Social reconstructions appear unadorned, since the divisions and barriers between private and public worlds have become blurred. But the worst crisis occurs when tensions between reified and consensual universes create a rift between the language of concepts and that of representations, between scientific and ordinary knowledge. It is as though society itself were split and there were no longer a means of bridging the gap between the two universes. Such tensions can be the result of new discoveries, new conceptions, their popularisation in everyday speech and in the collective awareness – for instance, the acceptance by traditional medicine of modern theories such as psychoanalysis and natural selection. These can be followed by actual revolutions of common sense which are no less significant than scientific revolutions. The way in which they occur and re-connect one universe with the other casts some light on the process of social representations and gives exceptional significance to our enquiries.

(d) *that the people who elaborate such representations be seen as something akin to amateur 'scholars' and the groups they form as modern-day equivalents to those societies of amateur scholars that existed about a century ago.* Such is the nature of most unofficial gatherings, discussions in cafés and clubs or political reunions where the modes of thought and expression reflect the curiosities that are voiced and the social links that are established at the time. On the other hand, many representations derive from professional works that are addressed to this 'amateur' public; I am thinking of those pedagogues, popularisers of science and journalists of a certain kind (Moscovici, 1976) whose writings make it possible for anyone to see himself as a sociologist, economist, physicist, doctor or psychologist. I myself have been in the situation of Agatha Christie's doctor who observes: 'Psychology's all right if it's left to the psychologist. The trouble is, everyone is an amateur psychologist nowadays. My patients tell *me* exactly what complexes and neuroses they're suffering from, without giving me a chance to tell them' (Agatha Christie, 1957).

Perhaps, after all, this volume appears too late in the day. Indeed, a number of my theories concur with those of various schools of sociology and of the sociology of knowledge in English-speaking countries. Farr (1978, 1981) refers, in a couple of articles, to the relation between the theories outlined above and theories of attribution, the social construction of reality, ethnomethodology, etc. However, from another point of view this volume seems to be appearing at just the right time for a reassessment of the field of social psychology in relation to related disciplines.

It cannot be denied that the programme for a sociology of knowledge, though often discussed, has not even begun to be realised. Indeed works such as that of Berger and Luckmann (1967) refer to a theory of the origins of common sense and of the structure of reality, but I believe that this theory, unlike my own, has not been tested. As to ethnomethodology, it originated from the distinction between the 'rationality' of science and the 'rationality' of common sense as applied to everyday life. It has examined this distinction by deliberately splitting the social fabric and then, in the light of attempts to restore the tissue's unity, exposing the social norms and conventions that constituted its continuity and texture. Once again, the result is a structure of reality stemming from a generally shared choice of rules and conventions.

I myself, on the other hand, have found it more rewarding to take advantage of the breaks which occur naturally and which reveal both the propensity of individuals and of groups to intervene in the normal sequence of events and to modify their development, and how they achieve their aim. In this way, it is not only the rules and conventions that come to light, but also the 'theories' on which they are based and the languages that express them. In my opinion, this is essential – social regularities and harmonies figure in a common representation and cannot be understood independently. Besides, the work of construction in which the sociologists are interested consists mainly, in our societies, in a process of transformation from a reified to a consensual universe, to which everything else is subordinated.

I have chosen these two examples to underline the affinities, but a number of others could be added. What they all have in common is their concern for social representations, and investigators would do well to recall Durkheim's advice: 'Since observation reveals the existence of a type of phenomenon known as representation with specific features that distinguish it from other natural phenomena, it is impractical to behave as if it didn't exist' (Durkheim, 1963).

Today, a high proportion of the sociological imagination is pre-occupied with consensual universes even to the extent of being more or less restricted to it. Such an attitude may be justified in that it fills a gap left by social psychology. But it would be better if there was a re-grouping of disciplines around this 'type of phenomenon known as representation' clarifying the task of sociology and giving to our own discipline the breadth of scope it so badly needs.

(2) A brief review of some of the major field studies

In a recent publication I had the pleasure of noting that, at last, American psychologists are prepared to acknowledge, though without actually naming them, the importance of social representations: 'Such tacit, global theories, as well as many more specific theories, including theories about specific individuals or classes of individuals, govern our understanding or behaviours, our casual explanation of past behaviour and our predictions of future behaviours' (Nisbett and Ross, 1980).

Or we might add, serve to conceal, ignore and replace behaviour. And since *Gedankenexperiments* or *Gedankenbehaviours* are at least as important in everyday life as they are in science, it would be a mistake to ignore them simply because they explain and predict nothing. But a lack of interest in anything written in languages other than English or for experiments carried out in another country – a lack of interest which, a generation ago, would have disqualified any scholar, whether in the United States or elsewhere – leads them to assert with total confidence:

There has been surprisingly little research on those beliefs and theories shared by the mass of people in our cultures. Heider (1958) was perhaps the first to emphasize their importance, and Abelson (1968) was the first (and nearly only) investigator to attempt to study them empirically. What little research has been done on people's theories has focused on individual differences in belief and theories.   (Nisbett and Ross, 1980)

Now it so happens that, at these precise dates, research on 'people's theories' was thriving and producing widely acclaimed results. I do not suggest that such research was superior to that mentioned, or even excellent in itself, but simply that it occurred and was not restricted to the study of 'individual differences'. If investigators in our field continue to see the whole of science represented by that of their own country, there will always be a Joe Bloggs or a Jacques Dupont to invent everything, like Ivan Popoff before them. Which is something we can very well do without.

As we said, it is during the process of transformation that phenomena are more easily perceived. Therefore we concentrated on the emergence of social representations: either starting from *scientific theories* – so as to follow the metamorphosis of the latter within a society and the manner in which they renewed common sense – or from *current events*, experiences and 'objective' knowledge which a group had to face in order to constitute and control its own world.

Both starting-points are equally valid since, in one case, it is a question of observing the effect of a change from one intellectual and social level to another and, in the second, of observing the organisation of a complex of quasi-material objects and environmental occurrences that an implicit representation normally encapsulates. The mechanisms involved are, anyhow, identical.

Common sense is continually being created in our societies, especially where scientific and technical knowledge is popularised. Its content, the symbolic images derived from science on which it is based and which, rooted in the mind's eye, shape common speech and behaviour, are constantly being touched up. In the process the store of social representations, without which a society cannot communicate or relate to and define reality, is replenished. Moreover, these representations acquire an ever greater authority as we receive more and more material through their mediation – analogies, implicit descriptions and explanations of phenomena, personalities, the economy, etc., together with the categories required to account for the behaviour of a child, for instance, or of a friend. That which, in the long run, acquires the validity of something our senses or our understanding perceive directly always turns out to be the secondary, modified product of scientific research. In other words, common sense no longer circulates from below to on high, but from on high to below; it is no longer the point of departure but the point of arrival. The continuity which philosophers stipulate between common sense and science is still there but it is not what it used to be.

The spread of psychoanalysis in France provided a practical example on which to start our investigations into the genesis of common sense. How did psychoanalysis penetrate the various layers of our society and influence our outlook and behaviour? What modifications did it undergo in order to do so? We investigated, methodically, the means by which its theories were anchored and objectified, how a system of classification and of the naming of persons and behaviours was elaborated, a 'new' language stemming from psychoanalytic terms was created and the part played by bi-causality in normal thinking. Apart from this, we explained how a theory shifts from one cognitive level to another by becoming a social representation. We naturally took political and religious backgrounds into account and stressed their role in such transitions. Finally, our enquiry enabled us to specify the way in which a representation shapes the reality we inhabit, creates new social types – the psychoanalyst, the neurotic, etc. – and modifies behaviour in relation to this reality.

Simultaneously we studied the problem of mass communications and their role in establishing common sense. In this case, common sense could be elevated to the rank of a major ideology; for such is the status of psychoanalysis in present-day France – comparable, in every way, to that of an official creed it became clear that, as far as evolution is concerned, the presence of a social representation constitutes the necessary preliminary to the acquisition of status. Moreover, we can state quite definitely the order of the three phases of this evolution: (*a*) *the scientific phase* of its elaboration from a theory by a scientific discipline (economics, biology, etc.); (*b*) *the 'representative' phase* in which it diffuses within a society and its images, concepts and vocabulary are recast and adapted; (*c*) *the ideological phase* in which the representation is appropriated by a party, a school of thought or an organ of state and is logically reconstructed so that a product, created by the society as a whole, can be enforced in the name of science. Thus every ideology has these two elements: a content, derived from below, and a form from above that gives common sense a scientific aura. Other investigations were concerned with more scientific theories (Ackermann and Zygouris, 1974; Barbichon and Moscovici, 1965), and our findings contributed to the formulation of a more general theory of the popularisation of scientific knowledge (Roqueplo, 1974).

In a second series of studies we examined more specifically the dynamics of technical and theoretical changes. To put it briefly, during the years 1950 to 1960, a vast diffusion of medical techniques and theories occurred in France as a result of an increase in medical consumption. Together with a new doctor–patient relationship, a whole new attitude to health and the body was rapidly transforming long-standing images and theories. One of the first to study the situation was

Claudine Herzlich in her work on the representations of health and illness. Her purpose was to highlight the emergence of a system of classification and interpretation of symptoms in response to what must some day be acknowledged as a cultural revolution in our views of health, illness and death (Herzlich, 1973). If one is nostalgic to see the disappearance of death from our awareness and from our rituals this dates from the time when confidence in the scientific powers of medicine was established.

A further study dealt with the social representation of the body. This revealed that our perceptions and conceptions of the body were no longer suited to the reality that was taking shape, and that a major upheaval was inevitable. We therefore analysed these representations; and in due course, under the influence of youth movements, the women's liberation movement and the spread of biodynamics, etc., ways of seeing and experiencing the body were radically changed. By taking up our enquiry again after this profound change of representations had occurred we were able to take advantage of something akin to a natural experiment. Indeed, a significant cultural revolution having taken place, we were in a position to observe its effects, step by step, and to compare what we had previously observed to what was now the case. In other words, we began to grapple with the problem of modification in social representations and of their evolution. This constitutes the bulk of Denise Jodelet's work (Jodelet and Moscovici, 1975) at the moment. But she was well prepared for such an investigation as a result of her study of mental patients farmed out among the inhabitants of various French villages. By observing this fostering over a period of some two years, she was able to describe, in great detail, the development of the relationships between villagers and patients and how, by its very nature, it gave rise to discriminations aimed at 'situating', in a familiar world, the mental patients whose presence was eminently disturbing. These discriminations, moreover, were based on a vocabulary and on social representations which had been delicately elaborated by the small communities. These communities felt somehow threatened by the harmless beings who had been placed in their midst by personal misfortune and institutional routine.

Finally, a wholly original study by René Kaës (1976) on group psychotherapy shows, on the one hand, how such groups produce certain types of representation concerned with what constitutes a group and how it functions and, on the other, how such representations reflect the group's evolution. There is no doubt that they have a cultural, not to say a scientific, significance and it is somewhat surprising to see them surface in such circumstances. Nonetheless, the fact remains that such representations canalise the flow of emotions and of fluctuating interpersonal relationships.

Denise Jodelet's collaboration with Stanley Milgram (Jodelet and Milgram, 1977) on the social images of Paris proves that urban space, or the raw material of everyday life, is utterly determined by representations and is by no means as factitious as we tend to believe. Moreover, it admirably confirms our contention that thinking is an environment, since nothing could be more pregnant with ideas than a city. The theories expressed in the first four sections of this essay have been corroborated by this first generation of investigations. Others bearing on culture (Kaës, 1968), intergroupal relations (Quaglino, 1979), educational methods (Gorin, 1980), etc. elaborated certain aspects we had overlooked, while studies of the representations of the child stressed the heuristic importance of the subject as a whole (Chombart de Lauwe, 1971).

VII The status of representations: stimulus or mediators?

(1) Social representations as independent variables

J. A. Fodor writes:

> It has been a main argument of this book that if you want to know what response a given stimulus is going to elicit you must find out what internal representation the organism assigns to the stimulus. Patently, the character of such assignments must in turn depend upon what kind of representational system is available for mediating the cognitive processes of the organism.   (Fodor, 1975)

A healthy concern with both the theory and the fact of representations can now be observed more or less everywhere. Thus what takes place within a society has become a major pre-occupation rather than simply how it creates and transforms the environment. But although such concern exists it is, nonetheless, essential to guard against traditional half-measures like those comprising the injection of a minimum of subjectivity and thought into the 'black box' of our brains or simply adding a surplus of soul to our de-humanised, mechanised world.

Indeed, if Fodor's text – which sums up a wide assortment of writings – is read with some attention, the use of two words cannot fail to astonish: 'internal' and 'mediating'. These terms imply that representations relay the flow of information coming to us from the outside world: that they are mediating links between the real cause (stimulus) and the concrete effect (response). Thus they are mediating, or chance causes. This re-conditioned behaviourism, to which we always resort at difficult times, is a clever piece of tinkering, but it is *ad hoc*, by definition, and not very convincing.

Here, we must stress the firm stand the theory of representations has taken in this respect: *as far as social psychology is concerned* social representations are independent variables, explanatory stimuli. This does not mean that, for instance, where sociology, or history is concerned what for us is explanatory does not itself require explaining.[2] It is readily obvious why this should be so. Each stimulus is selected from a vast variety of possible stimuli and can produce an infinite variety of reactions. It is the pre-established images and paradigms that both determine the choice and restrict the range of reactions. When a child sees its mother smile it perceives a number of different signs – wide-open eyes, distended lips, movements of the head – which incite it to sit up, scream, etc. Such images and paradigms portend what will appear to the actor or the spectator as stimulus or response: the child's arms stretched towards the mother's smiling face or the mother's smiling face lowered towards the child's outstretched arms.

Emotional reactions, perceptions and rationalisations are not responses to an exterior stimulus as such, but to the category in which we classify such images, to the names we give them. We react to a stimulus insofar as we have objectified it and re-created it, at least partially, at the moment of its inception. The object to which we respond can assume a number of aspects and the specific aspect it does assume depends on the response we associate with it before defining it. The mother sees the child's arms stretched out to *her* and not to someone else when she is already preparing to smile and is aware that her smile is indispensable to the child's stability.

In other words, social representations determine both the character of the stimulus and the response it elicits, just as in a particular situation they determine which is which. To know them and explain what they are and what they signify is the first step in every analysis of a situation or a social encounter, and constitutes a means of predicting the evolution of group's interactions, for instance. In most of our experiments and systematic observations we in fact manipulate representations when we think we are manipulating motivations, inferences and perceptions, and it is only because we do not take them into account that we are convinced to the contrary. The laboratory itself, where a person comes in order to be

Diagram

Current conceit

Stimulus

Representation

Response

Proposed conceit

Stimulus

Representation

Response

the object of an experiment, represents both for him and for us the prototype of a reified universe (see Farr's chapter). The presence of apparatus, the way the space is organised, the instructions he is given, the very nature of the undertaking, the artificial relationship between experimenter and subject, and the fact that all this occurs within the context of an institution and under the aegis of science, reproduce many essential features of a reified universe. It is quite clear that the situation determines both the questions we will ask and the answers these will elicit.

(2) *Social representations in laboratory settings*

Some investigations have sought to restore meanings and representations to laboratory settings and to corroborate, as far as possible, the theoretical postulate of their autonomy, without which both experiment and theory must forego much of their significance. In 1968 Claude Faucheux and I tried to prove that representations shape our behaviour in the context of a competitive game. We based our experiments on familiar card games. The one variant we introduced was that some of the subjects were told they were playing against 'nature', while others were told their opponent was 'chance'.

The first term evokes a more reassuring, comprehensible and controllable image of the world, while the idea of chance, underscored here by the presence of a pack of cards, recalls adversity and irrevocability. As we expected, the subjects' choice, and especially their behaviour, differed according to their representation of their opponent. Thus most of the subjects confronted with 'nature' spent some time studying the rules and working out some kind of strategy. Whereas, those subjects who faced 'chance' concentrated all their attention on the pack of cards trying to guess what card would be dealt, and didn't worry about the rules of the game. The figures speak for themselves: 38 out of 40 of those playing against 'nature' were able to rationalise the rules, while only 12 out of 40 of the others were able to do so (Faucheux and Moscovici, 1968).

Thus our inner representations, which we have either inherited from society or fabricated ourselves, can change our attitude to something outside ourselves. Together with Abric and Plon (Abric, Faucheux, Moscovici and Plon, 1967) we carried out another variant of this experiment. Here one group was told they would play against a computer, that the choices they would make would be programmed and that the computer, like themselves, would have to try to accumulate a maximum of points. The other group's aim was identical but in their case they were told they would play against *another* student like themselves, whose choices would be communicated to them by telephone. Once again, we observed different, or even contrasting, strategies and rationalisations according to the group. Understandably, a more co-operative relation to the *other* than to the computer emerged. Further experiments by Codol (Codol, 1974) concerned with the anchoring process of various representations of the self, of the group and of the task to be accomplished cast a peculiar light on their variety and impact in a competitive situation. Abric (1976), in a very ambitious and systematic experiment, dissected each of these representations and showed why they behaved as they did. An account of the wide range of results obtained will be published shortly.

In another series of equally convincing and straight-forward experiments, Flament, in collaboration with Codol and Rossignol (Codol and Flament, 1971; Rossignol and Flament, 1975; Rossignol and Houel, 1976) considered the same problem at another, more significant, level. Indeed, social psychology is largely concerned with the discovery of so-called universal mechanisms which, written in our brains or in our glands, are supposed to determine our every action and thought. They occur in society without being social. They are, furthermore, formal mechanisms quite unrelated to an individual or a collective content of any kind or to the history responsible for such a content. One of these supposedly unique and universal mechanisms is that of coherence and stability. This suggests that individuals try to organise their beliefs into internally coherent structures. Consequently, we prefer stable to unstable structures. The implied postulate can be stated thus: positive and negative interpersonal relations are determined by the principle of stability. The two propositions that sum it up – 'My friends' friends are my friends' and 'My enemies' enemies are my friends' – serve as immutable laws, unrelated to any implicit meaning and independent of any particular circumstance. In other words, the two axiomatised sayings form the basis of a syntax of relations between people and determine their own semantics or pragmatics.

Doubtless it was already obvious, before Flament, that such propositions apply only to 'objects' having a common frame of reference or that are situated along a cognitive dimension (Jaspars, 1965). But Flament's use of the theory of social representations enabled him to go both further and deeper. To begin with, he showed that each individual, who has to assess the relation between a number of other individuals, possesses a range of representations of the group to which they belong and of the kind of links that exist between them. These may be conventional or even somewhat mythical (e.g. the fraternal or Rousseauist group, etc.). The principle of stability will characterise such relations only if a person already has the notion of a basic, egalitarian, friendly group in mind. Then, he will try to form a coherent opinion of the members that constitute it. In other words, it is only in a social context of this kind that 'my friends' friends' must necessarily be 'my friends'. In such cases, Heider's principle of cognition and affectivity expresses only the particular group's collective norm and internal links, but not a general tendency. Indeed, Flament appositely shows that it is the representation of such a principle that gives particular prominence to the friendliness and egalitarianism of its members, and not the reverse. In representations of a different kind of group, friendliness and egalitarianism are not necessarily linked and do not have the same significance. Finally, it seems that the function of the stability principle consists in creating a social paradigm of positive and negative interpersonal relationships and that its significance depends on this paradigm. Which simply means that the principle of equilibrium, far from determining, is itself determined by how the context of interpersonal relations represented. And it is not really surprising that this had not emerged earlier.

Many contemporary studies in social psychology take as their paradigm such a group of like-minded people tending to have similar opinions and tastes and anxious both to avoid conflicts and to accept the *status quo*. But what they overlook is the fact that such a group is an objectification of the traditional, mythical notion of an ideal community. In this case, the tendency towards stability and coherence can well be seen as a determining factor of interpersonal relationships. But, if we then compare this social representation of the group to others, we will soon realise that such 'general' tendencies are really peculiar to it, that we have mistaken the effect for the cause. The enquiries carried out by Flament and his Aix-en-Provence team have made it possible for us to reinterpret Heider's theories through a re-assessment that takes into account the social and historical dimension of our perceptions and opinions of others.

We have referred only to a restricted number of experiments. Yet each of them prove, in its specific field (competition, awareness of others, etc.) that our postulate has a wide significance. Rather than motivations, aspirations, cognitive principles and the other factors that are usually put forward, it is our representations which, in the last resort, determine our reactions, and their significance is, thus, that of an actual cause. Through them society behaves somewhat in the manner of Marcel Duchamp; like this painter with his ready-made objects, it sets its signature on society-made processes and thus modifies their character. We hope to have demonstrated that, indeed, all the elements of the psychic field are reversed once the social signature has been set on them.

The lesson to be drawn from the above is that the present manner of proceeding – which we owe to Sherif and which consists in showing how psychic mechanisms are turned into social processes – should be reversed. For such is the process of evolution itself and, by following it, we shall be better able to understand it. It is only logical to consider that social and public processes were the first to occur and that they were gradually interiorised to become psychic processes. Thus, when we analyse *psycho*-social processes we discover that they are psycho-*social*. It is as though our psychology contained our sociology in a condensed form. And one of the most urgent tasks of social psychology is to discover the one in the other and to understand this process of condensation.

Final observations

I cannot conclude this exposition without mentioning some of the more general implications of the theory of social representations. First of all, the study of these representations should not be restricted to a mere shift from the emotional to the intellectual level and they should not be seen as solely pre- or anti-behavioural. If this were the case, there would be no point in dwelling on them. No, what is required is that we examine the symbolic aspect of our relationships and of the consensual universes we inhabit. For all 'cognition', all 'motivation' and all 'behaviour' only exist and have repercussions insofar as they signify something, and signifying implies, by definition, at least two people sharing a common language, common values and common memories. This is what distinguishes the social from the individual, the cultural from the physical and the historical from the static. By saying that representations are social we are mainly saying that they are symbolic and possess as many perceptual, as so-called cognitive, elements. And that is why we consider their *content* to be so important and why we refuse to distinguish them from psychological mechanisms as such.

In other words, we noticed, on various occasions, that social psychology tends to single out a simple mechanism, take it out of its context, and then to ascribe a general value to it – just as instincts were once singled out for a similar purpose. Some of these are pseudo-mechanisms, such as 'stability' or 'coherence', which appear to explain what they actually define. Since thought naturally tends to substitute order for disorder, simplicity for diversity, etc., to assert that thought tends towards coherence amounts to little more than saying that thought tends towards thought. Other mechanisms such as 'dissonance', 'attribution', 'reactance', etc. are seen as universal and are applied to all possible social fields, categories or contents. They are supposed to process certain information and to produce different information, no matter what. When assessing the majority of studies carried out on this basis, Simon concluded: 'When the processes underlying these social phenomena are identified, as they are in the chapters of this book, particularly those of the second and third parts, they turn out to be the very same information processes we encounter in non-social cognitions' (Carroll and Paine, 1976).

This is a disturbing coincidence, for *either* the social has an existence and meaning which must produce certain effects, *or* the study of these information processes, as isolated mechanisms, is a mistake that creates the illusion of a possible and easy contact with the essence of reality.

Social representations, like scientific theories, religions or mythologies, are the representations of something or of someone. They have a specific content – specific implying, moreover, that it differs from one sphere or one society to another. However, these processes are significant only insofar as they reveal the birth of such a content and its variations. After all, how we think is not distinct from what we think. Thus we cannot make a clear distinction between the regularities in representations and those in the processes that create them. Indeed, if we follow in the footsteps of psychoanalysis and anthropology we should find it much easier to understand what it is that representations and mechanisms have in common.

The second implication – and one which could have been foreseen – can be expressed in a few words: the study of social representations requires that we revert to methods of observation. I have no intention of criticising experimental methods as such. Their value is indisputable when studying simple phenomena that can be taken out of context. But this is not the case for social representations which are stored in our language and which were created in a complex human milieu. I am well aware that a number of my colleagues despise observations which they see as a cowardly abdication of scientific rigour, a sign of prolixity, laziness and fuzziness. I believe that they are over-pessimistic. Social psychology is no longer what it was half a century ago. Since then, we have come to appreciate the requirements of theory, of the accurate analysis of phenomena; but we have also come to appreciate the reverse, that is the limitations of theories that explain only what can be experimented upon and of the experiment as something to which reality is made to adjust. And what we require of observation is that it will preserve some of the qualities of experiment while freeing us from its limitations. It has succeeded in doing so for ethnology, anthropology and child psychology and we see no reason why it should not have similar results in social psychology.

But clearly, something more is at stake than the comparative merits of one method or another. And this has to be said unambiguously; quite apart from its technical merits experiment has come to stand for the exclusive association of social psychology with general psychology and of its departure from sociology and the social sciences. Doubtless such was not the intention of its founders, but that is the way in which it has evolved. Furthermore, its syllabi of research and teaching turn out psychological experts who are sociological ignoramuses. A return to observation would involve reverting to the human sciences. During the last decade these have made significant advances and have demonstrated that discoveries can be achieved without obsessive rituals, so that there might be worse fates than to take our place amongst them.

The third implication, which is a natural consequence of the second, concerns description. During a certain period we were preoccupied only with the explanatory mechanisms for attitude change, influence, attribution, etc. without giving much thought to collecting data. Such collecting is seen as a minor activity, a proof of intellectual sloth and even as downright useless. To devise hypotheses and to verify them in the laboratory seems to be the word of command to which we rally. But, contrary to appearances, this word of command has nothing to do with science. Most sciences – from linguistics to economics, from astronomy to chemistry, from ethnology to anthropology – describe phenomena and try to discover regularities on which to base a general theory. Their comprehensiveness consists mainly in the store of data at their disposal and the significance of the regularities revealed which successive theories interpret. I have no wish to analyse here the reasons for this word of command nor its negative consequence for our discipline. Whatever the reasons the fact remains that only a careful description of social representations, of their structure and their evolution in various fields, will enable us to understand them and that a valid explanation can only be derived from a comparative study of such descriptions. This does not imply that we should discard theory for a mindless accumulation of data, but that what we want is a theory based on adequate observations that will be as accurate as possible.

Finally, the fourth implication concerns the time factor. Social representations are historical in their essence and influence individual development from early childhood, from the day a mother, with all her images and concepts, begins to become preoccupied with her baby. These images and concepts are derived from her own school days, from radio programmes, from conversations with other mothers and with the father and from personal experiences, and they determine her relationship with her child, the significance she will give to his cries, his behaviour, and how she will organise the environment in which he will grow up. The parents' understanding of their child fashions his personality and paves the way for his socialisation. That is why we assume: '... that it is the transmission of understanding to the infant rather than his behaviour or his discriminative abilities which ought to be a matter of central concern to developmental psychologists' (Nelson, 1974. See also Palmonari and Ricci Bitti, 1978).

Our representations of our bodies, of our relations with other people, of justice, of the world, etc. evolve from childhood to maturity. A detailed study of their development might be envisaged which would explore the way a society is conceived and experienced simultaneously by different groups and generations. There would be no reason to see the civilised young adult as the prototype of the human race and thus to ignore all genetic phenomena. And this leads us to the more general concept of a link between the psychology of growing up and social psychology, the former being a social psychology of the child and the latter a psychology of the growing up of adults. In both, the phenomenon of social representations plays a central part, and this is what they have in common. If we added to these certain aspects of a sociology of everyday life – which has not, moreover, been adequately formulated – we might reconstruct a general science which would encapsulate a whole galaxy of related investigations. I see it as a concrete realisation of Vigotsky's remark: 'The problem of thought and language thus extends the limits of natural science and becomes the focal problem of historical human sociology, i.e. of social psychology' (Vigotsky, 1977).

This would be a science of consensual universes in evolution, a cosmogony of physical human existence. I do not ignore the difficulties of such an undertaking, nor the fact that it may be unrealisable, any more than I ignore the gap between such a project and the modest achievements that are our own to date. But I can't see this as a sufficient reason for not considering it and setting it forth as clearly as possible in the hope that others will share my faith in it.

Notes

1. Experiments by Tversky and Kahneman (1974) have happily succeeded in proving that this assumption is unfounded and owes its popularity to a misunderstanding that stems from artificial tenets.
2. We discuss social representations again after we have outlined the criticisms levelled at the concept of attitude which is, by definition, a mediating cause. In this way we hope to demonstrate the autonomy of social psychology and to include in the collective context a theory (i.e. that of attitudes) that has become too individualistic. The work of Jaspars and Fraser (chap. 5) lends much weight to this point of view.

2. Choosing ancestors: some consequences of the selection from intellectual traditions

IRWIN DEUTSCHER

Introduction

Although my students and colleagues tell me I am a symbolic interactionist, the mantle remains as uncomfortable as it was twenty years ago when the late Professor Arnold Rose asked me to contribute two chapters to a volume he was editing on symbolic interaction (Rose, 1962). As a young scholar I was flattered by his invitation, but, gathering up my courage, I asked him 'What is symbolic interaction?' His face flushed as he angrily shouted, 'It is what they do at Chicago!' And he turned on his heels and left me embarrassed at my ignorance. I hope in this paper to provide a somewhat clearer image of what symbolic interaction is.

Sociological social psychologies

Among American sociologists, there is a variety of social psychologies. Some of these imitate theoretical and methodological frameworks commonly found among their counterparts in psychology departments. By and large they do nothing different from traditional psychological social psychologists and do not do it as well. With that admittedly cavalier assessment, I will dismiss that group. There is another sociological perspective which is closely related to the Harvard structural–functional school of sociology and thus to the Americanized Durkheimian tradition. It is known as 'small group analysis' and is identified with such names as Bales and Borgatta (Hare, *et al.*, 1955). American sociologists have also found an endearing quality in the rambling insightful essays of Georg Simmel, although he appears to have inspired little empirical research.[1]

More closely related to our present concerns are the different social psychologies which have been developed by sociologists who derive their orientation from George Herbert Mead. Some of these call themselves social behaviorists and tend toward a positivistic stance in their research. Among them are some who describe their orientation as bio-social and can trace their descent in a direct line to Watson.[2] To further complicate matters, there are several groups of sociologists who call themselves symbolic interactionists.[3] One of these is identified with its founder, Manfred Kuhn, and is committed to developing and testing operational definitions of the self.[4] There are individuals who identify themselves as symbolic interactionists ranging from Stryker, who operationalizes Mead's concept of the self and employs rigorous positivistic methods in testing hypotheses derived from Mead (Stryker, 1962: 41–62), to Goffman whose original thinking seems to me to defy classification into any tradition.[5] For the purposes of this chapter, I will attempt to use the term symbolic interaction as it seems to me it is employed by Herbert Blumer who invented it in 1937 (Blumer, 1969a: 1).

Durkheimian sources in my own work

If I am a symbolic interactionist, then how do I fit Durkheim's apparently structural and deterministic image of society with the interactional and voluntaristic imagery of symbolic interactionism? My study of the relationship between what people say and what they do refers to Durkheim in three different contexts (Deutscher, 1973). One of these is a passing observation that such dissimilar sociological ancestors as Charles Horton Cooley (an early symbolic interactionist) and Emile Durkheim shared the assumption that human nature requires social constraints and that under such conditions there is an inherent conflict between one's private self and one's social self (ibid.: 61). My other two discussions of Durkheim are somewhat more extensive and, I believe, directly related to the concerns of the book. The first of these has to do with the nature of social statistics as a form of reality sui generis (ibid.: 114–16). We will consider Durkheim's interpretation of his suicide data later in this paper.

My final consideration of Durkheim in the 1973 volume was concerned with the issue of determinism vs. voluntarism in human behavior (ibid.: 273–4). Melvin DeFleur is one of the leading positivistic sociologists with a long history of experimental research on the relationship between attitudes and behaviors. I had been critical of his earlier work which assumed a direct relationship between the two. But in a paper published in 1969 DeFleur and his colleague Lyle Warner made what appeared to me to be a major breakthrough in their own thinking. They became convinced that an adequate theory of attitude must 'take into account the intervening situational variables which modify the relationship between attitudes and action' (Warner and DeFleur, 1969: 154). Although this position is a long way from Blumer's insistence that the intervening process is the legitimate and appropriate object of study in itself it is, nevertheless, a signal improvement over the older stance which searched for a simple relationship between an independent and a dependent variable. One of the two intervening variables which they seek to control is 'social constraint.' This variable was to become the theme of a number of studies during the ensuing years.

Warner and DeFleur borrow their definition of social constraint directly from Durkheim's conception of a collective conscience. This deterministic Durkheimian perspective brings them into sharp contrast with the more voluntaristic pragmatic perspective of the symbolic interactionist: for example they write, 'Sociologists hold it to be axiomatic that a person acting in relation to others is directly and indirectly compelled to *behave* as others expect' (*ibid.*: 155). This has indeed been the dominant sociological perspective, but the symbolic interactionists would not choose such a word as 'compelled.' Blumer, I suspect, would state the 'axiom' in a different way – something like: 'In attempting to construct his line of action, a person must *take into account* the expectations of others.' Whether or not the actor properly assesses those expectations, chooses to conform or deviate from them, is capable of carrying through her intentions, and other such contingencies is the stuff out of which inconsistencies between sentiments and acts are made.

In this introduction I want only to highlight the fundamental differences between 'to be compelled to behave as others expect' and 'to take into account what others expect.' This element of a compelling drive to conform, which is clearly present in Durkheim's concept of the collective conscience, is completely absent in W. I. Thomas's concept of the definition of the situation (Thomas, 1927)[6] and Mead's notion of the 'significant other' (Mead, 1934). This, then, has been a brief summary of some of the ways in which Durkheim's ideas have intersected with my own during the past few years.

The neo-Durkheimian social psychology

My understanding of this new French School is based upon materials I have received from Professors Farr and Moscovici: correspondence, bibliographies, reprints, a description of the colloquium, and papers presented at the colloquium (Paris, 1979). As I read those materials it appears that the link with Durkheim rests exclusively upon his concept of 'social representations' – always translated in English as 'collective representations.'

I am informed that this movement can be dated from the publication of Moscovici's *La Psychanalyse: son image et son public* in 1961. In that volume he refers to social representations as 'this neglected concept of Durkheim's.' In his preface to Herzlich's study of health and illness (1973: xiii), Moscovici describes collective representations in the language and style of the ethnomethodologist (quoted by Farr, 1977: 492 and 1978: 516): '[Social representations are] cognitive systems with a logic and language of their own... They do not represent simply "opinions about," "images of" or "attitudes towards" but "theories" or "branches of knowledge" in their own right, for the discovery and organization of reality . . .'

Farr recognizes the kinship between this statement and the position of the new phenomenologists in sociology, such as Berger and Luckmann, Cicourel and Garfinkel. In fact, it is remarkably close to Garfinkel's early definitions of ethnomethodology which condemned traditional psychologists and sociologists for holding to an image of human beings as 'judgemental dopes' (Garfinkel, 1964). The position seems neatly encapsulated in the description of the colloquium on social representations which identifies a common theme in the apparently diverse studies undertaken by the French School: 'The question raised each time concerns how people "theorize about" or "talk about" the experiences in which they participate and how these "theories" enable them to construct reality and, ultimately, to determine their behavior' (Moscovici and Farr, 1979).

It is clearly consonant with this orientation that Moscovici should note the structural context of attitudes – that 'it is not enough to consider the content of an attitude, the broader structure which integrates the content must also be taken into account' (1963: 238). In discussing his *La Psychanalyse*, Moscovici again defines a social representation, this time 'as the elaborating of a social object by the community for the purpose of behaving and communicating' (*ibid.*: 251). Here we have a statement of shared symbols which facilitate interaction. When psychoanalysis, for example, becomes objectified as a reality *sui generis*, we have not only a Durkheimian social fact but also the social construction of reality. The social fact becomes a shared symbol which enhances effective communication among individuals. It affects the way people perceive one another and relate to one another. Is this a bridge between Durkheimian structural theory and symbolic interactionist social psychology? We shall return to that issue when we consider the relationship between the two positions. I will leave this matter with Moscovici's conclusion that the language of psychoanalysis is incorporated into everyday speech. It 'becomes a common "dialect," pervades judgment, and directs behavior' (*ibid*.: 252).

In addition to its identification with Durkheim's concept of social representations, I am able to isolate two other features which appear to characterize the French School. One of these is its field methods which depart from traditional psychological research techniques. According to Farr, 'Where the contemporary Durkheimian tradition is most distinctive and most imaginative is in relation to non-experimental explorations of "social representations" in extra laboratory contexts' (1978b: 518). Examples of methods which lie clearly outside of the current psychological research style include Herzlich's unstructured interviews (1973) and content analysis such as that conducted by Moscovici of current mass media (1961) or that conducted by Marie-José Chombart de Lauwe of books and films relating to childhood during the past century (1971).

The third feature which seems to me to characterize the French School is that it is theoretically and methodologically iconoclastic – highly critical of the psychology that is. In their invitation to the colloquium of 8–10 January 1979, Farr and Moscovici identify this feature as one shared by symbolic interaction. The bits and pieces I have had the opportunity to read seem to suggest that the French School is a movement which seeks an alternative to dominant patterns of thought regarding human behavior and social processes. In this sense it is reminiscent of the Frankfurt School of Critical Sociology, of the radical sociology and psychology of the sixties, of ethnomethodology, of humanistic sociology and psychology, of the phenomenological movement in the social sciences – and perhaps of symbolic interactionism.

In sum, the neo-Durkheimians impress me as distinguished by (1) their commitment to the concept of social representations, (2) their methodological style and (3) their critique and rejection of contemporary fashions in theory and methodology. These characteristics will provide the basis for much of the comparative analysis which follows.

Emile Durkheim as ancestor

An over-simplified introduction

In his reaction to earlier nonscientific modes of thought as, for example, among the German Idealists, and in his enchantment with the great advances of knowledge made by positivistic science in his own time, Durkheim expounded a rigorous application of systematic logic and empirical evidence toward understanding human phenomena. He was truly a student of Comte. All could be known and understood rationally. All phenomena had their causes and were determined by other knowable phenomena. Durkheim appears to suggest that occasional expressions of free will – of independence from social constraints – are either aberrations or, if they begin to appear with greater frequency, can be viewed as indicators of the breakdown of society. One of Durkheim's great contributions was his introduction of this true scientific mentality into the study of human behavior.

All of this sounds like a description of the kind of psychology the French School is challenging. But is it? Durkheim was not a simple-minded man who thought in simple-minded terms. Let us focus in this section on three complex dimensions of Durkheim's thinking which may be relevant to the issues on hand: (1) his disciplinary chauvinism; (2) his understanding of the symbolic element in social life; and (3) his criteria for reliable and valid data.

Before discussing Durkheim's disciplinary chauvinism, we should remember one additional element in his thinking – one which will become important in our comparative analysis. The power of a social fact over members of a society was not only a determinant of beliefs and, to a lesser extent, of behaviors but, of equal importance, Durkheim saw this as a *consciously recognized coercion*. Social constraint is effective only because members are aware of it: 'A social fact is to be recognized by the power of external coercion which it exercises over the individual' (cited by Peyre, 1960: 20). In this respect Durkheim is a realist; social facts are objective realities *sui generis*.

Disciplinary chauvinism

Because Durkheim's central thrust was to establish the proper subject-matter for sociology and because of his tenacity in insisting that social representations, the collective conscience, and social facts were irreducible elements of study, he is sometimes misunderstood as denying the validity of psychology. Such a misunderstanding is especially possible in his insistence that suicide is a social fact and cannot be properly understood through the study of individuals. What he does argue is that social representations are something different from individual representations and that the latter is the proper sphere of study for the psychologist. His chauvinism is one of loyalty and commitment to sociology. Unlike some other types of chauvinism, it implies no contempt or disrespect for the study of human behavior at other levels. What he is contemptuous of is the scholar who fails to grasp the difference between the study of individual representations and social representations and the scholar who would reduce the latter to the former.

Although he makes a consistent and clear distinction between individual and social representations, Durkheim also discusses a 'social psychology.' He is not always clear regarding what this consists of, but at least at one point it sounds very much as if he uses the term synonymously with sociology: 'We see no objection to calling sociology a variety of psychology, if we carefully add that social psychology has its own laws which are not those of individual psychology' (Durkheim, 1951). If we interpret this within the framework of Simpson's argument that Durkheim 'could not foresee that one day we might be able to establish an individual psychology that would be inherently social' (Simpson, 1963: 3), it is possible to argue that the analysis of social interaction could be a legitimate area of study different from both the analysis of social institutions (Durkheim's sociology) and the analysis of individuals (Durkheim's psychology). As we shall see below, these are more than matters of taxonomy.

The symbolic element in social life

If Durkheim, in his self-conscious positivistic style, is sometimes a realist, there is also a great deal of idealism in his sociology. A symbol is something which stands for or represents something other than its objective self. It is an idea people have of a thing which is independent of the thing itself. Symbolism is a major feature of Durkheim's thinking. *The elementary forms of the religious life* (1961a) is essentially an analysis of religion as a symbolic force in society. He describes the symbol as a central factor in social representations of all sorts: 'Religion . . . [is] the system of symbols by means of which society becomes conscious of itself . . . All we mean by affirming the distinction between the social and the individual is that the above observations apply not only to religion, but to . . . all forms of collective life' (Durkheim, 1951: 312–13).

One American authority on Durkheim observes that 'the Meadian "verbal symbol" and the Durkheimian "collective representation" are virtually synonymous' (Hinkle, 1960: 278). Two American authorities on symbolic interactionism concur. Stone and Farberman state that:

The heart of Mead's work rests on the proposition that mind develops out of and sustains itself within an objective phase of experience. This objective phase of experience is, of course, what is captured in Mead's concept of the significant symbol or universal and Durkheim's concept of collective representation. In each case the symbol (or representation) is an objectification and universalization of particular experiences.   (1970: 108–9)

Stone and Farberman continue with a quote from *The elementary forms of the religious life* (Durkheim, 1961a: 260): '"Surely," Durkheim writes, "the soldier who falls while defending his flag does not believe that he sacrifices himself for a bit of cloth." And Mead also insists on the irrelevancy of the concrete symbol or object' (Stone and Farberman, 1970: 109). They provide a similar example from Mead's writing (Mead, 1934: 83) and conclude that Hinkle 'has incisively established the relationship between the significant symbol of Mead and the collective representation of Durkheim' (Stone and Farberman, 1970: 109, n37). These comments anticipate our comparative analysis. For the moment let us say that I do not believe that Hinkle's single paragraph on this matter establishes anything incisively. In fact, I will suggest later that there may be a great difference between Durkheim's concept of the symbolic element in social life and that of George Herbert Mead.

Durkheim's student, Marcel Mauss, sees an important part of sociology as the study of these symbolic systems which Durkheim calls social representations: 'The study consists of two parts: the collection and systematization of the ideas that constitute the collective representations, and the examination of the collective behaviour patterns that correspond to these representations' (Salomon, 1960: 255). What Mauss in his study of Eskimo society (1906) failed to recognize was that the beliefs conveyed to the ethnographer by the informants may be quite different from the behavior engaged in by members of the society. Durkheim recognized this possible divergence. 'Beneath all these [social representations] are actual, living sentiments, summed up by these formulae but only as in a superficial envelope . . . If, then, we ascribe a kind of reality to them, we do not dream of supposing them to be the whole of moral reality. That would be to take the sign for the thing signified' (Durkheim, 1951: 315). Durkheim proceeds to provide examples of the variety of responses from the 'average man' to the great societal symbols in which they all concur (*ibid*.: pp. 316–17). He discusses 'the distance between the social state and its individual repercussions' and concludes that 'it is a profound mistake to confuse the collective type of a society, as is often done, with the average type of its individual members' (*ibid*.: p. 317).

What is most remarkable to me about this distinction Durkheim is making between social ideals and individual realities is that it leads him to a position which seems to me to pose a dialectic driving force which could account for social change:

> ... in so far as we are solidary with the group and share its life, we are exposed to their influence; but so far as we have a distinct personality of our own we rebel against and try to escape them. Since everyone leads this sort of double existence simultaneously, each of us has a double impulse. We are drawn in a social direction and tend to follow the inclinations of our own natures ... Two antagonistic forces confront each other. One, the collective force, tries to take possession of the individual; the other, the individual force, repulses it.
>
> (*ibid*.: 318–19)

Durkheim's purpose here is to defend himself from attacks on his concepts of social representations and social facts as scholasticism. I am not aware that he ever considered the implications of his argument for a dialectic theory of social change. Certainly the American version of Durkheimian structural-functionalism does not. On the other hand, he clearly perceived the implications of his thinking for a sociology of knowledge.

In *Elementary forms*, Durkheim compares science and religion as bodies of belief which people act upon. Regardless of objective facts, scientific notions which do not fit are rejected:

> It is not enough that they be true to be believed. If they are not in harmony with the other beliefs and opinions, or, in a word, with the mass of the other collective representations, they will be denied: minds will be closed to them; consequently *it will be as though they did not exist*.
>
> (1961a: 486. Cited by Stone and Farberman, 1970: 105: my italics)

Whether they are religious or scientific, in order for beliefs to be shared or acceptable they must be in accord with other accepted beliefs or social representations. Otherwise 'they will be denied,' 'minds will be closed to them,' 'it will be as though they did not exist.' Durkheim is writing here of a concept which would be developed generations later: the social construction of reality – and unreality. This is a statement of a sociology of knowledge and a sociology of science. It suggests the type of research exemplified by Moscovici's *La Psychanalyse*: 'Today it is generally sufficient that [concepts] bear the stamp of science to receive a sort of privileged credit, because we have faith in science. But this faith does not differ essentially from religious faith' (Durkheim, 1961*a*: 486. Cited by Stone and Farberman, 1970: 106).

Peyre (1960: 25) observes that according to Durkheim the true function of society is to create the ideal: 'Durkheim proclaimed that society is a compound of ideas, beliefs, feelings . . .' (*ibid.*: 30). Idealism is strong in Durkheim's sociology. He shared with Mead and Blumer not only the notion that objects exist only if we take note of them, but also the concept of social objects as consisting of whatever we may take note of: 'it is not true that society is made up only of individuals; it also includes material things, which play an essential role in the common life' (Durkheim, 1951: 313). However, in our comparative analysis, we shall see that there is a difference in the way Durkheim and the symbolic interactionists perceive the operation of social objects.

Criteria for reliable and valid data

Turning from Durkheim's symbolism to his conception of data, we also turn from Durkheim the idealist to Durkheim the realist. He devotes the whole of the concluding section of his chapter 'How to determine social causes and social types' (in *Suicide*) to an essay on the distinction between 'defective' statistics which deal with motives and more acceptable statistics which consist of 'recording an accomplished fact' (*ibid.*: 148–51): '. . . what are called statistics of the motives of suicide are actually statistics of the opinions concerning such motives of officials. . . . Unfortunately, official establishments of fact are known to be often defective even when applied to obvious material facts. . .' (*ibid.*: 148)

Durkheim's student Maurice Halbwachs published his own study of suicide a generation later (1930) and, with both better data and better methods, verified Durkheim's findings. Parroting the master, Halbwachs insists that he is not concerned with subjective motives of individuals who commit suicide. 'Motives . . . are either subjective ideological constructs or arbitrary definitions laid down by the police or by coroners. He rejected any concern with them as unscientific' (Salomon, 1960: 258). It is puzzling that following his clear analysis of social representations and even society itself as composed of 'ideas,' there should be a rejection of data because it is an 'ideological construct.' Do not police and coroners reflect the collective conscience in their definitions? Is it not they and their likes who construct the very data with which Durkheim and Halbwachs *did* work?

Let us consider Durkheim's interpretation of his suicide data. His analysis suggests a remarkable stability of suicide rates within and between nations and within and between certain populations, such as urban and rural or married and not married or among religious denominations. His data also suggest a high degree of stability through time. One of the most common critiques of these observations is the argument that the data available to Durkheim were crude and unreliable, and therefore the conclusions he draws from those data are questionable. I think this is a fragile criticism. Reliability is essentially a matter of consistency or stability and that is precisely what is most remarkable about Durkheim's data. They are, in fact, highly reliable. Further evidence of reliability is provided by Halbwach's verification of Durkheim's findings at a later time, with new data, and more sophisticated statistical techniques. Any data which are so reliable – so consistent through time and between investigators – must be a valid indicator of something. The important question about Durkheim's and Halbwach's suicide data is, 'Of what are they a valid indicator?'

Jack Douglas suggests that not only are the data with which Durkheim worked unreliable, but also that what he actually worked with is the recording of norms of officials who reflect nothing more or less than what they perceive to be the values of the community. This is the basis for Douglas's argument that all such official data are social constructions of reality (Douglas, 1967). It is also the basis for suspicion of official data on the part of conscientious scientific analysts, such as Bernard Beck (1970: 27), who warns that 'most of these officially and semiofficially generated statistics are untrustworthy and misleading . . .' Harold Garfinkel, on the other hand, takes a different view when he observes that there are 'Good organizational reasons for "bad" clinic records' (1967: 186–207). There are many examples of the validity of consistent data once the source of their consistency has been properly identified. The most striking study of a social fact I have found is an analysis of 1000 New York City school children conducted in the early thirties (American Child Health Association, 1934). They were selected as a sample of children who had not yet had their tonsils removed and were submitted to a panel of physicians for diagnosis. Roughly 40 percent of the children were diagnosed as needing their tonsils removed. The remainder were again submitted to a panel of physicians and, again, 40 percent of them were diagnosed as needing their tonsils removed. The procedure was repeated until there were no longer sufficient numbers of children remaining. The percentage remained constant through each surviving cohort.

What these data suggest is that the question of how many people 'really' need their tonsils out or 'really' commit suicide is essentially unanswerable, except within the limits of a collective judgment about tonsils or suicide. It is possible that there was a dimension to Durkheim's notion of a 'collective conscience' which even he did not recognize. Durkheim believed in the objective validity of statistics enumerating the incidence of suicide, but rejected statistics on the motives of suicide as 'defective,' because they reflected opinions of officials. He proceeded with the data he trusted as if it did indeed reflect the rates at which people took their own lives and he attributed differences in rates to differences in social constraints. It may be that Durkheim provided us with an analysis of official and public norms about how many people of what types ought to be killing themselves. Is it any different from data which inform us of professional norms about how many children ought to have their tonsils out?

In a different context, Durkheim himself raises the question of what constitute valid statistics. In his critique of Quetelet, he accuses him of confusing the collective type of a society with the statistically average type of its individual members: 'The proper way to measure any element of a collective type is not to measure its magnitude within individual consciences and to take the average of them all' (1951: 319). This is reminiscent of Herbert Blumer's critique of public opinion polling (1948). It also describes customary contemporary statistical practices in both psychology and sociology. As with Durkheim's concept of the symbol, his concept of defective statistics will become central in the comparative analysis which follows.

Symbolic interaction, Durkheim, and the neo-Durkheimians

The Americanization of Emile Durkheim

In his preface to an edited volume of selections from the work of Emile Durkheim, George Simpson angrily denounces what he sees as an American corruption of the ideas of 'The Master' (1963: ix): 'To portray [Durkheim] as the father of the arid "functionalism" found in the works of Talcott Parsons and Robert K. Merton is a disservice ... This functionalism emphasizes but a single aspect of Durkheim's thought and, in my opinion, not the most important one.'

Let us take a brief glance at the history of American sociology in relation to Emile Durkheim.[7] The earliest systematic analyses of Durkheim's work were presented in two doctoral dissertations, both of which appeared in 1915 and neither of which were published in book form. Hinkle reviews the various criticisms they contain. It seems to me that one theme has persisted since the earliest American critiques of Durkheim appeared during World War 1. He is perceived as failing to allow for the volitional, acting, judging, interpreting, thinking, individual. The human being, according to these critics and others to follow, is viewed by Durkheim as a passive re-actor. Contemporary symbolic interactionists may see this as the major distinction between American functional sociology with its strong Durkheimian roots and their own brand of social psychology with its roots in the American pragmatic philosophers. The two schools have different answers to the question, 'to what extent does society create human behavior and to what extent does human behavior create society?'

The 1915 dissertation by Elmer Gehlke is a critique not only of Durkheim's social determinism, but also of his social realism. Hinkle comments that it 'is an expression of the individualism, nominalism, and voluntarism that are so characteristic of American sociology and so antithetical to social realism' (1960: 271). Yet Alexander (1978: 179) sees this same liberal ideology of enlightenment thought as 'the most important source for Parson's explicit emphasis on voluntarism ...' There is an enigma here.[8] We have seen that Durkheim was very much an idealist. Social representations, you will recall, are a compound of ideas, feelings, and beliefs. It appears that the American distortion of Durkheim, which Simpson attributes to Parsons and Merton,[9] pre-dates the ascendency of functionalism in American sociology. I do not know how to interpret this obvious and persistent historical mis-reading. Nor does the enigma end here.

If Talcott Parsons is the most influential American interpreter of Durkheim,[10] and if Durkheim is deterministic, then how does one account for the argument developed by Norbert Wiley? According to Wiley it was Parsons' *voluntarism* which revitalized symbolic interaction and other 'interpretive sociologies' after the appearance of *The structure of social action* (1937). That book 'was a systematic attack on ... various kinds of positivists' (Wiley, 1979*b*: 63–7). Parsons, the Durkheimian, is not only voluntaristic but he is also anti-positivistic. Wiley believes that Parsons provided a foundation for an interpretive sociology, but that he did not 'ever give a clear idea of voluntarism.' Perhaps that is why I never took note of these dimensions of Parsons' work or perhaps it is because voluntarism for Parsons is as it was for the classical economists – a freedom to make rational choices. But it seems devoid of human emotion, feelings, beliefs – of the freedom to define situations in a great variety of ways. It is this kind of voluntarism which lies at the heart of symbolic interactionism. The world does not appear as orderly as positivists assume. There are enigmas. It may be as the American poet Ralph Waldo Emerson wrote, that 'A foolish consistency is the hobgoblin of little minds' (in *Self Reliance*).

Returning to our history, Durkheim appears to have enjoyed continued neglect in America during the period following the First World War. In fact, pursuing the line of criticism from the earlier period, W. I. Thomas, one of the more important figures in early symbolic interactionist thinking, explicitly attacks Durkheim's social realism in the 'Methodological Note' found in his most important work, *The Polish peasant in Europe and America* (Thomas and Znaniecki, vol. I: 1918–20).[11]

Farr reminds us that both Thomas and Durkheim visited Wundt's laboratory in Leipzig and suggests that Mead 'started his symbolic inter-actionist social psychology from Wundt's concept of the "gesture" . . .' (Farr, 1978b: 505). Mead's distinction between the 'conversation of gestures' (the non-symbolic segment of social life) and 'the use of significant symbols' (symbolic interaction) may well have been stimulated by Wundt (Blumer, 1969a: 8–9). There is no argument about Wundt's 'folk psychology' influencing to some degree the thinking of both Thomas and Mead. But to 'visit' is not necessarily to be influenced or to approve. I would suspect that what Durkheim found admirable and useful in Wundt's laboratory was the model it provided for a positivistic method in the study of human behavior. This, surely Durkheim believed, was the kind of thinking and the kind of methods that must be applied to the study of sociology. Farr proceeds to observe that 'the psychology to which Durkheim took such strong exception was individual, not social, psychology' (1978b: 509). But our earlier analysis of Durkheim suggests that he seems to be using the term 'social psychology' synonymously with 'sociology' and that he had no concept of a social psychology as it was to later emerge in the works of Thomas and others.

During the thirties, criticisms of Durkheim begin to take on different dimensions. Harry Alpert complained of the vague and ambiguous meanings of such concepts as 'thing,' 'fact,' and 'constraint' in much the same vein as Farr's irritation some forty years later at the difficulties arising 'in the absence of any fairly precise delineation of characteristics of *"représentations collectives"* . . .' (1977: 500). Alpert is also critical of Durkheim for his assumption of a unilinear social evolution and his failure to include a 'verstehen . . . type of inquiry' (Hinkle, 1960: 284). Of critical importance is Alpert's accusation that 'Durkheim fails to recognize the role of the capta (that is, indirectly, the investigator) and is exclusively preoccupied with the data (the object investigated)' (*ibid*.: 283). This failure to recognize that the investigator must become part of the subject's definition of the situation persists as characteristic of contemporary positivistic research in sociology and psychology. Durkheim does indeed fail to recognize the manner in which the study of a social object alters the object itself, but then, so too did the rest of us until recent decades.

Wiley believes that the history of American sociology contains only two periods of clear theoretical domination: 'that of the Chicago School, from the teens until the mid-thirties, and that of the functionalists, from about 1950 until the mid- or late-sixties' (1979b: 793). What Wiley does not say is that these two schools were highly competitive, antagonistic and regional. They posed a confrontation between the declining pragmatism of the American Midwest – kept alive at the University of Chicago and its many satellites – and the thriving positivism and functionalism of the East. The theoretical and methodological distinctions between the perspectives are indeed blurred, but the depth of feelings and loyalties were not. It is no wonder that Arnold Rose, a spokesman for symbolic interaction, turned angrily on a young student who asked what it was and responded 'It is what they do at Chicago!' Although objective positivistic analysis would probably reveal otherwise, it is a social fact that the symbol of the Chicago School became G. H. Mead and the kinds of field research which were compatible with his theory. For Chicago, Max Weber meant *verstehen*; for Harvard–Columbia Max Weber meant organizations and institutions and, above all, Emile Durkheim through the works of Parsons and Merton became a towering figure in the structural–functional sociology which Wiley perceives as emerging victorious from the struggle with the Chicago symbolic interactionists. In addition to whatever objective realities may exist, such symbolic social representations must be taken into account in considering the choice of intellectual ancestors.

As late as 1960, Hinkle describes his article as 'an attempt to redress the neglect of Durkheim' (1960: 267). But it is my impression that American sociologists today recognize Durkheim as the father of sociology. The respect which Durkheim demands is so great that in 1970 two leading symbolic interactionists devoted a lengthy essay to the wistful proposition that 'In the final stages of his sociological inquiry, Durkheim would almost assuredly have accepted the position of social pragmatism ...' (Stone and Farberman, 1970: 110). For reasons which will be considered below, I suspect this is more wish than reality, but it is a reflection of the stature of The Master that nearly all American sociologists would like to claim him as their own.

For the liberal and especially the radical American sociologists caught up in the events of the late sixties and early seventies, the inherently conservative quality of Durkheim's thinking was more than troublesome. Like European students following the disturbances in major continental universities, they expressed open contempt for the likes of Durkheim and Weber who provided the foundations for a reactionary American functionalism whose sole purpose was viewed as supporting the decadent capitalistic system. Their reasoning was basically correct, even though their conclusions were dubious. Even from the sympathetic perspective of a leading American functionalist, it is clear that 'Durkheim's conservatism significantly limited his perception of society' (Coser, 1960: 211). According to Coser the problem of order preoccupied Durkheim throughout his career (ibid: 213).

Durkheim was committed to a unilinear notion of social evolution which implied a slow, orderly, natural change. The implication of this in contemporary American functionalism in sociology and British and American functionalism in anthropology is that what is is necessary or at least 'functional' and to radically alter any institution in society will have its repercussions on all institutions in society – a sociological version of the political scientists' domino theory. Although this gestalt conception of society is shared by symbolic interactionists, the implied conservatism regarding social change is not! That conservatism should be considered when one is choosing intellectual ancestors.

Durkheim and pragmatism

I have referred to the American pragmatic philosophers as the antecedents to symbolic interaction. It is to Cartesian dualism that Blumer is referring when he says that Mead 'reversed the traditional assumptions underlying philosophical, psychological, and sociological thought to the effect that human beings possess minds and consciousness as original "givens" . . .' (1966: 535). Nisbet, in fact, links Mead, Cooley, and Durkheim as rebelling against the turn-of-the-century obsession with individualism derived from that same Cartesian principle (1974: 108).

Like myself, Durkheim describes pragmatic philosophy as 'American' and it is the work of William James to which he largely addresses his lectures on pragmatism (Wolff, 1960: 386–436). Stone and Farberman find these lectures as bringing Durkheim to 'the edge of rapprochement' with 'the perspective of symbolic interaction' (1970: from their title): 'Durkheim's concern with pragmatism (especially the work of Charles Peirce, William James, and John Dewey) shortly before his death in 1917 is almost patent evidence of the direction his theoretical development was taking at the culmination of his sociological inquiries' (*ibid.*: 100).

It was to be in the work of Mead, they say, that the social pragmatism Durkheim needed was to appear: 'It is our contention,' they write, 'that [Durkheim] could easily have accepted Mead's *social* pragmatism, had it been made explicit to him at the time' (*ibid.*: 110). I am uneasy about their efforts at rapprochement. Durkheim's lectures were on philosophy, not on sociology, and I read them as consistently critical of pragmatic philosophy. Although he treats pragmatism with respect, he praises it not for its substance but for its positivistic assumptions: 'it makes truth "into something that can be analyzed and explained"' (Wolff, 1960: x–xi, citing the thirteenth lecture). Both Wolff (1960) and Nisbet (1974: 40) refer to the lectures as a critique of pragmatism.

The ideas of Mead and Cooley were still not available to Durkheim, but it is uncertain how convincing he would have found them. Stone and Farberman are aware that 'For Durkheim a collective representation was a social "fact" – a thing which in its symbolic form existed outside of man and constrained him into using it, like money or language' (1970: 111). Even they see the important difference between Mead's processual, developmental view of social action as created in the dialogue between the I and the Me, with its doubtful outcomes, and Durkheim's view of established external constraints which determine the course of human events.

The American pragmatic philosophers and sociologists and the functional sociologists and anthropologists appear to differ on one basic assumption which has broad repercussions for the sociology derived from those schools of thought. As Durkheim observed in his lectures, the pragmatists took a phenomenological position on the nature of social reality while the functionalists took a positivistic one. Pragmatists assume that reality is the creation of actors whose perspectives on each other and whose definitions of the social world create that social world. Sets of actors defining their worlds in concert will create different sets of worlds. Social realities, including images of the past, the present, and the future become social constructs. The functionalists on the other hand, as exemplified by Durkheim, assume an objective reality and seek to comprehend it.

It would seem that such contrary views of the nature of social reality would forever prohibit any convergence of the two perspectives. But are they as alien as this picture suggests? Perhaps not. Before turning to this matter of the social construction of reality, let us examine the philosophy of Mead as it is translated into a sociology by Herbert Blumer.

What is symbolic interaction?

The point of departure for symbolic interactionist theory is the image of the reflexive self. The ability to see one's self as an object is central. It is conveyed by Mead in his distinction between the I and the Me. Once the distinction is made, it follows that one can converse with the self, act toward one's self, attempt to see one's self as others do, and project imaginary lines of action between the self and others. In interaction the parties involved engage in this process and there is a constant modification which occurs as they take note of each other's gestures and talk, and otherwise define and re-define the social situation. In this process, the engaged parties fit their lines of action together. As Blumer puts it, they build lines of joint action. Underlying all of this and serving as a framework within which it occurs is what Mead calls the 'generalized other' – a concept which appears to me identical with Durkheim's notion of the collective conscience. All of this is part of what Thomas describes as the definition of the situation. From the definition of the situation it is an easy extension of other phenomenological links with Durkheim, such as the social construction of reality.

This brief summary of Mead's point of departure (1934) serves to introduce Blumer's conversion of Meadian philosophy into symbolic interactionist sociology. What is it that people take account of when they act? 'What he takes into account are the things that he indicates to himself. They cover such matters as his wants, his feelings, his goals, the actions of others, the expectations and demands of others, the rules of his group, his situation, his conceptions of himself, his recollections, and his image of prospective lines of conduct' (Blumer, 1966: 537).

For Mead, as well as for Blumer, 'an object is anything that can be designated or referred to' (*ibid.*: 539). The activity of human beings is formed around such objects as they perceive them in their environment. There is nothing inherently meaningful in the object. The meaning is revealed to the sociologist by the way people act toward objects. Objects are, then, things which must stand for something other than their objective selves; they are symbols. They are the fuel which powers our interactions: hence, 'symbolic interaction.' Surely, not all interaction is symbolic. There are stimuli in the environment to which we react to knee-jerk fashion; there are symbols which are so widely shared, whose meanings are so consensual, that it is hardly necessary to engage in a dialogue with the self or others to interpret them and act upon them. We do so routinely and automatically, and many of our habitual everyday encounters are of this nature. They are non-symbolic interaction. They account for the regularity and stability in social life.

It follows from what has been said that 'to identify and understand the life of a group it is necessary to identify its world of objects' (*ibid.*: 540). If one accepts the premise that 'the actor acts toward the world on the basis of how he sees it and not on the basis of how that world appears to the outside observer' (*ibid.*: 542), then the methodological implications become clear.[12] The investigator must attempt to imagine the world as do the actors under study.

Blumer points out that 'Mead's scheme definitely challenges' the basic premises of the contemporary American structural-functional imagery of society;[13] here we have a clear apposition of the Americanized Durkheim and symbolic interaction:

It [Mead's scheme] sees human society not as an established structure but as people meeting their conditions of life; it sees social action not as an emanation of societal structure but as a formation made by human actors . . . it sees group life not as a release or expression of established structure but as a process of building up joint actions; it sees social actions as having variable careers and not as confined to the alternatives of conformity to or deviation from the dictates of established structure; it sees the so-called interaction between parts of a society not as a direct exercising of influence by one part on another but as mediated throughout by interpretations made by people.   (*ibid.*: 543)

For the structural-functionalist, socialization is a matter of internalizing given norms and values of the society; for the symbolic interactionist it is a matter of effectively taking the roles of others. Social change is not an occasional event resulting from external forces operating on the social structure; for the symbolic interactionist it is a continuous process flowing from human interaction. For the structuralist, social disorganization is a consequence of the breakdown of social structure; for the interactionist, it is the inability of actors to mobilize effective joint lines of action in the face of a perceived social situation. Finally, Blumer insists that 'Social action, since it has a career, is recognized as having a historical dimension which has to be taken into account in order to be adequately understood' (*ibid.*: 544).

Blumer's symbolic interaction is hardly a popular position in American sociology. Maines (1977) has reviewed the range of critics. The positivists reject interactionism as untestable, since it is not possible to operationalize its concepts. Functionalists, in Coser's words, view it as 'an antitheoretical sociological theory that refuses . . . to transcend . . . the here and now' (1976: 156). Even critical theorists who recognize the common bond that the dialectic creates between their macro-theory and the micro-theory of the interactionists view the latter as 'overly subjective and voluntaristic' and argue that it 'lacks an historical concreteness' (Lichtman, 1970: 77; cited by Maines, 1977: 236).

This is not the place for an analysis of the criticisms of symbolic interaction. It is sufficient to bring them to your attention. But the issue of its a-historical quality requires some consideration. I do not believe that any event or process can be properly understood outside of its social and historical context. I also believe that much of contemporary social science is a-historical. This is partly a consequence of the very positivism which Durkheim advocated. Surely he could not have imagined that his own creative use of history as empirical data would be abandoned and replaced by the notion of experimental evidence as the only true source of knowledge. Although, when he recognized that science, like religion, was a social representation, he might have anticipated it.

One example in my own experience is the vigorous critique of my historical analysis of research on the attitude–behavior issue by a group of psychologists who are fully committed to experimentation: 'for the sake of progress in the social sciences, we hope that less effort will be expended in "looking backward" through distorted lenses' (Ajzen, *et al.*, 1970: 272). For those who 'believe in' experimental evidence, historical evidence becomes a distorted mystique – a social reconstruction of the past which does not reflect reality. The only history of consequence to experimentalists is the set of relevant experiments preceding their own.

All of this is reminiscent of the revolt against the new positivism in the nineteenth century, mainly by the German Idealists (Coser, 1971: 244–7). Dilthey confronted history with positivism in much the same manner as I describe the contemporary issue.

In a different way, the symbolic interactionists too are disdainful of history. When Blumer urges us to recognize that careers have an historical dimension, it is to their immediate past and future that he refers. The symbolic interactionist does concentrate on social processes but they are, in fact, processes under observation in the here and now. An examination of the works of major figures in the contemporary symbolic interactionist tradition would reveal little if any attentiveness to history. In their methodological texts both Glaser and Strauss (1967) and Bogdan and Taylor (1975) recommend that investigators do their field work with a *tabula rasa*. They should have no pre-conceptions and should observe 'everything.' Howard Becker once informed me that he adds his references to an article only after he has completed it and then primarily in order to make it appear acceptable to conventional readers. These people are among the foremost contemporary symbolic interactionists.

What may be the greatest challenge facing symbolic interaction today is the development of a method appropriate for the study of institutions and societies. Maines contends that Mead's major contribution is the argument that human conduct can only be understood within the context of the social structure in which it takes place (1977: 244). He reviews a great deal of symbolic interactionist research which he believes links interaction with social structure.[14] The linking concept which he suggests bridges the two in the idea of a negotiated order. For example, in *Awareness of dying* (1965) Glaser and Strauss employ as a key concept the term 'awareness contexts.' These are structural units larger than the observed interactions. Furthermore such contexts themselves exist under even larger structural conditions: organization, community, nation or society (Maines, 1977: 245).

Blumer has always seen symbolic interaction as relevant to the study of large social units (Rose, 1962: 179–92). His address to the Society for the Study of Symbolic Interaction at its annual meeting in 1978 was devoted to that topic.[15] Furthermore, Wiley refers to recent papers which probe the 'cognitive component of Durkheim's collective conscience' (1979*b*: 66). Handel (1979: 855) has provided a recent analysis concluding that structural and interactionist approaches 'are compatible and complimentary.' There does appear to be a growing literature, in addition to the work of Stone and Farberman and Maines' creative effort, attempting to link symbolic interactionism with the study of society as Durkheim imagined it should be.

Durkheim and symbolic interaction

Farr tells us that 'In the symbolic interactionist tradition of social psychology it is inconceivable to consider the individual as existing apart from the society of which he is a product' (1978b: 509). There is no doubt in my mind that Durkheim – original or Americanized – would agree. But, alas, Blumer would not, for the interactionist sees the individual not as a product of the society but as a producer of the society. Durkheim and Blumer agree as to the nature of a chicken and of an egg; they do not agree on which comes first.

It was suggested above that for the symbolic interactionist, all of society can be seen as emerging out of interaction. But Maines observes that the interactionist recognizes the limits on voluntaristic action. As organizations become more powerful, that power is delegated to a very few leaders while the masses find themselves relatively helpless, regardless of how well they take the role of the other, how effectively they interact, which objects they indicate to themselves and, generally, how they define the situation. In fact the reality of a large complex organization is one which frequently is defined in that manner by its members. Blumer makes this point of the relations which can develop between groups independent of the mass of members in general (1969a: 15–20, 57–60) and specifically in reference to industrial organizations (1947) and to fashion (1969b).

I have already noted the affinity between the ideas of 'collective conscience' and 'generalized other.' It is not difficult to find further parallels. Maines sees in Blumer's description of 'joint action' Durkheim's 'social fact': 'The joint action has a distinctive character in its own right . . . [It] may be identified . . . without having to break it down into the separate acts that comprise it' (Blumer, 1969a: 17). I find elsewhere in Blumer's writing a dash of 'social representations' and *un soupçon d'anomie*: '. . . the established patterns of group life just do not carry on by themselves but are dependent for their continuity on recurrent affirmative definition [social representations?]. Let the interpretations that sustain them be undermined or disrupted by changed definitions from others and the patterns can quickly collapse [anomie?]' (Blumer, 1966: 538).

I am uncertain as to the usefulness of such strained parallels, other than to remind us that great thinkers, regardless of their differences, may sometimes think alike. Robert Nisbet (1974), however, does not draw parallels. In his analysis of the essence of Durkheim's thought, he refers frequently to Mead and every reference suggests close similarity if not identity in their conceptions of the social world and social life.[16]

Nisbet views *Suicide* as 'a profound treatise in social psychology' and he praises its 'analysis of the social nature of human personality and of the relation of personality to social structures. Not for more than a decade,' says Nisbet, 'would the similar though fragmentary analysis of Charles H. Cooley and George Herbert Mead make their appearance in America' (Nisbet, 1974: 34–5). He argues that there is nothing in the concept of social representations or in Durkheim's description of it 'that would have been unacceptable to either Mead or Cooley' (*ibid.*: 61).

Nisbet has no 'doubt that if Mead had had to choose between being labelled a "social determinist" and any one of the labelings which rise today from reflexive, consciousness-oriented sociology or philosophy, Mead gladly would have chosen the former' (*ibid.*: 111). I find no reason to doubt this and I suspect that such contemporary Meadian 'social behaviorists' as Leonard Cottrell (1977) or Clark McPhail (McPhail and Rexroat, 1979) would agree. However, determinism of any kind is antithetical to the symbolic interactionist's position. There is no possible set of variables, social or otherwise, which can predict human behavior in the symbolic arena of group life. Behavior emerges out of the processes through which it is developed and outcomes, being contingent on definitions of the situation and on negotiations, may vary in unpredictable ways.

But Nisbet allows that 'social determinist' is 'an inaccurate label for Mead, and that it has been badly overworked for Durkheim' (1974: 111). Common to both of them is 'a view of the self that begins basically in society and its symbols . . .' But there also may be basic differences. We will turn below to the matter of the symbolic element in social life which both of these schools of thought appear to share. First, let us look more closely at the distinction between idealism and realism as it is reflected in these two schools.

Idealism, realism, statistics and symbols

Farr describes a parallel debate occurring in both sociology and psychology, using the words 'positivism' and '*verstehen*' to describe the sociological imagery, and 'behaviorism' and 'phenomenology' to describe the psychological distinction (1978b: 519). There are other words which carry the same basic semantics: introspective or subjectivist on the one hand and scientific or objectivist on the other, for example. Regardless of their merits, the distinction attempted is one derived from the philosophers' debate over realism and idealism. These differences are deeply entrenched in opposing theoretical and methodological positions in all of the contemporary social sciences.

We have considered Durkheim's idealism especially as it relates to his concept of social representations, which he describes as a compound of ideas, feelings, and beliefs. Yet he is generally assumed to be a realist and that was the basis for much of the early Chicago criticism of him. Although it is Durkheim's view that social representations are symbolic and that people must generate and support such symbolic systems in order for them to survive, it seems to me that he views their survival as essential for society and does not look kindly upon the alteration of social representations. This can only lead to a decline in the power of the collective conscience and to a breakdown of such venerable institutions as the family, religion, and the community. When such a breakdown unfortunately occurs, other institutions such as education must be strengthened to replace the old ones if stability and order are to exist in society.

If Durkheim is interested in stability and order, the symbolic interactionists are interested in process and change. If Durkheim is sometimes a realist and sometimes an idealist, symbolic interactionists appear to be idealists: 'The traditional position of idealism is that the "world of reality" exists only in human experience and that it appears only in the form in which human beings "see" that world. I think that this position is incontestable' (Blumer, 1969a: 22). But if Blumer is idealist in his assumptions he is insistently empirical in his methods. The scientist must observe and come to understand whatever 'reality' is created by people in the world. Furthermore, it appears that there is an objective world out there which is independent of the constructs of human beings. That real world can challenge and resist our images of it: 'This resistance gives the empirical world an obdurate character that is the mark of reality' (ibid.: 22). It turns out that, as with Durkheim, it is not so simple a matter to place Blumer as either an idealist or a realist. Both of these scholars seem to require some mix of idealism and realism. Can it be that the distinction is at best a heuristic one? Is it at worst a distinction which forces otherwise agile minds into one or the other extreme position which is inadequate as a conception of, or a method for, dealing with the social world?[17]

Let us consider how all of this bears upon the concrete case of Durkheim's conception of data as he deals with it in *Suicide*. We have reviewed his distinction between reliable data and that which is 'defective.' There are two levels at which such data need to be considered and Durkheim considers only one. It has to do with reliability, with the accuracy of recording, completeness, the clarity of definition, the consistency in reporting from different units, etc. The second level has to do with the definitions of what constitutes data – with the social meaning of data. At this level we ask, 'How do we create the reality of the first level?' For example, given the social representations of a society, what is the proper or reasonable frequency of suicide or welfare cases or tonsillectomies? The response to such questions as reflected in local statistics is, I submit, a social fact. But its coercive force is not one that people are aware of. It is not a conscious one. Doctors diagnose not out of fear of sanctions but because they are constrained to believe in these diagnoses.

Durkheim understood that social facts were composed of ideas, feelings, and beliefs. What he failed to grasp was that any reliable indicators of social facts (e.g., suicide rates) must also be social facts. In spite of his insistence that social facts can only be explained by other social facts, he nevertheless persists in the belief that sound data are an objective reality independent of 'ideas, feelings, beliefs.' He insists that those characteristics, when they enter into the construction of data, make those data 'defective.' To the contrary, if such data consistently reflect ideas, beliefs, and feelings then they too must be constituted out of such materials. As Jack Douglas suggests, the very data Durkheim employed were as much a social construction as the data he rejected (1967). This phenomenological view of the social construction of social data is one shared by the symbolic interactionists.

We have reviewed the manner in which both Durkheim and the interactionists share the idealism of posing a symbolic environment as a central feature in human society. Durkheim saw the symbol as a cultural phenomenon. It is a given which guides social life. It lies outside of individuals and exercises constraint upon them. It is what distinguishes individual representations from social representations. For Mead, the symbol was endemic. There is no individual; there are only interacting selves whose interactions are based upon the meanings with which they imbue the objects in their environment. If they fail to take note of an object it does not exist for them. When they do take note, they create a symbol of the object by interpreting it. With some exceptions, interaction is primarily built upon these symbolic meanings. Durkheim's symbols are grander, more distant from and external to the individual, and more limited: 'If then, we ascribe a kind of reality to them [symbols], we do not dream of supposing them to be the whole of moral reality. *That would be to take the sign for the thing signified.* A sign is certainly something ... but *after all it is only a sign'* (Durkheim, 1951: 315, italics mine).

The symbolic interactionist would reverse most of this. For Mead or Cooley or Blumer it is the sign or symbol which is important. The thing signified is after all only a thing of no importance in itself unless it resists the definitions imposed upon it. For the interactionists, to describe a symbol as 'only a sign' would be to deny their whole framework. The sign for them is the basis of social reality. Durkheim, like the interactionist, includes both people and material things in his definition of social objects, but the similarity stops there. For Durkheim, those material social objects are coercive external forces (*ibid*.: 314). The crux of the matter is that, although both depend heavily upon symbols in their analyses, for Durkheim they are external realities – social facts. For the interactionist, they are everyday interpretations constantly changing and routinely attributed to all that the actor takes note of. I suspect that the distinction between the individual and the collective conscience makes no sense to the interactionist. Durkheim treated psychology with respect as a different level of study and as distinct from sociology; symbolic interactionists do not. For them there is no individual conscience. They are in this sense more chauvinistic than Durkheim.

The new Durkheimians and symbolic interactions

Moscovici appears to share with the symbolic interactionists a dynamic, processual view of human behavior. It is a dialectic which challenges the validity of the static views so dominant in contemporary social science. After he finishes a thorough and extensive analysis of the state of knowledge regarding 'attitudes and opinions,' I get the impression that Moscovici has reservations about such concepts. In fact he sounds very much like Blumer on the concept of 'public opinion.' Moscovici suggests that 'the concept of social representations could usefully replace those of opinion or image which are relatively static and descriptive' (1963: 252). This statement also suggests, incidentally, that it has been many years since Moscovici attempted to introduce the concept of social representations into social psychology. In spite of his world-wide reputation, it appears that most psychologists do not take him seriously. It may be small comfort to learn that most sociologists do not take Herbert Blumer seriously either. All of this I suppose has to do with the sociology of knowledge: the right idea in the right place at the right time.

In that same paper Moscovici takes an unorthodox methodological position which is common among interactionists. He makes a distinction between verification and discovery in science, with a plea for discovery. Interactionists are inclined to avoid theory testing and are much more likely to attempt to develop what Glaser and Strauss call 'grounded theory' (1967). That is, theory based on direct empirical observation of social phenomena. This implies a predominantly inductive logic rather than the deductive one emphasized in testing theories.

This new Durkheimianism is, of course, a social psychology and as such is concerned with lesser units than total societies or social institutions. In that sense the affinity to symbolic interaction appears stronger than that to Durkheimian sociology. This is apparent in the concern for social situations. Farr cites Milgram to the effect that 'often it is not so much the kind of person a man is as the kind of situation in which he finds himself that determines how he will act' (Farr, 1978b: 510). In this statement Milgram simultaneously rejects traditional psychological conceptions of personality and traditional sociological conceptions of culture and society. What is left is a situation sociology – or social-psychology if you prefer.

Even at the situational level of analysis, very great differences in perspective and methodology remain. For example, the implication of most laboratory experimentation and small group analysis is that it is the objective features of the situation as presented by the experimenter to which the subjects respond. The interactionist, on the other hand, sees the situation as something which is defined by the parties who find themselves in it. For Abric and Codol, 'an individual's behaviour in an interaction situation is determined not by the objective conditions but by the subject's "representation" of this situation' (Farr, 1978b: 517). In Abric's own words, 'A representation is both the product and the process of a mental activity by which an individual or a group reconstitutes the reality with which he is faced and attributes to it a specific meaning' (1976: 106). This could be a direct quote from W. I. Thomas if the word 'situation' were substituted for 'representation.'[18] Apparently Abric, Apfelbaum, and Codol have been able to demonstrate experimentally the error of attributing objective reality to a social situation (Farr, 1978*b*: 517–18).

From my limited understanding of the French School, it seems related theoretically and methodologically to the symbolic interactionist perspective. Both the French School and symbolic interaction are iconoclastic, but symbolic interaction represents a venerated tradition in American sociology and its iconoclasm tends to be defensive. The French Durkheimian psychologists on the other hand seem to be generating a new perspective and they are on the offensive with their iconoclasm. Let me close this chapter with a few observations on the consequences of choosing ancestors and other concluding comments.

Consequences and conclusions

If my efforts at linkage seem strained it is because they are. The Durkheimian tradition is more closely linked to the positivistic and macro-sociological view of social life. Symbolic interactionism is more closely linked to the subjectivist and micro-sociological view. The differences emerging from such basic divergencies are massive. Yet we find two kinds of reality to contend with here. There is the obdurate world of the writings of those like Durkheim or Mead or Blumer and these writings will only bend so far. They are an objective reality. But bend they do to the definitions of them conjured up by those who take note of them. They become another kind of reality – social representations if you will. And that reality too must be taken into account as much as the reality of what they in fact wrote.

One of the principal features which identifies the French School is its commitment to Durkheim's concept of social representations. That worries me. To borrow a single concept in isolation from its context does not necessarily place one in a tradition. Durkheim was a careful systematic thinker and social representations are an integral part of a larger conceptual framework. I am not at all sure that Durkheim's image of society is the image entertained by the contemporary French School and I am certain that they share little with the Americanized Durkheim.

I see a close affinity with symbolic interactionists and other American phenomenologists such as the ethnomethodologists. This has nothing to do with whose side one is on or who appears to be a more heroic ancestor. Rather it has to do with a body of theoretical, methodological, and substantive literature. It has to do with where one searches for help in pursuing a perceived common interest. I submit that the phenomenological literature has considerably more to offer the French School than the structural-functional literature. It is, in short, more useful, and if this is American pragmatism, then so be it.

The iconoclasm of the French School suggests that it seek (in creating intellectual roots for itself) others who have been critical of current fashions in psychology and sociology. There is something to learn not only from Piaget, from Harry Stack Sullivan, and from Fritz Heider, but from lesser-known iconoclasts, such as Derek Phillips in sociology (1973) or Nehemiah Jordan in psychology (1968). From a symbolic interactionist perspective, to the extent that the French School defines itself into a Durkheimian tradition, that definition of its collective identity will have consequences for the kinds of knowledge it generates and the methods employed for developing that knowledge. Recall that both Durkheim and Blumer agree that when we fail to take note of something, it is as if it did not exist. The choice of ancestors and of intellectual traditions is also the choice of what one takes note of. Both Mead and Durkheim agree that this makes it a choice of what will be real and what will not.

Notes

1. Durkheim rejected Simmel's conception of sociology, surprisingly not because it was reductionist – a kind of psychology – but because Simmel's forms of sociation appeared a-historical to him (Wolff, 1960: ix).
2. Richard O'Toole, one of the leading researchers in this school, describes Leonard S. Cottrell, Jr. as the elder statesman among these social psychologists. Those social behaviorists whom I have met or read are openly antagonistic to Blumer's interpretation of G. H. Mead. See for example, McPhail and Rexroat (1979) and Blumer's angry response (1980).
3. A concise summary of this variety can be found in Warshay (1975: 29–34).
4. The works of Kuhn and such students as McPartland and Couch appear mostly in *The Sociological Quarterly*. The winter 1964 issue of that journal contains one set of them. For a comparison of Kuhn's 'Iowa School' and the 'Chicago School' of symbolic interaction see Meltzer and Petras (1970: 3–17).
5. George Gonos (1977) argues that Goffman's use of frame analysis reflects a structural orientation which is in direct contrast to the interactionists' use of the concept of the 'situation.' He sees Goffman as 'heavily indebted to Durkheim' (*ibid.*: 855 and n5).
6. There is an element of determinism in Thomas's analysis of the situation in his presidential address to the American Sociological Association in the sense that much of the experimental evidence he cites involves manipulation of the objective features of the situation. In his first published use of 'the definition of the situation' (Thomas, 1917) he examines the concept of primary groups developed by his contemporary, Charles H. Cooley (1909) and seems to view the definitions as imposed by the groups rather than defined in interaction. Thomas's 'definition of the situation' as an interpretive act is best understood

in conjunction with Mead's later analysis of the self and society and Blumer's concept of constructing lines of joint action. Later developments of Thomas's concept can be found in *The unadjusted girl* (1934: 41–50).

7. My historical analysis in these pages is heavily dependent upon Hinkle's analysis of 'Durkheim in American Sociology' (1960: 267–95). According to Hinkle, Durkheim is ignored by all of the major American theorists until after World War 1.

8. Alexander (1978: 180) attempts to resolve this enigma in part by highlighting the difference between Parsons' ideological individualism and his theoretical individualism, arguing that the two are unrelated.

9. My own thinking and research has been heavily influenced by Merton's 'arid functionalism.' A recent article by Gold and myself in an annual review of research in 'symbolic interaction,' (1979) leans heavily upon Merton's concepts of intended and unintended consequences as well as anticipated and unanticipated ones. These are the heart of his formulation of functional analysis.

10. Durkheim is one of Parsons' four stars in *The structure of social action* (1937), the others being Marshall, Pareto, and Weber. He devotes over 150 pages of that volume to Durkheim and four chapters deal exclusively with Durkheim's ideas.

11. I cannot find the 'explicit' attack to which Hinkle refers. Thomas does make passing reference to Durkheim in a footnote which suggests that the notion of social facts explaining other social facts is hardly worth the effort to criticize (1918–20, vol. I: 44, n1).

12. Blumer's most explicit treatment of methodology is found in 'The methodological position of symbolic interactionism' in Blumer (1969*a*: 1–60). Most of the Blumer articles referred to in this paper are reprinted in that volume.

13. As clear as this reference is, Blumer does not mention by name either Parsons or *The social system* (1951).

14. Maines finds a social organization perspective in 'two decades of interactionist informed research' (1977: 243) on urban or occupational issues at the University of Chicago. He cites Maines and Denzin (1977) as a source.

15. I did not hear that address, nor has it been published at the time of writing.

16. Nisbet (1974) is the most informative secondary source I have found for anyone wishing to establish a theoretical kinship between Durkheim and the Chicago School of symbolic interaction. He recommends Durkheim's *Moral education* (1961*b*) as the clearest exposition of the similarities in the thinking of Durkheim and Mead. Nisbet's book is also a scholarly attack on what he believes to be the current passing fad of subjectivism including ethnomethodology, humanism, and radicalism. Significantly, he does not include symbolic interactionism among these subjectivist fads.

17. McPhail and Rexroat (1979) are distressed by what they refer to as Blumer's 'waffling' and 'vacillation' between realism and idealism. Blumer denies any paradox and devotes a substantial portion of his rejoinder (1980) to a clarification of the need to entertain elements of both positions.

18. This is the central concern of Martin Orne in his consideration of 'demand characteristics' in experimental situations (Orne, 1962).

3. Attitudes and social representations

J. JASPARS and C. FRASER

1. The social nature of attitudes and social representations

Contemporary French research on social representations must present quite a few problems to social psychologists who are not familiar with the history of social psychology in France. According to Herzlich (1972: 303) the concept of 'représentation sociale' occupies a special place in modern social psychology, because it falls outside the predominant Anglo-Saxon influence and is related to a different European tradition.

Various French social psychologists (Moscovici 1963; Codol 1969b) have taken great pains to emphasize the difference between the cognitive tradition in social psychology and the recent work on social representations in France. As Farr (1978b) has pointed out, they invariably chose to contrast their approach with those cognitive approaches within social psychology which stress images, opinions, beliefs, personal constructs etc. Obviously the distinctive features of research on social representations cannot be its insistence on the subjective or psychological representation of objective social reality as a determinant of social behaviour, because 'the physical and objective properties of social stimulation and incentives have always been assumed to be less significant for the analysis of social behaviour, than their subjective counterparts' (Zajonc; 1969). Indeed Codol (1969b) points out that concepts like 'cognitive organization', 'cognitive structure' and 'personal constructs' share this notion with social representations, but at the same time he makes clear that the former ignore the *content* and the *social origins* of cognitive organizations. Moscovici (1963) in his review of attitudes and opinion research has suggested that the concept of social representation could usefully replace the concepts of opinion or image, which are relatively static and descriptive. Elsewhere Moscovici (1973) has stated that social representations are not simply 'opinions about', 'images of' or 'attitudes towards' the social world, but 'theories' or 'branches of knowledge' in their own right which are used for the discovery and organization of reality. According to Moscovici, social representations are systems of values, ideas and practices with a two-fold function. First of all they have the function to establish *an order* which enables individuals to orientate themselves in their material and social world and to master it, and secondly, they enable communication to take place among members of a community by providing them with *a code* for social exchange and a code for naming and classifying unambiguously the various aspects of their world and their individual and group history (see Farr 1978*b*).

It is quite clear that the functions attributed to social representations by Moscovici are to some extent similar to the functions which are characteristic of cognitive representations as studied in the Anglo-Saxon tradition. The most obvious example is probably G. Kelly's personal construct psychology in which both functions are explicitly mentioned and elaborated (Fransella, this volume). Cognitive research in social psychology has never limited itself to simply 'opinions about', 'images of' or 'attitudes toward'. Heider's psychology of interpersonal relations is perhaps the most extensive commonsense theory about social behaviour; the studies of the *Authoritarian Personality* did not stop at describing attitudes towards Jews and Negroes but – in an ever-widening circle of empirical covariations – stressed the underlying personality syndrome with its origin in childhood experiences (Brown; 1965); cognitive dissonance theory has developed over the last twenty years especially with regard to the motivational or dynamic implications of cognitive representations (Wicklund and Brehm 1976). Recent research on the representation of knowledge in long-term memory and especially the related research in computer simulation show that cognitive structures are not conceived of as simple one-dimensional representations of reality (Norman 1976; Schank and Abelson 1977), but as complex propositional networks or analogical maps. These recent developments in cognitive psychology show at least two interesting features. First of all it is clear that research on cognitive processing presupposes a social origin of such systems, in the sense that propositional representations rely heavily on structural and semantic properties of language, and secondly it is a condition *sine qua non* to specify the content of information to be represented, because it would otherwise be impossible to simulate understanding of natural language

(Schank and Abelson; 1977). The important changes which have taken place in the study of social cognition can be nicely illustrated by following the fate of the principle of cognitive consistency. In the original work by Heider (1958), Festinger (1957) and Osgood *et al.* (1957) this principle was proposed as a very general principle of cognitive organization of social information. It was in fact a Gestalt law dealing with perceptual unit formation in the social world (Heider; 1944). Gradually it became clear that it was unrealistic to assume that consistency would operate independently of the nature of the units formed. Even the earliest research by Jordan (1953) indicated that, for example, Heider's balance theory had to be modified in view of the differences found between perceived sentiment relations and other unit formation principles. The most important change, however, came many years later and can best be seen in the work by Abelson on belief systems and implicational molecules, and also in Gollob's subject–verb–object model of information integration (Wyer; 1975). This is not the place to discuss these publications in detail, but it is important to indicate that in the theory proposed by Abelson and Gollob consistency is still used as an all-pervading principle, which appears to operate more clearly under some conditions than under others. Presumably it does not operate at the lower level of script-based behaviour but at the higher level of interpersonal themes (Schank and Abelson; 1977).

Social psychological research on conceptual systems by Harvey *et al.* (1961) which followed in the footsteps of Adorno *et al.* and G. Kelly (1955) also indicates that content and structure cannot readily be separated. In a study conducted by Lamberigts (1980) it was shown that differences in cognitive integration implied content differences in conceptual structures. Subjects high in integrative complexity appeared to emphasize differences in sympathy when judging other people, whereas subjects low in complexity stressed differences in stability.

In another recent study by Hagendoorn (1976) it was shown that individual cognitive complexity, as measured by G. Kelly's repertory grid, depends to some extent on the nature of the role constructs used. In this study abstract and concrete persons, as defined by Harvey's conceptual systems test, appeared to differ in cognitive complexity only when familiar individuals had to be judged, but not when 'distant' individuals were evaluated. Apparently subjects characterized by concrete conceptual systems found it more difficult to apply abstract judgment to people they knew very well, but that does not mean that they cannot be just as complex as persons who process information in an abstract fashion, if they are presented with stimuli of more neutral content.

It should be obvious from this short review of 'Anglo-American' research on social cognition, and the recent studies on the relationship of structure and content of conceptual and belief systems, that at least some aspects emphasized by the French research on social representations are receiving more attention in research on social cognition. The functions of such systems for organizing and coding the social world have always been recognized, but the implications for social exchange have never been extended beyond the interpersonal level. Also, the growing awareness of the interdependence of content and cognitive structure as yet has not resulted in an attempt to uncover the social origins of such systems. However, these differences do not seem to constitute the most important distinction between social representations and cognitive structures. The fundamental differences, we believe are to be found elsewhere.

Perhaps they were obfuscated by the way in which the notion of social representation was introduced to non-French-speaking psychologists in Moscovici's Annual Review chapter on Attitudes and Opinions. It is not at all clear from the short and perhaps too modest reference to his own work which Moscovici makes in that chapter that he is introducing into the study of attitudes and opinions a completely different and European tradition in the social sciences which goes back to Durkheim's notion of collective representations. If he had used Durkheim's term or had referred to Durkheim's publications on individual and collective representations it would have been evident that what is social about social representations is not in the first place that such representations are representations of social reality, or that they are social in origin, but that they are social because they are shared by many individuals and as such constitute a social reality which can influence individual behaviour.

It is not necessary to spell out Durkheim's notion of collective representations here, because that has been done admirably by Lukes (1973) and to some extent by Herzlich (1972). It is important, however, to realize that the notion of social representations in the sense of Durkheim's collective representations is manifestly different from the notion of cognitive representations as developed in American (social) psychology. To a large extent such notions have been introduced in social psychology as a reaction to a behaviouristic S-R psychology in order to explain how response *differences between individuals* can emerge when objectively or physically the same stimulus is present. In the history of American social psychology the notions of cognitive representation and individual response disposition have been amalgamated under the influence of G. Allport's classic study of the attitude concept in Murchison's first edition of the *Handbook of social psychology* (Murchison; 1935). The result of this development has been that we have lost sight of the dual nature of attitudes and related concepts in social psychology (see below) and, more important perhaps, the collective nature of attitudes has been completely overlooked in attitude research during the last forty years.

In summary, it appears that the social nature of attitudes, as traditionally studied, differs in several fundamental ways from the social nature of social representations. Social representations are social in at least three different senses. (1) They deal with social reality mainly in the social structural and cultural sense. (2) They are social in origin and (3) they are widely shared and as a result they become part of social reality itself. Attitudes as the evaluative components of individual cognitive representations are social in the first sense, although much more emphasis is put here on the interpersonal aspects of social reality rather than on the structural and cultural aspects of social reality. Secondly, attitudes are usually defined as learned predispositions and as such are conceived as being social in origin though precious little research has been devoted to the study either of the development of attitudes or of the origins of the contents of attitude statements. Most importantly, however, attitudes are generally regarded as individual dispositions which were introduced in social psychology to explain differences between individuals in their reaction to similar stimuli. The notion that these dispositions might be shared by individuals belonging to the same social groups and the consequences of the social nature of attitudes in this sense have, however, never been considered.

The main purpose of this chapter is two-fold. First of all it is important to discuss in some detail the perverted development of the attitude concept, and secondly it is relevant to investigate what the consequences are for research in cognitive social psychology.

2. The individualization of the attitude concept

Allport's influential discussion of the attitude concept in Murchison's *Handbook of social psychology* has been criticized from the very beginning by various social psychologists. McDougall (1933) was probably the first to point out that Allport's conception of attitudes introduced into psychology a much too vague and global term, which was used to cover a multitude of facts of many kinds, including almost every variety of opinion and belief, and all the abstract qualities of personality, such as courage, obstinacy, generosity and humility, as well as units of affective organization. Recently Fishbein and Ajzen (1972) have been equally critical of attitude research, emphasizing that apparent controversies and inconsistencies are largely due to pseudoproblems created by conceptual ambiguity. They ask for rather serious reconsideration of basic assumptions and thoughtful theoretical reanalysis of problems confronting the field. It is not surprising therefore to see that previous investigators have been tempted to propose that the concept of attitude be dropped from social science (Abelson; 1972). In a way these controversial remarks are curious, since the concept of attitude became popular, according to Allport, because it brought peace between various schools of thought in psychology and appeared to be the culmination of convergent trends in experimental psychology, psychoanalysis and sociology in the 1920s. With the benefit of hindsight one wonders whether the introduction of the attitude concept has really solved anything or just obfuscated distinctions by being so elastic a concept. Allport seemed to be aware of this weakness and admitted 'that it might correctly be questioned whether a science reared upon so amorphous a foundation, can be strong'.

A clarification of the doctrine of attitudes was what was most urgently needed, according to his opinion. But in view of Fishbein and Ajzen's conclusion forty years later it seems that we still lack that clarification. It looks as if Allport overestimated the common thread running through the diverse conceptions of attitude in his time. Allport's conclusion was that in one way or another the essential feature of all conceptions of attitude was a preparation or readiness for response.

A conceptual analysis of the various notions of attitudes on which Allport bases this conclusion indicates, however, that he overempha- sizes this common thread. Before presenting his own definition of the concept of attitude Allport simply lists sixteen other definitions of the concept which were in use at that time, but he arrives at the conclusion just mentioned without any discussion at all. When one reads through the various definitions, it becomes clear that all except two refer indeed to the action, behaviour or responses of the individual, but it is by no means true that all definitions indicate specifically a state of preparation or readiness.

Using Allport's own omnibus definition and McGuire's detailed discussion of this definition (McGuire: 1969) as a guideline, a category scheme was developed, which allows a matrix notation of the attitude definitions mentioned by Allport. In all, eight categories appeared to be mentioned with sufficient frequency to be included in the analysis. The matrix of definitions and a description of the categories used are presented in Table 1. The matrix of definitions was interpreted as absolute judgment data (Coombs; 1964) and analyzed by non-metric multidimensional scaling. The results of the analysis are presented in Figure 1.

A superficial inspection of the matrix presented in Table 1 indicates already that the variation in definitions reflects more than one conceptual dimension. At least two dimensions are required to obtain a reasonable fit, as can be seen in Figure 1. Far from showing a common thread which would imply a unidimensional structure, the definitions imply two independent conceptual distinctions. There are on the one hand quite clearly a number of definitions which describe an attitude essentially as an evaluative mental state of efferent readiness, whereas other definitions emphasize that an attitude is a general afferent mental state, affected by experience. The very different nature of these definitions is nicely illustrated by comparing two authors whose definitions occupy opposite positions in the conceptual structure presented in Figure 1. As an example of the response conception of attitudes Droba's definition can be stated (Droba 1933). According to Droba an attitude is a mental disposition of the human individual to act for or against a definite object. As a contrast consider now Warren's perceptual definition, which reads:

When a certain type of experience is constantly repeated, a change of set is brought about, which affects many central neurons and tends to spread over other parts of the central nervous system. These changes in the general set of the central nervous system temper the process of reception. In terms of the subjective mental life these general sets are called attitudes.   (Warren 1922: 360)

The most important issue seems to be whether response states and perceptual states should be considered as one total intervening process or as two different states which possibly affect stimulus–response connections in different ways. That this is not merely a problem of historical importance is evident, for example, from an analysis made by Greenwald which leads to a distinction between a learning-behaviour and a cognitive integration position in attitude theory. Campbell (1963) has labelled these two positions the lever and template conceptions of

Table 1. *Allport's definitions of attitude* (Murchison, 1935)

	MENTAL	NEURAL	GENERAL	READINESS	AFFERENT	EFFERENT	EVALUATIVE	EXPERIENCE
1. BALDWIN	0	0	0	1	1	1	0	0
2. MORGAN	1	0	0	0	(1)	1	0	0
3. WARREN (1934)	1	0	0	1	1	1	0	0
4. CHAVE	0	0	0	1	(1)	1	0	1
5. CANTRIL	1	0	0	1	0	1	0	0
6. KÖHLER	0	1	0	0	1	0	0	0
7. BOGARDUS	0	0	0	0	0	1	1	0
8. THOMAS/ZN	1	0	0	0	0	1	0	0
9. F. ALLPORT	1	(1)	0	1	0	1	0	0
10. DROBA	1	0	0	0	0	1	1	0
11. LUNDBERG	0	0	(1)	0	0	1	0	0
12. EWER	0	0	0	1	1	1	0	0
13. KRUEGER/Rc.	0	0	0	0	0	1	0	1
14. WARREN (1922)	(1)	1	1	0	1	0	0	1
15. G. W. ALLPORT (1929)	0	1	1	0	1	1	0	1
16. MURPHY/M	0	0	0	0	0	1	1	0
17. G. W. ALLPORT (1935)	1	1	0	1	0	1	0	1

Notes: Cell values in parentheses indicate values that could not be fitted in a two-dimensional scalogram.

Each row indicates which elements, as defined below, were included in the definitions by the author mentioned on the left. This notation of course only enumerates the concepts used in the definition and neglects the way in which these concepts are related by the definition. Since the purpose of the analysis was to show that Allport's unification of the attitude concept was not justified a more refined analysis was not necessary.

1. Mental: Whenever the definition mentioned the words *mental* or conscious(ness).
2. Neural: Whenever the definition mentioned the words *neural* or *nervous*.
3. General: Whenever the definition mentioned the *general* nature of the state.
4. Readiness: Whenever the definition mentioned the terms *readiness*, preparation or tentative reactions.
5. Afferent: Whenever the definition referred to the receptor side of the S–R connection by expressions like, *incoming experience*, stimulus attention, sensory reception.
6. Efferent: Whenever the definition referred to the response side of the S–R connection by expressions like act, activity, reaction, adjustment, response.
7. Evaluative: Whenever the definition specified that the tendency was *for* or *against*, a certain object.
8. Experience: Whenever the definition indicated that attitudes come into existence through experience.

attitudes, but he argues that the two positions are functionally equivalent in their effect on behaviour. To illustrate this point Campbell uses a fictitious example of a hungry subject correctly recognizing a tachistoscopically presented stimulus more often than a person who is not hungry. The greater accuracy of the hungry person may, Campbell

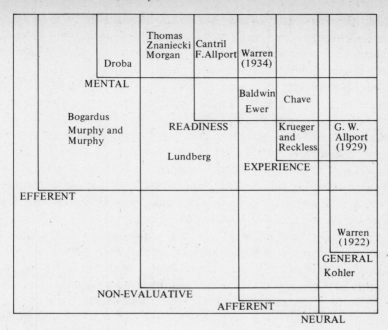

Fig. 1   A multidimensional conjunctive scalogram analysis of G. W. Allport's definitions of attitudes. The definitions (indicated by the name of the author) which are to the right and above a particular conceptual boundary (indicated by the concept in question) all include that concept as part of the definition.

argues, be due to a response bias, which leads to the identification of more stimuli as food stimuli, or the accuracy may be the consequence of greater sensitivity of the subject in discriminating between the two types of stimuli.

It is of course a moot question whether one can really speak in this case of functional equivalence, because the equivalence exists only in the reactions to the food stimuli, but not with respect to both food and non-food stimuli. It is precisely for this reason that the theory of signal detectability makes an explicit distinction between the observer as a sensor and the observer as a decision-maker. The relevance of the distinction made by signal detection theory for attitude research becomes clear when one exchanges Campbell's food stimuli for mesodiacritic minority group members (Tajfel 1969), that is a minority group whose members are moderately recognizable as belonging to that group (e.g. Jews). Many studies have shown that people who are prejudiced against such a group more often identify correctly persons as belonging to that group, but they do so apparently by classifying in general more people as being members of the discriminated group than by being more sensitive to the distinction between group and non-group members (*ibid*.: 1969). Prejudice does not operate as a more or less accurate template in this case, but as a response lever, which is more readily used by prejudiced people against other persons whether they do or do not belong to the minority group. It should be clear to anyone that one can hardly speak of functional equivalence when the difference can mean that one gets killed in the process. The theory of signal detectability is, however, only of partial interest for determining the afferent or efferent nature of attitudes, because the theory deals only with response *thresholds* (β) and perceptual *sensitivity* (d') whereas the problem of the dual nature of attitudes is much more general. Perceptual and response conceptualizations also distinguish two competing theories of attitude change, as McGuire (1969, 149) has correctly observed. According to perceptual or cognitive theory as advocated by Asch, attitude change involves not only making a new response to the old stimulus, but also a redefinition of the stimulus to which the response is made. The more response-oriented approach, such as the one proposed by Hovland and the Yale school, depict attitude change as a change of the evaluative response to the old stimulus. Here again is an example where it might be questioned whether both conceptualizations are functionally equivalent. Rather than just declaring that attitudes are both cognitive and affective in nature, and postulating that these components are possibly related, it might be better to consider cognitions and affects as separate entities, which together in a yet-to-be-determined way constitute the mediational process between eliciting events and the person's behaviour. This is, of course, exactly what, for example, Fishbein's expectancy-value theory of attitudes tries to do, by making a clear distinction between beliefs about an attitude object and the evaluative aspects of beliefs.

Although Fishbein's attitude theory (Fishbein and Ajzen; 1975) should be considered as an advance over previous conceptual treatments of attitudes, it is also clear that there are still quite a few problems in the approach developed by Fishbein. In the first place it is questionable whether cognitive and evaluative aspects of attributes of attitude objects are indeed related in a multiplicative way to direct evaluations of the attitude object (Jaspars; 1973). In the second place it is doubtful whether separate evaluations of the attitude object combine in a summative way, as is suggested by Fishbein's theory. As Slovic and Lichtenstein (1971) and Anderson (1974) have shown, it is likely that the processing of social information is more complex.

More important than these two objections, however, is the fact that there exists no intrinsic relationship between evaluations and beliefs in Fishbein's theory. It appears that the implicit evaluative response to each attribute of an attitude object is learned separately, through classical or instrumental conditioning. If this were true, one might assume that any evaluative response hierarchy might develop irrespective of the structure of a person's belief system, but simply determined by the person's individual reinforcement history. However, some relationship between evaluative responses and the habit family hierarchy of responses forming the belief system must exist, because (perceived) stimulus characteristics must play a role in the reinforcement process and depending upon the degree of (perceived) similarity between stimuli some generalization or reinforcement presumably takes place. In other words, given a particular belief system or cognitive stimulus representation, certain hierarchies of evaluative responses with respect to these stimuli are more likely than others. Another way of expressing the same idea is to interpret the belief system as a cognitive structure from which possible evaluative response hierarchies can be derived. In fact, the classical attitude measurement procedures of Thurstone, Likert and Guttman assume that such a relationship exists between the cognitive representation of attributes and evaluative responses to these attributes. This can be most clearly seen in Guttman's scalogram analysis (Guttman; 1944), where the evaluative response patterns produced by the subjects imply a unidimensional configuration of attitude statements, if the response patterns satisfy the criterion of scalability. The implicit assumption in this procedure is that subjects do not differ in their cognitive representation of the attitude statements, but only in their evaluation of the statements. Without that assumption it would be impossible to develop an attitude scale of the Guttman type. In other words, a cumulative attitude scaling procedure implicitly presupposes a *common* or *shared* cognitive representation in order to differentiate between the evaluative response patterns of the subjects. The same can be said of other attitude scaling procedures. A Thurstone scale only exists if there is sufficient agreement among the judges to produce a scale. Respondents are supposed to have a similar representation of the attitude statements and should produce similar reactions to statements which are adjacent on the scale. It is important to note that Thurstone originally presented five cases of the law of comparative judgment

(Thurstone; 1928) on which his method of attitude measurement is based. In the complete form of the law as described in the so-called Case 1, differences between scale values of statements are described as a function of *individual* discriminal processes (read sensations) and the correlations between these processes. The individual discriminal processes could be investigated by asking one subject to make the same judgment many times, that is, by replication over trials. In the other cases of the law of comparative judgment replication over individuals is substituted for replication over trials. It is apparently not recognized that this slight technical difference actually involves a very fundamental change from assumptions about the nature of an intra-individual cognitive process, to an inter-individual cognitive process, to an inter-individual social process of agreement between judges. Nevertheless, with a few striking exceptions (e.g. Newcomb; 1958), ever since Allport, attitudes have theoretically been considered as individual dispositions, whereas the available measurement procedures have implied on the one hand a common cognitive or shared representation of stimuli and on the other hand individual evaluative response tendencies. As Coombs has shown (Coombs; 1964) all methods of analysis for observations, which can be interpreted as relations between elements from different sets (such as persons' and attitude statements) are based on this notion of a common stimulus space to which differences between subjects can be related by assuming that the individual response patterns represent different ways of folding or picking up the stimulus configuration. Fishbein's proposal to measure beliefs and evaluations separately can be seen in the light of this development as the ultimate individualization of the attitude concept. In Fishbein's theory subjects can differ in their belief structure and/or in their evaluations of their beliefs. This is quite compatible with Fishbein's idea about an attitude change, which is seen as either a change in an individual's belief about an attitude object or as a change in the evaluative aspect of beliefs.

Theoretically Fishbein's individualized approach to attitude measurement had already been prepared by Campbell (1963). Campbell argued that the problem of attitude measurement is comparable to the problem faced by an animal psychologist who wants to investigate the acquired behavioural dispositions of an aged and experienced rat, which is shipped to him from another laboratory. In order to diagnose the residue of previous experience he would have to confront the animal on numerous occasions with a great variety of stimuli and observe the response to each of these stimuli. In this way he would obtain a stimulus–response matrix in which for each stimulus the conditional probability of a particular response would be given. Such a matrix could be analysed by multidimensional scaling techniques, which would produce a joint stimulus and response configuration of minimal dimensionality, or the stimulus–response matrix could be interpreted as the product of separate stimulus and response matrices (Jaspars, 1978). Although Campbell did not follow up his own parable of the visiting rat in attitude research, developments in multidimensional scaling have made such analyses possible. In fact Feeger (1974) has adopted this approach recently in his study of political attitudes in West Germany.

But now that we are able to analyse individual stimulus–response structures and belief-value systems, it is important to ask whether perhaps the implicit assumptions of classical attitude measurement procedures about the common cognitive representation underlying individual evaluative responses are justified. There are various reasons for assuming that such might be the case, but before discussing the available empirical evidence it is interesting to go back to attitude research, before Allport individualized the attitude concept and made it into a global stimulus–response disposition for the purpose of explaining differences in behaviour to objectively similar situations. The outstanding work in this respect is, of course, the famous study of the Polish peasant in Europe and America by Thomas and Znaniecki (1918–20), in which the concept of attitudes occupies such a central position that they suggested a separate scientific discipline – social psychology – for the study of attitudes.

3. Attitudes: the subjective side of social culture

In their famous 'Methodological Note' of the *Polish peasant*, Thomas and Znaniecki (1918, vol. 1, 1–86) present a completely different treatment of attitudes than Allport does fifteen years later. After some preliminary remarks about commonsense knowledge of social life and social problems, Thomas and Znaniecki point out that 'if social theory is to become the basis of social technique, it is evident that it must include both ... the objective cultural element of social life and the objective characteristics of the members of the social group ... taken as correlated' (*ibid*. 20). They suggest subsequently to use for the former the term social values or simply values and for the latter the term attitudes (*ibid*. 21). More complete definitions are given later in the same Note. 'By attitude', Thomas and Znaniecki write (*ibid*. 22), 'we understand a process of individual consciousness which determines real or possible activity of the individual in the social world', whereas 'by a social value we understand any datum having empirical content accessible to the members of some social group and a meaning in regard to which it is or may be an object of activity'. Although especially the description of social values is somewhat abstruse, the meaning of the term becomes clear from the examples given by Thomas and Znaniecki. A social value may be a foodstuff, an instrument, a coin, a piece of poetry, a university, a myth or a scientific theory. The contents of these social values differ in the sense that some of these values have a sensual content, whereas others have an imaginary content. The meaning of these values becomes explicit when they are taken in connection with human actions. The meaning of the foodstuff for example, is its reference to its eventual consumption; the meaning of a scientific theory, the possibility of control of experience by idea or action that it permits. Attitudes are the individual counterparts of social values, according to Thomas and Znaniecki. Thus the hunger that compels the consumption of food; the tendency of a spendthrift to spend the coin; the poet's feelings and ideas expressed in the poem; the interest in creating, understanding or applying a scientific theory – all these are attitudes (*ibid.*). Thomas and Znaniecki point out furthermore that an attitude is distinguished from a psychical state by its reference to activity and thereby to the social world. It is worth quoting Thomas and Znaniecki here *in extenso*, because their discussion of the difference between attitudes and psychological states is of crucial importance for understanding how different their view is from Allport's.

A psychological process is an attitude treated as an object in itself, isolated by a reflective act of attention and taken first of all in connection with other states of the same individual. An attitude is a psychological process treated as primarily manifested in its reference to the social world and first of all in connection with some social values. Individual psychology may later reestablish the connection between the psychological process and the objective reality, which has been severed by reflection; it may study psychological processes as conditioned by facts going on in the objective world. In the same way social theory may later connect various attitudes of an individual and determine his social character. But it is the original (usually unconsciously occupied) standpoints which determine at once the subsequent methods of these two sciences. The psychological process remains always fundamentally *a state of somebody*; the attitude remains fundamentally an *attitude toward* something.   (*ibid.* 23)

It is here that the difference between an individual psychological and a social psychological conception of attitudes becomes clear. For Allport,

Campbell, Fishbein and many other social psychologists an attitude is essentially a more or less permanent psychological state of an individual, whereas Thomas and Znaniecki view an attitude primarily as a reflection of the social world in the individual. If the latter view takes predominance over the former, it is obvious that attitudes of individuals will be similar to the extent that they share the same social environment. Attitudes conceived of as individual reflections of a common social environment, then, do not tell us very much about differences between individuals living in the same environment, but they might be very informative about individuals belonging to different social groups, such as Polish immigrants and Americans. It was Fraser (1978) who pointed out that this view is entirely consistent with the purpose of the study of the Polish peasant in America, because Thomas and Znaniecki want to explain the specific social problems faced by Polish immigrants as distinct from the problems of native Americans. They are not primarily interested in the question why certain immigrants behave quite differently from other immigrants in an otherwise more or less similar situation. They do recognize, to be sure, that attitudes may also reflect an individual's personal experience and distinguish him from other individuals belonging to the same group, but their primary aim is to make clear that attitudes are less general than universal psychological states. Thomas and Znaniecki (*ibid*. 27) remark that they 'find numerous monographs listed as psychological, but studying conscious phenomena which are not supposed to have their source in human nature in general but in special social conditions which can vary with the variation of these conditions and still be common to all individuals in the same condition.' 'It is this observation which leads to the statement that attitudes 'find also indirect manifestation in more or less explicit rules of behaviour by which the group tends to maintain, to regulate and to make more frequent the corresponding type of actions among its members' (*ibid*. 31). This statement has at least two important consequences for the study of social behaviour, one of which is already formulated by Thomas and Znaniecki. Adherence to rules by group members is, according to them, certainly due 'neither to the rationality of these rules nor to the physical consequences which their following or breaking may have, but to the consciousness that these rules represent attitudes of the group and to the realization of the social consequences which will ensue for him if he follows or breaks the rules' (*ibid*. 33). Thomas and Znaniecki thus appear to grant a super-individual status to shared attitudes, which can influence individual behaviour. The second consequence of this view is that one should not expect a strong relationship between attitudes and within-group differences in behaviour, because attitudes differentiate primarily between groups and not between members of the same group.

After all this, one may wonder why Thomas and Znaniecki still make a distinction between social values and attitudes, because if attitudes are just shared subjective interpretations of objective social reality, not much seems to be gained in explanatory power. Thomas and Znaniecki have been seriously criticized by Blumer for defining attitudes and values so inclusively as to be practically indistinguishable. The authors of the *Polish peasant* were well aware of this problem, but already in their 'Methodological Note' they reject explicitly Durkheim's point that the cause of social phenomena is to be sought, not in an individual but exclusively in another social phenomenon. They maintain that the cause of a social or individual phenomenon is never another social or individual phenomenon alone but always a combination of the two (values and attitudes). 'An attitude may be treated as a social phenomenon as opposed to a state of consciousness of individual psychology; but it is individual, even if common to all members of a group, when we oppose it to a value' (*ibid*. 44). The problem raised by Blumer is easily resolved, however, if one puts it in the perspective of the original study of Thomas and Znaniecki. *The Polish peasant* attempts to offer an explanation of the disorganization of immigrant life in terms of both immigrant attitudes and the values of the surrounding American culture. Because attitudes and values refer to different social groups, Blumer's methodological critique becomes largely irrelevant.

The relevance of the ideas developed by Thomas and Znaniecki for the study of attitudes and collective representations is that they show how similar both concepts originally were. We have lost sight however of the collective nature of attitudes, because attitudes have been impounded by social psychology and made into individual response dispositions of an evaluative nature, although classical measurement procedures were based on the implicit assumption of a common stimulus representation. Recent developments in attitude research and scaling techniques have led however to a complete individualization of the study of attitude, in the sense that not just response tendencies but also cognitive aspects of attitudes are seen as differentiating between individuals. If one assumes, however, that cognitive representations and/or response dispositions are collective in nature, because they have a common social origin, it is worthwhile to consider the consequences of such a hypothesis for attitude research.

4. Attitudes and social representations

Since attitudes, as we have discussed them above, can be thought to consist of cognitive representations and response dispositions, it makes sense to consider the consequences of the view presented by the social representation theory used by Thomas and Znaniecki separately for both components. Obviously either the cognitive or the evaluative response component of attitudes or both might have a common social origin and be shared by individuals belonging to the same social group. We will first consider the consequences of a common social origin of evaluative responses and then the implications of a shared cognitive representation. It is too early to present in detail a complete discussion of the implications of such an interpretation, but it is possible to consider here a number of obvious and possibly quite relevant consequences for the study of attitudes in social psychology.

a. The consequences of a common social origin of evaluative responses

The first consequence that should be considered is perhaps simply the effect of a common social origin on the *distribution* of evaluative responses. It was pointed out above that Thurstone's original law of comparative judgment (Thurstone, 1928), is based upon the idea that 'momentary fluctuations in the organism' lead to different sensations if the same stimulus is presented to an observer a large number of times, and that these sensations form a normal distribution on the psychological continuum. Essentially the same assumption is made when replication over individuals is substituted for replication over trials. However, if one assumes that the judgements made by the observers are not independent of each other in the sense that they have a common origin, it is unlikely that the so-called discriminal processes are still normally distributed. It is not easy to specify the function which would generate the distribution of correlated judgments made by observers, because we have neither a theory about the social process involved nor good data to test such a theory. It will be necessary to go back to statistical distribution theory (Kendall and Stuart; 1963) to deal with this problem adequately. Intuitively it is clear that a common origin will produce more agreement among observers than would be expected in the case of normally distributed judgments. In the extreme case of complete agreement among observers Thurstone's scaling procedure breaks down and a qualitative dichotomization of attitude items would result instead of a scale. If one still proceeds on the assumption of normally distributed judgments in the case of less than perfect agreement, scale values of attitude items tend to become more separated on the attitude continuum the higher the agreement among observers is. The important point then is to realize that scale values obtained in this way do not necessarily reflect an individual's ability 'to identify, distinguish and react to stimuli' (Thurstone; 1928), but rather the agreement among observers in this respect.

The relevance of this distinction can be illustrated easily with results from developmental studies. In an experiment on the development of national attitudes in Dutch children (Jaspars *et al*. 1972), it was found that preferential scale values for six well-klnown countries as determined by Thurstone's method of comparative judgment became increasingly separated with age. It would, however, be incorrect to interpret these results as an indication of individual cognitive differentiation with age. In fact from the age of eight onwards the children appear to be equally transitive in their judgments and hence do not differ in the extent to which they discriminate between the various stimuli. However, their individual comparative judgments begin to look more and more alike as they grow older, resulting in a much stronger separation of the stimuli. One needs a truly social point of view to realize that what appears to be a process of individual differentiation is in effect the emergence of a shared response hierarchy requiring a social explanation.

These findings do not necessarily imply however that the cognitive representations underlying the preferences have also become more similar. Data obtained in the same experiment on similarity judgments for the same stimuli suggest that this was indeed the case (*ibid*. 389) in that study, but there is no reason to assume that this is always so. In fact, the more interesting question is whether individual response hierarchies imply the same or different cognitive representations. In the latter case we would be confronted with highly personal, idiosyncratic cognitive representations, in the former with a social or collective representation shared by many individuals. It is the consequences of this difference which we want to explore in the next section.

b. The consequences of shared cognitive representations

Perhaps the first problem to consider is the relevance of the distinction between individual response systems and social representations for processes of *communication*. It is an almost trite hypothesis in social psychology to state that communication between individuals is influenced by the degree of similarity of their relevant cognitive representations. This general idea is interpreted in various ways, but usually no distinction is made between similarity in response tendencies and similarities in stimulus representation. More specifically one might ask the question whether accuracy of communication is, for example, influenced more by similarity in attitudinal responses or by the similarity of the underlying cognitive representations which are implied by these attitudes. In this form the general hypothesis becomes much more interesting. If similarity of latent cognitive representations is the only important factor, differences between communicators at the attitudinal response level should not affect the accuracy of information transmission. The only work which so far has attempted to approach the study of communication in this way is an experiment by Runkel (1956). In this experiment Runkel gave a short but relevant attitude questionnaire to both instructors and students in an introductory course in psychology. One might expect that communication between instructors and students would be more effective if students would share the attitudes of their teachers. Runkel predicted however that communication between instructors and students would not be affected by their agreement in this sense but by the similarity of the underlying cognitive representations. In order to investigate this problem Runkel determined first whether the responses provided by each student were co-linear with the responses given by his instructor, that is, whether both sets of responses could or could not be derived by unfolding from identical unidimensional cognitive representations. Runkel argued that, if it was possible to find such a common dimension, communication should be facilitated and result, for example, in better grades of students who are co-linear with their teachers as compared with students who are not co-linear in this sense. Runkel's hypothesis was clearly confirmed by the data. A significant difference in grades was found for co-linear and non-co-linear students, a result which could not be explained by differences in scholastic aptitude. Moreover there was no significant correlation between grades obtained by the students and the extent to which they exhibited the same attitudes as their teachers.

The study conducted by Runkel suggests immediately various other possibilities for communication studies. The most obvious one would be to study the effect of co-linearity in *persuasive communication*. From the point of view of social representation theory, most models of attitude change should be regarded as surface models (Jaspars; 1978). In virtually every experimental study of attitude change the attitude of source and receiver are represented as positions on the same attitude continuum. Most theories of attitude change simply assume a process of cognitive integration by the receiver, who arrives at a final judgment by weighing his own initial attitude and the position advocated by the source. No attempt is made to investigate whether the representation of the issues on which the attitudes are based is indeed the same. If the results of Runkel's study can be generalized, one would expect that co-linearity of the underlying representations would lead to larger change in attitudes, because information transmission would presumably be more effective or accurate in the case of co-linearity. Research on *the diffusion of innovation* (Rogers and Shoemaker; 1971) in which source and receiver have by definition different social representations shows convincingly, though sometimes only in anecdotal form, how ineffective attempts to change attitudes can be if differences in social representation are not taken into account.

Another point that becomes clear by looking at traditional attitude change studies from the point of view of social representation theory is that one can now also ask to what extent changes in manifest attitudinal responses also imply a change in the latent representation of the receiver. It may be that the difference between public and private change of attitudes is related to the distinction made between response changes and changes in cognitive representation. If the representation underlying a receiver's attitudinal responses is indeed a social representation, in the sense that his representation reflects in the first place the culture of which he is a part, then it becomes clear why such changes are much harder to accomplish than mere changes in evaluative responses. The results obtained by Moscovici and his colleagues on the *influence of minorities* show precisely this. A consistent minority is apparently able to bring about a change in representation, whereas a majority accomplishes usually only response compliance in conformity situations.

The implications of these ideas go, however, beyond the case of unilateral social influence situations. In conditions where at least two parties try to influence each other and attempt to resolve an interpersonal or *social conflict* through negotiation the same conflicts may be based on the same or different social representations of the relevant issues. In industrial conflicts newspapers usually only report the different claims or offers made by management and unions, but seldom deal with the social representations of both parties in the conflict. Still such representations may be extremely important in conflict resolution. In a series of experiments on social power (Verhagen 1975) it was shown that the influence of experts can be severely restricted by value coorientation among non-experts. The most interesting point in these experiments is that non-experts did not have to defend exactly the same position in the conflict with an expert. It was sufficient for them to share a social orientation in the conflict as opposed to the economical orientation of the expert.

Similar observations were obtained in the case of a serious conflict which arose a few years ago between a clinic for psychopathic delinquents in the Netherlands and the Ministry of Justice in the Hague over the restriction of freedom of the patients in the clinic. Negotiations between representatives of the two institutions lasted for a period of approximately two years, mainly because the freedom of movement problem was approached by both parties from completely different points of view. The representatives of the Ministry subscribed mainly to a custodial representation of delinquency, whereas the professional staff of the clinic maintained a socio-medical representation. It is interesting to note that a breakthrough in the negotiations occurred only after both parties began to discuss these representations and only then did they manage to agree on practical measures which were compatible with both representations. It was decided to reorganize the clinic in such a way that an intensive care unit could be established. This satisfied the representatives of the Ministry because security would be improved, whereas the staff accepted this proposal because it allowed for better treatment of the patients.

If such fundamental differences between social representations of groups can exist within the same culture, it should not come as a surprise that such differences may be even more marked when we consider differences between groups belonging to *different cultures*. As a final example it is interesting to refer to a recent study by Newman (1977) on the perception of deviancy in five different countries. In this study respondents were asked for a direct evaluative judgment of various deviant acts such as robbery, incest, appropriation of public funds, homosexuality etc. Respondents were however also asked to indicate to whom, if anyone, they would report such acts. The most frequently used categories were: reporting to the police, to the family or to no one at all.

A cursory inspection of the data published so far immediately shows that there are considerable differences in reporting between various countries in both a quantitative and a qualitative sense. Robbery, for example, is reported in 95 per cent of the cases to the police in New York, whereas the respondents in Orani, Italy, said so only in 50 per cent of the cases. Homosexuality is an interesting case, where qualitative differences appear to exist. In Iran it is very likely that one gets reported to the police if one is homosexual, in New York and in Italy 'no reporting at all' is mentioned most frequently, but in Indonesia homosexuality appears to be a problem to be dealt with in the first place by the family and the village head.

Although such results are interesting in themselves they do not provide us with an explanation. Again we will have to look for the social representations of control institutions and criminal acts if we want to make sense of the differences in reporting between the various countries.

The social representations of the various control institutions show interesting differences between cultures. For Indonesia, the representation appears to be simple and determined in the first place by the opposition between the police and the village head as control institutions, with the family occupying an intermediate position. The representation obtained for the Italian sample is more complex and the perceived difference between the family as a control institution and the local government is much more marked than the difference between the family and the village head in Indonesia. The fact that homosexuality is seen in Indonesia as a problem which concerns both the family and the local village head is a finding which is quite compatible with a social representation in which both institutions are seen as strongly related, but it would be hard to reconcile this result with the social representation obtained for Italy, where homosexuality is seen in the first place as an individual affair.

The point of this last illustration is simply to show that a much better understanding can be achieved if we go beyond the manifest responses which Ss provide in many attitude surveys and concern ourselves with the representations which are implicit in these responses. Systematic research of this kind would allow us to find out to what extent such latent representations are social in the sense that they are shared by individuals belonging to the same social groups. The few examples presented above suggest that this might indeed be the case in many circumstances. In that case attitudes with collective cognitive representations would show many of the features of social representations. If, furthermore, some of these attitudes proved also to involve collective response dispositions then the concept of social representation, but also the attitude concept itself, might provide a suitable basis for the social psychological study of ideology.

Summary

In this chapter we have argued that the most distinctive characteristic of social representations is that they are shared by many individuals and as such constitute a social reality which can influence individual behaviour.

It is shown that this notion was originally also part of the conception of social attitudes as studied by Thomas and Znaniecki. Under the influence of G. Allport the attitude concept became, however, more and more individualized and is currently interpreted as an individual response disposition sometimes combined with an individual cognitive representation.

It is suggested that it would be more useful to consider the attitudes as individual response dispositions based on collective representations. This is in fact an assumption made by various attitude measurement techniques.

Some consequences of such an integration of attitude research with research on social representations are discussed in the last part of this chapter.

4. Social representations: their role in the design and execution of laboratory experiments

ROBERT M. FARR

Individual and collective psychologies

When we trace the origins of psychology as an experimental and social science we note that Wundt chose to separate his experimental science from his social psychology. This he did deliberately and consciously, though historians of psychology as an experimental science have often failed fully to appreciate his reasons for this decision. Wundt had a very clear perception of the limitations of the laboratory science which he had established at Leipzig in 1879. Those who came after him, and who readily acknowledged him as the 'founding father' of experimental psychology, did not share his reservations concerning the limitations of his experimental science. This is an aspect of what Danziger has called 'the positivist repudiation of Wundt' (Danziger, 1979). Wundt's own answer to the limitations of his laboratory science is to be found in the ten volumes of his *Völkerpsychologie* (1900–20). These volumes have been virtually ignored by the official historians of psychology as a science.

Wundt's experimental science was a psychology of the individual whilst his social psychology (or *Völkerpsychologie*) was a collective psychology. The objects of study in his *Völkerpsychologie* were language, religion, myth, custom, magic and cognate phenomena. Had he been writing in the closing, rather than in the opening, decades of the twentieth century he would almost certainly have included science as an appropriate object of study in his collective psychology. He thus took cultural products as the objects of study in his collective psychology. He was prepared to make inferences about the nature of the mind of 'primitive man' on the basis of an analysis of the structure of the languages he spoke. Wundt thought it was necessary to supplement his laboratory science with the study of mind in society outside of the laboratory. The objects of study in his *Völkerpsychologie* were, in their

125

origin, the products of the collective experience of 'folk communities'. Language, religion, myth etc. could not have been invented, Wundt argued, by individuals, neither could these collective phenomena be reduced to, nor explained in terms of, the consciousness of individuals which Wundt had taken as the basis for his new laboratory science.

Not only could collective mental phenomena not be 'reduced to' phenomena at the level of the individual mind, but the techniques of investigation which were appropriate at this latter level were *inappropriate* for investigating phenomena at the collective level. The limitations which were inherent in Wundt's laboratory science derived from his reliance on introspection as his preferred method for investigating mental phenomena. He readily acknowledged that introspection was not an appropriate methodology for investigating man's higher cognitive processes. He argued this on the grounds that the mind of the individual could not by itself become conscious of forces of which it was the product, that is the processes of historical change and development. The study of the human mind as the product of evolutionary and historical change was the subject-matter of his *Völkerpsychologie*. This was his reason for treating this as a *separate*, though related, discipline to his laboratory science. Thus, *at the outset*, Wundt drew a clear distinction between psychology considered as an experimental laboratory science and psychology considered as a social science which treats seriously the evolution of mind in man. We can thus credit Wundt for this initial appreciation that *both* a collective *and* an individual psychology were necessary. His decision to separate the two, however, had certain unforeseen historical consequences which we must now trace.

The most important consequence, for the purposes of this chapter, can be seen in Wundt's influence on Durkheim. The many different ways in which Wundt exercised an influence on Durkheim are common knowledge amongst Durkheim scholars (see e.g. Lukes, 1973*a*; Giddens, 1978; Mauss, 1950, 1979). This is something of which most psychologists are ignorant as they only rarely read the literature of social sciences other than psychology. Durkheim had visited various German universities, including Leipzig, during the year 1885–6. He was impressed by what he observed. He was interested in the precision and rigour of Wundt's experimental research; and in his strategy of gathering around himself a team of fellow-workers who shared in the task of developing a new field of study and who initiated a journal in which they could publish the results of their research. He was subsequently himself to adopt a rather similar strategy when he established sociology as an academic discipline in France from his base in Bordeaux. Amongst psychologists Durkheim enjoys a reputation for having been the most antipathetic to psychology of all the major sociological theorists. This reputation derives, in large measure, from his insistence that 'social facts' are not to be explained in terms of psychological facts, for example in his classic study of suicide. This insistence, however, is little more than an echo and an amplification of Wundt's earlier insistence that his *Völkerpsychologie* was a separate enterprise to his laboratory science and involved a difference in levels.

The psychology to which Durkheim was so vehemently opposed was the psychology of the individual. He made a distinction between what he called 'collective' and 'individual' representations (Durkheim, 1898). He was quite happy to leave the study of 'individual' representations to the psychologist. They corresponded to the type of 'personal constructs' which George Kelly was later to study (see the chapter in this volume by Fransella). The study of 'collective representations', however, fell clearly within the province of sociology. Indeed Durkheim envisaged that some day there might be a sub-specialism within sociology (i.e. social psychology) exclusively dedicated to the study of 'collective representations'. The answering echo to Durkheim's plea was not to come until after World War II (see below). These collective representations were very similar to the objects of study in Wundt's *Völkerpsychologie*, that is language, religion, myth, magic, and cognate phenomena. What for Wundt had been a distinction between two forms of psychology – individual and collective – became, with Durkheim, a difference which separated two academic disciplines – psychology (focusing almost exclusively on the individual) and sociology (focusing almost exclusively on 'society'). This difference in 'levels' was the significant issue at stake in the famous Durkheim/Tarde debate in 1903–4 at the Ecole des Hautes Etudes Sociales in Paris (for an illuminating account of the debate and its background, see Lukes (1973*a*, chap. 16, pp. 302–13)). Each gave a lecture with the title 'Sociology and the social sciences' and this was followed by a third meeting in which they publicly debated their differences 'with much heat'.

The creative tensions which might have arisen from operating simultaneously at two different levels (i.e. the 'individual' and the 'collective') never really bore fruit. Even Wundt addressed himself to these separate, though related, issues during *different* decades in his long and highly productive career. McDougall wrote two text-books in social psychology – one at the level of the individual (1908) and the other at a 'collective' level (1920). The first was intended only as an 'introduction' to social psychology and the two together were originally intended as an outline of 'social psychology'. A major world war, however, intervened between the publication of the two volumes and each, separately, aroused significant opposition. The first volume was controversial because McDougall applied the term 'instinct' to account for human behaviour, whilst his second volume – *Group mind* – was controversial because he appeared to assign 'agency' to entities other than individuals. Both attacks forced him to revise his original formulation of the issues involved. F. H. Allport, the behaviourist, who attacked McDougall for assigning agency to such supra-individual entities as 'groups' also contributed both to 'individual' and to 'collective' themes within social psychology, for example his writings on institutional behaviour and public opinion, as well as his better-known text-book of social psychology (Allport, F. H., 1924, 1937). F. H. Allport differs from the other writers discussed above in that he did not believe that a *difference* in levels was involved when one moved from the individual to the collective. For him the ultimate reality was behaviour and only individuals behave. It was Allport's views, rather than McDougall's, which came to prevail, at least in the development of experimental social psychology in America. This accounts, at least in part, for the non-social ethos of much contemporary American and British social psychology. This helps to highlight the distinctly different perspective of contemporary French research on 'social representations' as set out in this volume. Deriving, as it claims to do, from Durkheim, it is a much more inherently 'social' social psychology than much contemporary research in American and British laboratories. It thus constitutes an important contemporary critique of the 'individual' bias of much social psychology. Herzlich (1972), in her review of French work on social representations, contrasts it with the dominant Anglo-American tradition: '. . . the concept of "social representation" relates to a different tradition: European and essentially sociological' (p. 303).

Instead of the tensions between different levels of analysis being creatively resolved within the one discipline (i.e. psychology) they ceased to be creative tensions once they resulted in a division of labour *between* academic disciplines. Durkheim (1898) cited, with approval, the arguments used by William James for psychology being a field of study quite independent of physiology. He made a similar plea that 'collective representations' ought to be studied quite independently of 'individual representations'. This led to a sharp separation between sociology and psychology. This separation posed problems for social psychologists who could develop their discipline on either side of this rather over-sharp divide. This is how it came about that there are now sociological, as well as psychological, traditions of social psychology. Elsewhere I have addressed myself to the issue of how one might set about the problem of reconciling the various traditions of social psychology which vie with one another in seeking to gain the attention of the modern reader (Farr, 1978*b*).

Social representations

The origins of the contemporary tradition in France in the late 1950s

The recent renaissance of interest amongst French social psychologists in Durkheim's concept of 'collective representations' commenced with the publication, in 1961, of Moscovici's study: *La Psychanalyse: son image et son public* (Moscovici, 1961). Whilst this book is now in a second edition in French it has yet to be translated into English. In choosing it as an illustration I am influenced by the fact that it is not yet available in English. In this pioneering study Moscovici refers to 'social representations' as this 'neglected' or 'forgotten' concept of Durkheim. This whole tradition of research in French social psychology represents a renewal of interest in the study of modes of knowledge and of the role of symbolic processes in relation to human action. Researchers within the contemporary tradition, consistent with the Durkheimian origins of the concept, stress the primacy of social, over individual, factors in the determination of human conduct.

Psychoanalysis was a convenient example, for Moscovici, of a 'new science' which was relevant to an understanding of human behaviour. Psychoanalysis, through its very circulation in society, becomes transformed into a social representation. 'A science of reality thus becomes a science *in* reality ... at this stage its evolution becomes the affair of social psychology' (*ibid*. p. 19, my translation). It is thus when a scientific theory is *published* that it may fall within the legitimate area of interest of the social psychologist. Lagache, in his preface to the original edition, felt it was necessary to explain to his readers why a social psychologist, who is not a psychoanalyst, should be writing a book on psychoanalysis. A theory, if it is to be effective, needs to be expressed in words (i.e. to be made *public*) and needs to be transmitted in written and/ or oral traditions. The creative act comprises the original formulation of the theory in some form of symbolic communication. The link here with studies in the sociology of knowledge is an obvious one.

In his study Moscovici traced how a scientific language became a common 'dialect' – how it pervaded judgement and directed human actions. Using the conventional tools of opinion polls and surveys Moscovici traced how a knowledge of psychoanalysis had diffused within various sectors of the French population in the late 1950s. He showed how the social representation of something as complex as a new scientific theory is not fundamentally an impoverishment, but is rather a transformation, of this theory. The appearance of a new language, he argued, is both a consequence of psychoanalysis being absorbed by a particular society and the means by which this process comes about. The existence of a dictionary of psychoanalytic terms (Laplanche and Pontalis, 1967) is further evidence, if such were needed, of just how widely psychoanalysis has diffused within French culture.

Moscovici used empirical methods to study the diffusion of a particular science within a particular culture at a particular point in historical time. It would thus serve as an excellent example of Gergen's thesis that social psychology is an essentially historical discipline (Gergen, 1973). This historical dimension is important in the work of the contemporary French school – especially in their field studies. Herzlich (1973) notes, by graphic references to the history of medicine, how the social representations which people form of health and illness have differed in different historical epochs *within* the one culture. She also notes, by referring to anthropological studies, how the social representations of health and illness, at any one particular point in time, may differ quite markedly as a function of culture. Similarly Jodelet and Moscovici (1976) are interested in studying *changes*, over historical time, in people's representations of their own bodies. Some of this work is cited in Jodelet's contribution to this volume.

Moscovici claims that any new theory or the application of any previously unknown technique might, potentially, have a similar impact in changing the culture within which it is conceived. The atomic bomb, he notes, through the political choices which it entails and the fears which it nourishes, has been a formidable school of physics for the majority of mankind. The world can never be the same place again once such a nuclear device has exploded amongst a population of humans. Theories can be just as explosive in their impact as nuclear devices, though the effects of their fall-out may not be so immediate. New theories could arise, for instance, from scientific voyages of discovery.

One could choose, for example, Darwin's voyage on the survey ship, HMS *Beagle*, or the space missions completed by American astronauts of the Apollo programme. The social, cultural and scientific repercussions of Darwin's theory of evolution have been profound. At a totally different level of initial impact we could cite photographs of the earth taken from outer space. These provide the average citizen of today with much more graphic and convincing evidence that the earth is round than the traditional arguments he might have learned at school against believing it to be flat. Pioneers are often themselves aware of the social repercussions of their own discoveries. This is evident in Darwin's reluctance to publish his theory until he had accumulated a great deal of evidence for it. It is also reflected in the remark that Freud is reputed to have made to Jung as they disembarked in New York at the turn of the century: 'We are importing the plague.' Moscovici quotes this incident, with evident approval, in the preliminary remarks to his study. They epitomise the point of Moscovici's own study, that is that scientific ideas and theories can change the nature of the world in which people live.

La Psychanalyse: son image et son public is a detailed case study carried out within one particular culture at a particular point in time. It is, therefore, only *illustrative* of Moscovici's more general thesis. His argument is thus much more general than the particular case study he initially chose as an illustration. He later goes on to make essentially the same general point in his theory of minority influence. Here he used experimental methods and the majority of studies were carried out in the laboratory rather than in field settings. The point of his theory of minority influence is that all truly creative geniuses are, almost by definition, in a minority of one until they persuade the majority to think in the way that they do or to see things as they see them. He is, thus, more interested in studying innovation and change than he is in studying conformity and the maintenance of the *status quo*. The time scale needed, however, for the successful adoption of an innovation within a society, is much greater than can be captured by any laboratory simulation of the process.

In the first part of his study of psychoanalysis Moscovici sampled the views and opinions of various sectors of the French population concerning psychoanalysis and their knowledge of this theory. Here he used the well-tried techniques of social enquiry – structured, and occasionally unstructured, questionnaires. The various samples comprised a total of just over 2,000 persons. In the second half of his study he carried out a careful content analysis of all articles relating to psychoanalysis which appeared in some 241 different journals, reviews, and newspapers during a fifteen-month period in the early 1950s. Moscovici thus not only sampled the diffusion of a knowledge of psychoanalysis – he also intercepted and analysed the information and propaganda circulating in the mass media relating to the object of his study.

The starting-point of Moscovici's study was the publication of a new scientific theory. Science is a topic as worthy of study as the religion, myth, and magic which were of interest both to Wundt and to Durkheim. As in his laboratory studies on minority influence, the interest lies in identifying how original ideas came, over time, to be accepted. As a theory psychoanalysis challenged traditional conceptions of man. He traces, in the second half of his study, how the Catholic press responds to a secular form of the confessional and how the Communist press handles a popular science which is non-Marxist etc. For a devout Catholic the *meaning* of psychoanalysis will be sought in the writings of churchmen and apologists on the topic. It may even be crystallized for him in the form of a papal encyclical. At the time of Moscovici's original study (i.e. the early to middle 1950s) the attitude of the Catholic Church in France to psychoanalysis had initially been one of suspicion followed by a period of amelioration and assimilation. The secular became assimilated to the sacred and this made it 'safe' for believers to take an interest in the new science. The response of the Communist Party in France, however, to the new science was, at that same particular point in time, a totally different one. This was the immediate post-war era when the cold war between America and Russia was the dominant theme in the arena of international politics. The Communist press handled psychoanalysis by rejecting it. Moscovici treated this press coverage as a case study in the dynamics of propaganda.

Discussions of how to 'handle' issues are common talk amongst those who work in the communications industry. It is a question of what sort of an 'attitude' one adopts or what 'stance' one takes with respect to a given issue. The term 'attitude' is used here in an almost Darwinian sense, which one rarely encounters in modern psychology, that is to refer to the often whole-bodied 'posture' of an organism towards some significant 'object' in its environment (see Darwin, 1872). In the second half of Moscovici's study it is social institutions, rather than organisms, which adopt these 'attitudes' of acceptance or rejection. An 'attitude' is thus a stance or a behavioural posture and is best conceptualised as such. The whole of the work of the French School is a critique of the more conventional research in social psychology which treats 'opinions', 'attitudes', 'personal constructs', 'images' etc. as more or less purely individual representations (for a critique of conventional research from this French perspective see Moscovici, 1963). In the field studies of the French School these 'attitudes' and 'stances' are socially negotiated and are usually studied by means of a content analysis of the messages diffused by the various media. Just as Mead was interested in analysing the 'conversation of gestures' which occurs when one animal orients itself with respect to another, so Moscovici is interested in analysing the dialogue and the war of words which pass between the institutions of a society and the mass of its citizens as they adapt to some momentous event or react to the emergence of some new science or idea.

The discrepancy between the field and the laboratory studies within the French tradition

In his foreword to the interesting study by Herzlich of people's representations of health and illness Moscovici describes

'social representations' in the following terms: . . . cognitive systems with a logic and language of their own . . . They do not represent simply 'opinions about', 'images of' or 'attitudes towards' but 'theories' or 'branches of knowledge' in their own right, for the discovery and organisation of reality . . . systems of values, ideas and practices with a two-fold function: first, to establish an order which will enable individuals to orientate themselves in their material and social world and to master it; secondly to enable communication to take place among members of a community by providing them with a code for social exchange and a code for naming and classifying unambiguously the various aspects of their world and their individual and group history. (Moscovici, 1973, p. xiii)

This definition of 'representation' is sufficiently majestic to encompass within its scope the study of any religion or myth or form of magic that might have appealed either to Wundt or to Durkheim. The idea of introducing science as a new category of representation into the pantheon established by the founding fathers is a modern and innovative idea. Moscovici's pioneering study of psychoanalysis was followed by others, some of which have already been alluded to above. There is Herzlich's study of the social representations of health and illness; the work of Jodelet and Moscovici on the social representation of the human body and changes, over time, in this representation. Jodelet is currently working on the social representation of mental illness, using the techniques of participant observation. Madame Chombart de Lauwe has written extensively concerning the 'myth' of childhood (1971). She has shown how 'childhood' is a social representation created by adults with powerful and real consequences for the children of those adults. These are refreshingly original studies which would stand up well in the searchlight of international scrutiny.

I am less sure in my own judgement about the possible international standing of the many laboratory studies carried out within this tradition of French research on social representations. This does not really surprise me because I believe there are important conceptual problems involved in applying the idea of social representations to laboratory science. If I understand the notion correctly, then one's representations of what science is and of what laboratories are for are bound to be of much greater significance than any particular pieces of research that might be carried out *within* those laboratories. Moscovici's characterisation of the social nature of representations (quoted above) is more directly applicable at the level of a scientific theory or of a research paradigm than at the level of a single experiment within such a paradigm. Is his description of a social representation not virtually synonymous with the common scientific endeavour which helps to keep a given group of scientists communicating with each other? It must relate to social exchanges which occur at the level of the scientific community. How can it possibly be captured and confined to something which occurs *within* the course of a single experiment, or even of a series of experiments? Social representations were born and nurtured in the wider society outside of the laboratory. They relate more directly to Wundt's *Völkerpsychologie* than they do to his laboratory science. There are some re-entry problems which need to be faced if the notion of social representation is to be successfully applied to the design and conduct of laboratory experiments. This is the issue I now wish to tackle in the second half of this chapter.

The laboratory as a social representation

The world of the observer

In the laboratory the world of the observer (i.e. of the experimenter) and the world which he observes (i.e. subjects performing laboratory tasks) are usually two quite different worlds. The implications of this distinction are rarely made explicit in the standard manuals of research methods. The sharp distinction between these two worlds first came into psychology with the acceptance of behaviourism. In Wundt's laboratory at Leipzig observer and observed were one and the same person. This early experimental psychology was thus inherently non-social in form. This was due to Wundt's reliance on introspection as his main technique of investigation within the laboratory.

When, with the advent of behaviourism, psychology became an 'objective' science, it was non-social both in conception and ethos though, in actual research practice, it was highly social. Observer and observed were now two different persons (or, perhaps more accurately, different organisms) and it was *behaviour*, rather than *experience*, which was the subject-matter of psychology. This opened up the possibility that observer and observed might inhabit two quite different worlds even though they encounter one another face to face in the context of the research laboratory. One of the early behaviourist textbooks, in which the author maintains a consistent methodological stance, was intriguingly entitled *The psychology of the other one* (Meyer, 1921).

I am indebted to Edgar Morin (1977) for first highlighting the importance of distinguishing between 'the world of the observer' and the world as it appears to that observer. He notes, particularly in the natural sciences, how the scientist, like the photographer, fails to include himself in that which he records. '... science has no scientific knowledge of itself and lacks the means of knowing itself scientifically. There is a scientific method for considering and controlling the objects of science. But there is no scientific method for considering science as the object of science still less (for considering) the scientist as the subject of this object' (*ibid.* p. 14; my translation). Whilst Morin is more broadly concerned with the effects of positivism and of science on man's conception of himself I am here concerned, more narrowly, with the effect of positivism on psychologists' conceptions of what a laboratory is. Positivism, within the history of psychology, took the form of behaviourism.

The world of the observer, in the psychological laboratory, is the world of other experimenters – those whom he has in mind when he *designs* his experiments and for whom he writes up an account of his investigations. There is indeed an agreed language, and even an agreed style, amongst those who comprise *the community of experimental psychologists* in terms of which members communicate with each other concerning the events which have occurred in their laboratories. Initially the future researcher is socialised into this community of other experimenters during his undergraduate and postgraduate studies. Surely it is at the level of the 'scientific community' of other experimenters (what Crane (1972) calls 'invisible colleges') that one ought to look for, and study, the operation of social representations? This brings us back to the whole conception underlying Wundt's development of a 'folk psychology'. Social phenomena, according to Wundt, are to be located at the level of 'folk communities', that is those who use a common language and, hence, share a common social reality. We have noted above links between Wundt's 'folk psychology' and Durkheim's notion of 'collective representations'. I think an error of translation has taken place, in the work of the contemporary French School, in the translation from field to laboratory. Instead of looking for the operation of social representations *at the level of the scientific community*, experimenters, instead, have been content to demonstrate how the representations which their subjects form of the experimental situation actually influence how they act *within* the milieu of the laboratory.

If one wishes to explore the role of social representations *in the world of the observer* then perhaps it is better to adopt the research techniques and general orientation of Lemaine and his collaborators (Lemaine *et al.*, 1977). In the context of accounting for the diversity of French research on sleep they investigated how rival teams of scientists in different laboratories came to adopt the research strategies which they did. This work generally is not considered to be within the tradition of research on social representations. However, it might be more profitable to follow up this line of investigation than to continue the current practice of conducting experiments *on* social representations using the traditional methodology of the laboratory experiment. The approach of Lemaine *et al.* is much more in keeping with the ideas and methods which inspired the field studies of social representations. They enable us to visualise and to articulate better the processes which are likely to be involved in studying how social representations operate in the world of the observer.

If social representations are a guide to conduct – and this is how Moscovici conceives of them – then how experimenters/observers behave in the context of the laboratory may be a function of how they represent to themselves and to others the nature of the scientific activity upon which they are engaged. If experimental psychologists believe, for example, that they are engaged in carrying out research in natural science (as opposed, say, to social science) then this must have a profound effect upon how they interact with their subjects and upon the design and layout of the laboratories in which they work. Thus 'representations' which the experimenter takes into account (or assumes) at the *design* and planning stage are likely to translate fairly directly into research practice in the actual *execution* of the experiment. Perhaps one ought to be looking here at the relationships between theory and practice in the psychological laboratory.

Elsewhere I have sought to demonstrate that *in actual research practice* there might be such a thing as a distinctly 'social psychological' *style of experimenting* (Farr, 1976). Differences in the theoretical orientation of the experimenter (e.g. a phenomenal/cognitive bias versus a behavioural bias) are consistently related to variations in actual experimental practice. Cognitive theorists, as distinct from behaviourial theorists, are much more likely to be concerned with how their subjects 'interpret' the experimental situation. In another article (Farr, 1978a) I sought to identify the social significance of the 'artifacts' which can arise in laboratory experiments. These artifacts arise because an experimenter 'represents' a social event (i.e. the experiment) as though it were not a social event. This may be because he subscribes to a model of the experiment which he derives from the natural sciences. This model affects not only his own planning and running of the experiment but also, afterwards, how he reports it to the scientific community. In describing 'the world *as* he observed it' the experimenter may fail adequately to take into account his own role as an observer and the effect he may have had on the world which he observed.

My evidence for the views expressed in the previous paragraph came from interpreting the 'accounts' which experimenters give of their research. Perhaps the best way to detect social representations is to use some sort of content analysis of written and/or oral communications. This is how they are usually detected in the field studies within the French tradition. By focusing on the 'accounts' which an experimenter provides for the benefit of *other* experimenters one is searching, *at least in the right place*, for evidence of social representations, that is in the world of the observer and at the level of the community. These 'accounts' can be 'interpreted' in much the same way as Harré and Secord (1972) suggested for the analysis of oral accounts. The main difference is that one is dealing, here, with the written text provided by an experimenter and intended for the eyes of other experimenters. Fortunately these texts are widely available in the learned journals. One is involved, here, in the explication of a written text rather than in the interpretation of an oral discourse.

The world as observed

This corresponds to the 'results' section in the formal report of most experimental investigations. Typically it comprises behavioural data relating to the performances on laboratory tasks of experimental subjects. The world of the experimental subject is not, however, the same world as that of the observer. Whilst the two meet face to face in the brief encounter of an actual experiment it would be wrong to assume that they *share* the same experience. It may seem strange, at first, to suggest that persons in face to face contact inhabit different worlds whilst the 'significant others' who determine the actions of the observer (i.e. the invisible community of other experimenters) are not themselves physically present in the laboratory during the course of the experiment. Experimenters and subjects cannot easily adopt *the same perspective* in regard to the significance of their social interaction. Most experiments inevitably involve an element of deception. It would be difficult, for example, for Milgram and one of his 'teacher' subjects to agree on the *significance* of the latter's button-pushing behaviour.

The *social* nature of the relationship between experimenter and subject is most salient at the point of recruitment and then again on the *threshold* of the laboratory, that is when the experimenter welcomes the subject on arrival and de-briefs him on departure. What happens in between arrival and departure is highly programmed and is rarely negotiable. This provides the experimenter with the 'data' for the 'results' section of his experimental report. The encounter is quite unlike anything which occurs spontaneously in the social world outside of the laboratory. In social interaction each interactant is normally free 'to assume the role of the other' with respect to himself (Mead, 1934). The interaction proceeds smoothly in so far as each of the participants is skilled at doing precisely this. In a typical experiment the most important 'other' (in the sense of Mead's 'significant other') for the subject is likely to be the experimenter in whose experiment he has just agreed to participate. His normal capacity to assume the role of this particular other may make him apprehensive on the grounds that he believes this 'other' will be evaluating him as a person on the basis of how he performs (Rosenberg, 1969). For a fuller exposition of the possible consequences of the subject's belief, see my paper on the social significance of artifacts in experimenting (Farr, 1978a). When, however, the experimenter 'assumes the role of the other' with respect to himself and to how he intends to act, that 'other' is usually another experimenter, that is some member of the scientific community. Experimenters rarely adopt the perspective of a subject in one of their own experiments. For certain notable exceptions to this general statement (e.g. Lewin, Asch, Festinger, Aronson and Carlsmith, etc.) see Farr (1976; 1978*a*). It is entirely consistent with the theme being developed here that the difference in perspective which characterises these exceptions should result in a different 'style' of experimenting, that is that the experimenter's representation of the human subject is likely to affect how he treats the latter in the actual conduct of the experiment.

It is worth highlighting a little more fully, perhaps, the social/non-social nature of the relationships between experimenters and subjects. In his highly original essay on the nature of the doctor/patient relationship Goffman (1961) traced some vicissitudes in the social history of the tinkering professions. When tinkers used to call at their clients' domiciles they had to exercise great caution in how they handled the property which was entrusted to their care. They often had to tinker with the object under the watchful eye of its owner. When tinkers ceased to be itinerants in search of work, however, and set up shop instead, this changed the social nature of the relationship between tinker and client. Customers now brought articles, which were in need of repair, to the shop. A wall or partition often separated the 'front' from the 'back' of the shop. As in much of Goffman's work this distinction between 'front' and 'back' regions is full of implications for the *types* of social interaction which can occur in the two locations. The separation between the two halves of the shop enabled the tinker to establish, and to maintain, a social relationship with his client in the front of the shop. Here the tinker could take his client's property into custody whilst being able to assure and, if necessary, to re-assure, his customer of his own technical competence to repair it. The tinker also returns the repaired article to its rightful owner in the 'front' of the shop and monitors the latter's response to the results of his work. In between these two social events the tinker can become highly technical in how he handles and relates to the object without his actions coming under the surveillance of its owner. He carries out this technical work in the 'back' of the shop, separated both in time and in space from his continuing 'social' relationship with the owner of the object.

Goffman then identifies the doctor's dilemma. The doctor needs to establish a social relationship with his client. As the same time he may need (to be able) to become highly technical about the latter's body. The problem is more acute for the doctor than it is for the tinker as the patient appears to be attached inextricably to his body. How the doctor sets about separating the patient from his body need not detain us here though it is an interesting topic in its own right. There may be some parallels in the relationship which experimenters seek to establish with their subjects. There is a certain phase within the context of the social relationship described earlier during which the experimenter assumes the highly technical role of being a scientific observer. We usually read about this phase in the 'results' section of most scientific reports. It constitutes 'the world as observed' by the observer. The experimenter, during this phase of the experiment, may adopt an attitude of 'civic inattention' to any item of a personal nature which the subject may wish to place on the agenda.

The laboratory

Just as the tinker lays out his shop to suit his needs so the laboratory is designed by the experimenter for his own purposes. Thus laboratories are likely to reflect, and to enshrine, their creator's conception of science. A laboratory is a place in a definite location (i.e. it has an address) as well as being a social institution. Subjects are invited to 'enter' it and are greeted on arrival. They are usually, but not always, volunteers. They enter, and leave, with their own impressions of what a psychological laboratory is. Laboratories have their own special 'atmosphere' or 'ethos' for those who work there as distinct from those who merely visit. A sociologist or anthropologist could easily, by means of participant observation, study the 'micro-culture' of such a laboratory. There is, however, a great dearth of such studies. The study of Latour and Woolgar (1979) of life in the Salk Institute: *Laboratory life: The social construction of scientific facts* is one such pioneering effort. It would be interesting to see similar studies carried out in psychological institutes.

One could explore the conceptions which experimenters have of the psychological laboratory. This has not been done so far as I know. It should be possible to predict just how such a social representation would vary as a function of the theoretical commitments of the person providing the account. One might expect, for example, clear differences between those who consider psychology to be a branch of natural science and those others who consider it a social science. Interesting new representations are beginning to emerge from those who consider psychology to be a 'cognitive science'. There were, of course, important historical differences in the design and layout of laboratories as between those who believed psychology to be the science of mental life and those others who believed it to be the science of behaviour.

In the world's first psychological laboratory Wundt accepted verbal reports of immediate conscious experience as the legitimate data of science. His stress on the immediacy of the experiences being reported led him to rule out retrospection as a legitimate form of introspection. For Wundt introspection was a type of 'inner perception'. In his laboratory he obtained introspective data under highly controlled conditions. The scientific rigour of the Leipzig laboratory stood in sharp contrast to the earlier informal use of introspection which philosophers used to indulge in from the depths of their armchairs. The preoccupation with precision in measurement on the part of these early experimental pioneers is reflected in the brass instruments of this early German laboratory science.

The laboratory is a device for isolating phenomena from the social contexts in which they occur naturally in the 'real world' outside. Historical events occurring between t_1 and t_2 in the course of an experiment threaten its 'internal validity' (Campbell, 1957; Campbell and Stanley, 1966) and, if not controlled for, may be confounded with the effect of the independent variable. Good experimental control is thus virtually synonymous with the isolation of the events studied from their location in space/time within a particular culture. The isolation and control which Pavlov achieved in his laboratories was an ideal towards which others have aspired. Scientists usually believe the results of their laboratory research to be generally true until someone else proves otherwise, that is, at least conceptually the experiment is, in some ways, the very antithesis of a historical event. The laboratory is, in a sense, 'a world apart'. It is so both geographically and conceptually. Madame Chombart de Lauwe (1971), in her highly sensitive field study of the world of childhood, identified how different groups of adults (e.g. writers, film-makers, city planners, architects etc.) create the world of childhood in which their children have to live. She entitled her study *Un monde autre*. The world of the child has to be understood by its contrast to the world of the adult. Similarly the laboratory might best be understood by way of contrast to the world outside of the laboratory. The 'laboratory' is an *other world* which experimenters create for their subjects to enter. Perhaps it too can be explored with some of the same imaginative techniques used by Madame Chombart de Lauwe in her study?

The very success of scientists in isolating the laboratory from the world outside makes it less likely that the social representations which incubate within its walls will readily diffuse in the society beyond those walls.

Freud's consulting-room was not so hermetically sealed off from the wider culture outside of it. Freud, as a scientist, responded to the real world problems and events which his clients brought with them into his consulting-room. It is thus perhaps natural that the results of his thinking, when made public, should reverberate within that wider culture outside of his consulting-room. Thus Moscovici can readily study the social representation of psychoanalysis in French society. It would be more difficult to study the social representation (and hence the cultural repercussions) of behaviourism or of experimental psychology. Elsewhere I have discussed behaviourism as a social representation (Farr, 1981).

With behaviourism there came into laboratory life the crisp separation, noted above, between the world of the observer and the world which he observed. It resulted in a dramatic reduction in the status of the human subject in the research process (Schultz, 1969; Adair, 1973; Farr, 1978a). It was no longer possible to say that experimenters and 'subjects' shared the same laboratory culture as they had done in Wundt's laboratory at Leipzig or at the Institute of Psychology in Berlin during the early days of the Gestalt movement. I refer here to the micro-culture *of* the laboratory rather than to the wider culture which experimenters and subjects obviously share by virtue of living in the same society. Many of the experimental studies of the French School on the role of social representations *within* the laboratory (e.g. the researches of Codol, Abric, Flament, Plon, Apfelbaum and others) depend for their efficacy on this wider culture which experimenters share with the subjects of their research. This shared culture is most obviously present in the common language which they speak. In those studies where it is assumed that a subject's representation of some aspect of the laboratory environment is the independent variable the experimental manipulation is invariably effected by means of subtle variations in the experimental instructions. Large differences in behaviour have been shown to depend on whether, in the context of an experimental game, one's opponent is described as a 'machine' or as 'another student like yourself' (Abric, 1976); or whether one is playing against 'chance' or against 'nature' (Faucheux and Moscovici, 1968); or whether the experimental task is described as a 'problem-solving' one or as a 'creative task' (Abric, 1971); or whether it is described as involving 'deduction and logical thought' or else as requiring 'the resolution of problems by several individuals collaborating together' (Codol, 1974).

In these experimental studies there is still a separation between the world of the observer and the world which he observes. The experimenter still remains 'outside of' his subject's cognitive representation of the experimental situation. He can only record the behavioural evidence on the basis of which he will be justified in claiming that the social representation made the difference. Whilst the experimentalists at Aix-en-Provence have conducted many interesting studies on the role of social representations in the dynamics of laboratory groups the experimenter inevitably remains on the outside of such groups. Indeed the individuals comprising the groups may form a group principally *because* the experimenter constitutes an important part of their environment. In these French studies the world of the observer and the world he observes still remain separate worlds. The experimenter, by means of his instructions, introduces the 'representations' into the minds of the individuals whose behaviour he then observes. The 'representations' are cognitive/individual but their mode of delivery is social, that is they are mediated by the experimental instructions. They are implicit in the language which experimenters and subjects speak and understand. It should not, therefore, be too surprising if the laboratory studies carried out within the French tradition do not appear too remarkably different from studies in cognitive science carried out in laboratories outside of France. They do, however, shed interesting further light on the social psychology of the experiment. The French themselves, however, do not seek to relate their laboratory studies to the predominantly American literature on the social psychology of the experiment.

On the social nature of representations and on the difficulty of investigating them experimentally

Whilst Durkheim chose to contrast 'collective' representations with 'individual' ones the members of the contemporary French School choose, instead, to talk only of 'social' representations. This could be a sign either of caution or of strength. It would be a sign of *caution* if they were unsure as to whether or not they can convincingly locate the social phenomena which they describe at a 'collective' Durkheimian level. Here 'social' is used in the *weak* sense of not being equivalent to 'collective'. In relation to Herzlich's study of people's representations of health and illness I have questioned whether, in actual practice, the social phenomena which she so sensitively portrays could be located at the 'collective' level (Farr, 1977). The structure of the accounts which she obtained seemed to me then to reflect the social context of the research interview in which they had been elicited rather than to reflect the structure of any arguments that might emerge at a 'collective' level. The choice of 'social' rather than 'collective' as the appropriate adjective to qualify 'representation' might merely indicate that the author is not claiming to be a follower of Durkheim. They are, after all, social psychologists rather than sociologists. The field studies within this French tradition are much more obviously 'social' in content than are the experimental laboratory studies. As forms of social psychology they are much more sociological than psychological. The laboratory studies, however, are much more psychological than sociological.

It could be a sign of *strength*, however, if 'social' is being used as a substitute for 'individual', that is there are no purely 'individual' representations. Indeed this is the precise strength of the French critique of the 'individual' nature of most Anglo-American so-called social psychology. If the term 'social representation' were to be adopted within the symbolic interactionist tradition of social psychology it would be used in the strong, rather than in the weak, sense, that is to deny that there is any such thing as an 'individual' representation. It seems to me that the term 'social representation' is often used in this 'strong' form in the writings of the contemporary French School, that is they are less gentlemanly than Durkheim had originally been about leaving scope for the non-social psychologist to explore 'representations'. In his foreword to the second edition of *La Psychanalyse: son image et son public* Moscovici talks of his ambition of setting out from this notion of 'social representation' in order to re-define the problems and concepts of social psychology. Social psychology could then be defined as being the study of social representations in much the same way as it was described, during the twenties, as being the study of social attitudes. By using the strong form of the notion it may even be possible to transform not just social psychology but psychology in general.

A strong form of the argument could be developed along the lines that *all* representations are social because language is social and language is involved in the creation and transmission of representations. This line of argument is consonant with Rommetveit's contribution to this volume. Language, it will be recalled, was part of Wundt's *Völkerpsychologie*. Wundt was aware of the close relationship between language and man's higher cognitive processes. Modern psychology has caught up on him. It is now highly cognitive and language-based. As language is inherently social, both in origin and use, it is psychology which is now the social science and not just social psychology. By this criterion even the experimental laboratory studies *within* the French tradition would qualify as a form of social psychology. They are not, as I have argued above, as inherently social as the field studies because the investigators were looking in the wrong place for the social representations, that is they were looking for reflections of them in the behaviour of their research subjects, rather than trying to identify their role in the world of the observer of those subjects. It thus takes the *strong* sense of the word 'social' as qualifying 'representation' in order to make the laboratory studies within the French tradition qualify as a *weak* form of social psychology.

Have contemporary French social psychologists now discovered the secret, which eluded Wundt, of being able easily to move between laboratory and field settings whilst still remaining faithful to the nature of the object of their study? Or, is there still an uneasy relationship between the field and the laboratory studies *within* the French tradition? I personally incline to this latter view. As previously mentioned in the transition from the field to the laboratory an error of translation occurred whereby the laboratory studies became confined to an exploration of the role of representations in the world of subjects, leaving completely unexplored the role of representations in the world of the observer. The role of social representations in the design and execution of laboratory experiments can, however, be explored *provided* one knows *where* to look for them and has some idea of *how* they operate. It is best to regard 'social representations' as being what Moscovici stated them to be, that is 'theories' or 'systems of knowledge' with a logic and language of their own. Properly applied the notion of 'social representation' could help us to arrive at a better understanding of how psychology came to be the sort of science it is and how it came to have the sorts of laboratories it does. The unit of analysis ought to be something as all-pervasive as a psychological theory, for example behaviourism. The implications of the theory for what goes on in laboratories can be studied by observing laboratory life. I have tried to suggest where and how social representations might be operating within the context of laboratory experimentation. I am not alone in feeling that there might be a difference in both style and content as between the field and the laboratory studies *within* the work of the French School. Herzlich (1972), in her review of the field, treats them separately and also implies that there is a clear distinction between them.

It is assumed in much of the above that 'individual' = 'non-social'.

This is true in terms of the way in which psychology has developed historically. It is also the force of the French critique of current orthodoxies in American and British social psychology. There is, however, an important other sense in which the notion of the 'individual' is a wholly social one. This, for example, is true of the study by Lukes (1973b) of 'individualism' as a key concept in sociology. In this study the individual almost has the status of being a 'collective representation' which characterises certain societies during certain epochs. It is, perhaps, one of the strongest representations to emerge in Western culture out of the Renaissance. It can best be understood, perhaps, by contrast to the caste system in India as described in Dumont's classic study (1980): *Homo hierarchicus*. The tendency in Europe and America to treat the individual as being responsible for his own outcomes is explicitly stated by Ichheiser (1949) to be a collective representation on the basis of which we praise and blame people for their successes and failures. It is also the representation which explains Lerner's 'just world hypothesis' (Lerner, 1980). This is the representation which is threatened if people do not get what they deserve and do not deserve what they get.

The American social philosopher, G. H. Mead, spent forty years of his life trying to inter-relate 'the facts of individual consciousness' with 'the facts of society'. Wundt, as we noted at the beginning of this chapter, chose to separate these two realms of phenomena. The one realm, that of the mind of the individual, was, for him, an inherently non-social one. The other realm – language, religion, myth, magic and cognate phenomena – was an inherently social one. Mead chose to inter-relate what Wundt had chosen to separate. Mead had been an enrolled student of Wundt's at Leipzig in the winter semester of 1888/9. Back in Chicago he reviewed the early volumes of Wundt's *Völkerpsychologie* as they appeared off the printing presses in Leipzig. The whole of Mead's social psychology developed from Wundt's concept of the gesture (Mead, 1934) and he saw in language the key to understanding the social nature of mind in man. Mind, for Mead, emerged out of interaction within a community of others who share a common language. Mind is thus rooted in social experience. Man's awareness of himself emerges from his interactions with others. Hence the individual is the *product* of social experience. It is now no longer possible to conceive of such a thing as a 'non-social' individual. Mead's thinking is still reflected in the symbolic interactionist tradition of social psychology within American sociology. Both Mead's social behaviourism and Blumer's symbolic interactionism are consonant with the strong version of the contemporary French research on social representations.

The notion of the individual which the philosopher Strawson developed provides Harré and Secord (1972) with their model for a new methodology in the social sciences. An individual is someone who can monitor his own behaviour and give an 'account' of it. This is an inherently social model of the individual. It is entirely compatible with the social behaviourism of the philosopher G. H. Mead. It is incompatible, however, with the forms of behaviourism which prevail within psychology. This is obvious from a reading of Harré and Secord's volume. This is because the social representation of the individual which prevailed amongst those behaviourists (principally J. B. Watson and B. F. Skinner) who were influential in the development of psychology as a branch of natural science, was a non-social one. Harré and Secord spell out the methodological implications of their social model of the individual. It would lead to a very different conception of the research process and of the laboratory to the one analysed earlier in this chapter. In the context of the behavioural orthodoxies, mainly of experimental research in psychology, their proposed 'new' methodology might appear quite radical. The term new 'paradigm' has been advanced to capture the radical nature of the break with the past which they propose. I am not so convinced that it is such a radically 'new' methodology (Farr, 1977), especially within social psychology where it has been fairly standard practice for some time to elicit self-reports. I also differ quite radically from them in seeing an important future role for laboratories and experimental research within psychology. My own approach is to use the social behaviourism of G. H. Mead in order to make sense of changes in states of awareness within laboratory contexts (Farr, 1978*a*). The simple point I wish to establish here is that there are important implications for *how* one does research depending upon whether one's representation of the individual is, or is not, a social one. This is true irrespective of whether one is interested in experimental research within laboratory contexts (Farr) or non-experimental research in field settings outside of the laboratory (Harré and Secord).

The idea of 'social representations' which emerges from the field studies of the French School is a potentially powerful force for the renewal of concepts within social psychology. In alliance with the views of philosophers and sociologists outside of France who similarly portray the individual as a social representation it could succeed in the process of re-socialising psychology, and not just social psychology.

5. The relationship between Kelly's constructs and Durkheim's representations

FAY FRANSELLA

In commenting on the debate amongst French social psychologists on the nature of representations, Farr states that 'They invariably choose to contrast their approach with those *purely cognitive* approaches within social psychology which stress "images", "opinions", "beliefs", *"personal constructs"*, "attitudes", etc.' (Farr 1978*b*, p. 514, italics mine). This stated contrast between representations (whether collective or social) and Kelly's personal constructs serves as a useful starting-point for an analysis of the relationship between the two. Are representations and constructs different? If so, in what ways do they differ?

Personal construct psychology

The model

Kelly (1955) is among the few in psychology who explicitly stated the way in which he wanted to view the individual. The model he chose was 'man-the-scientist'. Construing an individual 'as if' he was a scientist means that each of us is seen as attempting to organise the events with which we are confronted and, in so doing, to gain control over those events. This, in turn, enables us to predict events in the future. This control results from our noting that certain events are similar and thereby different from others. Having construed these similarities and differences we are able to anticipate subsequent events.

Using this model of the scientist, we are also seen as grappling with our own personal worlds on the basis of construct dimensions we have erected in the past. So, although it is assumed that the universe exists and the world of events is real, we each differ in our construing of those events, since we are each viewing them through a different system of constructs – it is in this sense that they are 'personal' constructs. While

Durkheim did not dwell at all upon the nature of the person who psychologically used representations, he was at one with Kelly in emphasising the living, on-going nature of human beings and how it is 'the creative capacity of the living thing to represent the environment, not merely to respond to it' (Kelly 1955, p. 8.).

Reductionism

Both men are in harmony again here. Both are against reductionism. In a paper first published in 1898, Durkheim comments that:

The psychological conceptions of Huxley and Maudsley, which reduce the mind to nothing more than an epiphenomenon of physical life, have no longer many defenders; even the most authoritative representatives of the psycho-physiological school have formally rejected them and endeavoured to show that such conceptions are not implicit in their principles.   (Durkheim 1974, p. 2)

A little later he continues:

For a psychologist the phenomenon of representation is only an assembly of representations. If these representations die as soon as they are born, then in what does the mind consist? We must choose: either epiphenomenalism is correct or else there is a memory that is a specifically mental phenomenon. But we have already seen that the first position is untenable, and consequently the second solution must be accepted if we are to remain consistent.
(Durkheim 1974, pp. 9–10)

Kelly focusses on the necessity for being clear about the boundaries between differing realms of facts. Each realm has its own system of constructs and its own language:

instead of saying that a certain event is a 'psychological event and therefore not a physiological event', we must be careful to recognize that any event may be viewed either in its psychological or in its physiological aspects. A further idea that we must keep straight is that the physiologically constructed facts about that event are the offspring of the physiological system within which they emerge and have meaning, and that a psychological system is not obliged to account for them.   (Kelly 1955, p. 11)

Its philosophy

Just as Durkheim had no model of the person, so he makes no explicit reference to his underlying philosophy. Kelly's philosophical system of *constructive alternativism* is implicit in his rejection of reductionism, but is made explicit in the statement that:

We assume that all of our present interpretations of the universe are subject to revision or replacement. This is a basic statement which has a bearing upon almost everything that we shall have to say later. We take the stand that there are always some alternative constructions available to choose among in dealing with the world. No one needs to paint himself into a corner; no one needs to be completely hemmed in by circumstances; no one needs to be the victim of his biography.

(Kelly 1955, p. 15)

The basic theory

Kelly's theory is set out in the form of a fundamental postulate elaborated by eleven corollaries and all logically extending from his philosophy. It is the most explicit theory in psychology today; every word in postulate and corollaries, every statement about relationships between constructs, the process of construing and change, is defined. Durkheim had no such explicit, precisely formulated theory, so any comparison between the two will be made at the appropriate time as the formal outline of personal construct theory is given.

The Fundamental Postulate states that 'A person's processes are psychologically channelized by the ways in which he anticipates events', and the first corollary (Construction) states that we 'anticipate events by construing their replications'. A construct is thus an indication that we have seen a structure or pattern in the events confronting us. We have seen that some events have common characteristics and so can be differentiated from other events. A construct is thus:

a representation of the universe, a representation erected by a living creature and then tested against the reality of that universe. Since the universe is essentially a course of events, the testing of a construct is a testing against subsequent events. In other words, a construct is tested in terms of its predictive efficiency.

(*ibid*. p. 12)

A construct, in turn, is an abstraction. By that we mean it is a property attributed to several events, by means of which they can be differentiated into two homogeneous groups. The invention of such a property is the act of abstracting. To construe events is to use this convenient trick of abstracting them in order to make sense out of them. (*ibid*. p. 120)

So a construct is a psychological representation of the universe, and for both Kelly and Durkheim the underlying mechanism is one of abstraction:

Everything goes to show that ... psychic existence is a continual stream of representations that blend into each other so that no one can say where one begins or another finishes. No doubt the intellect comes to make certain divisions, but it is we who introduce them into the psychic *continuum*. This process of abstraction allows us to analyse what is, in fact, an indivisible complex.   (Durkheim 1974, p. 12)

Kelly went on to elaborate his notion of the construct into a formal psychological theory, which Durkheim did not attempt to do. But why should he? He was a sociologist and was content to leave the notion of the individual representation for a psychologist like Kelly to expand.

But there is one very vital elaboration of Kelly's which makes the construct profoundly more complex than the representation; the construct is a vehicle for action. It is the means whereby we anticipate the future, with the anticipation being tested against subsequent events. Each of us has erected a set of construct dimensions based on our abstractions of some common properties seen in events flowing past us, and these then form the bases on which we predict or anticipate future events. What we predict is not the total nature of the future event, but simply that, for instance, tomorrow will only be similar to today in that both will include the rising and the setting of the sun. From the person-as-scientist model, the construct is seen as the hypothesis or mini-theory on the basis of which certain predictions are made which subsequently will be validated or invalidated.

The notion of 'testing' is crucial here. So far, as personal scientists, we have the hypothesis (based on our construing of past events), which gives rise to predictions about future events, and the present reality shows whether we were right or wrong in our prediction. But that most essential ingredient of the scientific enterprise is missing – the experiment. It is here that Kelly again goes way beyond Durkheim. For Kelly, it is our behaviour that is the experiment. It is the question we put to nature.

Instead of being a problem of threatening proportions, requiring the utmost explanation and control to keep man out of trouble, behaviour presents itself as man's principal instrument of inquiry. Without it his questions are academic and he gets nowhere. When it is prescribed for him he runs around in dogmatic circles. But when he uses it boldly to ask questions, a flood of unexpected answers rises to tax his utmost capacity to understand.   (Kelly 1970, p. 260)

It will be argued that this link between construing and behaving is of more significance than a simple elaboration of the individual representation, that it has implications for social representations as well. But before going on to discuss these implications of Kelly's ideas for work within the framework of social representations, there are a few other points of comparison to be made.

The non-verbal or pre-verbal construct

Farr (1978*b*) referred to personal constructs as 'purely cognitive'. One reason why people become convinced that personal construct psychology is all about cognition is that they equate constructs with verbal labels. But if we use the corollary stating that constructs are dichotomous and are the means whereby we discriminate between events within our environment according to their similarities and differences, then we can say that some of these discriminations can be verbalised and discussed, whilst others cannot. Channels are not limited to those symbolised by words.

A large portion of human behavior follows nameless channels which have no language symbols, nor any kinds of signposts whatsoever. Yet they are channels and they are included in the network of dichotomous dimensions with relation to which the person's world is structured.   (Kelly 1955, p. 130)

Durkheim likewise considered that representations were not by any means always available to consciousness:

Because it is convenient to call the conscious states of mind psychological it does not follow that outside consciousness there are only organic or biochemical phenomena.   (Durkheim 1974, p. 18)

Based on the results from Janet's experiments with hypnosis, he argues that:

Our judgments are influenced at every moment by unconscious judgments; we see only what our prejudices permit us to see and yet we are unaware of them.
                    (*ibid.* 1974, p. 21)

Here again Kelly, the psychologist, goes beyond Durkheim, the sociologist, by using the idea of pre-verbal construing to provide an explanation of some human emotion, and at the same time enables the range of convenience of his theory to extend and encompass living creatures other than humans.

For instance, a cat can discriminate between two tones of voice, one approving and the other disapproving, whilst having no idea that the words being used are the same in each case. It can make a non-verbal discrimination.

Another example of non-verbal discrimination might occur when a young boy, whose mother from time to time dresses up, comes all sweet-smelling to the bedside to bestow a gentle kiss on the cheek along with the admonition to 'be careful not to ruffle mummy's hair' and to 'be good while mummy is at her party'. The light goes out and mummy disappears into the night leaving the child alone in the dark and afraid.

Let us assume that the child can discriminate between nights when mummy kisses and cuddles and can be ruffled and when comforting noises come from downstairs when the light is turned out, from the non-ruffling nights with their subsequent anxieties and fears of being alone in the silence and dark. This boy grows up and has a girl friend, perhaps a bit on the cuddly, ruffly side. But she likes going to parties and will insist on 'dressing up' for the occasion and becoming 'untouchable'. No verbal labels here. But the discrimination formed in childhood is 'seen' to be applicable many years later and the young man has no way of explaining to himself or to his girl friend why it is he gets so irritable and anxious and unappreciative of her attractive party gear. But the 'seeing' is a perceiving and discriminating between events at a non-verbal level, and it is affecting this young man's feelings as well as his behaviour.

Contrary to Farr's statement (1978b) about the *purely cognitive* nature of the personal construct, I would argue that it is the representation that is purely cognitive in conception, and that the construct is an integral part of our feeling and behaviour. Kelly rejected dualism, preferring to think of bodily states (feelings) as part and parcel of the on-going human activity of trying to make increasing sense of the world. So feeling or emotion becomes construed in the context of transition, of process and change. When events do not fit with the constructions we place upon them and when we attempt to change these constructions, we experience some form of emotion. (For a detailed discussion of this issue see McCoy 1977.)

Thus, Kelly's psychology is about the whole organism. We cannot usefully be construed as consisting of separate parts, such as cognitions, affects, conations etc., with each part to be studied by a different set of people, and each set of people coming up with different theories, different methods of measurement and each producing findings that are not cross-referable. For such a divisive approach to the study of humans, tongue in cheek perhaps, Kelly coined the term *accumulative fragmentalism* (1965).

The organisation of constructs

The Organisation Corollary states that 'each person characteristically evolves, for his convenience in anticipating events, a construction system embracing ordinal relationships between constructs'. The use of the term 'evolves' underlines the on-going nature of life. But, taken as a whole, our construct systems are usually relatively stable, with individual constructs being changed as and when we see better ways of interpreting events. Some constructs are more resistant to change than others. For instance, core constructs are to do with our personal identities and radical change here can have catastrophic effects. Peripheral constructs are those that can be changed without serious ramifications to the rest of our construct system.

Just as constructs and representations are similar in being available to the conscious as well as the 'unconscious' mind, and are seen as being abstractions of events, so both are seen as being organised in some sense, that is, they blend into each other. But while Durkheim made a general statement about the nature of the relationship between representations, Kelly describes how such relationships might work and the effects different types of organisation may have on the effectiveness with which the individual goes about his daily life.

For Kelly, having a system of constructs means we are to some extent restricted in our range of actions. We cannot make sense of anything outside the system – outside there is only chaos. Our freedom is specified in the Choice Corollary, which states that one can choose 'that alternative in a dichotomized construct through which he anticipates the greater possibility for extension and definition of his system.' The basic point here is that we aim to increase the predictive power of our system, because in that way we gain increasing control over our environment. We can either aim to increase the meaningfulness of a limited range of events within a small world, or we can choose to put up with a certain amount of ambiguity on a day-to-day basis and extend our personal horizons so as to have a greater understanding of an enlarged world.

Constructs are organised hierarchically, and one important implication of this is the idea that superordinacy and subordinacy are relative terms. For example, *train* is a construct superordinate to *carriage* and *carriage* is superordinate to *compartment* and so on down the line. But, turned on its head, *carriage* is subordinate to *train* and *compartment* to *carriage*. It is possible that, in each person's system, there are one or two constructs which are subordinate to nothing else within that system, perhaps those concerning our philosophy of life, but nearly all constructs can be superordinate or subordinate, depending on their relative positions. Constructs can therefore be either dimensions which are placed over events or elements within the environment to be construed.

Thus, *carriages* and *compartments* are constructs, but also elements within the range of convenience of the construct *train*.

Hinkle (1965) in fact argued that the precise meaning and range of convenience of a construct can be specified in terms of its implications. The construct *sweet–sour* can be applied to the elements fruit, water and facial expressions, but not to boulders or trains. We talk of sour fruit, sour water and sour expressions, but the different contexts in which *sour* is used means that the subordinate and superordinate implications in each case will be somewhat different. Hinkle proposed that the identity of a construct could be defined by the implications or elements that were held in common in each case.

Durkheim apparently also pondered this problem of organisation and construct identity in relation to representations.

There is no justification for the supposition that representations are formed of definite elements or atoms that without losing their individuality go to the making up of various different representations. Ideas are not made up of bits and pieces which they exchange according to circumstances. The whiteness of paper is not the same as that of snow and the two appear in different representations . . .

He continues with his statement on organisation:

Everything goes to show that ... psychic existence is a continual stream of representations that blend into each other so that no one can say where one begins or another finishes.   (1974, pp. 11–12)

The construct and the individual representation

There are some fascinating similarities between the ideas of these two theorists, particularly in relation to the construing of change, abstraction, organisation and availability to consciousness. The major difference is that Durkheim's concept of the individual representation is descriptive and, as stated, mainly to do with cognitive activity.

For Kelly, the construct is the central unit, not only of our personality but of our total psychological life. We are, psychologically speaking, nothing but a bundle of constructs. These bundles differ from person to person in terms of content and structure. These construct dimensions, based upon abstracted similarities and differences in events, 'work' for us. They enable us to predict or anticipate the outcome of future events and we conduct the crucial experiment by behaving in a certain way. The validational outcome either passes unnoticed, or gives rise to despair (I always *knew* I was a failure), gives rise to anger (you see he *is* a bastard) or gives rise to joy (I really *do* believe he loves me after all). How the outcome of a behavioural experiment is construed will depend upon the question being asked.

Just as Durkheim was content to leave the individual representation to be used by psychologists, so may psychologists be content to leave the collective representation to sociologists. As might be expected, as stated by Durkheim collective representation does not fall within the realm of psychological enquiry.

social facts are in a sense independent of individuals and exterior to individual minds ... Society has for its substratum the mass of associated individuals. The system which they form by uniting together, and which varies according to their geographical disposition and the nature and number of their channels of communication, is the base from which social life is raised. The representations which form the network of social life arise from the relations between the individuals ... and the total society. If there is nothing extraordinary in the fact that individual representations, produced by the action and reaction between neural elements, are not inherent in these elements, there is nothing surprising in the fact that collective representations, produced by the action and reaction between individual minds that form the society, do not derive directly from the latter and consequently surpass them. (Durkheim 1974, pp. 24–5)

To study the interaction between these two distinct types of representation would seem to be a form of reductionism rejected by Durkheim. And yet Durkheim did consider there to be a connection between the two, but argued that the collective representation was at a higher conceptual level, or was more superordinate, than the individual representation.

The psychologist who restricts himself to the ego cannot emerge to find the nonego. Collective life is not born from individual life, but it is, on the contrary, the second which is born of the first. (Durkheim 1933, p. 279)

The connection between the individual and collective representation is more clearly spelt out in the following:

Society is a reality *sui generis;* it has its own peculiar characteristics, which are not found elsewhere and which are not met again in the same form in all the rest of the universe. The representations which express it have a wholly different content from purely individual ones and we may rest assured in advance that the first adds something to the second. (Durkheim 1961a, p. 16)

If it is indeed the content that is the prime difference between the two types of representation, then the psychologist does have entrée to this whole social area. There is nothing to prevent us from studying processes whereby the facts of social life influence the individual, particularly how they influence construct system development.

The social representation

The construct of the collective representation has evolved since Durkheim's time into the social representation. It appears to contain aspects of the individual representation which are then applied to groups. For some, at least, it is still a purely cognitive affair.

By representation system we mean the sum total of images present in the group and concerning the different elements with which the group is faced. Individuals confronted with objective conditions actually develop an internal perceptual and restructuring activity, which *must be considered a strictly cognitive activity*, one which allows them to integrate, understand, structure, and give meaning to these elements. The product of this cognitive activity on the part of each individual is what we call a representation. By analysing these representations, one can observe certain elements of the individual's or the group's subjective – or internal – reality.   (Abric 1971, p. 313 – italics mine)

The aim of Abric's study was to examine the role played by the representation of the task.

This representation of the task could be defined as the theory or system of hypotheses individuals work out regarding the nature of the task, its objective, the means to employ to carry out the task, and the behavior conducive to effectiveness. To the extent that this representation is shared by the whole group, it determines a collective representation of the given facts of the environment, that is, a social representation of the task.   (*ibid.*)

It is interesting to note that the terms 'collective' and 'social' representation are used synonymously. The talk of systems of hypotheses is very reminiscent of the language of construct theory, but how the representation links with behaviour is not explored. Abric is clearly content to let the representation be construed solely in cognitive terms.

Moscovici shows the cognitive relationship between the construct and the social representation even more clearly when he discusses how it differs from images, attitudes or opinions.

Because they determine both the object and the related judgement, and because they interact with one another, social representations are cognitive systems with a logic and language of their own and a pattern of implication, relevant to both values and concepts ... They do not represent simply 'opinions about', 'images of' or 'attitudes towards', but 'theories' or 'branches of knowledge' in their own right, for the discovery and organization of reality.   (Moscovici 1973, p. xiii)

This quotation is from the foreword to Herzlich's study of people's views (constructs, representations) of health and illness. But in neither the foreword nor in the work itself is there again any clear indication of the relationship between the social representation as a cognitive concept and related behaviour.

As we have seen, there is no theoretical difficulty in relating the personal construct to behaviour and feeling, but it is equally as applicable to the study and understanding of a number of individuals or a group as to a single person. Personal construct psychology has, in fact, two corollaries specifically concerned with interpersonal construing: Sociality and Commonality.

Sociality

Kelly saw the Sociality Corollary as providing the basis for a social psychology, for it states 'to the extent that one person construes the construction processes of another, he may play a role in a social process involving the other person'. By subsuming the way another sees things, we can have an interpersonal understanding and engage in a joint enterprise.

This in no way implies that we have a common understanding – we may totally misunderstand – but we are attempting to stand in another's shoes and see things as the other sees them. Our understanding of another's construing determines our subsequent behaviour. In ordinary conversation we constantly monitor others' reactions to what we are saying. If I interpret a listener's reactions as indicating that he is not understanding the point I am trying to convey, this will lead me to try another tack. If this seems to produce a more favourable result, I may well continue in this vein and, if he appears to become more and more favourable in his attitude, I will wax increasingly lyrical, until I suddenly notice that he has started shifting around in his seat. If I construe this as indicating that I have gone on too long and he has got bored with waiting for his turn to say something, I will stop.

All these interpretations of how he is construing the situation may be wrong, in which case I should enroll in a social skills training course at once. But the fact that I am attempting to see our interactions through the other's eyes means that our behaviour is interlocked. Kelly once commented that he had been called everything from an existentialist to a behaviourist, and it is easy to see how some can come to the latter conclusion. When the other attempts to construe my constructions, we are participants in an enterprise of interaction.

Commonality

Whilst the Sociality Corollary is a particularly important aspect of personal construct theory for the study of dyadic relationships and small group dynamics, the Commonality Corollary has more significance in relation to the social representation. Personal construct theory is, *par excellence*, a theory about individuals, as stated in the Sociality Corollary: 'to the extent that one person employs a construction of experience which is similar to that employed by another, his psychological processes are similar to those of the other person'. This does not mean that in order to construe things similarly people must have had similar experiences. It means that they must construe their experience in a similar way. 'It is not the similarity of experience which provides the basis for similarity of action, but similarity of their present construction of that experience' (Kelly 1955, p. 92).

So the individualist standpoint taken by Kelly does not preclude one from construing aspects of life from a group or cultural standpoint. We can stand on Mount Olympus and abstract certain common properties in certain groups of people and give the name 'cultures' to these similarities and differences. Or we can come down from that high level of abstraction and find that, as individuals, our construing leads us to expect certain attitudes and behaviours from certain people in certain settings. And, in turn, these people have certain expectations of us. If we conform, the *status quo* is maintained. If we deviate from the group expectancy, the personal construct psychologist would seek the explanation, not in the social process, but in the construing of the deviant or group of deviants (if that is how we wish to construe the asker of non-conformist questions). Norris (1977) did just this in her study entitled 'Construing in a detention centre'.

The question to be asked of all those described by society as deviant is 'what questions is this person asking, and what answers is he seeking by behaving in this particular way?' But we need not stop there. We can go on to ask of the conformists, 'what effect does the behaviour of these deviants have on the way you construe yourselves and them? Are you threatened by this behaviour? If so, what is the nature of the threat?'

It is possible for deviant behaviour to produce 'imminent awareness of comprehensive change in one's core structures'. For this is how threat is defined in Kelly's theory. If we have a personal belief that our particular culture is the best that there is, and we identify ourselves with that culture, then we will be severely threatened if we suddenly perceive that a minority group has gained sufficient strength to radically alter that culture. We can accept the threat and reconstrue, perhaps arguing internally along the lines that 'times change and, sad though it is, our culture is changing and so must I'. Thus the threat of deviance can produce change in the majority view. In this sense Kelly's theoretical approach is very much in accord with the ideas of Moscovici as expressed in his book *Social influence and social change* (1976).

But another, perhaps more common, response to threat is to show hostility. This is defined as 'the continued effort to extort validational evidence in favour of a type of social prediction which has already proved itself a failure'. If we are hostile to the minority group, we could keep it a minority by eliminating its members; or, less radically, we could prove to ourselves that these people are really no threat to us because they are pretty rotten human beings. We can force them to live in overcrowded conditions and give them a second-class education. This may well give rise to anti-social behaviour and illiteracy and so we have proved to ourselves that they are only a nuisance and not the threat that we had, for a few nasty moments, contemplated they might be. The snag is that the minority group may not agree to put up with the conditions forced upon them. And so the threat continues.

This discussion of a possible personal construct approach to deviance has exemplified the relation between behaviour, construing and emotion. Within Kelly's theory they are inseparable.

Research strategies

Theories are only of value in so far as they can be used both to formulate new questions and to seek new answers. In academic circles this is usually given the name of research or experimentation. The truly reflexive nature of Kelly's theory can now be seen. For not only are psychologists the same as all other people in going about their worldly business conducting behavioural experiments so as to test out their personal ways of construing the world, but they are also professional experimenters. Thus, from the standpoint of personal construct theory, the psychological experiment is always carried out within a social psychological context and can be studied as such.

Repertory grid technique

Apart from describing a complex theoretical system, Kelly also described the repertory grid as a technique for interpreting construct relationships in mathematical terms. The original grid format he proposed has evolved in many ways (see Fransella and Bannister 1977) and no doubt will continue to do so. As with the theory, its basic frame of reference is the individual and how the psychological space of that individual is structured. But Kelly points out that the Commonality Corollary enables one to look for aspects of a psychological space that is held in common between groups of people or within one group.

Group construing

Herzlich's work could be taken as a good example of the use of Commonality (1973). By a series of individual interviews, she elicited constructs which enabled her to isolate certain clusters of shared constructs concerning health and illness. She analysed the content of the interviews in detail and identified various types of respondent. The construct theorist might have taken the analysis a step further by attempting to quantify the differences between the groups by using a form of grid.

There are several studies that have used the notion of commonality and grid methodology in a social context. Weinreich (1979), for instance, has carried out a great deal of research on the development of identity in coloured immigrant children. Warren (1966) has studied the relationship between types of construing and social class grouping. Hoy (1977) has looked at the beliefs about alcoholism in both alcoholic and non-alcoholic groups. Orley (1976) has demonstrated the usefulness of grids in social anthropology by having Gandan villagers construe the spirits which form an important part of their mythology.

In a rather different type of study, Riley and Palmer (1976) elicited constructs from sixty individuals which were then pooled and analysed as a single unit. The elements to be construed were a variety of British and European seaside resorts. In this way, each resort could be described as having certain general characteristics as seen by all subjects. There is a marked similarity of approach here between construct theory and empirical studies of social representations. Milgram and Jodelet's social representations, described in 'Psychological maps of Paris' (1976), are along very similar lines. Milgram says 'We discern the major ingredients of that representation by studying not only the mental map in a specific individual, but by seeing what is shared among individuals' (ibid., p. 72). The only real difference between the two studies would seem to be the methods employed for analysing the individual's responses.

But a difference between construct research and representation research becomes apparent when one is concerned not only with the content of what we construe but also with the construing process and structure. Springing directly from construct theory we have, for instance, several studies on cognitive complexity (e.g. Crockett 1965) and on cognitive integration (e.g. Hinkle 1965). In the clinical field, Bannister (1960; 1962) examined the type of disordered thinking sometimes found in those diagnosed as suffering from schizophrenia, using the theoretical constructs of tightness and looseness. Bannister also developed an aetiological theory to explain this conceptual loosening (Bannister 1963/1965; Bannister and Fransella 1980). Tight construing is that which leads to unvarying predictions and loose construing to varying predictions. Changes in structure of construct relationships as the result of experience along this tight–loose dimension have also been shown to occur among those undergoing group psychotherapy (Fransella and Joyston-Bechal 1971).

As the grid was tailor-made for deriving mathematical relationships between constructs and the elements construed it has greatly influenced research within the field. But it can also equally well be used within some other theoretical context – that concerning social representations for example. But it takes the researcher a step further when used within the theoretical framework of personal constructs. For it can help demonstrate the relationship between construing and behaving. For example, voting behaviour in a coming British general election was predicted from scores on a grid (Fransella and Bannister 1967). Each of the seventy-four subjects named eight people they knew to serve as elements to be construed in political and evaluative terms. The best predictor of voting behaviour proved to be 'the ideal self' closely followed by the 'self'. This meant that if elements were construed as being *like I'd like to be* and also as *likely to vote Conservative*, the construer was herself likely to vote Conservative. This political affiliation also carried with it the idea that Conservatives were evaluatively 'good' and Labour voters 'bad'. What was 'good' and 'bad' was determined by the subject's political allegiance. Moscovici uses political construing as an example of the application of the social representation, but a direct link with behaviour is missing.

When we speak of social representations . . . there is no implication of any clear-cut division between the outside world and the inner world of the individual (or group); subject and object are not regarded as functionally separate. An object is located in a context of activity, since it is what it is because it is in part regarded by the person or the group as an extension of their behaviour. For example, any judgement of a political party depends upon the experience of the person who makes the judgement, and his definition of the party and of the political set-up. Not to recognize the power of our capacity for representation to create objects and events is like believing that there is no connection between our 'reservoir' of images and our capacity for imagination.   (1973, p. xi)

That some workers within the field of social representation research are coming close to using grid methodology to relate behaviour to representation can be seen in studies such as that of Abric and Kahan (1972). They showed very neatly that behavioural co-operation between partners was determined by the representation (construing) of the partner. Questionnaires 'asked for ratings on a seven-point scale of the subject's representations of the partner on a series of bi-polar adjectives' (*ibid.*, p. 132). This format could alternatively be described as a rating grid.

Similarly, Codol cites a previous finding showing that 'individuals have a tendency, generally, to fashion an image of their self according to which each one can assert that he conforms more closely to the situational norms than do others' (1974, p. 351). He then describes an experiment in which subjects' representations are manipulated.

It does appear from the body of work carried out within both representational and personal construct frameworks that both have a concern for the relationship between cognitive activity and behaviour, but the latter leads one to explore directly the link between these cognitive aspects and related behaviour in a way that the social representation model does not.

Conclusions

There is considerable similarity between the concepts of 'construct', as described by Kelly, and 'individual representation', as postulated by Durkheim, but also important differences. The chief difference is that the construct has an inbuilt action component, making for intimate relationships between thinking, feeling and behaving. The individual representation, on the other hand, is primarily a cognitive concept, whose relationship to behaviour can only be inferred. The same applies to the social representation.

It has been argued that the personal construct can be equally well compared with the social as with the individual representation. But, unlike the representation, it is supported by a very elaborate and explicit theory. Also the theory, with or without grid technique, enables workers to explore many avenues of human functioning, including thought process and content in both individual and group settings and the linkage between construing, behaving and feeling.

If I am correct in my own construing of some of the similarities and differences in these two approaches, there is yet another difference. Those interested in representations are concerned more with the study of human behaviour in the traditional experimental format than with interpersonal interactions, factors that facilitate change and so forth. This raises the prospect of research in the field of representations to enrich that which already exists within the field of personal construct psychology. There might, in fact, be a reciprocal relationship. Perhaps some cross-cultural research may evolve in which a common language emerges to enhance both orientations by cross-channel fertilisation.

Part 2
Identifying the representations implicit in theory and research

6. A theoretical and experimental approach to the study of social representations in a situation of interaction[*]

JEAN-CLAUDE ABRIC

In this chapter we are going to provide a summary and a synthesis of a body of research in which the experimental method is used to study the part played by social representations in the processes of interaction. This research uses as supporting evidence an interaction scenario which is called 'conflicting': the game known as the 'Prisoners' Dilemma'. Let us recall that this game brings into confrontation two individuals for whom one provides the ultimate aim of achieving maximum gain from a pay-off matrix. To be more precise, each individual can choose between two options (C or D in fig. 1) – the gain achieved on a given trial being at one and the same time dependent on the player's own choice and that of his opponent. This situation is interesting because it creates an interaction which brings into play two opposing kinds of motivation:

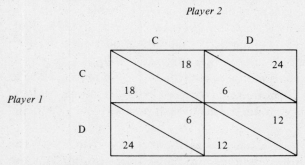

Fig. 1   The Prisoners' Dilemma matrix

(a) A 'co-operative' motivation which results in choice C on the part of

*Translated by John L. Carr

the two players, allowing them in the course of a series of trials to achieve maximum gain (which is the same for each of them)

(b) A motivation, or a temptation to defect, which leads to playing D (in the hope that the other has played C). Over a series of trials this choice of D does not permit the maximum possible gain: rather it permits a differential gain (i.e. I win less than I might have *but* more than the other fellow).

This game situation has enjoyed an enormous success in experimental psychology, for it has been perceived as a simple way of identifying the factors which lead subjects to co-operate or to compete. But the analysis of the hundreds of research projects undertaken in this area (especially in the United States) is singularly disillusioning: contradictory results abound and despite a number of attempts (Deutsch, 1962; Pruitt, 1967) no theory of inter-personal conflict has been successfully developed. It occurred to us, therefore, that one of the basic reasons for deadlock in these studies could possibly lie in the fact that they were all directed towards an analysis of the objective components of the given situation (type of matrix, nature of pay-offs, type of opponent etc.), without ever questioning *the significance of this situation* for the subjects involved in the experiment.

So the central hypothesis of our research may be expressed in these terms: the behaviour of individuals in interaction with each other is not determined by the objective characteristics of a situation but by the way in which this situation is 'represented'. By 'representation' we mean 'the end-product and the process of a mental activity by which an individual or a group reconstructs the reality with which he or it is faced and attributes to it a specific importance' (Abric, 1976: 106). This representation plays a fundamental role in the interaction because at one and the same time it defines what constitutes *reality for the subject* – the subject reacts to reality not as it really is but as he represents it to himself – and because it produces a network of anticipations and expectations which predetermine the relationship of the subject to his environment.

The primary aim of our research has therefore been to study the relationship between representations and behaviour, in order to show that the latter was truly determined by the representation of the situation.

The second aim was directed to discovering and analysing experimentally the characteristics of a social representation. As we shall see this second aim has at present only partially been realised.

I. Experimental studies on the role of representations in a game situation

On the level of an overall, rough analysis, the game situation seems to us to comprise four elements: oneself, others, the task and the context. We have therefore decided to study the role of the representation of each of these elements in the process of interaction and to study them one by one, leaving as a follow-up operation the study of the representation of the entire situation. Here I shall give only the main results obtained with regard to the last three elements (others, the task, the context). Work upon the role played by the representation of the self is too complex to be included within the limits of this chapter.[1]

1. *An example of experimental research into the role of the representation of the opponent*

(*a*) *The experimental situation:* the experiment involves 40 subjects placed in the situation of the Prisoners' Dilemma game and given non-competitive instructions (to make the maximum gain oneself without however endeavouring to beat the other person). *In the first part of the experiment* half the subjects think they are playing against a *student* opponent like themselves, the other half having been led to believe that they are playing against a machine (these two representations being induced by the experimenter). In reality, and without knowing it, all the subjects play against a fictitious opponent (who is none other than the experimenter himself) who in all situations adopts the same strategy (known as tit-for-tat). Each subject has fifty trials in this initial phase. He is then told the game is over and that in the second phase he will be up against another opponent (either a student or a machine). There are therefore four experimental situations.

In fact the game proceeds in the same way in the second phase (as in the first) with the partner continuing with the tit-for-tat strategy. In the four situations (control and experimental) no real change takes place: the effective opponent remains the same (i.e. he is still the experimenter) and his strategy continues unchanged. Only in the experimental groups does the image of the opponent change between the two phases.

(*b*) *Hypotheses*

General hypothesis: it is not the actual behaviour of the opponent but the representation of the opponent which determines the choices of individuals in a situation of conflicting interaction.

Table 1. *Experimental conditions*

	First phase (50 trials)	Second phase (50 trials)
Condition 1	student partner	machine partner
Condition 2	machine partner	student partner
Condition 3 (Control)	student partner	student partner
Condition 4 (Control)	machine partner	machine partner

Hypothesis 1: the representation of the opponent as 'human' fosters the development of co-operation; that of the opponent as 'machine' impedes it.

Hypothesis 2: change in the representation of the opponent in mid-game brings about an immediate transformation of the behaviour adopted in the first phase:

- a considerable and immediate drop in the level of co-operation when the change introduces the representation of the opponent as 'machine'
- an increase in the level of co-operation when the change introduces the representation of the opponent as 'student'.

(c) *Results:* the main results shown in table 2 and figure 2 confirm and verify our two hypotheses:

Table 2. *Proportion of co-operative choices*

	Control groups					Experimental groups			
	1–25	26–50	51–75	76–100		1–25	26–50	51–75	76–100
S–S	0.544	0.567	0.582	0.632	S–M	0.412	0.540	0.396	0.468
M–M	0.391	0.340	0.355	0.466	M–S	0.284	0.388	0.440	0.644

The representation of a 'human' opponent is more favourable to co-operation than a 'machine' opponent. Moreover, whatever kind of partner is encountered in the first phase the change in representation at the fiftieth trial totally transforms the subject's behaviour in the direction forecast by our hypotheses. In particular, when the transformation of the representation is made in the direction of a 'dehumanising' of the opponent the drop in the level of co-operation is spectacular. In our opinion this drop can be explained only by the fact that the transformation in the representation of the opponent changes the aims and the strategy of the subject: the very high level of co-operation obtained in this situation during the first phase demonstrates in fact that subjects have acquired an excellent cognitive grasp of the situation. This learning is swept away by the transformation in representation, or rather it appears inapplicable in a situation which the subject perceives as being radically different from the previous one.

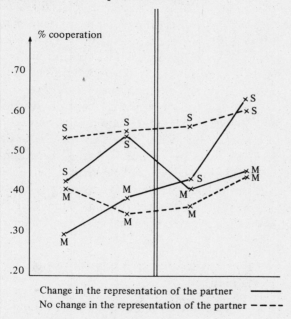

Fig. 2   Temporal evolution of co-operative choices

Questionnaires about the representation which we handed to subjects at the beginning and end of each phase enlighten us concerning these relationships between representations and behaviour.

We were accustomed in fact to asking subjects to choose qualifying adjectives to apply to each of the two opponents. The human partner would then be clearly differentiated from the machine by the fact that he was 'supple', 'adaptable' and 'reactive', whereas the machine was perceived as 'rigid', 'non-adaptable' and 'insensitive'. These characteristics of the representations allow us to understand the differences in observed behaviour: the 'reactive' characteristics of the human opponent permit and support an interactive behaviour on the part of the subject. On the other hand the imagined insensitivity of the machine renders such an interaction impossible and produces therefore a defensive type of behaviour.

When we study the evolution of the representations after the interaction we note that, even though the strategies employed are strictly identical, the differences between representations are maintained, at least in respect of the key dimensions: the capability of influencing and of reacting. This result seems to us to demonstrate how the initial representation plays the part of an interpretive filter: *the same behaviour is interpreted in a sense which is consistent with the initial representation.*

Tit-for-tat behaviour is interpreted as reactive when it is performed by a human opponent and as non-reactive if it is performed by a machine. Thus it is certainly the representation which determines the meaning of the behaviour and of the interaction, and not the reverse.

This research appears to us interesting for it shows not only that behaviour in the context of this interaction is determined by how the opponent is represented, but also it allows us to see the nature of the cognitive mechanisms set in motion by this representation: the representation constitutes *a reference grill for decoding and interpreting,* on the basis of which individuals attribute a meaning to the things they perceive; it also creates *expectancies and anticipations;* it immediately *categorises* and hence determines the circumstances of the interaction.

2.   *An example of experimental research into the role of the representation of the task*

This study has been elaborated in the course of extending previous research (Abric and Vacherot, 1975), and it uses the same experimental set-up, except that we introduce a new dimension into it: that of the representation which subjects form of the task they are given. In fact a basic criticism can be formulated in regard to most traditional experimental research. In their work, investigators behave as though subjects reacted consistently to a given situation. Scenarios mounted by experimenters are therefore considered at one and the same time to be accepted in an identical manner by the subjects and in the same way in which the experimenter himself interprets them. As far as we are concerned we think that, even in the controlled situation of the laboratory, the subject takes a more and more active part in identifying with the situation which leads him to attribute to it his own meaning, which is not necessarily that of the experimenter. From that point on one will be unable to interpret the results obtained except by providing oneself with the means of *locating and checking the meaning for the subjects of the given experimental situation;* in other words except by becoming familiar with their *representation of the situation* and more precisely with their representations of the task they are asked to perform.

The research we are about to offer intends therefore to show that:

(1) a single experimental set-up can give rise to different representations
(2) how subjects behave does not depend upon the objective character-
    istics of the task but upon their representations of it.

(*a*) *The different representations of the same task:* we do not propose to discuss in this paper the methodology we used to identify these representations. It is a matter of using the technique for the analysis of similarities pioneered by Flament (1981). This technique has allowed us to tease out two very different representations of the proposed task (the Prisoners' Dilemma):

– *an initial representation in terms of 'play'* in which the task is associated not only with notions concerning diversion or amusement but also with a situation which is unpredictable (chance, fortune) and competitive

– *a second representation in terms of 'problem-solving',* in which the task is associated with notions of difficulty, effort, rigour and complexity.

We note that the main differences between the two representations of the task are related:

– on the one hand to the presence in the 'problem' representation of a reference to a cognition on the part of the subject and therefore to the possibility of his 'control' of the situation, a dimension which we do not find in the 'play' representation

– on the other hand to the presence of a reference to a competitive aspect in the 'play' representation, an aspect totally absent from the 'problem' representation.

From this it is understandable that we may predict that each of these representations of the task will have a decisive effect on radically different behaviours and more specifically that the representation of the task as a 'problem-solving' one facilitates co-operation.

(*b*) *Behaviour and the representation of the task:* the observed results largely confirm this hypothesis. In fact we find (see table 3) that subjects who are confronted with an opponent in the Prisoners' Dilemma scenario are significantly more co-operative when they envisage the task in terms of problem-solving.[2]

Table 3. *Proportions of observed behaviours*
(with a partner)

| | | Representation of the task | |
		Problem-solving	'Play'
Behaviours	Co-operative	0.66	0.42
	Defensive	0.12	0.43

Furthermore, in this 'problem-solving' situation co-operation is the dominant behaviour. On the contrary, in the 'play' situation defensive behaviour appears significantly more often than in the 'problem-solving' situation[3] and, despite the experimental instructions, this defensive behaviour appears to be as important as co-operative behaviour.

To the extent that the subjects were confronted by the same Prisoners' Dilemma matrix and that they were all given exactly the same instructions, these results certainly prove that the subjects respond not to the objective characteristics of the task but to their own representation of that task.

(c) *The role of the different elements of the representation of the situation as they affect behaviour:* the results I have just presented were obtained in situations where the subjects imagined they were playing against a student opponent like themselves. We carried out the same research in a context where subjects thought they were interacting not with an individual but with a *machine*. The observed results are particularly interesting as they differ from those obtained in the context of the preceding experiment.

It appears in fact that there is an interaction effect between the representation of the task and the representation of the opponent (see table 4).

With a 'machine' as opponent the representation of the task no longer induces a difference in the levels of co-operation achieved by the subjects. Moreover, even if a tendency persists, there is no longer a significant difference in co-operative behaviour in the 'problem-solving' condition.

These results might appear to contradict the preceding ones if in fact they did not make clear the relationships which obtain between the different elements making up the *representation of the situation*. Indeed they demonstrate that if each element in this representation – here the

Table 4. *Proportion of observed behaviours with
a machine as partner*

| | | Representation of the task | |
		Problem-solving	'Play'
Behaviours	Co-operative	0.31	0.32
	Defensive	0.21	0.33

task and the opponent – has an important part to play this part can be understood only in relationship to the other elements present in the representation of the situation. More precisely, in the situation on which we are working we can say that *the representation of the task varies as a function of the representation of the opponent with whom one is performing it.* Not only do the subjects have *a priori* representations of the task, but these representations can vary according to the opponent assigned to them. It follows that this type of result calls into question, in a radical manner, most of the interpretations made by experimenters who have worked in the field of inter-personal conflict without checking on these essential determinants of behaviour.

To conclude on the subject of the results of this research we note that the 'problem-solving representation with a fellow-student as opponent' appears far and away to be the condition most conducive to the establishment of co-operation, that is, that in which the subject's performance (the number of points obtained) is at its highest. Now the distinctiveness of this situation is that it brings together the two elements in the representation which facilitate or allow harmonious behaviour. We may conclude from this – and it confirms similar results we have obtained from studying group creativity – that the best performance is achieved by subjects in contexts where their representations are in harmony with the objective characteristics of the situation.

3. An example of experimental research into the role played by the context of the task and by the social status of the subjects

The final piece of research that we shall give here makes use of an experimental task which is different from the preceding studies. In this work we have tried to study the effect of the context of the task upon behaviour.

In order to achieve this we have presented one and the same task under different guises, that is, a problem having the same logical structure has been presented in a variety of different concrete situations. Thus we have devised six different contexts having in common the representation of a mixed-motive situation of the Prisoners' Dilemma variety. Each context brings together 'two individuals in a potentially conflicting relationship' (see Abric and Mardellat, 1974); for example, a trade unionist and a manager in a situation of social conflict where they must make a choice between two options, the one 'conciliatory', the other 'hostile'. The subject is therefore asked to put himself in the place of one of the contestants and to declare the choice that he would have made in that situation. The six contexts studied offer a work scenario, a casino-gaming scenario, a freedom-fighter scenario, a publicity campaign scenario and a scenario involving the choice of a travel itinerary.[4]

Our first hypothesis is concerned with *the effect of the context*. The same logical structure produces different patterns of behaviour as a function of the representation induced by the context.

We have introduced into this study a second independent variable: the social status of the subjects. The same task was therefore given to higher business management on the one hand and to skilled workers from the same firm on the other hand. Our second hypothesis is concerned with *the effect of social status*: the subject decodes the information he receives and attributes meaning to the given context as a function of his own position in the social system. In other words, faced with an identical context the subjects' behaviour depends upon their own social status. The representation of a situation would therefore appear to be partly determined by the elements inherent in this situation but also in part by strictly social factors.

Taking into account the constraints and limitations of this chapter, we shall give only the results obtained on these two dimensions. The research itself was more extensive, since it was concerned also with the effect of 'social practice' upon behaviour (comparisons of the choice made by managers and workers with those made by the sons of managers and of workers).

The results confirm at one and the same time the effects both of the context and of the social status of the subject.

One certainly notes, in fact, that whatever may be the subject's social status the proposed context makes an important difference. It is not, therefore, the logical structure of the situation which determines choices but the meaning of the situation for the subjects.[5]

Table 5. *Proportions of conciliatory choices in each of the experimental contexts*

Status	Work	Casino gaming	Guerilla	Publicity	Strike	Travel itinerary
			Context			
Managers	0.96	0.35	0.56	0.52	0.84	1.00
Workers	0.96	0.52	0.50	0.29	0.48	0.50

Moreover, except in the first two contexts, one observes that managers make significantly more conciliatory choices than workers. None the less it is important to point out that in these situations the subjects were asked to formulate the choice made by *the person of highest social standing in the given context*. Consequently the results cannot be interpreted as displaying a more co-operative attitude on the part of the managers: more precisely, they show that, as a function of their social status, individuals attribute different intentions to the person involved in the context. 'The subjects appear to perceive the protagonist in a given situation as behaving more positively the closer he is to their own place in the social order. In this connection one must understand by positive behaviour not conciliatory behaviour but behaviour in line with the norms existing in a given social group' (Abric and Mardellat, 1974; 149).

If the 'work context cancels out the effect of social status' this is so, in our view, not only because it brings face to face two individuals whose social status is not made clear but also because it introduces into the situation a normative behaviour which is independent of status: in fact it is a question of refusing to decry a work-mate. Thus the salience of this norm over-rides the element of conflict in the situation.

As for the 'casino-gaming' scenario it offers a situation whose essential feature is one of being extraordinary and remote from reality.

Though rapidly presented, this research shows clearly that the meaning of a situation does not depend solely upon its logical structure, but upon its representation as induced, amongst other elements, by how the task is 'dressed-up' and the context of the task. The scenarios used in the experiments convey meanings and evoke behavioural norms. This representation and the responses to the context depend moreover on the social position of the subject in relation to the elements in the situation with which he is confronted. It therefore appears that all representations must surely be called 'social representations'.

II.   The characteristics of a social representation

The experimental research has allowed us to show that the behaviour of an individual or of a group is determined by its representations. But these studies also allow us to understand more fully the *nature* of these representations and to put forth hypotheses concerning their essential features. In this second part of the paper we are going to present our point of view on these matters.

1.   The notion of the 'nucleus' of a representation

The representation can be defined as comprising the totality of information, beliefs, attitudes and opinions which an individual has acquired with respect to a given object. All authors agree in adding that this aggregate is organised, that is, that the elements comprising a representation are inter-dependent and arranged in a certain hier-archical order. In our own work we have tried to analyse the nature of this organisation and our results have allowed us to formulate a general hypothesis which we can express as follows:
All representations are organised around a nucleus.
This nucleus is the fundamental element in the representation as it determines both the meaning and the structure of the representation.

The nucleus – or structural core – of a representation takes care of two essential functions:
– *a creative function:* it is through this component that the other elements comprising the representation acquire or change their meaning. It is that by virtue of which these elements acquire meaning and value
– *an organising function:* it is the nucleus which determines the nature of the links uniting the elements of the representation. In this sense it is the unifying and stabilising element in the representation.

2.   The nature and determination of the nucleus

The nucleus of a representation is determined on the one hand by the nature of the object presented, and on the other by the relationship which the subject has with this object. Or to be more precise it is, in the last analysis, the situation in which the representation is produced which will determine one or more central elements.

For example in situations of operational analysis one can consider that it is the element (or elements) which are valued for their functional significance which will be central. The studies of D. Ochanine (1978) in industrial psychology provide an excellent illustration of our point of view by demonstrating that in a professional activity the working images which guide the operator's behaviour are functionally distorted and that the components of the representation which are overvalued are those related to the nature of the task for the operator.

Conversely in normative situations – representations of social objects, of situations in which operational activities are associated with evaluative connotations or have socio-affective implications – one may presume that the valued elements, those which will comprise the nucleus, might, for example, be a strongly anchored stereotype or a strongly held attitude on the subject's part with respect to the object of the representation or an element of it. The investigations of P. H. Chombart de Lauwe (1963) seem to us to illustrate very well our point of view when they draw attention, for instance, to the fact that the representations of women in society are organised around what he calls a 'static core' comprising stereotypes of strong affective significance.

The nucleus is thus a sub-assemblage of the representation comprising one or more elements whose absence would either dismantle or radically alter the representation considered as a whole.

3.   The role of the nucleus in the evolution and transformation of a representation

We said that the nucleus was a creator and organiser of the representation. Taking account of these two characteristics we might add that it is likewise the most *stable* element in the representation, that is, the one which most resists change. In other words, the evolution of a representation – taking account of the rules of economy which govern cognitive phenomena – will start with the modification of the non-central elements or the peripheral elements. In fact the transformation of the nucleus calls into question the totality and structure of the representation. A representation is thus likely to evolve and change superficially by a change in the meaning or the nature of its peripheral elements. But it can only be radically changed when the nucleus itself is called into question.

4.   Elements of an experimental verification of the existence and role of the nucleus

The studies we have successfully completed and of which I gave a few examples in the first part of this chapter amount to a preliminary experimental verification of our theory concerning the nucleus.

In truth, we have been able to marshal evidence in the context of the interactions we have studied that the representation of the opponent was organised around a central component comprising a behavioural characteristic: *reactivity*. Indeed it is this component which gives the representation of the situation its meaning. In other words, for the subjects it both defines and distinguishes the features of the situation.

Put another way: it is the presence or absence of this element which constitutes for the subjects a state of affairs where co-operation is foreseen and allowed (reactivity being present) or not allowed (reactivity being absent). Consequently, it is undoubtedly this element which is central in the representation and which, by virtue of this fact, is the source of the observed behaviours.

The element of reactivity is certainly the nucleus of the representation in that it makes the interaction meaningful, *it structures how the situation is represented* and as a consequence it *determines the behaviour* of the subjects. Then again, our results confirm the fact that this is *the most stable* element in the resulting representation, that is, the one which does not change even if the information received contradicts it. The resistance to change of the nucleus is equivalent in the subjects to the process of reinterpreting the information they receive: the same piece of information is interpreted in line with the nucleus. For instance, subjects who have a representation of the opponent as non-reactive (i.e. those with a 'machine' as opponent) and who are confronted by behaviour which is in fact reactive consequently interpret this behaviour as being rigid and inflexible.

5.   Difficulties in locating the nucleus

In the present state of the methodology for the study of representations the locating of the organisation of the representation and of its nucleus poses enormous problems. Work currently in progress in our laboratory (see Flament, 1979) is precisely concerned with the attempt to develop methodological techniques suited to these analyses and it appears that the exploration in depth of techniques for *analysing similitude* might furnish a very rewarding method of analysis for our current needs. Alongside these studies we are at present also endeavouring to bring to a head *experimental techniques* for locating nuclei: techniques for the development and destruction of representations (the part played by suppressing or by introducing such and such an element into the production of a given representation) and techniques of analysing interpretative systems (exercises of interpretation starting from certain elements related to the object). Thus in the fullness of time we hope to provide ourselves with techniques of measurement and validation which will allow us to formulate a theory of social representations which is more developed and more concrete.

Conclusion

We have tried to show that the experimental approach could play a decisive part in the study of social representations. If indeed, as claim Moscovici (1961), Kaës (1968), Herzlich (1969), M.-J. and P. H. Chombart de Lauwe (1963, 1971) and others, it is important to study representations actually taking place in given social groups, it appears just as important to us to arrive at a description and an analysis of the mechanisms involved in the constitution of these representations and the link between representations and behaviour. Our studies amount to a first step in this direction. Despite their limited nature, they have allowed us to demonstrate that there is indeed a direct determining link between representation and behaviour. They may even – by means of the hypothesis of the nucleus – allow reflection and more fundamental theoretical research.

Notes

1. The reader interested in this subject can refer to my thesis on this theme (Abric, 1976: 173–217).
2. On an analysis of variance test, $F = 2.83 .05 < p < .01$
3. On an analysis of variance test, $F = 4.56 .05 < p < .01$
4. This study is the subject of a publication (see Abric and Mardellat, 1974) where the interested reader will find a much more detailed presentation of the experimental set-up and of the theoretical context of this research.
5. The overall X^2 is significant in the two situations at the level of $p < .01$.

7. Changes in the representation of the child in the course of social transmission[*]

MARIE-JOSÉ CHOMBART DE LAUWE

The social transmission of life styles, of knowledge, of systems of representations[1] and of values is not only carried out from one generation of adults to another, but also through the crucible of infancy, during the most intense years of training and socialisation. Through the socialisation of children, a complete social transformation is brought about. The young generation constitutes an arena for different ideological trends, for pressure groups and for those who maintain power in a given society. But social transmission cannot be reduced to a simple indoctrination of children: they themselves have an active role to play in their own education.

The interaction of the child with society varies according to the status granted to his age group and to the models presented to him by parents, teachers, childhood institutions, the media and his immediate environment. The social class of the parents, the socio-economic, cultural and geographical conditions of each social class create divisions in childhood, whereas institutions such as school and the mass media of communication tend to play a unifying role. Educational aims are in part deflected from attaining their target to the extent that children actually become like the models which are presented to them. This process of identification depends upon practices which are sustained by the milieu, the environment and by reason of the multiplicity of the representations to which children are exposed and which they try to reject or internalise.

I. Social transmission: an interactional process

Social transmission is both the site and the outcome of a field of explicit and implicit forces. The term 'process' expresses the dynamic character of the phenomena analysed. In order to make more explicit our psycho-

* Translated by Mlle Joelle Guillevout

sociological strategy, we will define social transmission as *a dialectic of psycho-social phenomena* which we have attempted to unravel.

At the heart of this process, the social representation turns out to be a central mechanism: it is, in fact, both a psychic mechanism, being an expression of the human mind, and a social mechanism in so far as it is a cultural product. It is thus located at the interface between the psychological and the sociological. It also facilitates communication between individuals and more particularly between generations by suggesting to children how they should perceive and interpret both objects and living beings.

The social representation of the child is among the most fundamental of representations both for individuals and for societies: furthermore, it is basic to social transmission, since it plays such a crucial role in shaping the personality of children. An interactional approach has proven itself to be particularly favourable in observing both the role and the genesis of social representations.

1.   The components of the field

The field of interaction in which these representations are constantly elaborated has been approached from various angles, sometimes from the direction of *society*, and sometimes from the direction of *individuals*. There is always the ever-present concern as to how to fit together again these two poles which have been arbitrarily separated to make them more manageable in terms of research practice.

Society: this is not a vague entity. It cannot be understood by simply introducing certain variables in isolation from one another on the basis of some experimental plan. We have coined the term 'universe of socialisation' to capture the totality of elements which contribute to the moulding of a young individual and which we define as a structured ensemble encompassing numerous conditions: socio-economic, spatio-geographical, institutional, cultural and ideological, all of which intervene in the socialisation of the child in a manner which is both general and specific. Each of these social dimensions can be broken down into variables which are more amenable to control for the purposes of research, as each child grows in a well-defined universe of socialisation.

Research has been carried out on:

The social category of the age grouping of children, or the socio-genetic category in society at large, by analysis of the child's situation, his status, taking into account the dimensions both of the immediate universe of socialisation and of the historical evolution which facilitates an understanding of these origins

the use of this category in the economy, publicity, etc.

the role of the images of the child in the imagination of adults

representations and models of the child presented to the children themselves.

The child: he is at one and the same time (*a*) an *individual* marked by his own personal history, in a constantly changing state, aspiring towards adulthood, but, at the same time, living each instant of his daily life in the present, (*b*) also *a member of a social class*, by virtue of his family and the milieu into which he is born and (*c*) *a member of a certain age group*, by virtue of a common status granted to all children in a given society, in this case, in French society.

This socio-genetic category has a particular status, that of being a dominated category. Being a category which is currently non-productive, it holds a secondary place in the wider society, except within its own institutions . . . and in general discourse! Other 'non-productive' categories include housewives, the aged and the handicapped who are generally assigned a marginal status in consumer societies. Childhood is a protected category; loved and the object of affectionate projections (Chombart de Lauwe, M.-J., 1976). From the perspective of the child two aspects of socialisation have been extensively researched. One analyses the interface between children and the representations of childhood conveyed by the mass media of communication. It also attempts to identify precisely how these representations are received, identified with and internalised; the constitution of these ideal models, and the remodelling of the self-image. The other bears on variations in practice and in the representations of children, according to contrasted universes of socialisation (for a variety of variables) or on standardisation by virtue of their common membership in an age category.

Intersubjective relations: children and adults find themselves in a relation of dominated category to dominant category. The notion of dominance, and hence also that of a power relationship, proves to be indispensable in this situation, both from a theoretical and a methodological point of view. The discourse of the producer and the receiver of representations always differs, even with respect to the same object, and this is particularly so when the object of the representation, that is the 'child' implies a relationship of dominance. In such a strongly affective relationship as that of the parent–child both sides are involved at a highly personal level.

The representation of each member of a dominated category is effected by reference to the model of the dominant category, according to two processes: a scaled-down identification (i.e. resembling the dominant model but with less developed characteristics) or inversion (i.e. with attributes that are contrary to those of the dominant model). The discourse of the dominant category over the dominated one betrays the values of a society. It is doubly interesting to analyse this discourse, because, on the one hand, the attributes which characterise the model of the dominant category are those which are valued by society at large and, on the other hand, the representations of the dominated are vested either with negative attributes, or with attributes which are valued in a compensatory world of fantasy, through a mode of thinking which is mythical in nature (Chombart de Lauwe, M.-J., 1972).

2.   Characteristics of the central object

If the central object of the research to be described is the social representation of the child and its variations, it is not really a matter of precise representations but of a system of representations tied to a system of values which, at times, takes on the aspect of a mythicising way of thinking, or that of a utopian ideal. We are concerned with studying how a society talks about a social category, how it sees and defines this category and the models of it which it holds up. It is in observing how the category functions that it is possible to perceive the role and the origins of the representation.

The conceptions and the images of the child have varied in the course of time, but the theme of the child rarely leaves us indifferent. The fact remains that every individual has been a child whose personality has been formed throughout his childhood, and this he extrapolates to his descendants who will, perhaps, compensate for his failures. For society, all hope of preserving the accomplishments of the past, of effectively carrying through the work of the present and of creating a 'better world' in the future rests with the new generation. Thanks to the mass media of communication, a collective discourse on the child has been inaugurated and has been growing considerably during the last ten years. It extends or multiplies often from an unrealistic image of childhood which becomes a symbol supportive of values.

A central objective of the work has been to find out if there is a central nucleus or foundation in the system of representations. We have observed variations in the representations as a function of how they are produced, broadcast and received and as a function of the ideologies and of the goals pursued by the transmitters with respect to different targets. The effects produced on the children as a result is the final stage in the process of social transmission. This has been analysed, either through the conditions which are imposed upon children themselves but which are conceived of by adults, or by means of the images which are presented to them.

II. The representation of the child in various types of discourse

The system of representations of the child which we are describing has emerged from a medley of complementary research: our personal work over the past twenty years, theses completed in our seminars and field research carried out by a specially trained multidisciplinary group: all in all, a series of works giving a detailed account of the research.[2] It will be possible here only to present a theoretical and methodological synthesis, as illustrated by certain results chosen from among the most important ones.

1. *The fundamental system*

The portrayal in French society of the child in literature, in printed or celluloid images, has been used to support the representations of the child conveyed largely by the mass media. Each character plays a role attributed to his corresponding age category either in real society or in a world of fantasy.

Various studies have been carried out, beginning with the analysis of the *child as a character*. The starting-point comprised a study of how the child is represented in novels, autobiographies, and secondarily in films for adults. Authors give free reign to their fantasies when they write for their peers, or their equals (Chombart de Lauwe, M.-J., 1971). Thus, they can express their fantasies and their desires in relation to their own idealised childhood, or with regard to the new generation capable of building a new society, either 'hoped for' or 'feared'.

The choice of the narratives was made according to the diversity of the writers: 'great writers' or those classified as such in literature, successful but forgotten authors and authors who have taken childhood as their main theme. A selection of narratives and characters was made from a

list of these authors. The guiding principle, here, was the represen-
tativeness of the different narratives and characters. More than repre-
sentativeness the methodological option must approximate that of the
mythology of which we must talk. In effect, it was a matter of finding all
the possible versions of the descriptions and the portrayals of childhood.
Seventy-five texts (twenty-five from before the 1914 war, twenty-five
between the two world wars, twenty-five from the contemporary period)
and fourteen films were retained. The richness of the material led to a
depth analysis which was more qualitative than quantitative. The
method was designed to answer, with the greatest precision, the
demands of the situation. It combines the techniques of thematic content
analysis, semantic analysis and the structural analysis of myths
(Chombart de Lauwe, M.-J., 1971).

Given the fundamental importance of this part of the research, we are
presenting the method which allowed us to highlight the most central
system of the representations. Although the other studies which have
been carried out have their own methodological characteristics, they will
only be cited for reasons of comparison.

1.1 Methodology

The first stage consisted of an analysis of the manifest content of the
narrative. A series of texts, which were as diverse as possible, were
broken down into units of meaning, taking into account everything
which was said about the child shown, commented upon and explained,
directly expressed or expressed by analogies, whether it was a matter of
images, concepts, and of representations offering, in several privileged
instances, an immediate reading of the significance (the image) within
the signification (the concept).

This first study led to the creation of *a dictionary of signs and themes*. We
succeeded in encompassing the semantic field of the word 'child' as well
as the positive and negative values associated with the term and its
equivalents; its analogues and antitheses were systematically registered.
But many of the statements conveyed attitudes, judgements and
situations which went beyond the semantic network of the word 'child'
or even of the broader term 'childhood'. Furthermore, statements
sometimes entailed several meanings. Hence the need to proceed with a
thematic analysis.

The following stage, *the creation of a code*, came about by choosing to
respect the richness and the diversity of the discourse on the child:
several codes and sub-codes have been progressively adapted from this

corpus. Four codes permitted the description: of the character in itself, of interactions between children and adults, of situations and of existential problems experienced by the adult characters or raised on their behalf. They were divided into more and more refined categories.

To better understand the operations, we shall begin with the label 'genuine'. It is a question of *an item which regroups a number of statements* in which the word itself, or one of its equivalents, has appeared, or again in which an element of behaviour, or an attitude of the character can be classified as expressing its genuineness. Other items such as 'true', 'exacting', 'present' etc. . . . are its semantic equivalents, as they are often associated with the same character. These items are regrouped into a *category* 'characteristics of the idealised child' which makes up a part of the *sub-code* 'the symbolic character and the idealisation of the child'. One of the components of the *code* 'the character in itself' carries three other sub-codes. In the sub-code related to the idealised character, another category brings together the statements dealing with the physical portrait, 'a significant portrait'. This category combines images, meaningful and more complex interpretations related to the body. A third category 'nature and the role of character' includes various statements which allows one to glimpse a direct symbolisation of the child and a form of mythicising thought, such as 'the true man-child', 'the instrument of destiny', 'a race apart', etc. (Chombart de Lauwe, M.-J., 1971).

This description clearly reveals that, although the analysis is part of the manifest content, *the latent content* is very quickly seized. The association of images and concepts appears frequently enough to allow us to deduce the meaning from the mere images. Systematically used equivalents have also permitted the inference of certain contents from partial and allusive discourse. *The longitudinal analysis, internal to each narrative*, was an indispensable part of the work, though it was too restricted to allow us to draw conclusions about the representations of the child in contemporary French society, and the evolution of discourse pertaining to the child since the nineteenth century. How can we tell if different narratives derive from a common system of representation? It is the analysis of values which gave us the clue to understanding system indicators.

Beginning with the semantic field of the word 'child', *opposing pairs* were revealed. The characteristics of the positive personality were quite obvious, along with those of the 'bad child'. Similarly the features of the situation are valued positively or negatively in accordance with the opportunities afforded the child whilst adults are evaluated in terms of their relations with the child hero. The pair of oppositions which induced an entire chain of evaluations seemed to be, at the beginning of the analysis, the 'genuine child' against 'the child modelled by society'. Following that, the pole 'modelled child' was associated with the 'adult norm', the research confirming that they both belong to the same semantic field. This new personality is the image and the model towards which modelled children tend and introduces a dimension of the future and of authority in relation to their present life. The two negative characters of the child and of the adult ended by inducing a negative representation of the society.

From the association of the system of both representations and values, two distinct languages *on* and *beginning from* the child emerged. The results offer a synthesis of the constitution of the mythicising thought which underlies the representations of the child in literary narratives and films. But, from a methodological point of view, it is worth while outlining how the different narratives fit within the latent system which was reconstituted.

After a *longitudinal analysis of each text*, a computerised card was established to record the presence and the associations of different sub-codes and categories. This permitted us, through rapid quantification, to follow the evolution of the stated narrative themes which were regrouped historically according to the three time samples indicated above. Moreover, thematic dossiers were compiled thus facilitating research into stability and change in the contents of representations by means of cross-references within the totality of texts. Characters were precisely classified according to the place they held in the overall system.

Each narrative expresses a more or less important part of a common latent myth. Table 1 tries to show this complex system in a schematic way. Each of the seventy-five principal works includes either the vast majority of the codes and sub-codes or, conversely, focuses more narrowly on some limited aspect of the common myth: the happiness of the small child, which portrays a small character which is much analysed in itself, in natural surroundings, a garden and in its own home or, conversely, the drama of a child – victim of his family, or socio-economic conditions, where the social framework predominates along with the relationship adult–child etc. Given the large number of units of meaning in the seventy-five texts it is only possible to show, in a highly schematised way, the general framework within which the analysis occurred. The four levels of refinement are not presented but only the codes, sub-codes and directly only some units of meaning.

Text number one illustrates the vision of a child who, letting himself be carried away in his dreams while waiting for his teacher, glances at the shapes that surround him and discovers a life in them that only children can understand. The characteristics of this child (*L'Enfant avec la figure* by Valéry Larbaud) are much richer than the few units of meaning indicated reveal. But the relationship to the adult is almost absent. The unit of meaning appearing in II is here 'capable of communicating directly with beings and things'.

The second example portrays a small, apparently life-like, character, a fragile child who is victimised by his mother, a tart; by a brutal step-father; and also by the educational system and, later on, when he becomes apprenticed, by the situation forced upon the working class (*Jack* by A. Daudet). These two texts overlap only slightly. The common units of meaning are, in fact, more frequent than is shown by this scheme, which only highlights certain dominant themes.

The third text, the richest one, is a narrative in which the greatest number of the main themes is present (*Le Lion* by Kessel). There are numerous aspects common to this text and the two preceding it. *L'Arbre de Noël* by Michael Bataille has a rather similar profile, but the relation to the adult is positive. The fuller texts allowed us to locate within the overall framework of the texts those which were confined to selected aspects of the discourse on the child and the portrayal of character.

To be even more precise, we must mention that some fundamental themes, such as the genuineness of the child, appear not only as attributes of character, but also in the other dimensions of the code: the relationships with the adults, with other children, situations, the concern shown for the great existential problems. In several narratives, they become actual leitmotivs. Finally, all the characters are described with nuances, and not in a monolithic fashion. The realistic characters possess faults which make them more human and closer to everyday children. Certain faults are tolerated, such as cruelty, because they are attributed to a natural state, while others only belong to the semantic field of the 'model bad child'. This schema must, therefore, be read with caution. If we could define this collection as a system, this only proved that it really functions as a whole in which each element derives its meaning from its location in the totality. This totality remains latent for the greater part of the time, and it is made conscious by only a few writers, even then perhaps unwittingly.

Table 1. *Schematic representation of the content analysis of the narratives*

CODES	The character in itself			Child–adult relations					Situations			Existential problems	
Sub-codes	I	II	III	IV	V	VI	VII	VIII	IX	X	XI	XII	XIII
Text 1		⊕		⊕	⊕				○	○			⊕
Text 2			⊕			⊖	⊖			⊖	⊖	⊖	⊖
Text 3		⊕		⊕		⊖	⊖	⊕	○	⊕	⊖	⊖	⊖

○ = unit of meaning
⊕ = with positive value
⊖ = with negative value

1.2 *The role of this system of representation in society*

The meaning of the two oppositional systems 'genuine child/society' is the questioning of the values attached to the world of adults. The two poles are not represented on an equal footing, their presence is more or less important. At times, society appears as a blur, all the narrative aiming at the enhancement of the small idealised child. Conversely, in other narratives, society becomes the focus of attention. It has destructive effects on the genuine child who becomes its victim. The authors analyse the procedures whereby society integrates and transforms the genuine child according to its own rules. In some cases, he only exists as a point of reference, thus appearing as a lost ideal. The relation between the two ways of existing is established through the diverse situations and reactions of the child. The confrontation can take place at a distance, as if the two worlds were only looking at each other or, on the contrary, it can be very violent. When existing in a favourable environment, such as nature, a garden, some old intimate quarter, the child bears witness, through his everyday life, to his 'other' way of existing, thus communicating directly with beings and things. At times, he submits to the constraints of adult life, behaving either as a passive victim, or revolting against it. The literary narrative gives rise to an affective language and to the evaluations and the imagination of a society or of a social group. Not all the writers go so far as to create a language starting from the child. However, the attributes of the child presented in a seemingly realistic way do not differ fundamentally from those of the symbolised child. The semantic universes of the two personalities are not opposed. The characteristics of the child portrayed in everyday terms are less exceptional than those of the genuine child.

Neither the novel nor the autobiography nor the film in themselves constitute myths. Science-fiction narratives, tales and passages from poetic and realistic novels are closer to the myth, for the following reasons: the small character appears there as unreal and thus he becomes the abode of the essence of childhood. As in the myth, these narratives transmit a message: behind what at first appears as a straightforward statement, there lies a hidden language. The fragmented myth is reconstituted from scattered sequences. A few narratives offer a frame which is almost complete, whilst others only cover one or a few parts of the system, as was pointed out with respect to typology. As in origin myths, the primary state conveys its meaning both to beings and things. A perfect nature, fixed once and for all, is the point of reference for old values. The child is the model of human-kind.

The universe of the child is situated elsewhere, as in all mythical narratives: either in the past, as in autobiographies and certain novels, or in the future, as in the science-fiction narratives where life and the organisation of the society take on entirely different aspects, or in some remote places unknown to the child, such as an African reserve (little Patricia, in *Le Lion* by Kessel) or on the banks of the Niagara (*Kid* by J. Giraudoux). Another element which contributes to keeping this universe at a distance and which applies to all the characters is the presence of a 'different world': this is the world of childhood which transfigures the everyday life, because the child sees realities beyond it which are not perceived by adults. These characteristics of the narratives signify the presence of a mythicising thought, as a latent form of a vivid myth which concerns the present society. Society is condemned for it is unfaithful to the idealised image of its origins.

In each of the media, produced for the same public and with the same objective, the totality of the narratives centred on the same object form a whole of which each is a component: the variability which it brings highlights, amongst other things, the social and individual character-istics of its creator. Consequently, how can the whole of the discourse on the child (here the object), represented differently in different media, be considered?

2.   Variations of the system

2.1   Representations of the child in publicity[3]
The purpose of these social representations is not to produce cultural objects which will be consumed, but to make children consume. This partly answers the question raised at the end of the previous section. The results of this study can be compared to those obtained in the analysis of the adult literature. Publicity gives priority to future adult consumers. It also stimulates children's desires. Nevertheless, it is the parents who spend money on behalf of children. In spite of the fact that publicity and adult literature pursue different goals, hence utilise different images of the child, both share certain adult representations which result from the discourses beginning with and about the child.

In publicity, the personality of the child serves also to indicate the true meaning of things and its presence evokes a manner of being which is different, more authentic. This aspect remains fundamental. Publicity, as a symbolic language, uses the social imagination but has, as its aim, the construction of an artificial reality. Literature often unmasks the oppressive character of social structures. Though the representations of childhood which it offers tend to encourage a regression, a return to the past, they can also create a desire for change and liberation. Publicity, by contrast, criticises only the archaic aspects of society, as its aim is to promote the consumer society and thus the projects of the ruling classes. It assumes the form of thinking in myths relating to the child because the image of the child is a psychological stimulus for the spectator. It is 'an ideological manipulation by means of an intermediate psychological manipulation'.

In the publicity image the child represents freedom, authenticity, and stands for the way to be followed. He is an exemplary model for the adult, who, thanks to the product which is associated with this image, gains entry to a world of progress. The model is thus prescriptive. Throughout her analysis N. Feuerhahn shows how the child is only a pretext for helping to increase the value of the product. The spectator invests the child with various feelings or projects his own onto him, this projection offering narcissistic gratification. The implicit relationship of the child to the adult is felt through this portrayal and the adult is also fascinated by the opportunity to dominate, whilst at the same time evoking his infantile self. The child almost never has a say, and when the portrayal shows an image in which both appear equal, the hierarchy is reintroduced by means of the accompanying text.

Finally, the characteristics of the representation of the child in the publicity make him 'a symbolic substitute for what is natural'. Advertising is built on a basis of mythical thought, but tends also to create utopias, since it aims at transforming society and proposing its most desirable and dynamic aspects.

Publicity also makes use of medical and psychological knowledge relating to the child. Products which are made for the child are given a label of quality because they are supposed to meet some of his 'needs'. Publicity thus contributes to the diffusion of certain information but, at the same time, it prescribes educational behaviour and medical treatment and defines the characteristics which specify the child at a given period. It thus offers models to its child viewers and tries to seduce them into becoming consumers as soon as they are old enough to choose and to buy the objects which are presented to them as desirable. The consumer is formed at a very young age. Publicity thus plays a double role in social transmission; creating both life styles and individual types.

2.2   *Representations of the child in relation to the built environment*

This is a completely different domain, where representations of the child play an important role in social transmission. This time, it is a matter of the ideologies *of planners, of town-planners, of architects who, because of their conceptions of the child, build environments which condition the practices and representations of children.* Taking the child into account in town planning would certainly imply a profound change in the organisation of the district but planners cannot escape from a mythicising way of thinking in relation to the child who is more often the pretext than the beneficiary in the development of new urban structures.

This ideology forms part of the facts which constitute the universe of socialisation of the child; the concept has been enlarged in meaning so as to include social awareness. It encompasses beliefs, representations, values, models and norms. It is a conceptual system. The myth is also a system, a narrative which interprets the world, but which does not have a basis in reality but depends instead upon the imagination and the symbolic. Mythical thinking makes the child unreal. Ideology moulds its practices.

A study was carried out simultaneously on the conceptions and images of different individuals and of groups who are in a position to control the organisation of the life styles of children. Five areas were chosen for observation according to several contrasting characteristics: urban or rural environment, old or new towns, and the place given to the child which may be: unthought-of and a source of difficulties, implicit, thought out as integrated within the overall society, thought to be apart, segregated.[4]

The social transmission followed in these observations takes as its point of departure the conception and status of the child, interwoven with its geographic and socio-economic conditions, in order to lead to the study of personalisation and the inculcation of culture. Two phenomena principally affect social transmission by means of psycho-social processes: the reading of the representations of a society through a study of the environment and the self-assertion of the child through its integration in the space, the tenure of which is only ceded to him by others.

The analyses of the representations concerning the child in the five universes of socialisation selected for the field studies were carried out starting from the positions adopted in speeches, lectures, charters or deduced from the place given to the child and from interviews when

Table 2. *Classification of the five locations used in the study of town planners and architects*

Environment	Urban				Rural
Town planning	New		Old		Old
The place given to the child	Segregated	Integrated	Un-thought of		Implicit
Areas chosen for observation	La Grande Borne Grigny	Villeneuve de Grenoble	Grigny II	St-Paul Paris IV	Villages in Lozère

there were no clearly explicit formulations available. We are only able to give here, by way of example, the most explicit systems of representations: those of the architect of La Grande Borne and that of the Charte de la Villeneuve, and representations arising from several sources which came to light concerning the adventure playground situated in the *IVe arrondissement* of Paris.

La Grande Borne: the ideology of the architect presents the child as a unique entity, without any social dimension, mythicised in a typical manner. Childhood must be lived in isolation. Children need dreams, solitude and even boredom in order to deepen their character. E. Aillaud builds on the hope of changing the world by separating children from adults, 'lost generation'. His system of representation is characterised by two oppositions: child/adult and the individual/crowd. In each instance the first of the two terms are given positive values and the second ones negative values. Providing collective facilities for children is excluded since it is the worst child who always imposes himself as the leader of the group. 'A child worthy of that name cannot play in an adventure playground': the child 'worthy of that name' is the authentic child, not deformed by the bad adult. School is perceived only negatively, as in mythical thought – it is a 'desert for the heart'. As a consequence the schools are situated on the outskirts of the district. Leisure centres are non-existent or recreated only as an afterthought to respond to the needs of child-minding, and to prevent the older children from being bored. The child, thought of in an idealised and abstract fashion, can only adjust to the environment in his dreams rather than by acting on it and transforming it. This situation is accompanied by many delinquencies on the part of children aged between eleven and thirteen years or thereabouts.

Villeneuve de Grenoble: the Arlequin district presented itself as a pilot experiment which accorded a high priority to children in the context of a project on continuing education. A charter set out the objectives: social segregations were to be eliminated and human relations modified. Children played an important role in the conception and functioning of the town. They were looked upon as social and political beings who were responsible and with a creative propensity of their own. The various fields of activity in their life, such as family, school, entertainment, had to be de-segregated as with the aged and with different social classes. Schools and day-care centres merged into unrivalled multi-purpose facilities, where the new culture was in the process of being born. There again, the hope for change rested upon the children, messengers of the new culture: it was a mission which, at times, was very difficult to undertake when their family did not belong to the project.

In each field, there are adaptations to the initial project which were either foreseen, acknowledged or sources of conflicts. It is not our purpose to describe the successive events which have characterised the history of these towns. The various discords which arose in the discourse over the adventure playground in the St-Paul district more easily illustrate how representations vary according to the position of the groups transmitting them.

The adventure playground in the St-Paul district: it is situated in a Paris district which is underdeveloped as far as local facilities for children are concerned. This project served to catalyse the attitudes of adults on the one hand, and the frustrations and desires of children on the other. The principal powers concerned were: elected representatives and the administration, associations specialising in the creation of adventure playgrounds, a parents' committee in the district and playground group leaders. The spontaneous reactions of the people living in the neighbourhood were also recorded. Everywhere, the further removed those responsible were from the concrete reality of the children, the more they froze them in a desocialised representation and turned them into a legend. This is where conflicts arose between those who had the power of deciding and the practitioners, especially when the latter adopted a non-directive attitude, which is their usual role in an adventure playground. Hostility in this respect, from neighbours, parents and leaders of private associations revealed the uneasiness of adults faced with the autonomy of the children when they took the playground for themselves, as if it had been an island of freedom. Here, as in many circumstances where the child appears to be the centre of interest, he rapidly becomes the stakes in debates and struggles from which he is excluded.

The evocation of the idealised child and of all its accompanying symbolism plays a significant role in the artistic creation of certain architects and writers, stimulated more by the image of a state of childhood than by any real children. In other cases, the presentation of a child which is likely to have a gratifying effect upon the adult who contemplates him is no more than a pretext: this child becomes an ornament of the life style or even a simple value-added unit of the dwelling, thus bringing everything back to the role that publicity wants him to fulfil.

III. Representations aimed directly at children: how they are used by this target population

Parallel to our studies into the character of the child in adult literature or films we have carried out research on:

1. *The character of the child in the media which concern children from seven to thirteen years old or thereabouts*
(Chombart de Lauwe, M.-J. and Bellan, 1979)

The authors, who are invariably adults, pursue other objectives: educational or playful, because they direct their writing to another target – the children. In doing so, they allow 'the child' in themselves to express itself. The nature and portrayal of characters are modified according to the images and conceptions of childhood which are held by the creators of this literature and to the more or less favourable reactions of their young readers and spectators, since that which they produce must be consumed and must make a profit.

Given the volume of the narratives produced and the stereotyped nature of the characters, the sample retained is enormous: nearly one and a half thousand little heroes culled from six hundred and forty-three titles, sorted into three types: the novel, where the verbal predominates; the comic and the film which are almost entirely iconic; and a particular type where the normative prevails: biographies of well-known children or narratives dealing with the childhood of famous men. A composite method was developed as much to deal with content analysis as to treating facts; this time, priority was given to quantification and the search for typologies.

As with the study concerning the media aimed at adults, we again selected three samples of narratives: the first sample was drawn from the second half of the nineteenth century and up to the first world war; the second sample from between the two world wars; and the final sample was drawn from the contemporary period. Thus it is possible to make both synchronic and diachronic comparisons between the representations offered to the two age categories in each epoch or between the representations intended for the same category in three different epochs. Another sub-division separated narratives aimed at children according to their different types.

The media intended for children can be considered as a socialising institution for the younger generation. This is a process of socialisation which operates within a given economic and cultural context. The economic importance of these media is considerable, as much from the quantitative, as from the organisational, standpoint.[5] It is a trickier matter to discern their cultural roots. This enormous market conveys various ideological trends but the ideology of the ruling classes is by far the predominant one. The image of society offered here is that of a censored and watered-down world. From a neutral or apolitical angle the distortions of reality allow one to see only a society without any burning social conflicts. The problems which arise are resolved by friendship, courage and morality. The working class scarcely exists. Sexuality does not exist. Overall, the world in which the little hero lives is either archaic, such as a village or the far-away universe of a jungle, or western, modernistic, of the type of 'new highly advanced society', where the characters benefit from television, aeroplanes and rockets. The writers avoid issues which are embarrassing or hurtful not only to children but to themselves. Imagination screens children from some aspects of existence and social reality which they have to face every day: sexuality, injustice and violence. The media which are not aimed at them, but with which they are in contact, such as the news on television, portray very cruel scenes indeed. Sexuality is widely displayed on advertising hoardings amongst other media.

The world of the child, as presented in the media reserved for youth, contradicts and compensates for the actual evolution of society. This is shown in the increase of natural and exotic contexts which has occurred since the nineteenth century, when urbanisation began to empty the countryside and when the mass of children began to live in cities. But other representations seem to have evolved in the same direction as the social transformations. Thus, the fact that pre-adolescents and youths acquire their independence at an earlier age corresponds to an ever-increasing autonomy of the characters: the little heroes direct the actions of adults, they have the status of adults, the existence of a family is mentioned less and less frequently. In fact, it is a matter of a reflected phenomenon which follows the broad outlines of a general evolution and which satisfies, on an imaginary plane, the young readers and spectators whose everyday existence remains that of dependence upon adults. This reflection of an objective phenomenon is even more clearly confirmed in relation to the image of the sexes which is derived from a separate analysis of the evolution in the characters of boys and girls. The attributes and situations which characterise the acquisition of autonomy in children are first to be found with boys, and the same evolution is evident in the case of girls, but with a lag of about one generation.

The representation of children in the media which are targeted at them is a complex phenomenon in which the real and the imaginary are inter-mixed, making up a rich tapestry of meaning. The status of the category of children is inverted because the media are addressed to them. Not only are children no longer dependent upon adults, but they ridicule them and even come to their aid. The little hero possesses aptitudes equivalent to those of an adult, but on top of this he is still a child, with a child's sense of humour and often his authenticity: he is a chimera made up of both adult and childlike features.

The characters are often mythicised and this trend has been on the increase since the nineteenth century: the percentage of those who remain frozen in the same form and who do not grow up has increased. In the narratives aimed at adults we note a parallel movement: authors focus on the question of the children's ages or kill off their characters or, in the case of adolescence, they turn this phase of life into a drama. Getting out of childhood is perceived as a painful experience. Calling society and the adult world into question, as a theme in the media aimed at children, also undergoes changes. Here we note a series of transformations; the characters are less symbolic, they carry within themselves an adult model of life, there are more adventurous characters who perform courageous actions and who are capable of overcoming obstacles before which adults have failed and sometimes even of saving the adults from danger; less naive humour, more comic and funny situations. The questioning of adult values is accomplished by revealing the contradictions and absurdities of adults, in a strongly caustic manner at times, and by the conduct of these little heroes and no longer by the statement of fundamental truths on the part of children.

2.   The field of representations of children:
the dynamics of social transmission

The final stage of social transmissions consisted of an observation of the mechanisms for the internalisation of representations by the children and the re-modelling of the self-image in the course of their development (Chombart de Lauwe, M.-J., and Bellan, 1979). The object conveys representations: the child character having been analysed and controlled, the interactional process is approached, this time from the perspective of the child as a receiver. Their perception and use of characters, which are relatively easy to obtain, are ways of approaching their own representations. The mechanisms of identification (i.e projection and introjection) can be discerned from the characters they choose as models. It is possible to grasp the field of representation already established in children and the hierarchy of values employed. The regulatory and cognitive roles and the personification of given representations as cultural objects in the child character are outlined. At times, however, the character in the mass media serves only to reveal representations which are interiorized by other means than through the media and, again, sometimes the character has a more direct influence in itself, or as a reinforcement of representations which are more or less well anchored. Sometimes, as a result of the reflection which the child undertakes in describing his 'hero' he reconsiders his own self-image. Some children then intend to adjust their behaviour to match that of their model. Imitation could boil down to little more than a party game; an imagination of their life or, especially with the approach of adolescence, it could occasion a remodelling of their own personality.

A survey was carried out on 1,200 children (half of each sex), from nine to twelve years of age, chosen from a sample stratified according to the degree of urbanization, first in a 'department', and then in the region of Paris. The children wrote two essays in response to questions, posed at an interval of one month, on the child character drawn from their media whom they admired the most (ideal model) and about the character they would like to be (identification model), whilst comparing themselves with that character. No list of characters was presented to them and they could express themselves as freely as they wished. It was not the immediate perception and reception of the characters which held our attention, but the lingering mnemonic trace and the interiorisation of representations offered by the adults as models.

The children's discourse is selective; it does not correspond directly to the exhaustive content analysis. Global comparisons of the discourses, however, enable us to highlight the specific character of children's representations. Their concentration on those aspects which they preferably retain expresses their interests. Children rarely describe, for example, the milieu in which their favourite character lives, but they give more details about it when it comes to describing the character they most want to be: the character often seems to be very different from their own self-image, which is perceived negatively by comparison, but the objects and situation which are envied offer a very desirable image of happiness. By studying systematic biases in the attributes of characters and by unifying the presentations of different little heroes, we can detect the presence of an expected model. A sort of *generic image* was found reflected in those characters which are more and more in evidence and dominant in the media aimed at children. (Out of more than two hundred characters cited by the children, some fifteen received 60 per cent of the votes.) This image, in part, distorts the model proposed by the adults. Various tests in the treatment of the data permit us to distinguish amongst the influences that change children's representations, between the models offered by adults, and variables linked to the psycho-biological and social characteristics of the children and to their status.

The example of the representations and values relating to sex illustrates in a particularly rich manner the general process of social transmission and demonstrates its different components. At first, account must be taken of the objects proposed, both quantitatively and qualitatively. The characters are more often boys than girls: 501 as against 382 in the most recent sample. Qualitatively, girls are often imitations of boy's models: a typological study based on a computerised classification technique showed that none of the types was associated with the sex of the character. This absence of a structural link between types and sexes does not mean that the mass media have become a universe where the equality of the sexes reigns supreme. The representation here was achieved by a process of reduction: most of the time, little girls are mere doubles of the male characters, but more limited and insipid. When traditional girl characters appeared they often played only secondary roles and they were never chosen as the ideal model or the model of identification by the schoolgirls who were interviewed.

Given what the media present, *the choice of the children as a whole* is indispensable as an analytic element for understanding the processes of integration: the girls are very ambivalent; 46 per cent of them chose a boy character as their admired hero and 4.8 per cent of the boys admired girl characters. The representation of masculine traits is such that they seemed clearly more desirable. The second part of the survey reinforced this attitude: 95 per cent of the boys wanted to become masculine characters and again a third of the girls were in the same category. Furthermore, a significant proportion of the girls refused to identify with a character, whereas a majority of these, in the first half of the enquiry, had preferred a masculine hero.

These first results, which clearly speak for themselves, were followed by an observation of *the field of representation of each sex*. A certain number of traditional stereotypes have been demystified by the totality of the children. On the other hand, other characteristics translated important differences in the systems of representations of girls and boys. These differences emerge more from the status of each sex, for the majority of items, than from the choice of the model. The numerous results which support this statement can be set in relief by a particularly significant test: this involves the description of the same character, at first a boy, then a girl, by the school-children of each sex. If the motives for choosing an admired character, as for choosing the character one would most like to be, already differ for the totality of characters (girls using moral and relational characteristics, such as 'smiling', 'good example', boys using characteristics which indicate the hero 'who succeeds', 'who dares'), these same motives appeared again in the discourses of each sex in regard to the same character, independently of whether it was a boy or a girl. Differences linked to the sex of characters clearly exist, since such attributes more easily qualify either one or other sex, but the most discriminating variable is the sex of the child being interviewed. Another result also showed the specific nature of the representations and values which have already been well internalised: in decoding the different attributes of the characters, their composite structure became apparent. Now the children, in their descriptions, break down the traits of the adult and of the child, and they carry out this operation according to their own status. Thus, boys perceive and describe characters in a more adult universe, where they live in an autonomous manner, with their friends and enemies, who are men. Girls place their heroes in a childish and protected (by the presence of the mother or of the school-teacher) universe in the company of children, which evokes a family or school setting. There again one must note that the aspiration of boys towards the adult world and towards autonomy and the restriction of girls to a more family orientated way of living and to interpersonal relations rather than to personal conquest constitutes one of the elements of the system of representations which is conveyed by the mass media aimed at children. But these latter accentuate such differences since they project them even into narratives where they do not figure: one can even find them when boys and girls describe the same character.

The data which were collected in the course of our observations of children in different universes of socialization converge when they deal with the practices linked to the status of the two sexes: everywhere the territory, known to, frequented by and appropriated by girls, is more restricted in comparison to that of boys.

Girls submit more easily to orders and their activities are more confined to the family circle. The effects of the different factors of socialization are self-perpetuating.

At the end of the enquiry children compared themselves to their heroes. This confrontation mostly led to a negative self-image, which was sometimes difficult to handle and caused a feeling of inferiority and only sometimes was sufficiently challenging to arouse an effort at self-reform. The mythicising of characters turned out to be an impediment to the development of certain children, since the models did not go beyond an infantile stage. In the discourses of these children frustrations also emerged: many of their desires found fulfilment only in an imaginary world, through their hero as intermediary. One can only, here, raise the problems posed by the place created for this age category in a consumer society where the process of growing up is little affected by direct practice and much affected by compensatory imagination.

The functioning of the system of representations of the child in French society has been identified with the help of the five principal studies. Several of the highlighted findings have served to illustrate in a concrete manner both stability and change in the system of representations and its associated values. It seemed to us useless to describe in traditional research language the series of hypotheses which were proposed in the course of the study. On the one hand, several of the studies which have been considered have each their own quite specific hypotheses and, on the other hand, in a social psychological work of this nature, we did not set out with a single hypothesis, but with a series of hypotheses to which answers were obtained in successive stages, which involved the generation of new hypotheses. The synthesis we have presented aimed at identifying the most essential aspects of the genesis and the role of representations in social transmission. It is a very large field which is likely to require further complementary clarification. New studies are already under way, particularly concerning the internalisation of social models by children. This constitutes the object of study of several specialists in France and in various other countries (see the symposium on 'The internalisation of social models' at the International Congress of Child Psychology, Paris, 1979).

In the light of our present knowledge, we can clearly state the following points:

The genesis of representations can no longer be attributed exclusively to social structures and their transformations. Social representations are built up in the course of interactions between individuals and their material and human environment, by practices which are responses either to the constraints of the environment or to the desires which it engenders. A whole dynamic process is needed to account for such a transformation.

If personality is powerfully structured in the course of early childhood, the individual re-socialises himself in response, on the one hand, to material and ideological changes (which themselves interact with each other) in the society in which he lives and, on the other hand, to his entering new roles corresponding to the different stages of life and to the events of his personal life history. The interactions between children and adults, and in particular their parents, thus evolve: the image of the father which the child discovers is modified in a two-fold manner: the expectations of the son are changed and the father is no longer quite the same, as the presence of the child influences him in return.

The social representation appears to be an instrument which allows the individual or the group to remodel their scale of values and consequently to readjust their behaviour. This central mechanism, in the interaction between individual and society, takes on a particular significance in the socialisation process which is brought about by the creation of that social category of age known as 'the new generation'. Such a process is dependent upon the power relationships between classes, social strata and social categories. The observation of this process starting from the representation of the child was stated, at the beginning of the study, as a fundamental hypothesis which has been confirmed. This has revealed an interactional dynamic. Social mechanisms (since the economic conditions for the production of goods underpins the representation due to the influence of ideology) and psychological mechanisms (perception, identification, internalisation) react reciprocally upon each other; this is why social transmission has been defined as a dialectic of psycho-social phenomenon, in which representations play a central role.

Notes

1. For definitions of 'representation' we refer to a series of books and articles mentioned in the bibliography: Moscovici (1961); Kaës (1968); Chombart de Lauwe, M.-J. and P. H. (1967); Herzlich (1972); Chombart de Lauwe, P. H. (1971; 1975); Baubion-Broye *et al.* (1977); Feuerhahn (1980).
2. Some books and articles that give a detailed account of these methods: Chombart de Lauwe, M.-J., Bonnin, Mayeur, Perrot and de la Soudière (1976); Feuerhahn (1978); Chombart de Lauwe, M.-J., and Bellan (1979); Chombart de Lauwe, M.-J., Bonnin, Mayeur, Perrot, Rieuner and de la Soudière (1979).
3. A thesis by Nelly Feuerhahn (1978) – a research worker at the Centre of Social Ethnology and Psycho-Sociology.
4. This research was carried out with a multidisciplinary team. See Chombart de Lauwe, M.-J. *et al.* (1976 and 1979).
5. See *Enfants de l'image* (Chombart de Lauwe, M.-J., and Bellan, 1979), ch. 2. In France, the turnover of the child book industry was more than 172 million francs in 1972. That of the press has amounted to more than half a billion for the last four years.

8. The representation of the body and its transformations[*]

DENISE JODELET

'At all times and in all places it has been man who has contrived to transform his body into a product of its own techniques and representations.' This lapidary sentence from an anthropologist, C. Lévi-Strauss, which introduces us to the study of the first sociologist to be interested in the body, M. Mauss (1950), points to the psychology of representations as being a privileged subject matter. For there is no doubt that it is in regard to the body that the study of representations most easily illustrates its character as social science, as claimed even here by R. Farr and S. Moscovici. This is so for two reasons: (*a*) research trends relating to the body which are current in the human sciences and (*b*) the special character of the body, being at one and the same time a private and a public object, the representations of which are closely linked with the psychological, social and cultural realms.

The study of the body and its representation

The coincidence appears striking, indeed, between the approach to the body in terms of 'social representation' and the perspective which has gradually emerged in the social sciences since Mauss emphasised the importance of social apprenticeship in the behaviour patterns related to the body. As M. Douglas (1975) reminds us, Mauss saw that: 'the study of bodily techniques would have to take place within a study of symbolic systems'.

Over the last ten years, which have been marked by a flowering of work on the body, reference to the notion of representation has been becoming more and more insistent. Some researchers, along with J. Blacking (1977), point to the 'need to study the biological and affective foundation of our construction of reality'. Others treat the functions and

[*]Translated by Leighton Hodson

211

uses accorded to the body, the practices, regulations and knowledge related to it, as so many instances where one may read of visions of man and of the world, expressions of a social make-believe, of a symbolic order and of a group identity (F. Loux and J. P. Peter, 1976). In all cases, whether implicitly or explicitly, we find the notion of social representation. And when the eye of the sociologist, of the ethnologist, of the historian either of ideas or of medicine surveys the representations concealed in habits to do with hygiene, food and sexuality, in techniques of breeding or maintenance, in scientific and lay forms of knowledge, its method of proceeding links up with that of the psycho-sociologist.

The representations thus apprehended are considered as the psycho-sociologist sees them: either as latent models referring to common systems of thought and value and assuring the coherence of the attitudes and behaviour within a given social regime, F. Loux (1977 and 1979); or as acts of social significance anchoring 'the most fundamental structures of the group in the basic experiences of the body', P. Bourdieu (1980); or as categories creating by analogy social and bodily experience since 'the social body constrains the way the physical experience of the body, always modified by the social categories through which it is known, sustains a particular view of the society', M. Douglas (1975). Such a convergence shows how relevant is the study of social representations to the social field in general. Dealing with the body, a reality which is both social and subjective, the approach of social representations must be developed along original lines (or perspectives) which we will delineate.

The succession of studies we have just mentioned highlights the social status of the body from two points of view: that of its determination and that of its inclusion in the debates which enliven the cultural scene. They show that the experiences, practices and physical states to which representations are linked are dependent upon regulations and social apprenticeships. They reveal also the way in which the body falls under the ever increasing sway of institutions of control in the medical, sexual, sporting domains etc. (Voltan, 1974; Brohn, 1975; Besin and Pollack, 1977; Bernard, 1978), and becomes thereby a subject of debate for anti-establishment and innovatory movements (from sexual liberation to ecology). Thus one can see models of thinking, alongside models of behaviour, altering ways of thinking about, and of experiencing, the body.

On this count, the body appears as a privileged subject for research on social representations, in that it enables us to rediscover the social deep within the individual. It also has something in common with objects which, by tradition, are held in check when one is seeking to delimit cognitive systems whose content and organisation vary according to different social groups. Here we have in mind researches which have taken as their subject: a scientific theory for example, psychoanalysis, S. Moscovici (1961/76); social roles for example, woman or the child, P. and M.-J. Chombart de Lauwe (1963 and 1971); socio-biological values for example, health and illness, C. Herzlich (1969); a collective good for example, culture, R. Kaës (1968). These are just so many socially significant objects around which gather the claims of conflicting ideas and values. They are institutionalised objects to which individuals have access only along socially approved channels and which they acquire through social communication (through the diffusion of information concerning models either of behaviour or socially codified practices). The incidence of these social phenomena will be all the more evident in the case of the representation of the body, in so far as this is captured, with peculiar acuteness – because people are today more open to contributions from other civilisations, from psychoanalysis, from techniques of physical training (bio-energy, primal scream) – in the mobility of ideas and fashions. The representation of the body has a certain historicity as an object of both thought and practice.

But the body has also a 'private', subjective, status which will lead those who study its representation to come to terms with the interaction of the social and of the individual at another level. Several elements contribute to this 'private' status of the body as an object of representation. In this paper, on the one hand, the anaclisis of the representation bears particularly strongly on the bio-physiological functions, of which Kaës here demonstrates the importance, alongside the socio-cultural anaclisis (see ch. 15). On the other hand, clinical psychologists like P. Schilder (1971) and F. Gantheret (1961), have shown how the 'body schema' and the 'body image', which are spatial representations of one's own body with a physiological basis and a libidinal structure, are able to account for bodily actions and the relationships which the subject maintains with himself, with others and with the world at large. This schema, which itself is partially dependent on the affective and interpersonal history of the subject cannot fail to appear again, at least as a residual trace or state of influence, in the mental re-construction of an object such as the body, which is rooted in subjective experience. Finally, it is enough to consider the role of immediate, concrete, experience. This is something which is recognised by all those doing research on social representations. A good example is the work of Jahoda (1979) on the role of immediate experience in the child's construction of economic reality. It follows that, however socially conditioned bodily experience and knowledge may be, they cannot fail, in the representation, to become part of a properly subjective universe of discourse which will come to modify the meaning and the content of what has been acquired socially.

The simultaneously 'social' and 'private' nature of the body makes us face up to three recurrent and interrelated questions which are at the heart of the present debate on social representations:

1 the relationship between social and individual representations referred to in other chapters in this volume (see I. Deutscher, R. Farr, S. Milgram)

2 the relationship between representation and behaviour (see J.-C. Abric, J. P. Codol, F. Fransella, J. Jaspars and C. Fraser)

3 the relationship between social representation and individual and social change (see M.-J. Chombart de Lauwe, R. Kaës, S. Moscovici). This overlaps with the, to date, little-studied problem of changes in systems of representations.

The investigations we have conducted on the social representation of the body are based on these questions. We now present some aspects and conclusions of our studies.

The representation of the body and cultural change

In wondering about how the body is understood, constructed and lived within the world of discourse and practice in our society, this study of its representation is concerned with how the body presents itself to social subjects. Meaning, by social representation, a form of knowledge, a cognitive elaboration which social subjects, defined by their group membership, effect under the influence of social forms of thought and collective norms concerning behaviour, by integrating the facts of their practical routines and their immediate experience. We were seeking to find out how the socially regulated relationship towards that social and private object, which is the body, is expressed and organised at the level of perception, of lived experience, of knowledge and of moral declarations.

Our exploratory study had a two-fold aim:

(i) to identify the mental categories, the cognitive and normative models which control lived experience and our knowledge of, and uses for, the body;

(ii) to grasp changes in the systems of representation in the different social groups and according to the state of social, cultural and economic circumstances in France.

This latter perspective is inspired by the theoretical reflections which Moscovici outlined when he was opening up this field of research on social representations (1961/76). He stressed, at that time, how important it was to treat representations as 'modalities of knowledge' and 'systems in the course of development'. Foreseeing, with his hypothesis of cognitive polyphasie, the possibility of a 'dynamic coexistence of distinct ways of knowing, corresponding to definite relations between man and his milieu', he was blazing the trail to an approach to the study of changes in the system of representation which took account of such 'social situations' as 'the movement of events and of interactional and cultural factors'. This view has hardly been exploited up to now in empirical research. The study of man's relationship to his body in both its social and historical aspects, of which we here present but a glimpse, sets the stage for an approach of this type.

This approach has been conducted in two phases with a view to comparing both diachronically and synchronically, the representations and positions relating to the body. The first study was based on a parallel consideration of two sets of depth interviews conducted at an interval of fifteen years; a second study aimed to isolate, by statistical analysis, the systems of representation of various groups (Jodelet and Moscovici, 1975; Jodelet, Ohana *et al.*, 1980). It is the results of the diachronic study which are more fully presented here; it constitutes a true 'natural experiment' which allows us to locate, in the representations of the body, transformations due to cultural changes.

In the course of the last couple of decades, such changes have been numerous and important, as much in the medical and health spheres as in the spheres of leisure activities, consumption, physical exercise and sport and also, as previously indicated, in the realm of ideas. They are, moreover, very noticeable for the public, who can note their effects in the commonest aspects of social life and exchange. The following brief indications, drawn from the statistical enquiry, bear this out. Thus people find that the treatment of the body in the media has changed in the last fifteen years; it is spoken about more frequently and in different ways (74% of replies). Whereas in the past the language of the mass media appears to have been equally characterised by moral meanings and restrictions (58% of replies), and by limitations on information or by the occlusion of certain aspects of the body (49% of replies), it seems, at the present time, to be characterised more by a change of style; more freedom, less hypocrisy, fewer taboos (55% of replies) than by any improvement in the information presented (only 37% of replies).

The accent, therefore, is on the change in approach to the body and its liberation. The view is the same when we consider social discourse. For 86 per cent of the people questioned the way in which the body is talked about has changed in the course of fifteen years. People talk amongst themselves in a franker, more open, way (60% of replies); certain prohibitions bearing on aspects of bodily life are fast disappearing. This is particularly obvious in the case of sexuality, if we are to accept the comments of 35 per cent of the subjects who see this as a consequence of the evolution in customs and ideas. Changes in private habits are also striking. Whereas 61 per cent of the people questioned had never discussed their bodies with their parents, 96 per cent of them stated that they discussed them with their own children, or intended to do so when they had children. It is obviously in matters of sexuality that prohibitions are being lifted, thus bringing about a veritable revolution in customs, if we go by the practice of nudity: 74 per cent of our subjects had not seen either of their parents naked; 80 per cent of them, however, are prepared to appear in the nude before their own children.

These few data are sufficient to highlight the social repercussions of this cultural change in one's relationship to one's body. They also highlight its meaning – a sense of liberation. This liberation has an impact on how people talk about, live with and think of their bodies. This finding emerges from a comparison over time (an interval of fifteen years) of the discourses we held on the body.

The cultural change in one's relationship to one's body has a direct bearing on how the body is represented. How our subjects express themselves, how they structure the field of their representation and organise their subjective bodily experiences, and how they choose the mental and normative categories which make up their conceptions of their bodies are all modified by this cultural change as we shall demonstrate when we have isolated the dimensions of an approach to the body which structures the field of the representation.

The development of the discourse and the structuring of the representational field

Besides a classic content analysis, the interviews were also subjected to an analysis which distinguised the different types of information on the basis of which subjects developed their discourses. This procedure for defining information, not by its special content but by the source from which it comes, has several advantages: (i) it sheds light on how representations are established and organised; (ii) it subordinates the content of statements to the processes by which they are elaborated and (iii) it brings out the structure of the discourse.[1] This approach was inspired by Moscovici's model for the dimensional analysis of representations and by my own analysis of the 'elements' of the representation, which I developed on the occasion of my research into the social representation of mental illness (1983). In this way four approaches to the study of the body have been distinguished which, based on different fields of reference – two subjective and two social – lead to the following modes of knowledge.

1. The approaches based on the subjective fields of reference reflect the relationship which the subject has with his own body: (*a*) '*bodily experience*' which includes all knowledge belonging to the domain of the direct experience of the body proper, by means of sensory or organic messages, somatic history and daily exercise. A person has some knowledge of his body by walking, by washing himself, by making love, by sunbathing, just as he feels it in pain, illness, emotion etc. This understanding can include experiences which are either imaginary or real, purely physical or psychological, belonging either to the present or to the past; (*b*) '*the relationship of the individual to his environment*' emerges as the role a person gives his body, the place which he reserves for it in carrying out his daily life and the image of it which is reflected in those around him. The external world, in which the subject is situated, is the starting-point for the body poised as the instrument for action, or establishing a relationship, for confirming its social position etc.

2. The approaches based on a social frame of reference include knowledge conveyed by social communication, which may be either formal or informal: (*a*) the approach based on '*social interaction*': the subject, in his approach to the body, makes appeal to facts which he gathered in the presence of a third party, or which he drew from his observations of others. Knowledge, transmitted by direct social communication (peers, specialists, doctors . . .), serves to fill out, and to refine, the representations. Others, in their actual bodily presence, are equally a source of information if one observes their presentation, their expressivity etc.; (*b*) the '*notional and normative*' approach: subjects will specify their knowledge of the body as a biological, cultural and social object, and determine their positions on the problems it raises by relying

on the education provided by the establishments and systems in which they are involved. First, there is the knowledge acquired through educational channels and the mass media, popular science etc. Secondly, there is the knowledge which they retain from carrying out their everyday, or professional, routines (the butcher's shop is frequently referred to by women to describe the workings of the body, just as men refer to cars). Lastly, there are all the points of view, principles and moral customs which subjects may borrow, knowingly or not, from the value and belief systems to which they subscribe, by virtue of their membership of particular social, religious or cultural groups.

The first two approaches are characterised by the involvement of the subject in his bodily experience; the last two presuppose a more distanced and abstract point of view. These approaches reproduce, at the level of the structure of the representational field, the duality of 'private body' and 'social body'. The comparison between them in table 1, which sets out the frequency of use of the different types of information in each of the interview samples,[2] shows that the discourses, for the most part, organise themselves around the first and the last approach. This dominance remains constant in time. In the two samples there seems to be little inclination to approach the body as the mediator of the relationship between the individual and the external world or as mediated by direct social observation and communication. And this is so to the benefit of approaches where individuals are personally situated, either in the uniqueness of a lived experience, of which their body is subject, or in the community of shared knowledge and rules, of which their body is object.

Liberty and involvement

However, beyond this general structure of the representational field the interviews are characterised from the one sample to the other by an evolution in mental attitude. A prime indicator of this phenomenon lies in the fluency of the discourses. For an identical number of words, the numerical importance of the references to the different categories of knowledge increases appreciably when one moves from the first to the second sample. The expression becomes freer and more committed. The statements are more varied, less redundant; the representation is richer and more subtly shaded in its dimensions. Fifteen years ago, subjects tended to focus on a limited number of themes and to reiterate their opinions. Now, however, the body presents itself as a more open, more

Table 1. *Approaches to the body according to sex and sample*

	Old sample			New sample		
	Total	Men	Women	Total	Men	Women
Bodily experience	1414 (35%)	579 (29%)	835 (40%)	2369 (38%)	1098 (35%)	1271 (40%)
Adjustment to the environment	475 (11%)	210 (10%)	265 (13%)	824 (13%)	400 (13%)	424 (13%)
Social interactions	330 (8%)	181 (9%)	149 (7%)	669 (11%)	356 (12%)	313 (10%)
Conceptual and normative approaches	1900 (46%)	1050 (52%)	850 (40%)	2419 (39%)	1255 (40%)	1164 (37%)
Total number of mentions	4119 (100%)	2020 (100%)	2099 (100%)	6281 (100%)	3109 (100%)	3172 (100%)

accessible, field of exploration, a more active field of preoccupation. Liberty and involvement are today the hallmarks of discourse on the body.

Another indicator of this phenomenon lies in the evolution of references to the different registers of information which emerges from table 1. Taken all in all, less importance is now attached to received opinion and custom. The approach to the body is, therefore, less abstract, and less distanced, than it used to be. The expressly socialised aspects of the body are blurred in the representation in favour of elements which reflect more directly the subject's own body. This shift of emphasis reflects subjects' personal involvement in their discourse. It also reveals the interplay between prohibitions and social models. One can hypothesise that, in the development of discourse, one is governed, either by the concern to be reticent about one's body or, on the contrary, by the need and the wish to talk about it. Choices relating to received opinion and custom would convey, therefore, the effect of a constraint, a holding back; those relating to the experience of one's own body would convey a greater acceptance of physical experience, and so a freer position. The anchorage in lived experience would imply likewise a harmonious, non-conflictual, relationship with one's own body; whereas recourse to a set of abstract formulations would be a way of enrolling one's body in the problematic issues of one's time and in the conflicts which result from them. These hypotheses are consonant with the statements made here by R. Kaës concerning the double anaclisis of representations. They enable us to indicate one of the loci in the representation where the effect of liberation comes into play: the opposition between 'private body' and 'social body'.

Male body/female body

Another point of change stands out if we consider, still with reference to table 1, how the male and the female discourse has evolved: that of the opposition: male body/female body. The impact of cultural change affects the outlook of each sex differently. Women who, in the past, had a more open relationship with their lived bodily experience than men, remain stable in their manner of approaching it today. On the other hand, the approach of men is shifting, with references to their own bodies more in evidence, balancing the net reduction in developments of an impersonal nature.

Other data, based on the comparison, subject by subject, of the relationship between appeal to lived experience and abstract statements, corroborate the fact that the position of men approaches that of women in according a lesser place to abstraction and a greater place to the body proper. Thus it appears as if men, in the first sample, take refuge in the impersonal more than women do (significant at the 0.01 level). In the second sample this is the only category for which there is a marked scatter in the distribution of men's answers, and this mainly in the single domain of lived experience. Knowing that the increased dispersion signifies less agreement on the norm we may conclude that the current male discourse is marked by greater freedom. On the other hand, the analysis of the evolution of the discourse, according to the different phases of the interviews,[3] or according to the increase in references to one single approach from one sample to another,[4] reveals, in women, a tendency to relate more readily, today, to abstract developments, and to oscillate between lived experience and reflexive distancing. In this overlapping women reveal a body consciousness which is more vigorously invested with ideology. What does this mean?

The fact that the change in customs and ideas has a differential impact according to sex indicates that men and women are located in the field of quite specific social pressures from which they escape by different paths. If the evolution of male responses is evidence of a phenomenon of liberation in the relationship which they maintain with their own bodies, the free and candid relationship which women had, and preserve, in their lived experience, like their tendency to encompass conflicts of an ideological order, leads us to look elsewhere for the effects of social pressure. As the content of their discourse shows, women adhere to the claims of the feminist struggle which denounces their alienation and their reification. Liberation, for them, is less a question of lifting prohibitions than of emancipation in relation to an imposed condition. Thus, for women, it is the social definition of their status, and the equally constraining image of their bodies, against which they rebel ideologically. For men, it is the repression of lived experience, and a narcissistic relationship to their own bodies, from which they break free. The structure of the dialogues carries the traces of this situation and bears witness to it.

Body–object/body–machine

This dynamic of change between the sexes, brought about by the waning of a double standard, will be illuminated by the results of a word association test on the word 'body' which was carried out on the occasion of the second series of interviews. The associations seem to be governed by a double process: evolution in regard to form but hysteresis and retentivity in regard to content.

Indeed, the associations aroused by the word 'body' are numerous and reveal a wide range of individual differences (Moscovici, 1976). If one refers to the laws of word association, one may detect there a sign of originality in the mental production; and a sign of liberation in relation to systems of norms and values, which ordinarily assure the stability of cultural frequencies in word association. In this respect, men show a greater verbal fluency and an idiosyncratic lexical range. With women the vocabulary is less rich and its frequency of use higher; this redundancy reveals a tendency to homogeneity. It all seems as if, for men, the liberation of thought took on a very individualistic form whilst for women it bore the mark of group solidarity. Is this the mark of a condition or of an ideological effect?

But the most instructive feature lies in the differences between the sexes in semantic content, the most striking aspect of which concerns the emphasis on anatomy and organic functions. Female associations yield a body 'cut up into small pieces' where anatomical elements are juxtaposed. The listing of them, which is fragmentary, does not concern the internal parts of the body, but elements which have either a connection with the outside, whether it be to do with contact or appearance (hands, eyes, face ...) or an erotic connotation (breast, mouth, flesh ...). Men approach the body as a 'functional whole': they produce associations which reflect images of material or functional wholes (cellular mass, cybernetic machine, official assembly ...); and are alone in mentioning the internal organs; they call to mind states of organic change with connotations of anxiety (death, accident, suffering ...). This is not the case with women, whose associations have a euphoric tone, which contrasts with those of men in associations relating to physical potential: where men say delicate, ephemeral, woman say life, procreation, robustness, energy.... These associations yield an implicit vision which is still lively in each sex, despite the denials of modernity, and one which opposes 'woman-object' and 'man-machine'. This opposition masks another: female vitalism and male anxiety. We shall come back to this. Another difference merits attention: that observed in the symbolic universe. Certain poetic reminiscences or phonetic associations denote a distancing with respect to the proposed stimulus. This type of usage is characteristic of men, as if, the body remaining a taboo object, they were looking for a means of escape. Women do not escape by means of a play on words, but have a marked tendency to locate the body in a debate which is either psychological or moral.

Word associations appear to us to be quite expressive of the dynamics of change in the representation of the body which locate it, in a somewhat conflicting way, between the poles of tradition and of modernity. The contents of the associations reveal a traditional image of male and of female bodies; their form is indicative of the way in which men and women encompass modernity: on the private level and in freedom of expression in the former case, and by a communality of shared circumstances and ideological emancipation in the latter case.

The different indicators which we have just examined bear witness to the indirect and unconscious effects of cultural change on the structuring both of discourse and of the general features of the semantic field of the word 'body'. They indicate, each in their own way, but in a perfectly concordant manner, the points where the mobility of representations and the dynamics of their change are situated, as well as the stakes and conflicts: freedom, involvement, rehabilitation of one's own body in the face of social constraint, in the form of norms and ideology. We shall find other expressions of this mobility by exploring the two main approaches to the body. The limitations of this chapter do not allow us to tackle the whole of the field of the representation of the body.

The restoration of one's own body and the onrush of hedonism

The effects of the liberation movement will be felt directly in one's understanding of one's own body. The analysis reveals various modes of knowledge, recovering experiences of varying richness and importance: sensory information (sight, touch, other senses); movement, sporting activities; pleasurable bodily states (experience of well-being, sensual and sexual pleasure); inner awareness (consciousness of the body in general or of bodily functions); morbid bodily states (pain, discomfort, illness, deprivation); bodily changes (growth, biological evolution, sexual development); medical treatment and aftercare; contacts with the natural, material and social environments; bodily appearance (physique, dress, attractiveness); experiences of psychological origin (dreams, fantasies, emotions). These different elements of information constitute the 'lived experience', a special sector of the field of representation, the diachronic comparison of which can be seen in table 2.

Table 2. *The dimensions of bodily experience in the two examples*

	Old sample			New sample		
	Total	Men	Women	Total	Men	Women
Sensory information	132 (9%)	37 (6%)	95 (12%)	124 (5%)	72 (6%)	52 (4%)
Movement	135 (10%)	57 (10%)	78 (9%)	217 (9%)	116 (10%)	101 (8%)
Pleasurable bodily states	87 (6%)	44 (8%)	43 (5%)	358 (15%)	182 (16%)	176 (14%)
Inner awareness	187 (13%)	81 (14%)	106 (12%)	124 (5%)	67 (6%)	57 (4%)
Morbid bodily states	271 (19%)	148 (26%)	123 (14%)	340 (14%)	166 (15%)	174 (13%)
Bodily changes	135 (9%)	46 (8%)	89 (11%)	287 (12%)	86 (8%)	201 (16%)
Treatments and care	66 (5%)	31 (5%)	35 (4%)	114 (5%)	57 (5%)	57 (4%)
Contact with the external world	41 (3%)	16 (3%)	25 (3%)	209 (9%)	90 (8%)	119 (9%)
Bodily appearance	221 (16%)	60 (10%)	161 (19%)	326 (14%)	136 (12%)	190 (15%)
External manifestations	29 (2%)	6 (1%)	23 (3%)	51 (2%)	25 (2%)	26 (2%)
Imaginary experiences	74 (5%)	39 (7%)	35 (4%)	157 (7%)	76 (7%)	81 (6%)
Emotional feelings	36 (3%)	14 (2%)	22 (2%)	62 (3%)	25 (2%)	37 (3%)
Total number of mentions	1414 (100%)	579 (100%)	835 (100%)	2369 (100%)	1098 (100%)	1271 (100%)

The change which stands out most clearly concerns the perception of bodily states. Whereas the taking into account of negative states, like grief, illness etc. was dominant in the first sample, which had little access to bodily pleasure or well-being, it is, on the contrary, to pleasurable states and sensations that subjects turn today when it is a question of knowing something about their own bodies. Certainly morbidity is far from being absent from their thoughts, but it is less vital, and this attitude goes along with a reduction in the attention paid to all those internal messages which were earlier of undoubted importance. Detachment with regard to the bodily interior is matched by an opening out to the external world with the taking into account of contacts with the environment, a mode of understanding the body which also involves sensuality, whether the sensation comes from contact with the natural elements or from the presence of other bodies.

It is as if modernity, over and above a greater liberty of expression, brought with it a change in the relationship to the body, which is now invested with sensuality. It does not seem that the effect of lifting prohibitions, now permitting the open expression of what previously was done without comment, could by itself explain either the onrush of the hedonistic, sensual and sexual dimension in its massive and systematic form or the fact that it operates at the expense of functional preoccupations and of the awareness of painful or morbid states. On the other hand, the thematic analysis of the interviews reveals a representation marked by the decline of the 'body considered as a biological organism', closed in on its functioning and its failings, and the rise of the 'body considered as the locus of pleasure', open to the world and to others. In the restoration which subjects are making of their lived experience, the dimension of pleasure invades the whole field of feeling: there is an extension of the palette of pleasurable sensations; a deployment of the milieu which both stimulates and reveals something of the body; at a sensory or active level there is the dominant role accorded to the human environment in the discovery of oneself. With the emergence of enjoyable awareness the reversal of positions in regard to inner awareness is accompanied by a change in the selection and interpretation of bodily messages. Gone is the so-called 'silence of health' and the one and only voice of illness; the sensations retained are no longer those strictly connected with organic functioning, but those which result from the multiple ways of living one's corporeity. One loses interest in the biological body searching through inner awareness for a sense of life, often associated with a sense of pleasure.

This analysis is confirmed by the replies to one of the questions in the statistical enquiry concerning the understanding of one's own body. Subjects had to indicate the four circumstances in which they were most aware of their bodies, making their choice from a list of twenty experiences referring respectively to morbid states (being ill, having a pain . . .), functional states (digesting food, being out of breath . . .), to forms of activity (making an effort, sport . . .) and to sensual pleasure (making love, sunning oneself, eating well . . .). Hedonism and activity won out over morbid and functional messages. Over the whole range of replies, categories of bodily awareness reflect in 45 per cent of cases the world of pleasure, in 22 per cent the world of action, in 20 per cent states of morbidity and in 12 per cent functional states.

Furthermore, the combination of the four replies given individually has permitted the establishment of a typology of lived bodily experience, which characterises each individual by the dominant category of his understanding of his own body. Two major types of approach emerge according to a dichotomy which opposes pleasure and activity to morbidity and functionality. This opposition may be interpreted, in the light of the preceding analyses, as an expression of the opposition between two modes of relating to the body; modern and free versus traditional and restrained. Within this dichotomy 56 per cent of subjects are included with a clear preference for the first approach (37% versus 19%). The remainder of the sample (44%) refer jointly to the two other approaches in their bodily awareness. One can see, therefore, that at the present time the lived experience of the body proper includes a marked preference for sensual and dynamic experiences. That this orientation should be dependent on cultural diffusion becomes evident if one considers the distribution of the types of lived experience, according to age and level of education, which mediates a greater or lesser familiarity with models of recent thinking. More of those under thirty-five years of age are of the hedonist/active type than are those over thirty-five. Those with higher education are distinguished by over-scoring on the pleasure and action categories, and by under-scoring on the morbid and functional categories, in comparison with those who have a lower level of education and who present the opposite tendency (X^2 (significant at the 0.001 level)). Thus the models of thought have succeeded in producing representations which, when collectively shared both in their categories and their content, will structure the representation and the experience that each one has of his own body.

Performing power/vital power

The cultural differentiation in the relationship men and women have towards their bodies is confirmed in the typology of lived experience: men are directed more towards a state of awareness which is organic in character, women towards one which is pleasurable in character, conveying thereby their greater freedom and the positive and vital tone of their lived experience already established at the level of word associations. However, they are far from excluding the morbid – functional dimension and if we return to the diachronic comparison of male and female positions (table 2), we notice that the two outlines converge today in their apprehension of negatively toned states. In fact, the content of the interviews makes it apparent that, in this case, the representations are modified by an experience which is organic in origin.

There is a change in the meaning conferred on morbid states which follows a trend which goes in somewhat opposite directions for each sex. In the first sample men, who worry more than women over their inner bodies, showed rather hypochondriacal preoccupations. In the second sample, their morbid attention is attenuated, but it is focused on a new pole of concern with the fear of deprivation experiences covering the loss of such attributes as hair, teeth, organs, limbs. With women the awareness of morbid states remains stable but, with time, attention is displaced more towards pathology. Whilst pathology increased sharply in importance, loss and symptomatic states, like pain, decreased as important topics of concern. Is it not possible to see, in this two-fold movement, an effect of the change in customs and norms not only on perceptual categories, but also on the expression of fantasies? Fear of castration is more openly felt in men, whilst in women the affirmation of a less restrained body, which is more active both physically and in professional life, causes the emergence of anxiety in the face of threats to bodily function. The importance conferred on various morbid states, besides corresponding to a fact of current experience, may convey either a manner of perceiving the body which is socially approved (e.g. sobriety of dress in the Judaeo-Christian tradition; or sobriety of thought as the only legitimate form of knowledge ensuing from the prohibitions on pleasures of self-attention, among others) or the expression of certain anxiety states related to the body. The evolution of representations shows that what morbidity loses in normative weight, it gains in expressive value.

This expressive value is under-pinned by basic experiences linked to the status of each sex and to their role in the processes of production and reproduction. As proof, the following data from the statistical enquiry can be cited: when subjects are asked if they happen to feel their bodies as a brake, or as an obstacle, the men, for whom this is the case, mention essentially obstacles to the achievement of physical, intellectual and work tasks; women point to restraints related to illness or states of discomfort or blocks of a psychological nature (X^2 significant at 0.001 level). Once again we find here the counterpart of the two visions of the body of which we previously caught a glimpse, especially in the word association test. On the one hand there is the male pattern of 'body-machine', an instrument subject to norms of output and a working model which encounters within itself limits to the demands of efficiency. On the other hand, there is the vitality, expressed by women in the euphoric vein of plenitude and fecundity, of an organism whose strength is intrinsically limitless but which is also vulnerable by dint of external events. Now these same subjects, when invited to say what they fear most for their own bodies, specify, in the case of men, the loss of organs and assaults on the integrity of the body; in the case of women, handicaps and restrictions of capacity bringing with them a complete bodily impotence (X^2 significant at the 0.01 level). The connection between bodily 'brakes' and organic anxieties shows quite clearly that anguish hinges in men on the necessities of a working activism; in women on the preservation of a vital potentiality. And what is at stake, in this organisation of the representations, are the respective statuses of the productive body. These statuses are socially and sexually different for each sex. Here we have the example of a process by which the elaboration of representations and the meanings with which their categories are charged setting in motion the interplay between imagination and social and vital functions or practices. In other words, it concerns the entanglement between the subjective and the social in the elaboration of the representation, which was a problem that we evoked at the beginning of this chapter.

Social models and organic conceptions

This is an entanglement which may favour an upheaval in individual experience under the influence of social changes. A striking illustration of this is provided by the change in conceptions of pregnancy and childbirth which is a consequence of the gradual change in beliefs and mental attitudes, as much in politics as in medical practices. The meaning of words, just like the meaning of acts and their physiological and psychological repercussions, is transformed with the introduction of new values. Our study of changes over time took place at two key moments in the history of female sexuality in France: the introduction of painless childbirth for the first phase, the campaign for the voluntary termination of pregnancy for the second phase. A comparison between the contents of the two dialogues reveals the effect of the corresponding ideas and practices. In the first sample, women stressed the importance of pregnancy represented as the execution of a major biological function, lived through in shame because it bore the sign of sexuality and distorted the appearance of the body. As for childbirth nothing was said about it directly. On the other hand, all subjects, including the men, spoke of the technique of painless childbirth as a scientific achievement which permitted an escape from the religious curse of suffering and as a victory for knowledge and voluntary control over the body.

This perspective is turned on its head in the second sample. It is childbirth, in fact, which is put forward as a revealing act in which a specific power is made evident. The importance accorded to abortion as a female campaign and act of choice, the development of gentle techniques centring on the pregnant woman during labour, have directed attention more to the fact of birth than to that of pregnancy. Pregnancy, however, is depicted as a happy physical condition, desirable because desired, there for all to see. Through both pregnancy and childbirth, a uniquely feminine power is confirmed in relation to a sexuality which is free of all guilt. Yet, at the same time, no one any longer seeks either to assume or to avoid the pain, which is stigmatised as both natural and medical 'violence' against the body, justifying the application of external means to alleviate it. 'I would never have forgiven my child for having suffered in bringing it into the world', said a young interviewee who had chosen to give birth after spinal injection in spite of the risks of which she was fully aware. We have come a long way from: 'In pain shalt thou bring forth children.' We are here pinpointing the effect of social changes on the active and mental relationship to a major biological fact. With the weakening of Christian morality, the affirmation of feminine power in the choice and act of childbearing, and the reintegration of sexuality and pain, the framework of traditional thought is burst asunder. Old categories take on another meaning and are re-organised in accordance with a viewpoint which profoundly modifies both lived experience and conduct. This demonstrates, furthermore, the circular nature of the relationship which exists between representation and behaviour.

Thinking of the body in terms of action and power, women deny its socially created character as an object, not only at the level of the explicit discourse, but also on a more or less unconscious level in how they approach their own bodies. Hence the outline of their representation will differ from that of men. Such is the case for the importance accorded to sensory information and physical appearance through the play of normative and ideological pressures. Let us return to table 2: the sensory data show an overall fall which can be explained by the drop in the number of references recorded by women whereas with men, the references, whilst remaining constant when expressed as a fraction, actually double numerically. This is evidence of a profound change in attitude. All the women in the first sample took cognisance of their bodies through vision, either directly or through a mirror. No more than half of them proceed in this way in the second sample. The comparable figures for men are three-quarters in the second sample compared to half in the first sample. Moreover, the men include all sensory messages within their field of awareness: these include skin and touch sensations, as with women, but also, in a more marked way than women do, sensations of taste, of smell and of hearing. Do women forbid themselves a sensory relationship with their bodies so as not to risk presenting themselves to men and others as objects whilst, in their freedom, they discover a new richness in lived experience? This is a hypothesis which is confirmed by the replies concerning physical appearance which are outwardly similar: a lesser overall importance which can be particularly ascribed to a drop in the declared interest of women whilst men, on the other hand, were decidedly more numerous in allowing themselves to take into account their appearance in terms of physique, dress and aesthetics. A similar tendency can be found in regard to bodily treatment and care: feminine replies remain constant but male interest increases in questions of body care to the detriment of medical treatments and care.

And just as the change in values and knowledge, brought about by changes in social practice concerning the freedom of procreation, has modified the image of childbearing on the cognitive and experiential levels, so too change in the norms relating to female and male bodies affects, not only lived experience, but also knowledge. One finds, in fact, that the changes in the relationship to one's own body meet with an echo in the realm of scholarship. Anatomical physiological representations bear the mark, in their evolution, of the lack of interest in the biological as this is manifested in lived experience. They present, as table 3 shows, a more fragmented rather than a whole character, with the descriptive

Table 3. *Elements of the anatomical–physiological representations*

	Old sample			New sample		
	Total	Men	Women	Total	Men	Women
External anatomical parts	209 (39%)	92 (36%)	117 (42%)	252 (44%)	180 (49%)	72 (35%)
Internal organs	203 (38%)	104 (40%)	99 (35%)	251 (44%)	150 (41%)	101 (49%)
Systems	54 (10%)	30 (12%)	24 (8%)	35 (6%)	22 (6%)	13 (6%)
Functions	72 (13%)	31 (12%)	41 (15%)	35 (6%)	16 (4%)	19 (9%)
Total number of mentions	538 (100%)	257 (100%)	281 (100%)	573 (100%)	368 (100%)	205 (100%)

and enumerative points of view dominating over any analysis in terms of procedures. This is a general tendency which is strong today. As much as the decline of interest bearing on organic functioning these data show the gain in value of all aspects of corporeity, which is as wholly cathected in the realm of knowledge as it is in that of lived experience. But the most striking feature of these data resides in the fact that changes in the positions of men and women, in regard both to appearance and to functional anxiety, have an impact on the selection of the bodily elements from which each sex constructs its anatomical representation. The comparison of the two samples reveals that external parts of the anatomy are now more distinct in the masculine representations whilst, by contrast, women are more preoccupied than previously with the organic (X^2 significant at 0.001 level).

These changes in the structure of the anatomical images unconsciously reflect the re-organisation of the approach to the body in the two sexes. The new latitude allowed to men to interest themselves in their appearance directs attention towards the external body; the fading of the body-as-object in favour of the body-as-activity in women turns attention away from the external body to the internal. The cognitive image given by the first sample is matched by the traditional vision which the word associations convey; that of the second sample proposes a schema expressing both freedom and modernity which leaves its mark on bodily experience as a result of the change in norms and cultural values and in ideologies and social practices. These results lead one to think of the representation as a sedimentary phenomenon, the more or less conscious layers of which are displaced according to their own particular rhythms in a dynamic which has an antagonistic character, as S. Moscovici (1976) noted: 'Creativity and redundancy in representations explain both their great fluidity and their no less great inertia, antagonistic qualities to be sure, but an antagonism which is inevitable; it is on this basis that they are always being transformed whilst surviving quite well.'

The psy-body, locus of conflicts between the individual and society

A dynamic phenomenon functions also on what could be described as a horizontal plane, that is between the different representational fields constituted as a system. With the advent of a liberated body, normative constraint, which is less internalised, will be projected outwards and will be experienced in more acute form as societal oppression. This is what changes in the second dominant field reveal. This is the field which refers the approach to the body to the received ideas and norms transmitted by the formal channels of communication. The importance of the social, abandoned at the level of the body as it is experienced, re-appears as aggression at the level of the body as it is thought. This reversal is brought about by a re-working of the informative facts which are used to decide and fix its points of view on the body; a re-working which leads to a change of frameworks and mental categories.

The conceptual and normative field is organised around three domains of reference relating to, respectively, a scientific, a speculative and a practical approach. The proportion of responses in each of these areas in the two samples (table 4) alone shows how the way of conceiving of the body has changed. With the reduction in importance of the sphere of the biological being confirmed, the body is more often approached in a psychological and social perspective, or even within the framework of moral and philosophical reflection (X^2 significant at 0.001 level). Less strongly defined by its organic materiality, the body changes nature: it becomes a 'natural symbol' to adopt a term used by M. Douglas (1975), expressive of the subject and engaged in the interplay between the social and the ideological. In order to think about the body an ever-increasing appeal is made to the human sciences: it is inserted in a network of determinations and meanings whereby it becomes a 'psychological locus' and more particularly a 'social object'. This is accompanied by change in the way in which the relationships between body and mind and between body and society are treated which we shall illustrate briefly, with the help of an analysis of a few of the themes appearing in the discourses.

In the first sample, the psychological approach, based on the dualism of body and mind, was characterised by a set of problems centred on the control of the body, ranging from the simple mental regulation of physiological mechanisms and of muscular and visceral functions, to the instrumental mastery of resources and organic capacities with a view to accomplishing the desires and intentions of the subject, and even to the domination of an animal nature by a voluntarist discipline.

In the second sample, the dualist model is blurred in favour of a global perspective where the relationship between mind and body involves the adjustment of the individual to his environment. This is how interpretations in terms of psychosomatics become dominant, explaining physical metamorphoses and bodily reactions and changes as the expression of intra-psychic conflicts or as the consequence of the

Table 4. *The dimensions of the conceptual and normative approaches in the two examples*

	Old sample			New sample		
	Total	Men	Women	Total	Men	Women
Biological sciences, medicine	877 (46%)	475 (45%)	402 (47%)	567 (24%)	316 (25%)	251 (22%)
Other natural sciences	61 (3%)	46 (4%)	15 (2%)	44 (2%)	32 (2%)	12 (1%)
Social sciences, psychology	369 (20%)	209 (20%)	160 (19%)	947 (39%)	435 (35%)	512 (44%)
Philosophy, cultural norms	311 (16%)	161 (15%)	150 (18%)	518 (22%)	278 (22%)	240 (21%)
Practical knowledge	282 (15%)	159 (15%)	123 (14%)	343 (13%)	194 (15%)	149 (12%)
Total number of mentions	1900 (100%)	1050 (100%)	850 (100%)	2419 (100%)	1255 (100%)	1164 (100%)

difficulties confronting the individual socially. The fusion of the mental and the bodily leads to abandoning the question of the control and of the instrumentality of the body and to the recognition in the case of the latter of specific demands, needs and language. The spontaneous expression and satisfaction of these specific characteristics are hindered by the dictates, codes of conduct, conventional customs and formal regulations which determine the maximal use and functioning of the body. Finally, it is in terms of opposition and of demands that the body, now that it has become the vehicle of the psychological, is situated in regard to the social.

This is a point of view we meet again when we in fact approach the question of the relations between the body and society. The first sample of respondents thought of the social insertion of the body in terms of its being determined. They underlined its dependence on social regulations whether it was a matter of manners, or of eating habits, or of dress or of the control of sexuality and basic needs etc. Socialisation appeared, therefore, as the means whereby the animal body became human. Conformity with this social order was laid down as being a matter of course within a perspective of social integration. The only and rare cases where this ascendancy appeared to be harmful related to the imbuing of sexuality with guilt as a result of religious and educational taboos without this, however, calling into question, on other levels, the internalisation of social models experienced as necessities.

It is quite otherwise in the new sample of respondents for whom social adjustment becomes a major preoccupation. If, to believe what subjects say, moral prohibitions on sexuality no longer carry any weight, education and social codes and rituals, by way of contrast, are considered to be an obstacle to the freedom of life and of expression of the body. Incidentally, it is less the socialisation of the body that is attacked so much as its transformation into a social object, its standardisation in the consumer society and its direct involvement in social relations. People, especially women, fasten with disconcerting insistence on the ill effects of advertising and of fashion which impose models which one is forced to obey without any commitment. All this only reveals the significance of a feature of our age: the incessant hammering, through publicity, of male and female images which are uniform in their youth, vigour and beauty. Added to this is their denunciation of a system which, under the guise of a fallacious taking into account of the body, turns it, instead, into both the means, and the goal, of consumption. But here is something new – this taking up again of contested issues is coupled with the formulation of a malaise which is felt on the psychological and physical level, in so far as subjects are confronted by an equally frustrating alternative: either to yield to the pressures to be like everyone else, which permits a gain in seduction and security in interpersonal exchanges, but which persecutes the body and loses its identity in a world of objects; or else to reject this pressure, which allows one to dissociate the body from this world and allows its nature to be respected, but which lays one open to the risk of social and professional failure or of sexual and emotional isolation. Here are some other targets for criticism: the pressures of urban life and of industrial productivity which entail a body which is automatised and constrained, excluding the sensuous enjoyment of everyday life, and relegating pleasure to the sphere of sexuality alone 'so that society may continue'. There is no way of escape from this constraint and automation other than the flight towards nature, the hedonism of private life and relationships with others, nor is there any response other than violence.

These indications are corroborated by the statistical enquiry. The influence of modern life on the body is emphasised by 70 per cent of the people questioned. Of these, 63 per cent denounce the normative pressures which society inflicts on the life of the body through fashion, through the constraints of the social or work environment, rules of conduct and etiquette etc. And 40 per cent point to the pernicious consequential effects of the social context, together with the nervous and biological disorders which result from the way of life or from the unprovoked assaults of the environment and the contempt for bodily needs. And in evaluating work, around 52 per cent of the replies highlighted the fatigue and the physical ailments which result from it, 35 per cent of replies concern the unbalancing effects of work and 24 per cent the lack of availability of one's own body which results from it.

Towards the body-subject

Thus cultural diffusion, by making prominent the viewpoint developed by the psychological and the social sciences, provides new conceptual tools, new normative frameworks for thinking about the body, and changes the meaning of traditional categories and the hierarchy of values. This re-organisation occurs in direct contact with the facts of the everyday life of the individuals. It enables them to interpret their social experience and to locate themselves in the modern world. In this process the body takes on new meanings. With its status and its sufferings called into question by the way in which society functions, it becomes the place where the conflicts between the individual and society are experienced and expressed.

This is a view which will be pushed to the limit by those who are most actively involved in the social movements leading towards a new conception of the body: militants from the movements for sexual liberation, proponents of a new politics of the body and those skilled in new bodily techniques. Their avant-garde practice leads them to sketch the image of a future body. This is an image of something uniquely material and impulsive; positively stated in opposition to the pressures of conformity; freed from the masks of a socialised exterior, defended in the uniqueness of its demands and of its bio-rhythms in the face of functional definitions, medical control and the constraints of industrial production. It is a somatic singularity with its own history and it possesses, by virtue of its symptoms, its reactions and its gestures, a power of language. This is a language which expresses personal identity and truth and gives access to new forms of communication between one body and another. In so far as the feeling of social oppression gains strength from the demand for freedom of desire and for individuality in bodily expression, and in so far as this opposition is conveyed at times in the form of violence, either suffered or repulsed, the body in its libertarian stance, and in its results, emerges as being endowed with the powers of social change.

Within the network of determinations, where the individual sees himself as trapped and dispossessed of his quality as subject, is there not, in the making of the body the centre of its own particularity, in endowing it with expressive powers, in granting to its revolts a power for effecting change, a sort of transfer, a delegating of subjectivity? The body has appeared on many occasions as a system of opposition. The opposition between female body/male body is levelling out. That between social body/private body is indistinct. The body-as-object is everywhere decried; it heralds the advent of the body-as-subject.

These indications prefigure the symbolic evolution of the body in modern consciousness. To trace this evolution was a logical conclusion to the study of a social representation which, as a social product, we have shown (i) that it has a profound influence on the relationship which an individual maintains with his own body at the level of lived experience and of conduct whilst (ii) at the same time, it bears the lineaments of social thought.

Notes

1. The procedure used involves a reversal in perspective to that which is generally adopted in the treatment of depth interviews. Instead of isolating the contents of different statements and then re-grouping them according to *a posteriori* categories we were forced to characterise the different statements by the type of information to which the subjects had recourse in order to develop their points of view independently of the particular contents of those views. This analysis was conducted with the aid of a coding grill comprising more than 100 items descriptive of the different types of information used by subjects. These items were grouped into four classes according to the source of the information which led to the different approaches to the body.

2. The coding grill served as the base for the quantifications which were necessary for the diachronic comparison between the two bodies of interviews. The comparison must be carried out on homogeneous protocols. We worked on the first twenty-five pages of the typewritten re-transcription of the interviews (this number corresponds to the shortest of the transcriptions we obtained and to an average interview length of around 90 minutes). The coding of references according to the different types of information was carried out page by page. Each use of an item was repeated only once per page without taking account of cases of redundancy at the level of contents. In the final phase we summed up across the totality of pages, the number of mentions collected for each of the items of information. It is the total of the different mentions of items which is at the base of the tables presented in the text.

3. The comparison of the relevant importance which the different approaches receive as the interviews unfold was carried out by coding mentions in blocks of five pages. It appears that men begin, in both samples, their exploration of the body by minimising lived experience but, whilst in the former sample their penchant for abstract developments increases as they advance in their discourse, in the new sample, they depart from this attitude in favour of accentuating lived experience: rational defence yields to the spontaneity of personal involvement. As for the women they change both in the manner of their approach to the body and in the course of their development. They are more clearly orientated towards lived experience at the start of the interview, more so in the former than in the recent sample. By contrast they show a stronger tendency in the new sample to allow abstract discourse and appeal to lived experience to co-exist as the interviews develop.

4. The increase, in percentage terms, in the number of mentions relating to each of the approaches, in the second sample compared to the first, is as follows:
   Lived experience: men 89%   women 52%
   Conceptual normative approach: men 19%   women 37%

9. On the system of representations in an artificial social situation[*]

JEAN PAUL CODOL

Introduction

The experimental approach always limits the researcher in a number of ways because it involves the taking into account of generally simple and precisely defined variables which can also be manipulated. It requires any analysis undertaken to be based on concepts which, due to the requirement that they should denote quantifiable phenomena, are often subject to definitions which are more rigorous than those commonly allowed in other modes of investigation.

The experimental study of representations is particularly subject to the foregoing constraints: first, because the idea of representation in the various disciplines covers, as is well known, a very wide and imprecisely delineated field; secondly, because the underlying concept is one of the most complex and semantically diverse concepts in the human and social sciences.

The experimenter must define representations in an operational context, and so the study of them in the laboratory involves a notable reduction in the richness of these associated ideas.

Consequently, it is hardly surprising to find that psychologists in general, and experimental social psychologists in particular, have mainly approached the question of representations from a *cognitive* perspective. This approach undoubtedly accounts only in part for what we understand by a representation, particularly one which is termed 'social'. It seems obvious, in fact, that one cannot achieve a comprehensive study of social representations without an interdisciplinary cooperation in which each, in accordance with the traditions of his own specialism, makes but a limited contribution to the amassing of a wider corpus of knowledge.

I am not here suggesting that the study of social representations can be

[*]Translated by Dr Geoffrey Woollen

completely divorced from a cognitive approach: But care is required with terminology here: a fairly widespread current usage would restrict the term 'cognitive activity' to intellectual operations alone. This definition, however, is far too restrictive and would lead to a strictly reductionist viewpoint which is quite unacceptable (Codol, 1969b). In fact, cognition, in its original derivation, has to do with a far broader range of phenomena, denoting *all the activities whereby a mental apparatus classifies information into types of knowledge.* In no way can this ordering be reduced to a series of formal operations – some sort of alchemy of neutral elements (however complex) which somehow is carried out quite independently of people's psychosocial experience. For at all stages of cognitive processing – that is the selection, transformation and organisation of information – the following can be expected to impinge: opinions and attitudes; affectivity; emotions; the attribution of meaning; value judgements, etc. What is more, the pieces of information themselves are more often than not social in origin, and the resulting knowledge is not expressed within an empty framework. The items of information, quite to the contrary, are wedded to all the kinds of social experience relating individuals to each other: attraction and repulsion; influence; power; the need for approval; the desire to be different, etc. Within this plurality of phenomena, knowledge develops and is disseminated. To the extent that they can be defined as 'products and processes of the mental reconstruction of reality by one human mind aided by another' (Moscovici, 1979), social representations incontrovertibly partake of the nature of cognitive phenomena – even if certain of their characteristics partially escape being included within this framework.

It is not irrelevant to note the reference to a 'mental apparatus' with respect both to cognition and to social representation. For we must accept that each individual integrates, appropriates, modifies and creates, at any given moment, the social forms of knowledge belonging to the cultures and groups in which he is involved. So however numerous may be the agencies (such as institutions, powers, laws, the media) which mediate and underlie social representations, in the final analysis it is always individuals who convey and articulate them.

Hence it is quite legitimate, by observing and questioning subjects, to endeavour to snatch glimpses of social representations reflected in individual patterns of behaviour.

In fact, the difficulty both with cognition and with representations lies not at all in their social character, which is confirmed by all the evidence, or in how they are expressed in individual behaviours, but in their content and in the mechanisms which sustain them.

On the question of *content*, it is admittedly very difficult to propose any general rule at all. The content of a representation obviously depends principally upon the object to which it relates: at a particular moment in time, in the context of a given culture and within a particular group, any object, whether it be a material or symbolic one, could be the object of a social representation. Psychoanalysis, illness and culture are examples; so too are the town, the family, woman and the child; so too are friendship, the body, the group, the house, master and pupil, any technical tool, God, the person or myself.[1]

So what we urgently need are monographs which isolate the origins of a particular representation, its anchorage in a tradition and its development in popular lore, its functional significance for the group which conveys it, and its relative importance in the social life of institutions and of people. The analysis one carries out cannot but be a multi-disciplinary one: at one and the same time historical, ethnographical, political, sociological, juridical, etc.

As far as the *mechanisms* and the processes whereby representations are elaborated and communicated are concerned, they can only be understood in a dual and doubtless highly complex way which involves, on the one hand, both intergroup and interpersonal relationships and, on the other hand, the more specific cognitive mechanisms whereby individuals first perceive and then reinspect reality.

The experiments and findings which are briefly presented in this chapter do not claim to be any kind of study of the *content* of particular social representations. Their aim is merely to indicate some mechanisms – fairly general ones, it is hoped – whereby representations come about. Or, more specifically, we are dealing with the relations which form between the representations of distinct objects which are simultaneously present in the same situation.

To determine these, our experimental procedures are designed to test the relationships which exist between the representations of self, of others, of the task and of the group in an artificial laboratory situation in which several people are brought together.

II. On the interdependence between the representations of the self, of others, of the group and of the task in an experimental situation

A very simple idea prompted this research. It is that no single object, whether it be concrete or abstract, material or symbolic, is ever considered in isolation. It is always understood cognitively and placed within a situation which is more or less complex, in a series of relations with other objects relating to the same situation. As a result, to assign meaning and content to a particular object will alter the meaning and content of the other objects in the same situation. Borrowing from the terminology of the psychology of perception, Moscovici (1961) labelled this phenomenon *anchorage*. For our purposes, anchorage can be taken to denote the *interdependence, in the cognitive universe of individuals, between the representations of different objects within the same situation.*

By experimentally varying, in the course of several separate, but directly comparable, studies, three of the main elements of representation around which the life of the group is organized – the *task* (Codol, 1968, 1969a); the *others* (1970a); and the *group* itself (1970b) – I obtained results which confirm the validity of the above definition at least as far as small groups are concerned. In particular, I demonstrated how by changing the representation of *any one* of these elements, this very perceptibly modified the way in which the members of the group represented *all the other* elements of the situation (see also Codol, 1972).

Although the analysis carried out separately in each of these experiments produced clear evidence of a 'representational system' in group situations, yet it would not indicate either the *strength* or the *type* of relationships which link together, in the minds of these subjects, the representations of the task, of others, of the group and of themselves. More detailed findings on the relative importance of these links within the cognitive universe of each group member could, then, not only enhance our knowledge of small groups but also shed more light on the sorts of mechanisms which may be operating in such groups in the elaboration and change of representations.

Here, various hypotheses can be put forward, and a preliminary résumé of the experimental procedures which we adopted will enable them to be stated with greater clarity.

Procedure

Two types of experimental situation were used:

Experimental situation I
Eighty-one groups of three female students, divided into three separate experimental groups, were observed. A detailed presentation of the

three experiments will be found in the articles quoted above. For our present purposes it is sufficient to say that in each case the task was a decoding one, with rules which made it into a kind of group game.[2] These rules also allowed each group member to adopt, during the course of the game, behaviour that was either *cooperative* or *competitive* in some degree, such patterns being observed by the experimenter. In each experiment, the instructions stressed the importance of individual performance in carrying out the task.

Before the experiment, either the collective/cooperative or individual/competitive nature of the task, or of a particular group member, or of the group as a whole, was manipulated by the experimenter. A variety of techniques, all pretested as to their reliability, were combined according to the experimental conditions (words of greeting, preliminary questionnaires, introductory tasks, etc.).

When the rules of the task had been explained, a pre-experimental questionnaire was given out to ascertain the Ss' representations of the task, of the other group members, of themselves and of the group as such. A post-experimental questionnaire identical to the first was distributed on completion of the task, and this enabled the experimenter to follow how the representations evolved. For, while the Ss were involved in the task, other experimental manipulations were effected. In half the cases they were intended to *reinforce* and in the remaining half to *contradict* the initial manipulations. To take two examples, the use of confederates or the order of presentation of the information to be processed during the task could encourage Ss who had initially envisaged the situation as cooperative to exhibit what in fact was competitive behaviour.

The questionnaires were closely coordinated with the experimental instructions, and dealt only with the 'cooperative–competitive' aspect of the representations. This was achieved by having each question contain an equal number of items denoting cooperation and competition, as previously established by a double preliminary survey conducted on a sample from the same parent population. For each object of representation, the Ss were required to tick as many as they liked of the items which, in their opinion, corresponded to the object being considered. The 'degree of cooperation' of a S's reply to a question was obtained by establishing the ratio of the number of items she had ticked in replying to the question.

To enable the interdependence of representations to be evaluated from these results, the correlation coefficient (Bravais-Pearson's r) for the degree of cooperation in the replies to each pair of questions was computed for all the Ss in each situation, and also for the pre- and post-experimental questionnaires.

Experimental situation II

Twenty groups of two, three or four subjects (57 in all), all-male, all-female or mixed, were made up at random from a student population. *No pre-experimental manipulation was performed by the experimenter.* The task was an extremely simple one: the groups were expected, within a time limit of 6 minutes, to make up one or more coherent sentences from fifty letters of the alphabet printed on small wooden squares. In the allotted time, each group was supposed to construct the most original sentences it could, whilst using as many as possible of the letters. The task was in three parts, with three different batches of letters.

It was announced that:

1. the participation of each member in the work of the group would be rated by an observer on the given dimensions (number of letters used, creativity), according to precise criteria which had been established on the basis of previous experiments[3]

2. a group score would also be established by adding together the individual scores.

However, in both cases, no scores would be announced until the Ss had filled in a final questionnaire.

As in the preceding experimental situation, two questionnaires (pre- and post-experimental) were devised with the object of recording the Ss' representations (bearing on the twin ideas of 'creativity' and 'logical problem-solving') with respect to the task, the other members, themselves and the group as such.

Hypotheses and results[4]

Before we turn to more specific hypotheses, we must present two preliminary hypotheses which are likely to have some bearing on them. They are of general significance and concern respectively:

(a) the likely evolution in time of the strength of the relationships linking an individual's cognitive universe with the different representations which were engendered, and

(b) the impact of a particular representation on how the representational system itself is structured.

(a)   Evolution of the degree of interdependence between representations

Given that, in the experiments summarized, we were studying the links between representations at two specific moments, that is, *before* performance of the task (by pre-experimental questionnaire) and *after* its completion (by post-experimental questionnaire), it was pardonable to indulge in some *a priori* speculation as to the likelihood of finding a change in representation between these two moments.

It is, for instance, quite clear that *before they perform the task,* the Ss' representations can reflect only the very fragmentary information derived from the experimenter's manipulation (in experimental situation I) or their interpretations of the instructions (which were precisely the same in each experimental condition); whereas *after they have carried out the task,* the Ss' representations will have been enriched and/or modified as a result of their own experience of the behavioural and affective life of the group during the performance of the task.

The following very simple hypothesis may be stated whilst we are on this subject. Any new situation (whether or not it involves, as here, the life of a group) is first of all cognitively understood 'as a whole' by the Ss involved: the constituent elements or aspects of it are not at first recognized as being distinct. Consequently, each S's system of representations must be, at this stage, to some degree *syncretic*. However, the knowledge which individuals acquire through their own experience and their personal involvement in the situation (in this case, the life of the group) must eventually result in their being better able to distinguish between the separate elements. One can suppose, then, that the individuals' representations of these different aspects *will become increasingly independent of each other.*

If this is the case, it was to be expected that the degree of relationship between these representations, as expressed by the correlation co-efficient employed here, should be stronger on average before, rather than after, the performance of the task.

Our observations convincingly confirm this hypothesis: in both types of experimental situation the correlation coefficients effectively demonstrate (see Codol, 1974) that *the links between representations are both stronger and less differentiated at the beginning of the experiment than at the end.*

(b) Semantic relationships between represented objects

The second hypothesis was that the experimental manipulation of the representation of a particular object would probably not have the same repercussions on the representation of the situation as a whole (and hence on the representations of the other constituent elements of it) for every object considered. Specifically, it was to be expected that, due to the all-inclusive nature (semantically) of the concept 'group' (including as it does both 'others' and 'myself' as objects of representations), the experimental manipulation of how the *group* is represented should have a more decisive impact on how the situation as a whole is represented than would have been the case for varying experimentally the representation either of the *task* or of *a particular member of the group* (since these are semantically independent of one another).

The results for experimental situation I (the second was inappropriate for this purpose) show that this is indeed the case: it was the condition where the representation of the group was varied experimentally that the interdependence between all the representations attained its maximum value.

(c)   Specific interrelations between representations

On the subject of the specific interrelations between each pair of representations, several hypotheses were propounded. These are based on two common principles:

The *first* concerns the *functional importance* and the *normative character* of each object as it is represented within the situation, particularly in relation to its effect on the determination of behaviour.[5]

Insofar as success in performing the task was given as an explicit objective in all of the experiments, it was legitimate to suppose that, from the beginning, the *task* should appear to the Ss to be the most important element in relation to this functional dimension. If this is so then actions ought to be resolved primarily in terms of their relation to the task. In other words, we expected the task to become the reference point, the model, the rule, the behavioural norm for subjects.

Admittedly, since in both experiments group situations were set up, the *group* as an object might well also have taken on a distinctly normative character, inducing subjects to adopt patterns of behaviour centred on the group. However, given that in experimental situation I each member possessed, in turn, the individual power of decision in the situation and where, moreover, performances were calculated individually, it is understandable if the situation as a whole should appear to subjects to be more task- than group-orientated. In experimental situation II, where it was announced that both individual and group scores would be established, the group might be expected to retain a certain degree of normativeness, greater anyway than that pertaining to it in experimental situation I.

For the objects *self* and *others*, it was fairly safe to assume that each member, in determining his own actions, would attach greater functional significance to himself than to others.

– The *second* principle deals with a process of *social comparison between self and others*. I have shown elsewhere (see Codol, 1975, 1979) that there is a general tendency for the individual to form an image of himself according to which he declares himself to approximate more closely to the norms of the situation than others (what I called the 'superior conformity of self' phenomenon or 'PIP effect'). Specifically, it was observed in experimental situation I (see Codol, 1969a) that in groups where cooperation was defined as the work norm, each tended to see himself as being more cooperative than his comrades, whereas in those groups where competition was perceived to be normative, the prevailing tendency was to consider oneself as being more competitive than colleagues.[6]

Combining these two types of hypothesis allows us to formulate reliable predictions concerning the interrelations between representations of the task, of the group and of the self. In particular, comparative hypotheses can be made concerning the strength of the relationships between (*a*) the representation of others, or (*b*) the representation of self, with the representations of the task and of the group.

For if first, in the context of these experiments, the task is more normative in character than the group, and if secondly, the hypothesis of the superior conformity of self is well founded, then we might expect that:

the representations of self (*S*) and of the task (*T*) should be more strongly related than the representations of others (*O*) and of the task (*T*)

$$(T \times S > T \times O)$$

the representations of self and of the task should be more strongly related than the representations of self and of the group (*G*)

$$(T \times S > G \times S)$$

finally, that the representations of self and of the group should be more strongly related than the representations of others and of the group

$$(G \times S > G \times O)$$

An inspection of the experimental evidence confirmed these hypotheses in every particular (see Codol, 1974).

(d) The respective centrality of different representations

Applying to representations the theory of central traits which Asch (1946) demonstrated for cognitive elements, it might be worth while to attempt to determine the degree of centrality which each of the representations studied occupies in the Ss' representational systems. The method of analysis is a very simple one: since Wishner (1960) showed that the most central elements in a cognitive structure are those which are most highly correlated with the other elements, we can say that the higher the average value of its correlations with other representations, the more central is a particular representation.

It was difficult to predict *a priori* just how central each of the particular representations would be in a S's cognitive system. However, the core of any such representational system cannot be independent of the phenomenon of the superior conformity of the self, stated above, which means in particular that the representation of self should, overall, be more centrally situated in each S's cognitive universe than that of others.

Similarly, in experiments where the importance of efficient individual performance is stressed, it would have been surprising if the functional importance of each object in the situation was not closely related to the centrality of the corresponding representations within the S's representational systems.

Taking into account the various experimental conditions in the two studies, the results suggest the following hierarchy for the centrality of the representation: representations of *self*, of the *task*, of the *group* and of *others*.

The fact that the representation of self should be the most central in the representational system can come as no surprise. It has long been known that the image which an individual has of himself is essentially linked to the totality of his other representations and perceptions.

The subsequent order of representations, though, is distinctly more relevant to our theories; it is *task – group – others*, and corresponds exactly to the order established for the *functional importance* of each object of representation in the determination of actions. This would seem to indicate that the performance to be accomplished was the filter through which the Ss viewed the situation as a whole. Hence it is easy to understand why the representation of the task is more central than the representations either of the group or of others: the Ss' attention and perceptions were more sharply focused on their success in the task than on interpersonal relations within the group. The discrepancy between the representations of self and of others (the latter being, under all experimental conditions, the most peripheral representation) further shows that the representation of others played only a very minor role in a S's representational system – just as its functional importance in determining actions was minimal.

Overall, it seems that the centrality of a representation in a representational system depends on the normative character of the object which is represented in its relation to the whole of the situation in which the Ss are actually involved. The fact that, in these experiments, a great deal more stress was laid on the Ss' task performance than on the interaction between individuals within the group led to their representational systems being geared accordingly.

III. Conclusion

(1) This body of observations enhances our understanding of some of the mechanisms underlying the system of representations within a group situation.

Three separate principles, combined in different ways, appear to account for the interrelations between the various representations.

(*a*) The task, the group, others and self, by virtue of their meaning within a particular culture (which also defines the roles they play in any group situation) – are not directly comparable elements.

So the first principle hinges on *an object's degree of generality, complexity or 'globality'*: an object (for instance, the group) both semantically and in individuals' representations of it, may include several other objects (self, others...). Consequently, the effect of varying a particular representation on how the situation as a whole is represented will depend directly on the 'globality' of the representation which is changed.

(*b*) However, the complexity or 'globality' of a representation gives no prior indication of its *functional importance*, specifically as a determinant of behaviour.

Hence our second principle is concerned with the normative character of each of the objects of representation within the concrete situation in which the Ss are involved, and its role in the overall objective of the group. For all the groups in our experiments, there was one such overall objective: to achieve the best performance. The task thus appeared to be the object of primary functional significance in the situation and, as a result of this, became the point of reference and the norm for behaviour.

The respective centrality of each representation within a S's representational system seems to be directly related to the perceived normative character of the objects which are represented. Having focussed their perceptions on the successful completion of the task, the Ss represented the group and the others as elements of fairly secondary importance in the situation.

(c) The third principle bears on *a process of social comparison between self and others*. It is based on a hypothesis dealing with the interrelations between how different elements of the situation are represented according to the normative character of these elements: that is, each person tends to consider himself to be abiding more closely than others by the norms and requirements of the situation. Our experimental findings seem to justify this hypothesis, in particular by establishing that the stress laid on individual performance in the task of each group results in each member of the group considering himself more competent than the others to complete it.

(2) Nevertheless, it would not be realistic to claim that these results are generally valid in every group situation. Groups where elements other than the task have a normative character can easily be imagined. In such groups, the representations of objects in a S's representational system are likely to be placed in a different order to the one we observed here. Hence a combination of factors different from those we have isolated could produce markedly different results. For instance, in situations where the focus of attention is on the *group* itself, or on a *leader*, the superior conformity of self-hypothesis would indicate a stronger link between the representation of self and the representation of the group or of the leader than between either of these latter two and the representation of others.

So even if our reported results are strictly dependent on the particular situations in which the Ss were placed, it is legitimate to suppose that the different *principles* advanced here have a much wider validity, in that they go significantly beyond the question of how representations are organised in group situations. We may indeed suppose that, whatever kind of situation is experienced by individuals, the links between representations are dependent both on the (culturally determined) semantic properties of the objects which are represented and on the perceived normative importance of these objects in terms of the situation. On the basis of other observations a further supposition appears to be justified: that the superior conformity of self-principle is involved not only in social situations, but also in those situations where no other person is directly implicated. The desire for a positive self-image (seeing oneself as being suited both to the situation and to one's social reputation) can easily accommodate the absence of the other.

(3) Does the fact that persons (oneself or others), a group or a collectively-performed task are unequivocally *social objects*, and secondly that they are examined in the light of a situation which, even if artificial, can be termed *social*, necessarily imply that the representations of these objects are *'social'*?

This cannot be stated with certainty, for it must be admitted that, in accounting for these representations and their interrelations, what was examined was each S's responses. That is, the relationships of interdependence studied here are undoubtedly the product of intra-individual cognitive processes. If these analyses had been carried out, not at the level of the individual subject but at the level of each group, would we even then have been justified in claiming that we had grasped representations which were *social?* This is not certain either: representations may be termed 'social' less on account of whether their foundations are individual or group than because *they are worked out during the processes of exchange and interaction.*

The complexity of the problem may now be seen, for in fact the representations formed by each S in these experiments did not occur in a social vacuum.

Admittedly, we might posit that, *before interaction*, each S's representations (as recorded by pre-experimental questionnaire) could depend solely on the personal relationships existing between each of them and some aspects of the situation. However, it is extremely difficult to believe that a S could enter a laboratory unburdened by all sorts of prior representations – whether social or not – as to the group, himself, others, etc.[7]

In any case, the problem clearly exists in a different form *after the experiment*, when interpersonal and social relationships have been established during the performance of the task. May we speak here of *social representations*, whereas before they were *individual representations?*

In this connection, let us draw attention to the following interesting fact, common to both experiments:

It has been seen that, in experimental situation I, before any process of interaction was instituted, representations were *induced by the experimenter*, so that, with very few exceptions, all the members of the same experimental group did indeed represent the situation as a whole *in the same terms* (i.e. of cooperation or competition). Yet it will be recalled that in half of the groups an experimental manipulation *contradicting the initial one* was performed whilst the task was in progress, which led Ss to behave in ways which were in conflict with those they themselves had anticipated. What was then observed? In all cases, the Ss' final representations (derived from post-experimental questionnaires) *had been modified in the direction of the behaviour actually adopted by the group in the situation* (see Codol, 1972).

Incidentally, when no experimental manipulation was performed, as in experimental situation II, it was commonly found that, prior to the experiment, Ss in the same group formed *different* representations of the same situation, some seeing it in terms of creativity, and others in terms of problem-solving. Yet *at the end of the experiment, in almost every group, all the members represented the situation in the same terms* (i.e. *as creativity or as problem-solving*).

And so, in the two experimental situations, the processes of interaction, communication and influence which were operating within each group resulted in group members forming representations which differed from those they held initially.

In the light of these findings, it seems legitimate to employ the term 'social representations', always bearing in mind that, in the examples presented here, the requirements of experimental design resulted in a dramatic simplification of situations which, in everyday life, are much more complex.

Notes

1. To take a representative selection of themes forming the basis of studies of social representation, to which bibliographical references are made elsewhere in this book.
2. For a fuller exposition of the general structure of this basic task and for some indication of further possibilities in its use and adaptation, see Codol and Flament (1969).
3. This was not, in fact, the case, as behaviour was not observed during the task.
4. All these experimental results (computations made, coefficients derived, etc.) have appeared in an earlier article (Codol, 1974). They will not be reiterated in this present study, which is primarily intended to convey an *idea* of the method and of the sort of experimental results obtained.
5. To evaluate the functional importance of each object of representation within the situation, from experimental situation I, the mean coefficients of

correlation between each representation and the Ss' behaviours over the game as a whole were calculated. These latter, whether cooperative or competitive, had been objectively recorded in this experiment.

6. A whole series of experiments using different populations and various methodologies has confirmed the general validity of this phenomenon. For detailed presentation and discussion of these, see Codol, 1979.

7. The fact that representations *prior to the experiment itself* are a feature of the experimental situation is a fact that may be very clearly observed in experimental situation I: it is shown in the degree of difficulty the experimenter may experience in changing one representation or another. For example, in those group situations, it was much easier to create representations of cooperation than representations of competition.

10. Social representations, inter-group experiments and levels of analysis[*]

WILLEM DOISE

1. Introduction

If for the last dozen or so years social psychologists, especially experimentalists or former experimentalists, have been willing to talk about a crisis within their discipline, our belief is that in reality the problem is a much older one. It reflects efforts to bridge a dichotomy between psychological and sociological explanations, a dichotomy which had already been acknowledged in the work of Wundt, and one which has re-emerged in several famous controversies, as for instance that between the 'sociologism' of Durkheim and the 'psychologism' of Tarde. But if such controversy has been with us for a long time, so have efforts to move beyond it and to integrate the two systems of explanation. Moscovici's research on social representations is located directly within this dynamic, its objective being to 'define an object of social psychology which is pertinent both to the individual level and to the collective level and of which the content has a clear social value. The ideal being that it can lend itself to a continuous description...' (Moscovici, 1979, p. 4). The various contributions to this volume demonstrate that studies on social representations have begun to realize this objective.

2. Social representations and levels of analysis

Research on social representations, including that collected together in this book, reflects no less than other research an important characteristic of work as a whole in social psychology: its scattered nature. Theoretical approaches in this area of the human sciences exhibit a pattern of diversification in which specific initiatives are confined to very limited problems. Where aims have been more ambitious it has seldom been

[*]Translated by Angela St James Emler

255

possible to arbitrate between the competing claims of rival approaches. Nevertheless, some systematization can be imposed on this diversity. Thus we have been led to distinguish four levels or types of analysis (Doise, 1978).

I.   The first of these levels of explanation is confined to the study of 'psychological' or 'intra-individual' processes which are supposed to account for the manner in which an individual organizes his experience of the social environment. Research on the treatment of complex information or on cognitive balance exemplifies this kind of approach.

II.   A second level is concerned with 'inter-individual' and 'intra-situational' processes; the many experiments using game matrices and studies of the attribution of characteristics to others are representative of this type.

III. The third kind of explanation makes use of differences in 'position' or 'social status' as intervening variables to account for variations in situational interactions. Here the individuals who participate in the experiments are no longer considered to be interchangeable. Recent studies of power and of social identity often resort to explanations of this kind.

IV.   Finally, some experiments are based on an analysis of the general conceptions of social relations which individuals bring with them into the experimental situation, and they show more particularly how such 'universalized ideological beliefs' result in differentiated, indeed discriminatory, representations and behaviours.

These distinctions would be of very limited interest if they aimed only at replacing the classical dichotomy between psychological and sociological explanations with a four-fold division. If we hold with these distinctions it is because they constitute a first step; it is necessary to distinguish first in order to achieve, in the end, a better unification. In effect, we believe that if social dynamics can be conceptualized at one of these levels it is no less true that the conditions under which these dynamics are realized are shaped by factors relevant to other types or levels of analysis. We will demonstrate this later with respect to research specifically in the domain of inter-group relations. But how is this framework for analysis relevant to the study of social representations? Let us apply it to some of the contributions to be found in this book.

The bias towards balance is most often studied as a process of psychological functioning with the traditional explanation for it being given at the first of our four levels. Claude Flament refines this particular level of explanation even further by distinguishing two axioms which intervene in this bias, but he also shows how the way in which they operate in the individual is conditioned by the ideological universe that a situation evokes in him – an analysis, in other words, at the fourth level.

In similar vein, J. C. Abric and J. P. Codol study more especially the interindividual and situational dynamics of a level II analysis, though they show that these interactions are modulated by the intervention of representations which are independent of these situations, and which, through the effects of the experimenter and his instructions, in some manner link them to the more general dynamics present in a society.

The research of M.-J. Chombart de Lauwe shows how social representations which reflect the specific position of a social category, that is that of the child, are situated within a set of social relations. She thus deals with the dynamics of level III but articulates them with a dominant discourse within a society (i.e. level IV). Jaspars and Fraser show how a central notion in social psychology, that of attitude, has been studied above all as an individual disposition (i.e. level I), but that it also necessitates a cultural approach (i.e. level IV), as was the case with the earliest work in this field. A number of authors show that though social representations are general they are re-worked and re-generated in a specific manner by individuals.

There are therefore at least two kinds of generality which must be taken into account in the study of social representations. First, there are indications of a certain generality in the content of the representations themselves, and second there are postulated general mechanisms of an individual, inter-individual or positional nature which can account for transformations in these general contents. The study of social representations thus spans many different levels of analysis and benefits from their articulation. Moscovici (1979, p. 7) attributes a certain automony to social representations as compared to the consciousness that individuals can have of them:

Assuredly, individuals do think them and do produce them but in the course of exchanges, of co-operations, not in isolation. Once produced, they live a life of their own, move, combine, attract and oppose, giving birth to new representations while old ones disappear. They have in common with categories of thought that they are the categories of a subject, collectively understood, and with the phenomena of reality that they are independent and follow their own laws. In consequence, all representations should be understood and explained, beginning with the one or ones which have given birth to them, and not by starting directly with such and such behaviour or such and such an aspect of the social structure.

To explain the transformations of representations in a way which takes account of their previous forms raises our fourth level of analysis. To explain them equally in terms of individual, inter-individual and positional dynamics returns us to an articulation of the levels of analysis. Elsewhere (Doise, forthcoming) we have developed a conception of experimentation which is suited to such a task. It entails the submergence of experimentation in social reality as a whole so as to bring to light the dynamics of this reality by exaggerating them, restraining them, opposing them, in other words by transforming them, if only momentarily. Here we return to the examples provided by experiments on inter-group relations to show how experimentation involving the articulation of different levels of analysis readily allows one to study transformations in social representations. For indeed, social representations do intervene in most inter-group research of a psychological nature either as dependent variables or as independent variables or as intermediate variables.

3.   Levels of analysis and inter-group relations

Different models have been used to provide an account of particular aspects of inter-group relations. Certain of these models begin from a level I analysis, as for instance the categorization model which was first studied with respect to perceptual judgements. It entails an accentuation of similarities between stimuli belonging to the same category and an accentuation of differences between stimuli belonging to different categories. This categorization process has been described by Tajfel (1959a) who studied it experimentally in terms of judgements of the length of physical stimuli (Tajfel and Wilkes, 1963). But in another experiment, Tajfel, Sheikh and Gardner (1964) showed that the process could account for certain characteristics of social stereotypes. A stereotype is, by definition, the perception of a correspondence – whether 'true' or 'false' will not concern us for the moment – between membership of a group and the possession of a certain characteristic. The process of categorization is equally involved in value judgements based on regional accents (Tajfel, 1959b).

In the same way some of our own research (Doise, 1976, pp. 195–9) has verified that an accentuation of differences and similarities occurs in judgements based on membership of different groups, as the categorization model would predict.

But this psychological process not only accounts for perception of the social environment; it intervenes equally in actions effected on this environment; actions which can often result in a differentiation, indeed in a discrimination, between categories.

Certainly, other intra-individual models have been advanced to explain inter-group phenomena. Thus the different uses in this area of psychoanalytically derived models have been discussed at length by Billig (1976). If processes of a psychological nature are undoubtedly involved in inter-group relations – because it is always individuals who participate in these relations – the problem still remains of articulating these individual dynamics with those of a more collective nature.

Other studies touch on the relations between groups in analysing more specifically the inter-individual and intra-situational relations involved. Thus Rabbie and Horwitz (1969) explain the discriminatory effect of sharing a common fate in terms of anticipatory interaction being easier with those who share the same fate and being more difficult with those who are acquainted with a different fate. These analyses derive typically from level II, as in fact do most of those employed by Rabbie (1974) in an impressive body of research on co-operation and competition between groups. The classic research of Sherif *et al.* (1961) on the same problem was based on analyses at this same level; in effect the idea behind the project was to account for the forms of interdependence between the individuals comprising a group and the relations between groups.

Tajfel has developed a theory of social identity which is particularly suited to encompass the dynamics of level III. It is located directly within the articulation between the individual and the collective. The individual, searching for a positive self-definition, builds this definition on his category membership and to this end seeks to introduce a positive difference between the category to which he belongs and other categories. From this can be derived not only the importance of prior category membership in a given situation, but also the necessity of being familiar with the specific relations which exist between the categories involved in an interaction situation. This situation can serve either to reinforce or to undermine existing relations of differentiation between these categories and thus determine, as research by Brown (1978) and by Branthwaite and Jones (1975) shows, the different behaviour of members of categories. Reference group theory has also indicated the importance of studying the respective social positions occupied by groups in accounting for the behaviour of and the representations held by their members.

One can hardly think of an experiment on inter-group relations which does not directly involve level IV variables. Indeed, the phenomena of categorical differentiation, of co-operative and competitive interaction between groups, of differing social identities, all presuppose the existence of values diffused in a society which determine the dimensions on which groups define themselves in relation to one another. Some experiments (e.g. Turner, 1978; Turner and Brown, 1978; Van Knippenberg, 1978) have studied the varied effects of these value dimensions, which correspond to social representations. Peabody (1968) has proposed a method for studying the characteristic evaluative bias of the representations of different groups. He verified that there could be a certain 'objective' consensus accompanying differential evaluations. This was the case in the Philippines for inter-group representations of Philippinoes and Chinese. The descriptions given of the Chinese were more towards a 'tense' pole (self-mastery, economic, serious) while those of the Philippino group were more towards the 'relaxed' pole (spontaneous, generous, gay). Such differences agree with the economic positions which the two groups respectively occupy in relation to one another. But if the members of different ethnic and socio-economic groups share a certain consensus in the description of their characteristics, agreeing about dimensions principally linked to their socio-economic positions, they nevertheless evaluate these dimensions differently.

There is an important consequence to this. The differential evaluative dynamic, which Peabody's method is able to capture, allows groups to bend in their favour a 'tension' which other groups might have introduced into some area of social life. It involves, therefore, a dynamic which unfolds at the level of representations and general evaluations but which allows groups, at opportune moments, to register their own originality and their identity in the unfolding history of their relations. Let us again emphasize that evaluations shared by an entire population still allow different subgroups to respond differently in the same situation. Ideological truths are in some sense 'deep structures' generating multiple and varied expressions reflecting the dynamics of relationships between social positions. We are concerned here, therefore, with an interaction between factors located at levels IV and III.

4.   Points of articulation between different levels of analysis in research on inter-group relations

The distinction between four kinds of experimental approach corresponds to a division of labour amongst social psychologists; different schools give preference to different levels of analysis. Each experiment offers a framework for analysis situated at one of the levels described and therefore it has to 'neutralize', even to let escape other important aspects of the situation being studied; aspects which could only be captured by the application of a different framework. Such an autonomy of levels is an indispensable stage in the work of social psychology, but it is only a stage which must be incorporated with complementary work on the articulation of the analyses undertaken. The social actor is at the same time an integrator of information in terms of distinct processes, a participant in interpersonal and positional dynamics, and an active supporter of norms and of ideological representations.

We would now like to show how an articulation of the levels of analysis described above has already been initiated in various studies. We shall review combinations of different levels of analysis and cite experiments in the area of inter-group relations which are located at each of these points of articulation.

A.   *The intra- and inter-individual levels of analysis*

This articulation returns us to a consideration of the relationship between dynamics which are essentially psychological and those which refer to specific characteristics of the interaction between individuals. Research manipulating relations between individuals who must be evaluated by the subject can be considered to be situated at this level of articulation. Thus one of the hypotheses in an experiment by Bruner and Perlmutter (1957) is derived from such an articulation. It states that the category memberships which differentiate amongst a collection of people will exert a stronger effect on their description when these people are presented simultaneously to a subject than will the same categories when they characterize people presented separately. Simultaneous and separate presentations of people belonging to different categories affect the process of information integration differently. Willis (1960) also shows that a quite simple feature of a situation – the inclusion of two or three individuals possessing a common characteristic – gives rise to an integration of information which necessitates an adaptation of the models being used.

In research carried out with Deschamps (Deschamps and Doise, 1975) we were able to show that the process of categorising intervenes differently in situations which differ from one another only slightly. One experimental condition (without anticipation) involved subjects in describing members of a category without being told that they would subsequently need to describe members of another category. In a second condition (with anticipation) the subjects who were to describe members of the first category had been warned in advance that they would also have to describe members of another category. In this latter condition the categorization process intervenes much more strongly than in the first condition.

Certainly in the research just cited the manipulation of level II factors has been slight and in one way or another simulated. Although they did not involve encounters between real people the differences introduced into the situation have, even so, been sufficiently strong to affect the psychological functioning being studied. In an experiment by Turner (1975), the situation studied is a little more realistic, involving subjects who must pay or evaluate other subjects present whom they cannot, however, identify. The theory underlying this experiment was located at the point of articulation between levels I and II. The individual will seek a positive self-evaluation and self-differentiation in a manner which varies as a function of the social situation in which he finds himself. If he can manage it by differentiating himself from other individuals, even those of his own group, an inter-individual differentiation will be observed. If he is only able to do so through a differentiation of category adherences, this will happen. Though these predictions are verified, the results seem equally to indicate that an already established inter-categorical differentiation inhibits the subsequent appearances of inter-individual differentiation, whilst the reverse is not the case. What is important in this research is that the individual achieves his need for individual self-evaluation differently according to the characteristics of the social situation.

B.   Social status and the intra-individual level of analysis

The previously mentioned research by Willis (1960) relates to level I processes whilst involving the intervention of level II factors, but it also introduces the effect of level III factors in the integration of information.

Male and female students were required to evaluate photographs of boys or girls. If a contrast effect characterizes judgements based on the overall set of photographs, both the more and the less attractive, an equally clear effect differentiates judgements of the male and female photographs. Male and female students generally evaluate more favourably sets of photographs representing individuals in their own respective sexual categories. The boys manifested this bias more strongly than the girls. Sexual category membership intervenes, then, in a differential manner in the calculation made by subjects about the informational elements presented to them. In other words, the respective social positions which the subjects occupy during the course of socialization, and the representations which are involved in this, mediate the manner in which subjects elaborate their judgements in Willis's experiment. Elsewhere, in our research with Deschamps (Deschamps *et al.*, 1976) we have obtained an analogous result; boys, much more than girls, accentuated differences between masculine and feminine photographs.

An interesting way of articulating levels I and III can be found in developmental social psychology. Here Kohlberg advances the hypothesis that differentiations corresponding to social categories which occupy specific positions are established in a definite order. Differentiations based on size and power will be established first in children and then corresponding to these, the differentiation of the sexes would appear:

It appears likely, then, that children's stereotypes of masculine dominance or social power develop largely out of this body stereotyping of size–age and competence. Children agree earliest and more completely that fathers are bigger than mothers, next that they are smarter than mothers, and next that they have more social power or are the boss of the family.   (Kohlberg, 1966, p. 102)

One can explain thus that:

... the 6-year-old boy is a full-fledged male chauvinist, much more so than his parents, and he is that way regardless of how he is brought up in a society that fosters role differentiation. Fortunately later stages of cognitive growth qualify, moderate or undo this male chauvinism.   (Kohlberg and Ullian, 1974, p. 213)

But it could be that male chauvinism even at this age is only the other side of the coin. In fact we have studied the evaluative aspect of inter-sex representations in boys and girls from seven to thirteen years (Deschamps and Doise, 1975). The girls, just as the boys, attribute more value to their own sexual category. But if for the boys this bias remains constant across the age range studied, in girls the degree of value attached to their own category is an inverse function of age. After nine to ten years they begin to attribute a greater number of negative traits than before. These results also suggest that sexual differentiations are established in several stages. Girls progressively modify the evaluation of their own category before integrating it with the difference in position occupied by the sexual categories in our society.

Another interesting example of articulation between levels I and III is provided by Vaughan (1978), who articulates the historical change in New Zealand in relations between the white majority group (Pakeha) and the indigenous minority group (Maoris) with the ontogenetic development of bias in favour of one's own group. There has been a relative increase in this bias during the last few decades amongst Maori children, whilst it has decreased a little amongst the Pakeha children. But in every epoch it is the relatively older children who show this change faster. Thus they are becoming conscious more rapidly of the historical changes that are occurring in the relations between the groups.

C. Ideology and the intra-individual level of analysis

Much research has had as its explicit aim a study of the links between certain characteristics of systems of belief and characteristics of psychological functioning. We could recall in this respect the research which has examined links between, on the one hand, more or less rigid adherence to an established order (Authoritarianism) or to a cause (Dogmatism) and, on the other, a certain rigidity in cognitive functioning. The context within which these studies were initially conceived was the study of inter-group relations. However, the type of explanation which was elaborated in the course of this research was centred on the personality syndrome pole and rather neglected an actual study of the ideological pole.

Other research directly studies commitment to particular ideologies, for example racism, and its effect on level I processes such as perceptual accentuation. With respect to this we would cite the research by Secord, Bevan and Katz (1956), which begins from the presupposition that belonging to the categories Black or White is emotionally more important to those Americans expressing strong racial prejudice than to those who show less prejudice. It follows from this that the first type of individual compared to the second will more strongly accentuate differences between pictures of blacks and pictures of whites on traits supposed to represent the negroid type (black skin, broad nose, curly hair, thick lips, etc.). This is indeed what these researchers found when they asked subjects to describe on different scales the physiognomic characteristics of fifteen people from their photographs, ten photographs depicting people with more or less negroid features, whilst the others were of whites. The segregationist subjects in fact perceive more negroid characteristics in all the photographs than the 'neutral' subjects, accentuating the difference between the ten photographs considered to represent 'blacks' and those representing whites. On this point it is also interesting to note that other subjects, who belonged to a group which was strongly anti-segregationist, gave results intermediate between segregationist and neutral subjects. One might suppose that those who combat segregation do so precisely because they have become conscious of the unjustified importance which membership of different races assumes.

Likewise, Pettigrew, Allport and Barnett (1958) were able to observe in South Africa a perceptual difference between Afrikaaners belonging to a strongly discriminatory culture and Anglophones not speaking Afrikaans who were more recent immigrants and less immersed in a culture of racial discrimination. The Afrikaaners showed a stronger tendency to attribute pictures to perceptually opposed categories (white and black) than to intermediate categories (coloured or Indian) in a procedure involving the stereoscopic presentation of two photographs often representing individuals of different races.

D. Social status and social interaction

We have carried out several investigations on the links between forms of intra-situational encounter and established adherences to social groups. Thus, in a mixed motive game situation (Doise, 1969), two pairs were required to interact, but in each condition the composition of the pairs was differently organised. Depending on the experimental conditions, the encounter involved either two pairs of young people of the same nationality (four French or four Germans), two couples each consisting of a French and a German subject (mixed groups), or a French pair and a German pair (heterogeneous groups). This last condition was, therefore, the only one involving an encounter in which membership of the experimental group coincided with membership of the national group. It was also in this condition that subjects showed relatively more antagonism with regard to the other couple. No difference was detected between homogeneous groups and mixed groups which had in common a lack of coincidence between established membership differences and

opposition between parties in the game situation. Some anthropologists (e.g. Levine and Campbell, 1972; Jaulin, 1973) have
suggested that the crossing of allegiances between groups makes the
regulation of conflicts in a society easier. Indeed, how can the process of
category differentiation function in a situation of crossed categorization
constructed in such a manner that for each individual some members of
his own category and some from another category distinguished on the
basis of one criterion share membership of another of his categories
distinguished on a different basis? There should be a growth of
differences between the two categories distinguished on the first basis,
but also a growth in differences between categories distinguished on the
second basis. At the same time there ought to be an accentuation of
differences within one category, because it is by definition composed of
individuals belonging to two different categories according to another
criterion. For the same reasons and at the same time there ought to be an
accentuation of similarities between members of the same category and
between members of different categories who nonetheless share
membership of a category according to some other basis for
categorization. There will therefore be conflict between accentuation of
similarities and differences within categories and across the boundaries
of categories. One could thus expect these opposing tendencies to
reduce category differentiation. This is what we found in an experiment
with Deschamps (Deschamps *et al.*, 1976), by crossing adherences to
sexual categories with membership of two experimentally created
groups.

An articulation between levels II and III was also studied in an
experiment by Doise and Weinberger (1972/73). In situations either of co-
operation or competition between male and female students, intersex
representations, reflections of an important social division, were modified with predictions derived from the category differentiation model.
In the same way in encounters between apprentices and collegians,
modifications in the situation (one-to-one or two-to-two encounters)
modified images reflecting the respective social positions of these two
categories of subjects (Doise, 1972). All these experiments therefore
effectively articulate factors belonging to analyses at levels II and III.

E.   *Social interaction, social status and ideology*

To conclude this enumeration of forms of articulation, some examples
will be given of articulation between three different levels of analysis.

Research by Lerner (1971) on the victim constitutes a prototype for the articulation of levels II and IV. The influence of the ideology of a just world differs according to the interaction situation (victim remunerated or not, involvement of the observer, continuation or termination of intervention). But certain studies have also explicitly introduced category membership as either shared or not shared with the victim. Thus Katz, Glass and Cohen (1973) confronted white subjects with a victim who was either black or white, to be administered either weak or strong shocks. In accordance with their prediction based on the ambivalence of the situation, they found that the black victim to whom the strong shocks were to be given was more depreciated. A significant inter-action was found between the intensity of the shocks and the race of the victim.

The dominant ideology stresses heterosexuality over homosexuality. Nevertheless, certain characteristics of a situation may lead subjects to favour attribution of an unfavourable characteristic to members of their own category. Bramel (1963) induced certain subjects to believe that they had homosexual tendencies. These subjects subsequently found a greater number of homosexual themes in an analysis of a Thematic Apperception Test protocol if it was attributed to another student (someone similar to themselves) than if the protocol was attributed to a prison inmate. In attributing a little-appreciated trait that one possesses to others like oneself, one conserves a good opinion of self, but on the other hand one hesitates to attribute one's own characteristics to representatives of social groups who do not rejoice in the same prestige as members of one's own group. Edlow and Kiesler (1966) obtained analogous results for another characteristic generally evaluated negatively, indecisiveness. The attribution of little-valued characteristics occurs both as a function of category membership and of specific evaluations that subjects receive in a given situation. It is indispensable to articulate the analyses of levels II, III and IV if such attributions are to be understood.

5. Conclusion

Let us return to the study of social representations. Certainly, they are to be studied by sociologists and historians who should relate them to the historical development of a society. But it still remains to be explained how the historical dynamics are actualized through psychological dynamics. If social representations have life it is because they are lived by individuals, co-ordinating their actions, organizing into groups and occupying different social positions in relation to one another. The transformations which these representations undergo reflect at the same time the functioning of individuals, their modes of interaction with one another, and their positions in the social order. The study of the overlaps between all these dynamics is incumbent on social psychology which, we hope we have shown, is in possession of the means to accomplish it.

11. From the bias of structural balance to the representation of the group[*]

CLAUDE FLAMENT

Introduction

Some aspects of Heider's theory of structural balance can be translated by saying that the bias of balance is the expression of the representation of positive and negative interpersonal relations. Breaking away from that perspective, I will show that the bias of balance has to be decomposed and explained by two different mechanisms. One is the simplification of cognitive structures in situations of stress. The other is the intervention of a schema of formal equivalence, made possible by the tie that exists, in the representation of the group, between friendship and equality. My intention is to show that this mechanism operates within an overall image of society as antagonistic and 'multi-groupal'.

Heider's theory of structural balance (1946) is well known, as well as Zajonc's remark noting 'the distressing fact that twenty years after the original statement of the principle of balance, practically no research has ever gone beyond a mere attempt to demonstrate the validity of the fundamental statement' (1969, p. 353). For ten years, I have been trying, like so many others, to *explain* why the definition was valid. For this purpose, I have chosen to adopt the perspective of the experimental study of social representations, relying on the mathematisation of balance given in the theory of *graphs* (Flament, 1970).

When Heider considers that balance is a principle of cognitive organisation, which depends upon a naive psychology, this can be translated as follows: the principle of balance organises the representation of positive and negative interpersonal relations: more cautiously, some authors, Zajonc in particular, prefer the notion of a *bias* which organises the answers obtained in certain experimental situations.

Before proposing a few observations regarding the possibility of

[*]Translated by François Rosso

269

rapport between 'bias' and 'representation', I wish to specify that the answers to which Zajonc refers are those of subjects who had been asked to learn, to build, to modify, to complete or to choose structures outlining the relations of friendship between *fictitious persons*. In such a 'social vacuum', and if one assumes that the subjects do not answer at random, one may think that they refer to a social model – a representation. It is necessary then to say to which model they refer, and to ask why this particular one is evoked. If they do not refer to a social model, one can only suppose that the subjects use purely formal rules, the utility of which is to enable them to answer, with a feeling of being rigorous, some questions which scarcely bear any meaning. This assertion is made by Leonard who successfully managed to retrieve the notion of balance using non-social material (he talked only about building blocks in a construction game which either fit together or do not). Leonard (pers. comm.) has obtained new and more subtle results which appear to depart too radically from the analogy for the hypothesis still to be retained, and I will be content to seek a social representation behind the structural balance.

Biases, schemata and representations

When one wants to study a representation, one asks questions – which could be precise or otherwise – to which subjects respond: these questions could range from a choice between two pre-coded words to completely open-ended questions. If no kind of structure can be observed in the answers, this may be for three reasons:

1. One does not know how to locate a structure which remains hidden.
2. One does not know how to find the appropriate questions for engaging the sought-after representation.
3. The sought-after representation does not exist.

If a structure can be observed in the answers, then it is possible to talk of a *bias* (for example, the bias of balance); this term ought to have a purely technical meaning, that is a systematic deviation of the answers with regard to a norm (for instance, correct answers in a learning experiment; random responses in an experiment involving the completion of structures – these being classical examples in the study of balance). The fact that one finds a bias when one is looking for a representation may lead one to confuse the two. This is certainly due to an exceedingly simple conception of representation. Being a relatively stable cognitive structure, the same representation can manifest itself differently in different situations (e.g. in response to different questions). It is then convenient, in order to explain the observed bias, and to know the target representation, to find the mechanisms which shape the responses as a function of the echoes which the questions evoked in the field of the representation. I will use the word 'schema' to describe this kind of cognitive mechanism.

If one endeavours to distinguish clearly the schemata of representations, one will become aware that there is no specific schema which is unique to a particular representation. At any rate, that is my hypothesis. These relatively general schemata are normally studied independently of research on representations: logical schemata, such as those studied by Piaget, rhetorical schemata (analogy, metaphor), psychoanalytic schemata . . .

It is not enough to identify a schema which is likely to produce a bias; it is also essential to explain why this general schema should operate in this particular case. In the bias of balance, one can isolate a bias of the transitivity of friendship ('my friends' friends are my friends'); the schema of transitivity is well known to Piagetians (Bullinger, 1973). It will be necessary to show that it really is this schema which is responsible for the bias, and why the representation of friendship (or of something else) requires this logical schema to account for the structure of the responses.

It is by answering this question, by identifying how the representation interacts with the logical schema, that makes it possible to discover some important aspects of the representation.

My starting-point – close to Heider's theory – was to consider that the bias of balance translated the structure of interpersonal relations, both positive and negative in their representations. Does a schema of balance exist? Harary (1953) defined the theory of balanced graphs before having any knowledge of Heider's conception of balance. Physicists have, in ferromagnetism, a theory of 'frustrating triangles', which is isomorphic with Harary's theory. And it must be said that some presentations of these theories suggest a schema of thought which seems so natural that one would readily hypothesise that a psychological schema of balance does actually exist.

I did not have to wonder about this for long: experimental results suggest that, as far as interpersonal relations are concerned, one has to decompose the bias of balance into two, and hence find several explanatory mechanisms. In doing this, it is not at all obvious that it is a matter of a single study of the representation of interpersonal relations, and one of our problems will be to find the object whose representation is translated by the observed biases.

Decomposition of the schema of balance

There have been many studies analysing the structures triangle by triangle. It is known that the eight possible triangles can be grouped into four categories, as is shown in figure 1.

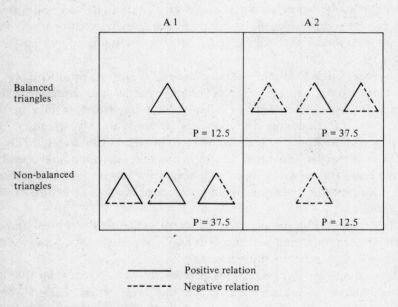

Fig. 1   The eight possible triangles

Four of the triangles are balanced; the meaning of columns A1 and A2 will be seen shortly. I have called P the percentage of appearances of each of the four cases under the hypothesis that positive and negative answers are equiprobable.

Examining closely the details of the experimental results (whenever this is possible), one finds that, whereas the balanced triangle of the A1 type (3 positive relations) always has a strong appeal for subjects, this is far from being the case with balanced triangles of the A2 type (2 negative, 1 positive). (This fact, at the level of the raw data, is perhaps masked by the greater possibility of the second case which is three times that of the first.)

In an experiment of which we shall have more to say later, Pichevin and Poitou (1974) were led to calculate an average preference ranking for the eight triangles (fig. 2).

	A 1	A 2
Balanced triangles	1.9	5.5
Non-balanced triangles	4.4	4.4

Fig. 2 Average preference rank for the four types of triangle. Based on the study by Pichevin and Poitou (1974)

Only the balanced triangle of the A1 type has an average rank significantly different from the average rank which would result from chance (4.5).

Such results suggest that the answers obtained in the experiments concerning balance are not organised according to a single principle, the principle of balance, but suppose the existence of two psychologically distinct processes.

To aid in the search for these processes, it is convenient to rely on a formulation proposing two axioms instead of one (Flament, 1968 and 1979). In the experimental cases which interest us (connected graphs), it is sufficient to postulate the following axioms:

A1: if a triangle has 2 positive sides, the third side is positive.
A2: if a triangle has 2 negative sides, the third side is positive.

One can see then that, in figure 1, columns A1 and A2 regroup the triangles to which the axioms A1 and A2, respectively, can be applied; in the row of 'balanced triangles' appear the triangles where the relevant axiom can be verified; and in the row of non-balanced triangles appear the triangles where the relevant axiom, on the contrary, is not verified.

A generalisation applying to any kind of graph has been proposed (Flament, 1979):

A'1: no cycle has exactly one negative link.
A'2: every cycle of odd length has at least one positive link.

Axiom A'1 is Davis's *clustering* axiom (1967); the writer has proposed to name A'2 the 'parsimony axiom'. Indeed, in a graph for which A'1 can be verified, one has any number whatsoever of groups of friends, each without internal hostility; if, moreover, A'2 is verified, there is balance, and the number of groups of friends, then, does not exceed two. This remark is essential for understanding the link between the parsimony axiom and the psychological hypothesis to be proposed here.

The axioms of parsimony and stressful situations

It is known that stressful situations modify cognitive structures, generally either in the direction of simplification or of 'polarisation'. This process, when applied to a representation of interpersonal relations which satisfies the 'grouping' axiom (i.e. a number, which may be high, of groups of friends), leads to a simplified (i.e. 'parsimonious') representation comprising a single group or, at most, two groups. The axiom of parsimony tends then to be confirmed, and the representation is in balance – without the action of a possible schema of balance being supposed.

The following hypothesis is therefore proposed: let there be two situations with the sole difference between them being that one is under stress, the other being (relatively) normal, then the responses of subjects will always confirm axiom A1, but will confirm axiom A2 more often in the stressful, than in a normal, situation.

In order to test this hypothesis, Rossignol and Flament (1975) manipulated stress in two different ways:

1. *'Success–failure'*: before the balance questionnaire, subjects underwent a mock intelligence test. Some succeeded, others failed, massively and publicly. This is denoted by S or F.
2. *'Preference–truth'*: this is a variation in the instructions of the balance questionnaire: 'Answer quickly, without thinking; say which you prefer the most'; 'Say what, according to you, is the truth, think carefully.' This second instruction is thought to be more stressful than the first. This is denoted by the P or T.

This gives four situations: the most normal is SP; the most stressful is FT; in between are ST and FP, concerning the order of which no particular hypothesis is stated.

The eight possible triangles are presented to the subjects by eight such phrases as 'my friends' friends are my friends', to which the subjects assign a mark on a five-point scale. From the answers, two acceptance scores are calculated, one for each axiom. The results are presented in figure 3 with the score varying from −2.5 to +2.5, zero being the neutral point.

	SP	FP	ST	FT
AXIOM 1	1.67	1.41	1.30	1.25
AXIOM 2	0.07	0.64	0.71	0.82

S = Success
F = Failure
P = Preference
T = Truth

Fig. 3   Acceptance scores for each axiom

The results, essentially, confirm the hypothesis: axiom A1 is always strongly accepted (even though in the three stressful conditions one can detect a slight drop in the rate of acceptance, which we are unable to explain); axiom A2 is accepted only in the stressful conditions. It is worth noting that the three stressful conditions differ hardly at all on either axiom.

The experiment was repeated (Pichevin and Rossignol, 1976), using structures which were more complex than triangles (relations between five persons); the results are less clear, but, after a precise formulation of parsimony (Flament, 1979), the tendencies appeared to be identical.
We are thus led to conclude:

1. The balance schema has no psychological reality.
2. If the way in which positive and negative interpersonal relations are represented sometimes confirms the axiom of parsimony, it is for very general psychological reasons (the action of stress on cognitive structures), which are of no interest to us here.

It is conceivable that stress modified the representation itself; it is more satisfying, however, to postulate the existence of a schema which modifies how the representation is expressed. Such a schema – of a psychoanalytic nature – has been studied by Rossignol and Houel (1976).

It remains for us to identify the psychological schema which is implied by the confirmation of axiom 1: this is where the representation of the group – and no longer the representation of interpersonal relations – makes its appearance.

The axiom of 'grouping' and the schema of equivalence

Formally, axiom A1 simply states that the relation of friendship is transitive (in the form of A'1, the transitivity may not be total). It is this transitivity ('my friends' friends are my friends') which we have to explain, directly or indirectly.

All authors admit that friendship is thought of as being symmetrical (i.e. the bias of reciprocity). Moreover, one can conceive that friendship is also a reflexive relation (everyone being his own friend, though this may make little sense).

Therefore, formally, friendship is thought of as having the properties of a relation of equivalence. All of which suggests that the representation of friendship may be governed by the schema of formal equivalence:

1. The relation of friendship is thought to be a particular instance of the more general relation of equivalence.
2. Every relation of equivalence, once it is mastered as such, is transitive.
3. Consequently, the relation of friendship is thought to be transitive, and axiom A1 is confirmed.

If the first point is conceded, the initial question – why is friendship transitive? – can then be replaced by a new question: why is friendship considered as an equivalence?

But the first point needs first to be established. For that purpose, Flament and Bullinger (1977) have studied the answers of children aged from 5 to 10. A considerable number of these children are unable to master, or master only incompletely, the formal schema of equivalence. Therefore, by questioning them according to the techniques of the Piagetians, one may hope to record different kinds of reasoning depending upon age (though the developmental aspect as such does not interest us here). It is necessary to check whether each child uses the same mode of reasoning in a physical task (the equivalence of the size of discs) as in a social task (friendship).

Physical task (discs): the experimenter used wooden discs of similar diameter, but of different colours; these discs were aligned on a board,

DOLLS

		CLASSIFICATION	OSCILLATION	RELATIONS	
	CLASSIFICATION	4 ($6\frac{5}{12}$)	2 ($7\frac{3}{12}$)	–	6 ($6\frac{8}{12}$)
DISCS	OSCILLATION	3 ($7\frac{5}{12}$)	6 ($9\frac{4}{12}$)	1 ($10\frac{1}{12}$)	10 ($8\frac{10}{12}$)
	RELATIONS	–	4 ($8\frac{8}{12}$)	13 ($9\frac{2}{12}$)	17 ($9\frac{0}{12}$)
		7 ($6\frac{10}{12}$)	12 ($8\frac{9}{12}$)	14 ($9\frac{2}{12}$)	

Fig. 4 Division of the 33 children according to how they treat the two situations (figures in brackets refer to the average ages of the children expressed in years and months)

and could be compared only by placing a disc on top of one of its neighbours. Questions relating to the equivalence in size of different discs called for a comparison to be made between discs which were not adjacent to each other in the array.

Social task (dolls): the experimenter laid out the dolls in a line before the child; he stated the feelings (of friendship or of hostility) between neighbouring dolls. The questions concerned the feelings between dolls which were not placed next to each other.

Each child undertook both tasks. The analysis of their answers allows us to identify three types of reasoning which are similar for the two tasks.

(1) *Treatment by classification:* the attribution of properties to objects (discs or dolls) enables children to divide the totality of these objects into equivalent classes (eventually in a fluid way if several properties conflict). This treatment of the task is particularly noticeable amongst the very young children.

(2) *Treatment in terms of relations:* the relations between the objects belonging to different pairs are considered as being part of a single unique relational field, and may therefore be organised (e.g. to give a reasoning based on transitivity). This treatment of the task is especially found amongst the older children.

(3) *Oscillation between treatment by classification and treatment in terms of relations*: for example, the child may create a local set of relations grounded, for different pairs of objects, on different properties.

Figure 4 shows that 70 per cent (23/33) of children treat discs and dolls in the same way. For the others, the developmental spread is minimal.

I conclude that the relation of friendship is thought of according to the schema of formal equivalence which implies transitivity (axiom A1). There is therefore no need to explain this transitivity, but what has to be explained is why friendship relations are considered as social equivalence.

Friendship and hierarchy

The fact that friendship and equivalence go together may seem natural: to be friends, people must resemble one another, have the same tastes, belong to the same social level. Is this not, though, too naive a psychology?

With others, I have studied the relationships between friendship and hierarchic equality (Flament, 1971; Flament and Monnier, 1971a and b). For instance, *on the one hand*, we have described a hierarchy and asked whether the relation between such an individual and such another one belonging to the same hierarchy, is a 'rather friendly' or 'rather hostile' one. Table 1 shows the results for three parallel sample surveys:

I. Subjects: students from Aix-en-Provence. Hierarchy: among the students in a work situation.
II. Subjects: students from Aix-en-Provence. Hierarchy: among the staff of an administration.
III. Subjects: pupils from a *lycée* in Geneva. Hierarchy: among the pupils.

Table 1. *Percentage of 'rather friendly' responses concerning pairs of individuals*

	Hierarchic equality			Hierarchic inequality	
	Higher level	Middle level	Lower level	Consecutive levels	Non-consecutive levels
I	25	40	51	70	40
II	45	49	68	57	40
III	26	37	31	78	30

One can see that the relations between equals are thought of as rather negative, except when it is matter of individuals sharing an equally lowly position in an administrative hierarchy; by contrast, individuals situated unequally, but consecutively, in a hierarchy (direct hierarchic relation) are fairly easily seen as being friends.

On the other hand (see Figure 5) we have presented pairs of individuals as being either on friendly or hostile terms (Flament and Monnier, 1971*b*), and have asked whether they were 'of equal rank' in a hierarchy or not (subjects: pupils from a *lycée* in Geneva; structures: among pupils).

	Equal	Unequal
Friends	55%	45%
Enemies	53%	47%

Fig 5. Percentage of responses 'equal'/'unequal' in rank concerning pairs of individuals described as being either 'friends' or 'enemies'

The differences in percentages in the results would be interesting to comment on if they were not so negligeable. From these results, one can conclude that it is far from being automatic that there is a relationship between friendship and equality. This would seem to contradict the conclusion from the previous section of this study. Then, however, we were studying the reasoning of children treating, independently, friendship and formal equivalence. Here, what we have studied is the relationship between friendship and hierarchical structures, in which social equality, quite a particular thing, cannot be reduced to the formal aspects of equivalence.

In a hierarchy, it is inequality, dependence, which characterises the situation. And one may wonder whether, in such a situation, the kind of friendship which is evoked is of the same nature as the friendship which is studied in classical experiments about balance. Let us note that the results in table 1 exclude the transitivity of friendship (friendship between consecutive levels should imply, by transitivity, friendship between non-consecutive levels). The subjects mention a very particular type of friendship when they make such comments as: 'In an administration, it is a good thing to make friends with certain people.'

The 'social vacuum' in which experiments about balance are carried out might lead one to suppose that it is the notion of friendship in general which is operating there. Our results suggest that such a general notion of friendship does not exist, and it is necessary to find something more consistent. It will be shown that the notion of 'friendly and egalitarian group' can fulfil the demands of this search.

The egalitarian group

Friendship and equality are bound up together in the idea of group, as our students present it when, at the beginning of a course, they are asked for a definition of the notion of group: a group is a gathering of individuals who have positive affective relations with one another (negative relations are never mentioned); they have activities, aims, ideas, attitudes, etc. in common; they are not differentiated, except perhaps in the organisation of a successful activity, and then equality is regained through equity. They are not in a hierarchy (except in the responses from students from a military college!).

This idea of the group, drawn from our pedagogic experience, is confirmed by a systematic study by Poitou (1978, chap. 6). Poitou shows (chap. 4) that the notion of group, as it is found in the theories of social psychology (which makes itself out to be scientific), is only this very idea, infinitely more subtle, articulated and argued! This convergence of naive and academic psychology is, for Poitou, ideological in nature (in the Marxist sense of that term). The history of this ideological notion may reveal to us its present mode of operating, and suggest some confirmatory experiments.

Thinkers of the Enlightenment, preparing the way for the industrial revolution, affirmed that society ought to be free, egalitarian and brotherly, as the motto of the French Republic still proclaims. Freedom and equality – essentially judicial – allowed a wage-labour market to be created; brotherhood was supposed to lead to equity whilst ameliorating the eventual inequalities which would result from the effect of the conflict between protagonists on this labour market.

Writing after the numerous revolutionary crises on the nineteenth century, Durkheim (1893, 1898) could no longer believe that a harmonious society would result from these grand principles directly governing the relations between individuals within society. He reports the analysis at the level of the group – the working group, primarily, which has 'the moral power of restraining personal egoisms, and of maintaining in the workers' hearts a stronger feeling of their common solidarity, and also of preventing the law of the strongest from being applied so brutally . . .' (Durkheim, 1893, p. xii).

These considerations did not remain in academic dissertations. They can be found, from the beginning of the century, in many texts of bourgeois origins concerning relations within business and industry: for example, in the news bulletins of firms (edited by the employers) exalting the 'one big happy family' and the 'spirit of the enterprise'. For Poitou, the ideological role of the notion of group is therefore obvious: affirming solidarity between all the members of the firm makes it possible to deny any antagonism between social classes, between workers and employers. The industrial changes of the middle of the century (e.g. the ever-increasing importance of supervising grades, of white-collar workers) has widely developed the efficiency of this ideological role. Indeed, these white-collar workers, most of them descended from families of self-employed workers, are, because of these origins and their own type of integration in the enterprise, particularly sensitive to the idea of the latter as an egalitarian and brotherly group. This was when the theory and practice of group dynamics developed most strongly.

But I consider that this is not the whole story of the notion of an egalitarian and brotherly group. One must also refer to the many millinerian currents of social thought in the West: Christianity, social utopianism . . . What is new in the philosophy of the Enlightenment is the affirmation of universal equality. Before, equality was reserved for some categories of people (e.g. Roman citizens, Christians, etc.). Thus Spinoza (seventeenth century), from whom Heider has drawn much of his inspiration (1979), enunciates (*Ethics*, III) some propositions quite similar to Heider's theory of equilibrium, but he very often circumscribed the field of their applicability to individuals 'of the same class or the same nation'.

I consider, then, that the contribution of bourgeois ideology, as far as our problem is concerned, is that it authorises and even forces us to think of the egalitarian and brotherly group as possibly being composed of any type of individual and, notably, of individuals who are in a relation of social antagonism.

We can therefore expect that, if the structures of friendship subjects have been asked about apply to *differentiated* individuals, the schema of equivalence works only for each sub-structure where the members are not differentiated.

In fact, the fictitious individuals mentioned in the experiments are always differentiated, even if it is only through their names. One must therefore ask oneself about the frontier of differentiation, and/or the pertinent criteria of differentiation; beyond which the structure is no longer a unique group.

The image of the group and differentiation

Thanks to the experiments about the relationship between friendship and hierarchy, we know that insisting on the hierarchic aspects is enough to suppress the reference to the notion of an egalitarian and brotherly group. In the absence of particular information concerning how hierarchical groups actually work, there is no reason to suppose that the hierarchical differentiation will be compensated for in terms of equity, so the idea of the group cannot wholly apply here to the structure.

Poitou's analysis shows that the ideological role of this is to conceal, not the hierarchic differences which exist within the firm, but the antagonisms of class which cut the hierarchy in two: workmen and supervisors. Consequently, one may expect to find out that the idea of a brotherly group appears again if one presents a hierarchy explicitly situated in a firm – at least when one questions the persons who are most sensitive, according to Poitou, to the influence which the predominant ideology exerts in this field, that is the middle-level supervisors in the organisation.

In the same firm, Aloisio (1970) has questioned on the one hand the departmental managers and, on the other, the operatives (workers); using five hierarchic levels well defined within the organisation (operative, foreman, departmental managers, vice-chairman, chairman). He asked if, 'in a firm like yours', the relations between two persons, whose hierarchic ranks only were mentioned, were likely to be 'rather friendly' or 'rather hostile' towards each other. For both of the categories who were questioned, vice-chairmen scarcely have any positive relations, either between themselves or with the others; which seems to reflect a real situation of conflict within the firm to which the subjects belong. Apart from that, each category describes the organisation in very different ways: for the departmental managers, some conflicts do exist (between vice-chairmen; between operatives and foremen – two levels of blue-collar worker in a situation of antagonism) but, essentially there is no division between the top and the bottom of the hierarchy; ties of friendship create relations between everybody, at least indirectly, through the departmental managers themselves, who ensure in this way the cohesion of the 'family' which the organisation forms. On the other hand, for the operatives, two groups are antagonistic; manual workers (operatives and foremen, all friends) and management.

Poitou emphasizes the essential role of the idea of an egalitarian and brotherly group in the process of masking the fundamental socioeconomic antagonisms, and an experiment carried out by Pichevin and Poitou (1974) demonstrates this in a way that deserves to be discussed. The subjects have been led, by means of constructing structures, to arrange the eight possible triangles in order of preference.

Three conditions were presented:

1. *'Control' condition*: the three fictitious subjects are designated by names only.
2. *'Differentiation by age' condition*: in addition to the names, it is specified that one of the subjects is forty, the other two are twenty.
3. *'Differentiation by social class' condition*: in addition to the names, it is specified that one is a managing director, the other two are workers. The experimenter has questioned French students and African students studying in France (the names mentioned being French for the French subjects and African for the African subjects).

In the 'control' condition, the friendly group (i.e. entirely positive triangle) reaches the following rank preference: 1.9 for French students, 2.3 for African students. The ranks of all the other structures was around 4.5, which is the result to be expected from chance (one can refer to the results obtained with French students in fig. 2). Figure 6 shows the results concerning the 'Differentiation' conditions.

The 'class opposition' of employers and workers is without doubt as well known (superficially) to the African students as it is to the French. On the other hand, the opposition by age does not mean the same thing for the two populations: for the French, the matter actually is the 'conflict of generations', which is a very significant phenomenon; for the Africans, it is a remaining trace, still very present, of the organisation of precapitalist African societies in which differences of generation indicated positions in social relations. From Poitou's perspective, one therefore must not be surprised that the structure '40 year-old against 20-year-old' is equally preferred by the Africans to the structure 'managing director against workers', whereas the results are different for the French.

But one ought to remark (and this Pichevin and Poitou leave out) that the differentiation by age exerts an influence on the French subjects: the

Differentiation	By age		By class	
Subjects	French	African	French	African
	3.0	4.5	4.7	4.0
	3.2	2.1	1.2	2.0
Best rank amongst the other structures	3.6	3.8	4.3	4.3

○ = 40 years of age, or managing director

□ = 20 years of age, or workers

Fig. 6   Mean rank of preference. Based on the study by Pichevin and Poitou (1974)

'perfectly positive' structure reaches only 3.0; and the structure '40 year-old against 20-year-old' reaches 3.2, whereas the other two structures which include two 'negative' and one 'positive' bond, reach the figures of 6.1 and 5.4 . . .

Our conclusion therefore ought to be – unlike the analysis completed by Pichevin and Poitou – that the differentiation by age does affect French as well as African subjects. The difference between the responses of these two populations is caused by the fact that the age difference refers, for African people, to a general model of society as divided into antagonistic classes by age, whereas for the French this difference does not refer to any such general model (either of society or of the family).

From these results, we can conclude that, in experiments about structural balance, the image of the group which emerges is that of an egalitarian and brotherly group. Moreover, these experiments record the image of society as 'multigroupal' and antagonistic whenever differentiations are relevant for a population. The previously mentioned experiment has been partly replicated, affording the experimenters a few insights into the models of 'unigroupal' or 'multigroupal' situations (Audierne, 1973). Only French people have been chosen as subjects. Only the 'control' (absence of differentiation) 'differentiation by social class' conditions were run. It is a pity that the differentiation by age was omitted. One can observe the same tendencies as in Pichevin and

Poitou's experiment. But, in addition, subjects had been asked to describe a concrete situation in which each structure was likely to apply as a way of commenting on the structures.

In the 'control' condition, that is the 'perfectly positive' structure – which is predominant – it is thought of as 'normal' and so there is little comment made about it; on the other structures, comments are made by imagining some traits of the protagonists' personalities.

In the 'differentiation by social class' condition, the predominant structure (employers against workers) is 'normal'. The most interesting result is how the structure which presents employers and workmen as friends is commented upon:

it is the Ideal Society (about 10 per cent)

it can exist in a small business, a family business or a craftsman's business (about 40 per cent)

the three men know one another outside the business (school, national service, sports centre . . .) (about 50 per cent).

Conclusion

In these various studies starting from the analysis of the bias of balance, I concentrated my research on explaining the bias of transitivity in friendship. After showing that the schema of formal equivalence is responsible for this bias, I have dwelt on the thesis: friendship and equality, in general, do not go together, they do so essentially in the representation of the egalitarian and brotherly group.

This representation projects itself, according to the case studies, into the whole of the structure under study, or into several sub-structures of this structure. Although this is not the problem we are dealing with here, the writer ought to recall the representation of a 'multigroupal' society, each segment of which, being sufficiently homogeneous, allows the idea of an egalitarian group to operate. Poitou's analysis suggests that these segments have to be defined by reference to class antagonism. It appears that these antagonisms play an important role, but it is possible that they do so mostly by proposing to subjects a common model for the division of society. Other divisions might be meaningful only for some of the subjects. The study of these 'multigroupal' representations remains to be carried out.

Part 3
The representations of cities and of urban space

12. Cities as social representations

STANLEY MILGRAM

Let me begin this chapter with a few general comments on the guiding concept of social representation. I shall then deal with its application to urban psychology.

Introductory remarks

For purposes of convenience, we take Durkheim's ideas of *conscience collective* as our starting-point. But in doing so we recognize that theories concerning the relationship of belief systems to social structure extend beyond this eminent sociologist. The major nineteenth-century social thinkers were concerned with the relationship between modes of consciousness and the structures of society. Within our own century, a substantial body of thinking has evolved under the rubric of 'the sociology of knowledge.' Thus a first obligation is to recognize that in addressing this topic we are working within a very substantial intellectual tradition, one which has approached the problem of social representations from a number of theoretical angles, not all of them compatible. Durkheim, for example, could not accept Marx's idea that such shared ideas were merely epiphenomenal derivatives of the economic structure of society.

If we examine the index of a standard contemporary text in social psychology, we will find little or nothing under the rubric of social representations. However, it would not be true to say that traditional social psychology has failed to deal with social representations, but rather that it has studied such phenomena under other labels. For example, the study of racial and ethnic stereotypes, which has received substantial attention in American social psychology, focuses on widely diffused beliefs that explain and evaluate social objects, while often predisposing the person to act toward such objects in certain ways.

Contributors to this volume have interpreted 'social representations' to mean several different things. It is useful to be clear about these distinctions. Thus far I have dealt exclusively with the notion of social representations in the sense of shared beliefs, theories, etc., following Durkheim's conception.

Of course, social representations can also mean something quite different, namely, how individuals represent the social world, whether or not such beliefs have a shared basis. This seems to be the meaning intended by the editors in their initial invitation – their concern is 'how people "theorize about" or "talk about" the experiences in which they participate and how these theories enable them to construct reality and ultimately to determine their behaviour.'

Such a view is, of course, far more general than what Durkheim had in mind in his concept of *conscience collective*. First, Durkheim contrasted shared beliefs with *conscience individuelle*. *Conscience collective* is a social phenomenon, concerned with social objects, produced through social interaction, and possessing the properties of *exteriority* and *constraint*, which are defining criteria of all social facts.

If we abandon this social emphasis to study how individuals theorize about their experiences, then we can see that within social psychology such topics as 'attribution theory' and 'implicit theories of personality' have systematically explored this issue. Indeed, it would be hard to exclude even Piaget from this camp, for he has certainly been concerned with the manner in which people develop theories about the physical and social world. Professor Farr's emphasis, however, is quite different. He argues that research should have a more phenomenological flavor or, more precisely, that it is important that we understand things from the actor's point of view. I myself think this is important. But – to return to our starting-point – we cannot equate this approach with Durkheim's concept of *conscience collective*, or with the methodology Durkheim wished to impart to sociology, with its unremitting emphasis on the objectivity of social facts.

One further general comment. One of the inspirations for this volume has been Moscovici's important work: *La Psychanalyse: son image et son public*. Let us note a special feature of this work. Moscovici has shown how a pre-existing system of thought – namely, the theories of Freud – is altered in the process of being assimilated into society. This is an extraordinarily interesting project, but it needs to be distinguished from the more general processes whereby society itself elaborates social representations using experience and the facticity of events as its raw material, rather than a pre-existing theory.

Having made these general comments, I would now like to proceed to an account of some research on the city as a social representation.

Cities as social representations

We start with the notion that people have some idea of what the city they live in is like. They have a map of the city in their minds, often fragmentary, that shows how various streets and avenues come together, and where certain neighborhoods are situated in relation to each other. They may also have attitudes about different parts of the city, and memories of different experiences associated with particular locales. This is not an especially revolutionary idea. Nor is it limited to social scientists. Indeed it is part of common-sense understanding, implicit whenever a newcomer asks a resident for directions in a strange city. In doing so, the newcomer assumes that the person he addresses possesses a representation of the city superior to his own. The ordinary person knows that people harbor representations of a city in their heads, and he knows further that some representations are more complete than others.

The task for the social scientist is to externalize these 'maps,' to get them out of the informant's experience and onto paper in complete and observable form. Once this is done it becomes possible to see how accurate the person's map is, where it distorts reality, what degree of structure it possesses, etc. It would also be possible to see what degree of consensus there was in the maps of many individuals and to explain their functional significance.

'Mental map' is, of course, too simple a designation for the corpus of information which individuals possess about the city, for although such schemata contain geographic components, in varying degrees they also harbor images of architectural details, attitudes toward different areas of the city or their residents, and numerous personal associations. Nonetheless, the cartographic emphasis has an element of validity in that individuals must have some spatial representation of the city in which they live, if only to enable them to move from one part to another. Moreover, the concept of the mental maps has proved useful in giving focus to the efforts to externalize the complex aggregate of ideas, attitudes, and information which individuals possess about their cities.

Psychologists have not been the only persons interested in psychological maps. Geographers such as David Stea (1969*a* and *b*), Peter Gould (1967), and Thomas Saarinen (1971) have tried not merely to describe cognitive representations but also to develop concepts for analyzing such maps. Stea asks: 'What are the elements out of which people mentally organize large geographic spaces?' and concludes that people think in terms of *points* (New York, Chicago, Canada, etc.). Further, he concludes that these points may be arranged in some *hierarchy* (some are larger, more important, desirable, etc.); that the areas are *bounded* with clear or fuzzy lines of demarcation; that people think in terms of *paths* connecting different points and whether *barriers* block any pair of points. Stea says that 'it matters not a whit that we cannot directly observe a mental map . . . If a subject behaves as if such a map existed, it is sufficient justification for the model.'

In typical studies employing these concepts, subjects are asked to make distance, direction, or size estimates of geographic points. Average results are then compared to the objective reality, the point of interest being the type of deviation from reality contained in the mental images. Thus Griffin (1948) argues that the relative areas ascribed to various regions reflect the importance individuals assigned to them. (Some of us have seen the map of the 'New Yorker's idea of the United States,' in which the city occupies a vast area of the country, and the Midwest is shrunk to a fraction of its actual size.)

Another question concerns the manner in which individuals use mental maps in everyday life to locate themselves in the environment or navigate from one point to another. The question of orientation was raised as early as 1913 by Trowbridge, and continues as a lively issue. Stea suggests that two very different mental approaches may be used in moving from one point to another. In one case, the person proceeds on the basis of a set of specific operations, so that the map consists less of an overall image than a sequence of directional instructions tied to specific cues. The person starts off in an initial direction until he comes to cue[1], such as a building or landmark, at which point he turns right or left until he gets to cue[2], and so forth, until his destination is reached. In a second strategy, the individual proceeds not in terms of a sequence of operations but through a generalized image of the city. Through successive approximations, he zeroes in on the target, constantly referring his position to his knowledge of the city's structure. This second strategy allows for the use of alternative routes, whereas the former method does not. Moreover, Stea points out that in the specific sequence method, 'if you miss a cue, you're lost.'

A final question, of particular relevance to the theme of this volume, is the degree to which such mental maps of cities may be considered 'social representations'. The fact that a person has some model of the environment does not, in itself, indicate that it is shared by others, or that it is in some manner the product of social interaction. A sailor stranded on a deserted island, for example, may form a subjective map of his environment which remains nothing more than the product of his individual cognitive processes. What then should be the criteria that determine whether such models of the environment ought to be considered social representations?

The first, and easiest to satisfy, is that the internal models represent social rather than nonsocial objects. This criterion is met by the very definition of the subject-matter; for cities are, *par excellence,* the products of intensive and prolonged social activity, containing the material embodiments not only of one's contemporaries, but of the accumulated labors, decisions, and values of earlier generations. Moreover, the city is not merely the product of social activity, it is the very form through which the most intensive of human social activity is given expression.

A second criterion, one which we shall have to establish by evidence rather than fiat, is that such representations are themselves the products of social interaction with the physical environment. We know, of course, that people are perfectly capable of elaborating maps of their environment even when left on their own. Generally speaking, it will be the *shared* character of the maps which will establish their social origin, just as it is the shared character of the linguistic forms of a community that indicates that language is a cultural rather than an individual product. Of course, this is not a foolproof criterion. Certain physical features of the urban environment may impress themselves on all individuals exposed to them, in the absence of actual social influence (perhaps by virtue of their impressive perceptual properties). Only detailed examination of the mental map of a number of individuals will reveal the degree to which such maps are socially mediated.

The third criterion that would qualify mental maps as true social representations is the presence of social meanings as an integral part of their construction. We may ask, therefore, whether such representations of the urban environment are limited to physical, geographic elements, or whether social categories interpenetrate them at significant points. Finally, we will want to know whether such representations are utilized only as individual cognitive tools, or whether they serve larger social functions.

Elsewhere (Milgram and Jodelet, 1976), I have described in detail the results of a study of mental maps in Paris which I carried out with Denise

Jodelet, then at the Maison des Sciences de l'Homme, and with the generous aid of Serge Moscovici. I shall summarize some of the findings of that study, then move on to report a complementary study of mental maps of New York.

Mental maps of Paris

To begin, our 218 subjects, drawn from each of the twenty *arrondissements* of Paris in proportion to their numbers, were asked to draw a map of Paris in which they were to mention all the elements of the city that came to mind. They could illustrate their maps with monuments, squares, neighborhoods, streets, or whatever else occurred to them. They were told that their sketch should not resemble a tourist map of Paris, but should express their personal view. Let us consider some of the maps drawn.

Map 1. This was drawn by a 25-year-old commercial agent with university degrees in physical chemistry. His first entries on the map were the Boulevards Saint-Germain and Saint-Michel, then the Faculté des Sciences at Jussieu, confirming that his student experience remains dominant. The modern structures of the Zamanski Tower at the Faculté des Sciences and the 50-storey Maine–Montparnasse office tower are prominently shown. Young people, more often than their elders, include these contemporary elements, as if the mental maps of the old were memorized a long time ago and cannot include these recent additions. Rising in the northwest, the massive office complex, La Défense, is given an almost projective significance, as it hovers menacingly alongside the city. The map expresses the central dilemma of contemporary Paris: how can it preserve its distinctive character, formed in earlier centuries, while coming to grips with modernity?

Map 2. This was drawn by a 50-year-old woman who, at the time of the interview, lived in the 12th *arrondissement*. However, for fifteen years she had lived in the 4th, which she drew with scrupulous detail, even to the point of showing the one-way streets for cars. She centred her map not on Paris as a whole, but on the part which had special meaning to her. Yet she was able to link her personal experience to highly public landmarks, like the Louvre and the Palais Royal. Perhaps it is characteristic of Paris that one can readily fuse private and public aspects of life through the network of streets and landmarks.

Map 3. This was by a 33-year-old butcher who lives in the 11th *arrondissement*. At first the map looks confusing, but when looking at it

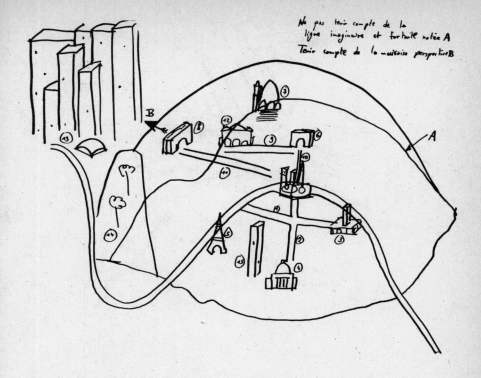

Map 1   Drawn by a 25-year-old who included new building at La Défense (far left) as well as the area which he knew best as a student

Ne pas tenir compte de la ligne imaginatire et fortuite notée A
Ignore the imaginary and accidental line labelled A

Tenir compte de la mauvaise perspective B
Notice the [better?] perspective B

The map is numbered in the sequence in which it was drawn

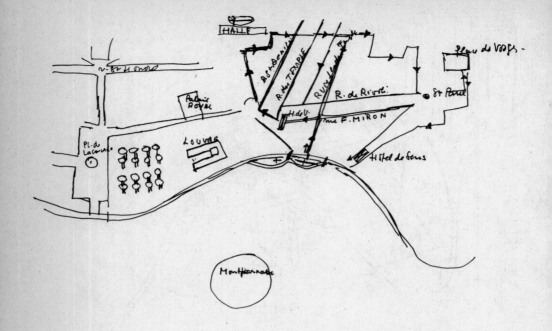

Map 2   A 50-year-old woman centred her map on the particular area which she knew best, but linked this with her own favourite landmarks

 1 Ile St Louis
 2 Ile de la Cité
 3 Hôtel de Ville
 4 rue F. Miron
 5 Châtelet
 6 Les Halles
 7 rue St Denis
 8 rue du Temple
 9 rue du Parc Royal
10 place des Vosges
11 Hôtel de Sens
12 quai aux Fleurs
13 Notre Dame
14 Montparnasse
15 Palais Royal
16 Le Louvre
17 Les Tuileries
18 Place de la Concorde
19 rue St Honoré

This is the subject's list in the order in which she drew the points on the map

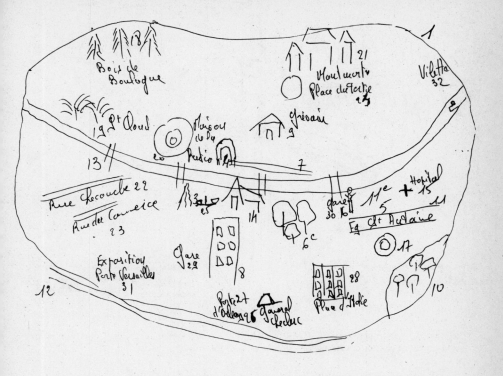

Map 3   A butcher's map includes the slaughterhouse of La Villette and his home area, yet distorts basic geography, particularly the curve of the Seine

  1 Le contour
  2 La Seine
  3 Tour Eiffel
  4 Arc de Triomphe
  5 Mon quartier le 11ᵉ
  6 Jardin des Plantes
  7 Champs-Elysées
  8 Tour Montparnasse
  9 Musée Grévin
 10 Bois de Vincennes
 11 Fg St Antoine
 13 Les ponts sur la Seine
 14 Notre Dame
 15 Hopital St Antoine
 16 La Bastille
 17 La Nelieu

 18 Bois de Boulogne
 19 Les fontaines de la Porte St Cloud
 20 ORTF
 21 Montmartre
 22 Rue Lecourbe
 23 Rue du Commerce
 24 Place du Tertre
 25 Le Palais de Justice
 26 Ave Général Leclerc
 27 Porte d'Orléans
 28 Les Tours de la Place d'Italie
 29 Gare Montparnasse
 30 Gare de la Bastille
 31 Palais des Expositions, Porte de Versailles
 32 La Villette

Subject has omitted some numbers and place names from map, which is numbered in the sequence in which it was drawn

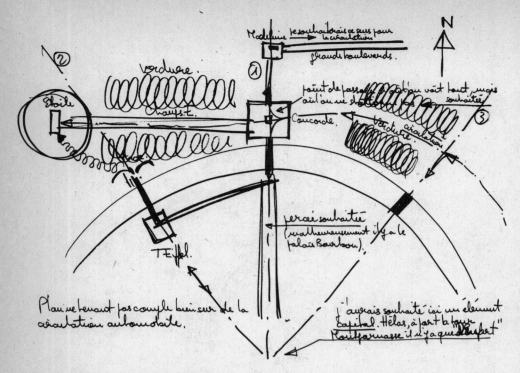

Map 4 A visionary map of Paris, which was drawn by an architect, portrays some imaginary new avenues as well as projected monuments

je souhaiterais ce sens pour la circulation grands boulevards
I would have the traffic on the *grands boulevards* one way only, in this direction

point de passage d'où l'on voit tout, mais où l'on ne stationne pas
a thoroughfare with a panoramic view, where parking would be forbidden

percée souhaitée (malheureusement il y a le palais Bourbon)
a proposed through road (unfortunately, this is blocked by the Bourbon palace)

j'aurais souhaité ici un élément *capital*. Hélas, à part la tour Montparnasse il n'y a que 'Denfert'.
I would like to have a *major* feature here; but apart from the Martparnasse tower, there is only 'Denfert'.

Plan ne tenant pas compte bien sûr de la circulation automobile
This map of course takes no account of motor traffic

1 Concorde
2 Etoile
3 Madeleine
4 Seine
5 T. Eiffel
6 Trocadero
7 Ponts
8 Axes 1 2 3
9 vers Montparnasse

closely you can see the elements of his life circumstances. He does not forget to include his home area, which is something of a hidden one to most subjects. Nor does he neglect La Villette, where the major stockyards and slaughterhouses of Paris are. You can imagine his visits to the great exposition hall at the Porte de Versailles to see displays of meat-cutting equipment, motorcycles, and perhaps cars. Faubourg Saint-Antoine, of revolutionary significance, is placed on the Left Bank, where it would seem to belong politically. Most confusing, perhaps, is the inverted curve he has given to the Seine; the placing of elements along the river seems out of line with reality. Yet even if the Etoile, the Maison de la Radio and the Porte de Saint-Cloud deviate from their true place, there is still meaning in their topological sequence.

Map 4. A mental map is not limited to reality, but may include visions of how a city ought to be. The architect who drew this map organized the city around the Place de la Concorde. He saw a major avenue stretching south from the Place, over the Seine, piercing the Chambre des Députés, and continuing south into the heart of the Left Bank. It terminated in an impressive structure (as yet unrealised). From that point, a broad avenue would sweep northwest to reveal the Eiffel Tower, and another would sweep northeast, leading to the colonnade of the Madeleine (displaced from its present location). Such mental maps are fanciful. Yet Paris as it exists was born first as a set of ideas, and the Paris to come is also germinating in the minds of architects and city planners. This mapmakers' concern with problems of car traffic represents a realistic attention to the city's most severe environmental problem.

It is clear the subjects did not merely draw their maps from personal, direct experience with the city. They learned them, in part, from other maps. Street maps of Paris, prepared by technically skilled cartographers, are an inherent part of contemporary Parisian culture. Probably not a single subject could have drawn an accurate map of the city, showing its form and basic structure, without recalling maps he has already seen. But through selection, emphasis and distortion, the maps became projections of life styles, and express the emotional feelings of the participants.

Moreover, neither the city, nor the mental maps of the city, are simple collections of elements; they are structures. It is the essence of structure that displacing one element has consequences for the other elements to which it is linked.

Finally, a map that a person draws of his city is not his mental map, but is only a clue to it. He may not be able to draw very well; he may have images in his mind he cannot put on paper. But the sketch is an opening into his conception of the city.

The sequence that emerged as subjects sketched their maps of Paris may tell us what was uppermost in their minds when they thought of the city. What is most important is probably what comes out first. With this in mind, we asked each subject to number each element as he drew it on the page. Most subjects began their maps of Paris by drawing a rough egg shape designating the city limits. Paris possesses a clear boundary and its inhabitants are conscious of its form. The boundary is sharply etched by the *périphérique*, a highway wrapped around the city, separating the city from the densely populated suburbs, and providing a contemporary moat-in-motion to replace the historic walls.

Within the city there are almost 1,000 different elements included in the maps drawn, but only one feature was the first entry of a large number of participants: the Seine. After the city limits are sketched, this is easily the most popular item. It is not only a basic geographic fact of the city, but its most salient psychological feature as well, and much of the subjects' subsequent mapmaking revolves around it.

But there is a serious distortion in the way the Seine is represented. In reality the path of the Seine resembles a wave that enters Paris at the Quai Bercy, rises sharply northward, tapers slightly as it flows into separate streams around the islands, initiates its flat northernmost segment at the Place de la Concorde, then turns sharply in a great bend at the Place de l'Alma to flow out of the southwestern tip of the city. But in their drawings, 91 percent of the subjects understated the river's degree of curvature. Several pulled it through the city as a straight line, and it was usually drawn as a gentle arc, of slight but uniform curvature. Because the course of the river is made to resemble a gentle, convex arc, some subjects forced the river through the Bois de Boulogne, allowing no space for the Auteuil and Passy districts. Accordingly, these districts are eliminated or displaced to the Left Bank.

Why does this distortion occur? Quite clearly it reflects the subjects' experience. Although the Alma bend of the Seine is apparent in high aerial views of the city, it is not experienced as a sharp curve in the ordinary walk or drive through the city. The curve is long enough to obscure the pronounced turn of the river.

After the Seine, Notre Dame and the Ile de la Cité were set down most often as first entries. These three elements are at the very heart of the idea of Paris. Lutèce was born on the Ile de la Cité; Notre Dame was constructed there 800 years ago. The sequence in which subjects enter features in the hand-drawn maps recapitulates this history.

Unlike a city such as New York, whose psychological core has shifted continuously northward, the psychological centre of Paris has remained true to its origins, building outward from the Seine, never shifting its centre away from its historic root. The remarkable stability of the 'heart of Paris' gives a permanent dimension to the city's psychological structure.

Altogether, our subjects entered 4,132 elements in their maps – an average of nineteen for each subject. If the city did not give its inhabitants a sense of its structure, we would find little agreement among the subjects. But time and again we find the same locations showing up. Indeed, about half the 4,132 elements are accounted for by only twenty-six locations. A city is a social fact. We would all agree to that. But we need to add an important corollary: the perception of a city is also a social fact. It is not only what exists, but what is highlighted by the community that acquires prominence in the mind of the person, and in this sense a city is as much a collective representation as it is an assemblage of streets, squares, and buildings.

To supplement the method of 'free recall' used in drawing maps of the city, we gave our subjects forty photographed scenes of Paris, which they were asked to identify. Correct recognition showed that a scene was an active part of the subject's representation of the city, even if he or she did not include it in his map. All of the groups that were shown the photographs, whether professionals or workers, recognised the same four scenes with the greatest degree of accuracy: Etoile, Notre Dame, Place de la Concorde, and the Palais de Chaillot. What distinguishes these scenes is not so much their beauty as their monumentality, special historic significance, and scenic grandeur. Each has come to be indelibly associated with Paris, not merely within the city, but abroad as well.

In the mental representation of a city, two quite separate geographic locations may be collapsed into a single imagined site. Thus, many Parisians mentally combined the nonsectarian Monument de la Déportation (located on the Ile de la Cité) and the Mémorial du Martyr Juif (located in the Saint-Paul district) into a single place, believing there is only one such monument, rather than the two that actually exist. Porte Saint-Martin was frequently misidentified as Porte Saint-Denis, highlighting the psychologically interchangeable character of the two arches.

Class factors shaped the maps of the subjects by segregating rich and poor residentially, and also by transmitting a class-linked culture to various parts of the population. Thus, Place Furstenberg is recognised by 59 percent of the professional subjects, but only 17 percent of the workers; UNESCO headquarters by 67 percent versus 24 percent. The icons of the city, however, are recognised equally by all groups, acting as integrative elements.

When a city lacks fine squares and architecture, mediocre places are widely publicised because they are the best of what is available. But in Paris, a surfeit of riches creates the opposite situation. Competition for a place in the mind is fierce: many worthy places are excluded. Thus Place Félix Eboué, which has an impressive and monumental fountain, is recognised by less than half of the Parisians, while 87 percent of the subjects cannot identify Place Rodin. Place d'Israel, which could serve as an architectural showpiece, sinks to virtual obscurity – identified by only 4.47 percent of the subjects.

Location plays some part. But, more critically, the data highlight how the mental maps of Parisians are not only individual products, but important social constructions. Any one of those last sites possesses sufficient aesthetic value to serve as a widely known feature of the Parisian environment. If society chose to publicise Place Rodin, the square could become as famous as (God forbid) the urinating statue of Brussels. Social definition determines, through selection and reiteration, which features of the city acquire importance in the mental maps of the inhabitants.

The photographic recognition test tells us about the knowledge of specific landmarks, but we wanted a more general picture of the known and unknown parts of the city. Accordingly, we provided each subject with an illustrated map of the city, which we overprinted with the boundaries of the eighty administrative districts (quartiers). We asked each subject to study his map and indicate the ten quartiers with which he was most familiar, and those that were least familiar to him.

The five most familiar quartiers are centered on the Latin Quarter and Ile de la Cité. The next five choices are near to this cluster, but also extend to the Champs-Elysées and Etoile. When subjects were asked to list the quartier they knew least well, we found a striking movement away from the centre of Paris to the neighbouring arrondissements.

These data, translated into respective arrondissements, outline a ring of unknown areas around the core of Paris. Curiously, the boundary between known and unknown parts of the city retraces part of the route of the last wall of Paris, the fermiers Généraux. Although the wall was torn down in 1859, its effects stay in the mental maps of contemporary

Parisians, with the city's least familiar parts lying outside the original wall boundary.

The residential patterns of Paris create a class basis to known and unknown parts of the city. Generally speaking, the wealthier people live in the western part of the city, and the poorer classes live in the east. It is not surprising, therefore, that the areas least well known to the working class differ from those of the middle-class professionals.

Ethnic groups – with the exception of North African districts and the Jewish quarter around Saint-Paul – do not figure greatly in the mental maps of Paris. The city does not have the multiple ethnic concentrations found in New York, and areas are not branded with an ethnic label. Paris, before the last war, had areas which were rich in residents from particular provinces, and subjects still identify the quarters around the Gare de Montparnasse as Paris des Bretons. On the other hand, the Chinese community that once flourished behind the Gare de Lyon was not represented in the maps of contemporary Parisians.

Subjects placed the very poor in the northeastern districts, while the wealthy are overwhelmingly situated in the 16th *arrondissement*, at the western edge of the city. This is a sharply differentiated perception, with no geographic overlap between the two groups. The criminally dangerous areas of Paris were put down as the 18th and 19th *arrondissements*, with the greatest threat to personal safety in the Goutte d'Or *quartier* (which houses many North African immigrants).

The deepest affection for the city was reserved for its central historical areas. The best-liked *quartiers* fell in the 6th, 4th, 1st, and 5th *arrondissements*.

A comparison with mental maps of New York

Somewhat similar methods were used in a study of how New Yorkers mentally represent their city. I will describe these results briefly in order to compare them to the Parisian findings. The subjects for the New York study consisted of 332 residents who returned a questionnaire which appeared in a local magazine. From this pool of responses we reduced the number to make the final sample proportional to the actual population in each of New York's five boroughs: 34 percent Brooklyn dwellers, 23 percent from Queens, 20 percent each from the Bronx and Manhattan, and 3 percent from Staten Island. Of the subjects, 47 percent are male, 53 percent female, and their ages range from 14 to 72. With a median age of 32, they have lived on the average for 25 years in New

York and, for the most part, are rooted in the professional middle class.

Let me begin the discussion with an account of some differences between the maps of New York and those of Paris. As indicated above, Parisians know that Paris is shaped like an egg, with a river curving through it. It has fixed, clear boundaries and, once you cross the *périphérique*, you are outside the city. But the representation of New York is different; the city has a clear psychological core, centered on Manhattan, but it is unstable at its outer boundaries. New Yorkers are not certain whether 'New York' means only Manhattan, the five boroughs (which politically existed as part of New York City since 1898), or the larger metropolitan area. About 25 percent of the subjects depict only Manhattan on their maps; 50 percent drew the boundaries to include other boroughs, and 25 percent also included the fringes of New Jersey. Many New Yorkers are uncertain whether areas such as Bay Ridge, Glenn Oaks, and Pelham are contained within the meaning of the concept of New York City.

The image of Manhattan is so powerful that it obscures for the residents many admirable features of other parts of the city. There are numerous examples in our findings of the way in which Manhattan dominates the subjects' conception of New York. For example, subjects were asked to indicate the most beautiful areas of the city. Seven of the ten most cited areas were in Manhattan. Of the 32 areas mentioned as most familiar by 10 percent or more of the respondents, 22 were in Manhattan, 5 were in Brooklyn, 3 in Queens, 2 in the Bronx, and none in Staten Island. It must be remembered that only 20 percent of the sample reside in Manhattan, while 34 percent reside in Brooklyn.

It became clear from our study that the knowledge which typical New Yorkers have of their city is not merely knowledge they have gained from direct experience. They have also acquired second-hand knowledge, attitudes, and beliefs about the city. Thus, their responses to many of our questions reflect 'conventional wisdom' about the city rather than its deeper reality. For example, in one of our questions we asked subjects to identify locales in the city that they find particularly beautiful. Here we find that the typical thinking is circumscribed by a set of social boundaries. These boundaries define the 'fashionable areas of the city'. Whatever lies outside these boundaries tends to be ignored in responding to this question. For example, by any standard of urban design, Ocean Parkway is an impressive and beautiful thoroughfare, but it hardly appears in any maps. This is also true of the Grand Concourse. The latter was designed by a Frenchman, Louis Risse, at the turn of the century; it is as broad as the Champs-Elysées, with cross streets passing through tunnels beneath the boulevard. Yet, because it lies outside the ambit of what is socially fashionable, it remains a virtually unmentionable locale.

Even within Manhattan, we find the subjects' knowledge of the city to reflect a socially generated picture of the city. Audubon Terrace, at 155th Street and Broadway, is one of the most impressive architectural ensembles of New York; but it is located in an area populated by blacks and Hispanics. It is not only off-limits geographically, it has also been expunged cognitively from the minds of New Yorkers. It scarcely figures in the maps of our subjects. There is an urban culture, transmitted to residents, that highlights certain parts of the city while suppressing a knowledge of other parts. In this sense, mental maps are social facts, not just individual facts.

Neighborhoods

The single most important element in the social representation of a city is the *neighborhood*. The concept of neighborhood itself reflects more general modes of how we organize knowledge of social life: neighborhoods are either good or bad, fashionable or undesirable, and always connote something of the economic, ethnic, and racial characteristics of their inhabitants. From a simple idea of spatial location, the concept of neighborhood comes to be imbued with properties derived from fundamental ideas of social hierarchy.

Moreover, the neighborhood becomes a component of the individual's social identity. That is why when you ask a person what city he comes from he will tell you without blush, but when you ask about his neighborhood, the question may be considered too personal for casual conversation: for the neighborhood is a status-differentiating component.

The neighborhood, therefore, is the principal means whereby the merely geographic and physical characteristics of the city are given a social meaning. Although New York does not possess the numerically labeled *arrondissement* structure of Paris (so convenient for pigeon-holing people), it possesses more than a hundred recognized neighborhoods, all of which can be placed on a continuum of social desirability.

Neighborhoods high in this continuum need not always have the most desirable physical features. Consider New York's upper East Side, the area which our subjects designate as the most desirable. Unless an apartment overlooks Central Park, it is an area devoid of breathing space, consisting of stone towers built on acres of unrelieved pavement. Park Avenue is a fuming canyon of hydrocarbons. It is a wonder not only that people will pay exhorbitant Park Avenue rents and maintenance charges, but that they are willing to live there at all. We note that Harlem, which in popular imagery possesses only rat-infested slums, actually contains a considerable amount of attractive housing. But none of this figures in the public image of these two areas. The images are social constructions that are linked to, but not wholly identifiable with, the facts.

The social representation of an area often represents a simplification and exaggeration of the dominant theme. It is as if each neighborhood has to be characterized by some simple, socially potent description. Often the image of an area will be dominated by the social character of its inhabitants. In New York this often translates into ethnic or racial identification; and one pronounced difference between the mental maps of New Yorkers and Parisians is the greater degree of ethnicization in New York. We asked subjects: 'Different ethnic groups are sometimes concentrated in specific areas of a city. Please identify some of the ethnic areas of New York City which you are aware of.' The responses to this question reflected the ethnic complexity of New York City, and the high degree of salience which ethnicity possesses. A total of fifty-one labels were mentioned by our 100 respondents, covering almost every neighborhood in the city.

Of the total number of responses made to this question (1,646), 81 percent (1,329) converged on seven ethnic groups: black, Jewish, Italian, Puerto Rican, German, Irish, and Chinese. Blacks were listed by 85 percent of the subjects, Jews by 87 percent, Italians by 82 percent, Puerto Ricans by 67 percent, Chinese by 60 percent, Germans by 51 percent, and Irish by 41 percent. At least 5 percent of the subjects also mentioned Greeks, Scandinavians, Poles, Ukranians, Arabs, and Indians.

New York has a greater ethnic pluralism than Paris. But New Yorkers also have a greater tendency to define a neighborhood in ethnic terms – Little Italy, Chinatown – and so forth, and this plays an important part in the New Yorker's representation of his city.

One can go further and say that in New York ethnicity, and above all race, is the prepotent classificatory principle. Anyone penetrating the euphemisms of polite speech recognizes that when a middle-class New Yorker asks: 'Is this a good neighborhood,' he generally means, 'Is this a neighborhood free of blacks?' Numerous other variables map onto this racial schema. For example, when subjects were asked to indicate areas about which they were fearful, the results correlated strongly with the presence of black and Hispanic minorities. Approximately three-fourths of the 439 responses to this question converged on fifteen geographic areas. The most frequently mentioned residential area inspiring fear was Harlem, reported by 32 percent of the subjects, the South Bronx, the Lower East Side, Greenwich Village, and Bedford Stuyvesant. Almost all of the fears mentioned involved fear of some crime: robbery, mugging, rape, or murder.

Neighborhoods in New York, as in most cities, have identifying labels attached to them: Murray Hill, Morningside Heights, Riverdale, etc. A neighborhood label, once affixed, has important consequences for the inhabitants. For outsiders, it reduces decision-making to more manageable terms. Instead of dealing with the variegated reality of numerous city streets, the resident can form a set of attitudes about a limited number of social categories and act accordingly. Thus a mother will instruct her child to stay out of Harlem, or a mother may judge that a boy who lives in Riverdale is probably acceptable for her daughter. Thus the mental map of neighborhoods is not superfluous cognitive baggage, but performs important psychological and social functions. And the consequences are indeed ramified: the reputation of a neighborhood may influence where a businessman decides to open a shop, where banks invest money, and it affects public policy. In New York City, banks engaged in a policy called 'redlining', that is, defining certain neighborhoods as being unsuitable for investment. A practice such as this may create a self-fulfilling prophecy. The decision to refuse mortgage loans to a neighborhood increases the likelihood of that neighborhood's further decay. The negative conception of an area may thus produce its own reality.

The existence of neighborhoods implies that cities not only have external boundaries, but important internal boundaries as well. But what establishes the boundaries of an area? There appear to be two schools of thought. The first is that sharp discontinuities in the objective features of areas determine neighborhood boundaries. These may consist of physical barriers, such as a broad street, a change in the economic and social characteristics of an area and, perhaps most important for New York City, the racial and ethnic composition of the inhabitants. A somewhat different view has been advanced by Gerald Suttles in his important book *The social construction of communities*. While acknowledging that all of these factors play a part in defining the boundaries of a neighborhood, he asserts that in the last analysis, the neighborhood is a creative social construction. He points out that most often the neighborhood boundary is an arbitrary street or intersection, rather than a physical boundary. Thus, in New York City, Harlem 'begins' on the north side of 96th Street. The demographic approach, which equates the neighborhoods with particular concentrations of ethnic or racial types, is less interesting for Suttles than the question: 'How are varying proportions of racial, ethnic and income groups selectively highlighted in the reputation of local communities?'

In my own view, both principles are operative. Objective factors are, of necessity, reflected in mental maps, but such representations often exaggerate, simplify, or distort social facts. Moreover, there is a continuous dialogue across the two domains. People cannot forever hold on to the image of an area as a pleasant neighborhood if it has decayed into a brutal slum. But there is frequently a time-lag between the actual state of an area and its social reputation. Or a neighborhood may slowly improve without this being reflected in its general reputation for many years.

In my discussion of mental maps of New York and Paris, I have concentrated on the way in which the individual is the recipient of information about his urban environment. This is, of course, only part of the picture. Suttles, and more recently my colleague Dr Peter Salins, stress the process whereby the social images are actively constructed. For any one person, the images are built up from a composite of information received from direct experience, other individuals, and the media. The media constantly evaluate places in articles, news reports, etc., often from a specific point of view. Moreover, individuals personally familiar with a place, and those who are not, voice opinions about a place. These not only become part of the reputation of an area, but may critically affect how a person perceives a particular neighborhood. Direct observation itself is only partially accurate, because what the person perceives from a complex visual and social field may be highly selective and dependent upon his expectations. The social reputation of a locale may direct his attention to features consistent with that reputation, and constrain the person to report in terms of the social judgments he had previously internalized.

Social representations are the product of a multitude of persons. Not all of those persons, of course, need play an equal part in the formation of the urban image. Those occupying dominant positions in society have greater influence, prestige, and access to the media than the poorer elements of society. They are therefore in a better position to impose their own conception of what is desirable and what must be avoided. The opinions of the powerless concerning their neighborhoods may be more readily discounted.

Moreover, business and real estate interests that have an economic stake in their investments expend considerable effort to create a favorable image for particular urban areas through the extensive use of advertising and public relations devices. Durkheim argued that the *conscience collective*, the attitudes and sentiments shared by members of a society, pertained only to societies that did not possess a complex division of labor. In a complex society, numerous groups compete to impose their viewpoints, and the 'conventional wisdom,' far from being a spontaneous emergent, may often be shaped by the manipulative efforts of influential economic interests.

Concluding remarks

The representations which people have of their cities contain many idiosyncratic elements, but I have been impressed in my research by the degree to which people's knowledge about a city, and how they feel about various parts of the city, are social facts, and not merely individual facts. The reputation of Harlem or Greenwich Village exists outside any specific individual, but is lodged in a general community consciousness. Moreover, such representations exhibit the constraints Durkheim ascribes to social facts. It is not merely that the individual knows that Harlem is an undesirable neighborhood; he cannot choose to live in Harlem without jeopardizing his own social standing. He will be directed toward those neighborhoods that correspond to his own social position, or that reflect his social goals. The person's social identity is bound up with the neighborhood in which he lives and the social connotations attached to that place. The social representations of the city are more than disembodied maps; they are mechanisms whereby the bricks, streets, and physical geography of a place are endowed with social meaning. Such urban representations, therefore, help define the social order of the city, and the individual's place in it.

13. The representation of urban space: Its development and its role in the organisation of journeys*

J. PAILHOUS

When Professors R. Farr and S. Moscovici invited me to present some work at a colloquium on social representations (Paris 1979) that I had conducted into the representation of urban space, I at first expressed mild surprise. In the twelve years that I have been carrying out research, this is the first time I have been called upon to present some of my work within the context of social psychology – which only goes to show how watertight the sub-disciplines of psychology are. My interpretative frameworks, methods and critical standpoints are in fact mainly allied to what is commonly known as cognitive psychology. I had indeed an inkling of a cognitivist current within the heart of social psychology without, however, being able to determine its exact content. What precisely, for example, might be the meaning of social representation in relation to image or spatial representation? Is there, moreover, any more to the distinction drawn between 'social representation' and 'image representation' in Piaget's sense – in other words, representing an object to oneself in its absence – than the remnants of an old philosophical debate on 'nature–nurture'? As both terms are different aspects of the same philosophical position this might explain their current peaceful co-existence in mutual ignorance of each other. It is therefore in all modesty that I offer one research perspective amongst others, leaving until afterwards the clarification of this question.

In this chapter, I shall be writing about urban space, in other words, the process of modelling which transforms physical space into this complex reality which is the town. I shall be more particularly concerned with space as it is involved in journeys. From this point of view, the town presents two major characteristics: a structural complexity of space, and the attainment of a goal which cannot be seen directly

*Translated by Anne Duff

311

by the subject and which he must, therefore, necessarily represent mentally. We know in psychology that this representation is closely dependent on the type of activity in which the subject is engaged. The tourist, the taxi-driver, and the worker who make their daily journeys from home to work, etc. have different representations of the town in general and of the space involved in journeys in particular. How a representation of space is developed on the basis of this activity and how this representation of space, in turn, enables one to plan a journey are questions which will be considered here as of prime importance.

It is today impossible to address this type of question without referring to the work of K. Lynch (1960). In his opinion, the primary role of the image of the environment is to permit mobility and the attainment of goals. He stresses that 'in the process of way-finding, the strategic link is the image of the environment; the generalised mental picture of the external world that is held by an individual. This image, which is the product both of immediate sensation and of the memory of past experience, is used to interpret information and to guide action.' Moreover, although each representation is individual and its essential content is only rarely, if ever, communicated, it is nevertheless linked to the collective image.

In this volume, Milgram illustrates and develops theoretically the link between the collective image and the individual representation. He discusses not only the functional aspects of this link, but also, and more especially, its significance, and its emotional aspects.

At the same time, in the Soviet Union, Shemyakin (1963), who is interested in topographic representation, made an interesting distinction between the representation of journeys linked to the subject's immediate activity and the representation of the spatial relations between the 'objects' which make up this space. This latter type of representation is characterised chiefly by its panoramic nature. Basing himself on observations concerning the comparative orientation of blind and sighted subjects Shemyakin concluded that representations of the former type are absolutely necessary for the development of the latter. Furthermore, on the ontogenetic plane, he demonstrates the dominance of the first type of representation during early stages in the development of a topographic memory. This is a result which, on this point, compares with those obtained by Piaget and Szeminska (1948).

If I have cited these two authors (i.e. Milgram and Shemyakin) as a part introduction to my own studies (although, at the time I began my work on this topic, I was unaware of their existence), it is because they bear witness to attempts, both in the United States and in the Soviet Union, to use cognitive psychology, in its fundamental aspects, in order to understand situations outside of the laboratory. These field studies, in turn, have proved fruitful to theoretical developments in cognitive psychology. It is with this in mind that I shall briefly present a series of personal studies on urban space.

We will, therefore, be studying individual representations of a social object – the town – in which the subjects carry on their social activities (e.g. their work, if they are taxi-drivers). These individual representations will have both a content and a structure, even if one considers only their functional aspects, such as the planning of journeys. Two points, therefore, can be made:

(1) In concerning ourselves with the functional aspects of action, we are not concerned with motives: *we are investigating the how and not the why*.
(2) The commonality found between the individual representations (i.e. the means of action) derives from the possible common activity (e.g. of taxi-drivers) and from the uniqueness of the object. *From the same causes, the same effects*.

This makes these studies unique in relation to the classic works on social representations.

1. Co-ordination of the rules governing journeys and of spatial images

To begin with, it must be stressed that the analysis of the rules governing journeys has been clearly distinguished from the analysis of images. Broadly speaking, it is fair to say that works on the representation of urban space (including those previously quoted by Lynch and, to a lesser extent, by Shemyakin) have made only a poor distinction between these two aspects. After a statement of principle on the decisive role of the activity of the subject in the use and construction of the image, the authors rush on to analyse such images as can be inferred, for example, from drawings. However, we shall see that it is a precise analysis of how journeys are organised which, *at a later stage*, will permit the analysis of images. It is true that it is the operational and symbolic concepts, as well as the dominance of the former over the latter in Piagetian theory, which encourage this type of distinction.

I consider it worthwhile, in view of the fact that I shall be making extensive use of them in interpreting my own results, to recapitulate briefly some important elements of Piaget's position. In their *Représentation de l'espace chez l'enfant* (1946), Piaget and Inhelder define representation in this way: 'it consists either in evoking objects in their absence, or, when it enhances perception in their presence, in filling out perceptual information by referring to other objects not visible at that moment in time'. As it stands, this definition is too broad for our problem; this is due mainly to the spatial character of the work carried out by taxi-drivers. Piaget gives representation the narrow meaning of a mental image in the formation of the symbol (1945). On the spatial level, the image arises from what Piaget terms 'geometric intuition'.

The image does indeed play a special role in the geometric field in that it is itself spatial in character. In *L'Epistémologie de l'espace* Piaget (1964) develops this theme, starting from an example: 'in the case of numbers, the number 4, etc. . . . . None of these images is a number. On the other hand, if you ask the subject to symbolise a square, the expressive image tends towards a genuine isomorphism with the object signified'.

This image does not result from perception alone, but rather from perceptual activity – which is something quite considerably different. The latter amounts to 'co-ordination at an operational level – between the foci of attention and perceptions proper'. The image is an 'internalised imitation', which is not a faithful copy of the object itself, but one which contains accommodations suited to the action which this subject will bring to bear on the object. Thus, 'everyone knows that the lay-out of a strange town can be worked out and remembered better by walking around it alone and being responsible for one's own wanderings, than by following a companion who acts as a guide' (*L'Image mentale chez l'enfant*, 1966), even though the sensory data remain comparable in the two cases. The intervention of actions as essential components is all the more necessary in that it is almost always a case of 'images with multi-sensory connections', that is relating to complex actions which is precisely the case in journeys within urban space.

The image, in Piaget's works, plays the part of a sometimes indispensable auxiliary. An auxiliary, in so far as, for example, the transformation of an arc into a straight line necessitates an invariance of length in order to create a correct image. This invariance is subject to the notion of conservation. Conservation in no way relies on the image but, on the contrary, exerts an influence over it. It is indispensable in so far as, if the (symbolic) knowledge of the state, E_n, resulting from the (operational) transformation, T_u, is not sufficiently precise, then there can be no comprehension either of the state, $E_n + 1$, nor even of the transformation, $T_u + 1$.

Thus, travel within urban space amounts to a close inter-connection between the operational activity (or transformation) and the imaginal activity (or representation) of the states. The stability of the spatial configuration encountered in the town, and the fact that it is impossible to perceive the goal directly, make planning the action both possible and necessary. This planning of the action, which for the most part takes place before it is carried out, is, at the level of skill attained by taxi-drivers, rarely questioned during the actual course of the journey.

One can, therefore, distinguish, on the one hand, an image of the town – which we know depends on the activity of the subject – and, on the other hand, an (internalised) operational activity of creative changes in this image at the end of which the journey has been planned. It is the result of this planning, in so far as it can be observed in the journey actually carried out, which we shall now analyse.

The analysis of the co-ordinations between image and rule, as far as urban space is concerned, involves meeting several necessary conditions:

1. That the subject has a global image of the town (and not simply of the journey from home to work, for example).
2. That his image of the town is stable i.e. it should not evolve in the course of the experiment.
3. That he encounters obstacles (temporal or spatial) in the attainment of his goals, so that he must use his representations in a precise manner.

From this point of view, the profession of taxi-driver fits the bill exactly.

1 – 1 Analysis of journeys

This analysis was made by setting taxi-drivers spatial problems (getting to appropriately chosen addresses) without allowing them to consult the map. In regard to the problems which the drivers solved, it brought to light two types of network. The distinction between these two types of network lies, not in their spatial properties, but in the differences in behaviour which were observed. The first, the primary network, characteristically supports a *behavioural algorithm* or, more precisely, behaviour governed by an algorithm. According to Trahtenbrot (1964), an algorithm is an instruction to carry out a number of operations, in a given order, and permitting the solution in a finite number of steps of all problems of a prescribed type. Behaviour algorithms have given rise to numerous studies (Newell and Simon (1972) in the United States, Landa (1959) in the Soviet Union, Vergnaud (1968) in France). What are the instructions in this instance? It has been found that when the driver is using this network he takes the route which makes the minimal angle with his goal. This is effectively an algorithm. Some consequences of a spatial nature are implied by this algorithm; for example, the fact that it must not have gaps or dead-ends.

The secondary network supports a heuristic procedure, that is one which includes intermediate goals, a reasonably large field of forecast and a certain flexibility (cf. Bresson, 1965). The only rule which the subject really applies is to regain the primary network. Not only does this rule increase the distance to be covered, it also does not always turn out to be effective, as witness the mistakes made and the fact that these latter increase with distance from the point of departure from the primary network. Let us limit our analysis of journeys to these simple facts and draw from them consequences regarding the image of urban space.

1 – 2   Analysis of spatial images

In view of the characteristics of the image in the spatial field, which have already been mentioned, and the essentially flat nature of a town such as Paris, where the experiments took place, we have assessed spatial representation by means of drawings, which is indeed the classic method. Subjects were asked to arrange a certain number of places within the town, paying respect, as far as possible, to their relative positions. The distortion, therefore, can be analysed between the real geographic configuration and the image which the subjects form of it. However, in order to analyse this distortion (whose origins, we know, are to be found in the activities of the subject), one still needs relevant and fairly precise descriptive categories – something often lacking in this type of study.

Once again, we have had recourse to Piaget's theory (1946). It is a matter of identifying the spatial relations which subjects retained in the course of their activity. Now, our subjects are *adult* subjects and so have available a certain number of possible options which they have acquired in the course of their development.

Generally, space for the child begins with elementary topological intuitions; in other words, it is based on qualitative links which appeal to relations of proximity, order, separation, etc. These relations, which take no account whatsoever of distances and angles, are independent of the elongation or the foreshortening of the shapes used. The relation of proximity, amongst all the topological relations, seems best to express the fundamental character of this space (Grize, 1964). Built up by degrees, topological relations do not strictly permit the construction of a coherent system beyond a certain level of complexity.

The next stage involves the adoption of a privileged viewpoint, that of the subject, in order to co-ordinate the forms. Projective space enables one to establish notions of straight and parallel.

The final stage is the creation of a 'euclidian' space, which entails the conservation of angles and of distances. Initially, the co-ordinates of euclidian space are nothing more than a vast network which extends to all objects and which includes relations of order referring simultaneously to these dimensions; left–right, up–down, in front–behind.

So, by adulthood, our subjects have at their command this battery of possible options. Which are selected at the level of representations?

Once again, we shall be very succinct: the analysis of distortions between the drawings and the town shows that, at the level of representations, there exist two types of locality which are distinguishable by the nature of the relationship between them.

The first type of locality displays only a very slight distortion from the true geographic outline; not only are the general topological and projective relations conserved, there is also a very good approximation to distances and angles.

By contrast, the second type of locality displays considerable distortions (in particular, a large over-estimation of distances). These localities are indexed to those of the first type by the relation of proximity. Thus, the Paris Observatory is near Place Denfert-Rochereau. Near, but in almost any direction.

If the results of the drawings are compared with those which are obtained from an analysis of journeys, one finds that the first type of locality corresponds to the primary network, whilst the second type of locality corresponds to the secondary network.

Here we broach an important point concerning the necessary co-ordination between rules and images. Even if the rule of the primary network, which consists in taking at each crossroads that route which forms the minimal angle with the goal, is algorithmic, nevertheless the subjects cannot see the goal and so must estimate its direction by using their representation of the locality. This rule, therefore, on its own, does not guarantee the attainment of the objective, despite its algorithmic character; it must be supported by an appropriate image of the locality. If the direction of the goal is judged wrongly, a procedure which consists in choosing the route which forms the minimal angle with the *estimated* direction of the goal could not possibly lead to it. It can be seen, therefore, that rule–image co-ordinations are critical to judging the relevance of action. The representation enables the operator to calculate, in an internalised manner, the results of these possible actions; it implies a programming of the devices which are used to support the calculations, and of the rules of calculation which generate the sequences of operations.

Related experiments have demonstrated, in all those who use a town, the existence of primary and of secondary networks. Their scope, their variety, and even their clarity are not as great as those of the taxi-drivers, but the essentials are unchanged: on the one hand, algorithmic rules and faithfully represented localities; and, on the other, heuristic rules and localities indexed to the first type. One can assume that such a network would prove most useful, both from the point of view of journey-making and from that of the 'feeling' which inhabitants have about urban space. This feeling is important in the study of the migrations which are desired by town planners.

The formal heterogeneity of the images and the inter-connection between this heterogeneity and the rules governing journeys – the surprising results of these experiments – pose numerous problems about the relationships which exist between *ontogenesis* – the main object of Piaget's interest – and *learning*.

This work has allowed us to analyse – in an admittedly highly elaborate way – how image-operation co-ordination functions in the planning of journeys, that is in the last analysis a person's functional understanding of urban space. The question is raised, at the end of the study, of the process of understanding itself and, more precisely, of the processes whereby spatial images are constructed.

2.   The elaboration of the image

How, on arriving in an unknown town, do we construct this 'strategic link which is the environmental image' (to adopt K. Lynch's expression)? As it stands, the question is intrinsically interesting, the more so because there is very little information available on this topic. However, as well as this, the observation of the process whereby the image is formed is also essential for the understanding of its role in action. It is, however, essentially for a theoretical reason that this study was undertaken.

In order to elaborate his image during his first outings in a strange town, the subject has various means at his disposal which he could use. We have already come across some of these means, in connection with the creation of spatial relations between elements of the field – topological, projective, and metric relations – and there are many more besides. Now, as B. Inhelder (1954) puts it, 'if, in the course of his evolution, man develops the instruments of knowledge, he still needs to know how to use them'. To explore how this use is organised, currently a very controversial question, is the basic reason for these studies.

The objective of our studies, therefore, will be to identify, at each level of the observed image in the course of its construction, the instruments which are brought into play, their order, and their co-ordination. I shall try to put on one side these preoccupations in order to accompany you on a walk through the images, starting from the initial void of the subject who arrives in a strange town, and ending with the subject who is an expert in journey-making. A formal and functional walk, admittedly, but one in the course of which the form will be seen to take shape (Pailhous, 1971).

We carried out an experiment in the classical sense of the word and this, I know, may be surprising. This type of method, in our opinion, seemed to be indispensable in this particular context. One cannot state, as many authors do, that the image is dependent on the activity (i.e. the journeys) and not control that activity. This is what would have happened if we had surveyed large masses of people arriving in strange towns.

We do not intend here to detail the principles and conditions of the experiments. It is sufficient to say, simply, that adult, town-dwelling, subjects followed planned routes (which were the same for everyone) in a town [Paris] which was totally unknown to them. The length of the routes (70 kms) and the duration of the experiment ($6\frac{1}{2}$ hours) enabled subjects to develop images at a sufficiently complex level. Indications of direction and map drawings allow the content and the structure of the representation of space to be analysed throughout its development (see figs. 1 and 2).

First level: the establishment of initial bearings
We are here concerned with accurately determining the mechanisms which underlie the development of initial bearings (the angular position

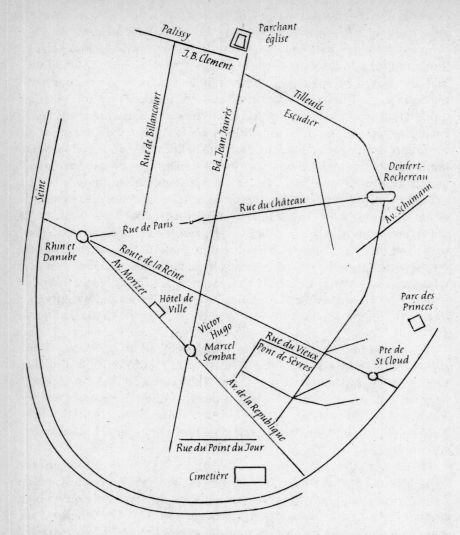

Fig. 1   Drawing by the subject F. R. after 2½ hours experimentation in the town of B-B (suburb of Paris)

of a non-visible place in relation to the actual position of the subject: this direction being indicated with the arm), in a situation where the subject's only sources of information are his own journeys. Indeed, during the subject's first journeys, the angles made by the streets, as well as their length, are the only pieces of information he has with which to judge direction.

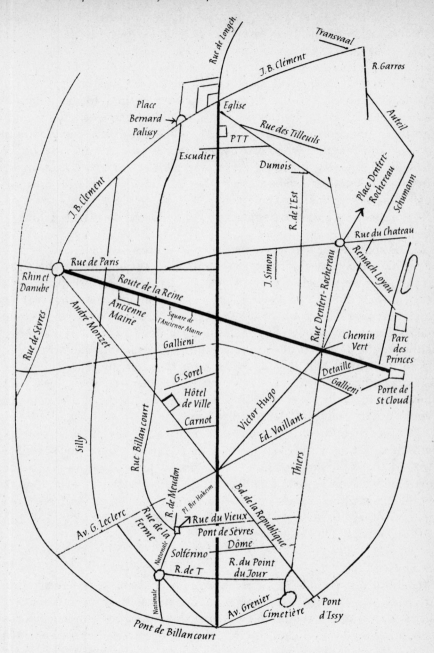

Fig. 2 Drawing by the subject F. R. after after 6½ hours experimentation (final drawing)

Having said this we do not propose, for the moment, that the subject should make use of these bearings; he could either develop them for future use or else give us an answer which could be interpreted as an artifact of our method of enquiry. Nor do we require that he should be able, strictly speaking, to make use of angles or lengths; in fact, the subject can select weaker criteria: for example (i) time, for the length of streets and (ii) right, left, and straight on, for the angles. At any rate, errors in direction result from a poor estimation of the parameters of angles and lengths; whether this be, for example, in the case of the former, due to the difficulty subjects experience in measuring angles from within cars, or else because 'to the right' involves an error of angle, etc. It is easy to illustrate this role:

(i) the subject is asked to define the direction of the place from which he has just come;

(ii) the subject is asked to sketch the route he has just taken.

If the subject does not use metric relations, so that, for 'to the right' means any angle between $0°$ (go straight ahead) and $180°$ (turn right back), then there will be a weak correlation between the (vague) direction proposed by the subject and the direction which one could deduce from the drawing by taking into account angles and distances. However, a strong correlation is noted between the direction proposed from the outset and that deduced from the drawing. From this, we conclude that, in order to develop his initial bearings, the subject uses metrics, since whatever criteria he employs, he uses measurements of angle and of length to calculate directions.

We see, therefore, at the most elementary level, that in order to work out the direction of the place from which he has just come, the subject is led, in the very simple space comprising his initial journeys, to use extremely elaborate instruments (metrics, in this instance), even though he makes serious mistakes and is aware of them. He could have used much weaker instruments – relations of incidence or of 'next to' – whose subsequent use we shall see.

Second level: loops

An entire section of the subject's activity consists in processing the directions elaborated during the first stage within a 'hypothetico-deductive' framework and in correcting these directions and structures according to the extent to which the hypotheses are verified. All this happens during what might be called 'loops', that is when the subject crosses, or passes again, a point he has already passed.

An example of this can be given: as subjects tend to attribute a value of 90° to the angle made by a street crossing their own route, two streets which 'empty into' the same road are seen as been parallel. When the subject arrives at the crossroads of these two, so-called parallel, streets he can draw his own conclusion as to the real value of the angles, or, at the very least, as to their non-parallelism!

There are many other corrective procedures (such as alignments, but to further elaborate these here would be of no value). Be that as it may, two phenomena are noted at this second level: (i) the establishment of reliable structures with places which are well situated in relation to each other and (ii) an ever-increasing degree of complexity, which makes memorisation impossible if the subject continues to operate in the same manner.

Third level: the appearance of the primary network
The establishment, at the level of representations, of a reliable network enables a subject situated at any spot in this network to indicate accurately the direction of other points in the same network. The subject, moreover, knows how to reach all these points. The frequent appearance of new roads makes it impossible for him to remember all the routes covered. Furthermore, to choose but one example, the fact of passing the same crossroads several times gives this crossroads a privileged status, as well as favouring the formation of a network which allows one to reach any of the crossroads in this sub-assembly. Given that the bearings of these crossroads are precise in the subject's mind and that the network of pathways connecting them is reliable, he can then apply the rule of the minimal angle between the roads in the network in conditions of total effectiveness (*a priori* efficacy).

Although the subject creates a primary network, he retains, at least, a certain amount of information about the places he has passed through which are not in the primary network. These localities, which form the secondary network, are indexed to the crossroads and pathways of the primary network and they enjoy only relations of proximity with the primary network. The phrase, 'it's near', appears frequently in the subject's speech. These are the assemblies which form what the subject calls the nuclei. Indexation activity is intense. Since the size of these nuclei is relatively restricted, the subject can either see points within the nucleus directly and so reach them, or he can reach them most often by relying on visual signs (turn right after the red cafe) which are, altogether, intra-labyrinthine signs (Blancheteau, 1969).

Fourth level: the growth of the primary network by the extension of neighbourhoods

The fourth level is the one which we observed in taxi-drivers. It is interesting because, once a primary network has been set up, its growth occurs by means of completely different mechanisms. The indexation of points in the secondary network to nodes in the primary network, which characterised the previous level, leads to the enlargement of neighbourhoods. The neighbourhoods of the nodes which constitute the crossroads of the primary network can then overlap each other: a certain number of points are seen as being 'near X' and 'near Y'. As a result of this the direction of a point in the secondary network becomes all the more precise in that this point is at the intersection of a greater number of neighbourhoods. This process therefore enables the point in question to become a point in the primary network. Thus, a point very close to a crossroads in the primary network has few chances of being situated at an intersection of neighbourhoods and therefore of becoming a crossroads itself. This contributes to making the primary network a web of almost equidistant threads and always permits the subject, by using an efficient algorithmic rule, to arrive close to the point he intends to reach. Experimental data on this problem can be found, already, in previous experiments which compare experienced and inexperienced taxi-drivers (Pailhous, 1970). Several examples of it were also found in the final test of this experiment. At the fourth level the subject is only dealing with very weak relations (the most important being the relation of proximity); but these relations, though weak, allow him to construct a coherent space. Far from being in the position of the children observed by Piaget and Szeminska (1948), the subjects behave as if they 'knew' that these nevertheless very elementary relations retain to a certain degree, in a complex space, metric relations between their component parts.

2–1   Some consequences

The analysis made here of the elaboration of the image demonstrates that how the techniques of spatial knowledge are applied differs quite markedly from how they were acquired in the first place. In constructing their image subjects, in fact, do not use their spatial techniques in the order in which they were acquired (the hypothesis of a microgenesis imitating ontogenesis). A complex process is observed in this application which testifies to the existence of rules governing the management of instrumental techniques peculiar to a class of problem.

The cognitive elaboration which we have analysed here reveals the subject's operational activity when the universe of reference, which he has constructed at the level of representations, expands (in this case, the expansion of a spatial image resulting from the covering of new routes).

Several points can be underlined:

(i) how the spatial image is used becomes increasingly distinct, as it develops, from how it was constructed. Initially, the image is heavily dependent on the routes actually covered by the subject. Each of the four levels which we have distinguished marks the progressive abstraction of the image from the preceding levels, which opens up new possibilities for the subject;

(ii) the tools which the subject used to construct his image are more powerful at the beginning of its development than when the image is already reasonably well structured. Nevertheless, this image continues to improve (see level 4); the complexity of space plays a determining role here. As has frequently been observed (e.g. in the case of breakdown), the subject, in this type of situation, co-ordinates different types of activity within the same problem area: algorithmic procedures enable him to arrive fairly easily at a state of affairs close to the solution, with weaker rules being developed for certain classes of events. These latter classes of event are characteristically linked to events at the first level. In the elaboration of the image one notes that the elements of the first level are formed before the classes of the second level appear.

But perhaps the question which will most fully capture the attention is that of the real initial level of the subject. As a matter of fact, the situation differs, for example, depending upon whether the subjects who are constructing an image of a totally unknown town are town- or country-dwellers. Experimental surveys have shown this.

In the experiment which we have presented here, the subjects are town-dwellers. In other words they know, though not consciously so, which is the relevant image – that is the one which permits easy journeys. They therefore have acquired *already* the rules for the management of their instruments in order to construct the image of the town. Country-dwellers, on the other hand, have the same repertoire of spatial instruments at their disposal (a set of journeys, topology, co-ordinates, metrics, hypothetico-deductive reasoning) as the town-dwellers, but they do not know how to use them, because they do not know which type of image is relevant; they do not realise that the direction of the goals must be precisely mastered, etc. The same would probably apply to town-dwellers in a country environment.

This throws some light on the problem of transfer which, in this instance, appears to be one of organisational rules (and not simply of observable responses). What the subject acquires is very different according to whether or not he has mastered the rules of management. In the absence of these rules, a professional training, for example, should make their acquisition a top priority.

As can be seen in these interpretations, Piaget's theory, by identifying the cognitive instruments – here those which constitute the representations of space – permits one to identify, at each moment in the subject's performance, the presence or absence of some of these instruments. As it also offers a panorama of the subject's 'competence' at a given age – here, the stage of formal operations in the adult – one, therefore, can evaluate the processes of acquisition within this comparison between competence and performance. However, it says nothing at all as to how this acquisition is itself organised. The Soviet tradition of research, in particular Galperine in his 'Essais sur la formation par étapes des actions et des concepts' (1966), is specifically concerned with this issue. In particular, it permits the re-instatement, in a different context, of the functional concept of 'management rules' which has been put forward to interpret the strategies behind the way in which instrumental knowledge is applied.

Without going into the conceptual detail of this theory, it is worth noting that by characterising action in terms of its goal and its 'orientational base', and by breaking it down into the operations of orientation, executing, and surveillance, one can then express more simply how the spatial image itself is acquired. In fact, this theory sets itself the task of following the elaboration of an action by identifying the form it takes (from the material right through to the intellectual); its degree of generalisation, all the greater when the subject takes into account only those aspects necessary to carry it out; its level of reduction, that is the subject's capacity to implicitly 'understand' certain operations; and its level of assimilation, which essentially illustrates the phenomenon of the automation of action.

As far as the representation of urban space is concerned, this theory enables one to distinguish clearly, at an equivalent structural level, between subjects who are accustomed to urban space and those who are not, when both groups are confronted with a *new urban environment*. In fact, the orientational base for the actions of these two groups, as well as their orienting activities, are completely different. The internalisation of the conditions necessary to effect a journey which implies, as we have seen, a precise knowledge of the direction of the goal, is very good in the first group and non-existent in the second. Country-dwellers must therefore disengage this orientational base since they have to fashion a new course of action.

3. Conclusions

It goes without saying that competence in the field of social representations cannot be accomplished overnight, so I have not attempted it. In actual fact, my paper has two objectives:

(1) I have modestly tried to state that, among the vast (and elsewhere decisive) questions of a political, ideological and economic nature which are raised by the urban habitat and which pervade the subject's 'representations', there are certain material, even basely material, conditions which the image of urban space needs must fulfil if it is to permit such an elementary activity as that of making a journey. The built environment can be more or less favourable to this type of picturesque storage, which is not to say that a town which is conceived so as to facilitate this particular aspect would be a pleasant one in which to live. However, I think it is one dimension to be taken into account and it is surely not in contradiction with the other dimension. For instance, the diversification of the environment (easily identifiable reference points . . .) which is often advocated as necessary for the quality of emotional relationships, is also necessary for journey-making. At any rate, a town in which travel is difficult is also a town in which the quality of life might be said to be of an insufficient standard (at least as far as this point is concerned!).

(2) My second aim, in the context of this volume, was to strike a fairly un-socio-psychological note on the representation of a highly socialised object. Finally, therefore, I wished to enquire into the different attitudes and methods which one could adopt with respect to one and the same object: a town, and the same 'concept': representation. Indeed, to my mind, this raises a question: are these the efforts of different sub-disciplines which converge in order to grasp a reality which is complex? In that case, why do we meet so infrequently? Or is it, perhaps, a division of labour aimed at masking, at least partially, the reality of this subject?

Part 4
Language, social representations and culture

14. The role of language in the creation and transmission of social representations

RAGNAR ROMMETVEIT

1. Introduction

Let us assume that we as social scientists are doomed to seek knowledge *in* and *about* a pluralistic, only fragmentarily known and only partially shared social world, a world fraught with ideological conflicts and uneven distribution of power, knowledge and expertise. Imagine, moreover, that the devil for some obscure reason wants us to remain ignorant about what happens when mortal men communicate under such extremely complex, though interesting, conditions. What kind of strategy would he then adopt in order to prohibit human self-insight?

His most efficient bait to us scholars of human communication, I shall argue, are *seductive, monistic assumptions about our language and the world*. Such assumptions allow us to pursue our academic trade with formal rigour and academic success while evading practically urgent and basic existential issues of human intersubjectivity. It is no wonder, therefore, that so many of us so often yield to the devil's seductive monism.

I shall in the present paper argue that current psycho-, socio-, and 'linguo'-linguistic research paradigms indeed have in common a basically monistic outlook, and that mainstream scholarly research for that reason provides us with very little insight into the role of language in the creation and transmission of social representations. My major constructive aim, though, is to spell out some important implications of an alternative, consistently pluralistic, set of assumptions.

What happens when an implicitly monistic outlook is replaced by an explicitly pluralistic paradigm is a subtle, though significant, transformation of some basic questions concerning human communication: what from a monistic position appear as 'dynamic *residuals* in the construction of human intersubjectivity' must within a pluralistic theoretical framework be examined as basic *constituents* of mutual

331

understanding. A major part of my paper will hence be devoted to an exploration of aspects of human discourse, such as *reciprocal role taking*, *actual and reciprocally assumed control*, and *naive* (and in some sense: self-fulfilling) *faith in a shared social world*.

2.   Monistic assumptions in mainstream scholarly research on language and human communication

I have elsewhere (Rommetveit, 1978) tried to show how the notion of linguistic competence within transformational–generative linguistics – when assimilated within psycho- and sociolinguistic research – has made for a general strategy of 'negative rationalism'. The essence of this general strategy appears to be an explication of natural language in terms of invariant meanings and 'propositional content' *and* the assumption that actual language use can be scientifically explored and understood only *qua deviance* from hypothetical, idealized conditions of human discourse. The practice of reading one single unequivocal literal meaning into a set of only partially determined semantic potentialities thus paves the way for the assignment of 'propositional content' to sentences *in vacuo*.

What invariably happens to words when trapped in scholarly nets of negative rationalism, however, is that very significant – though often negotiable – semantic potentialities get lost. These are potentialities mirroring options with respect to categorization and attribution *in* and *about* a multifaceted, pluralistic, only fragmentarily known and only partially shared *Lebenswelt*. And this has to be so, because utterances have meanings only in the stream of life and because our mastery of words borders on our imperfect knowledge of the world and only partially explicable ontological assumptions (cf. Wittgenstein, 1968, p. 739). Polysemy and ambiguity due to the manifold of possible social realities and human perspectives can thus be evaded, but never *eliminated* by recourse to prestigious, but monistic, 'conceptual realities' or by lexicographical legislation. We may for instance attempt to disambiguate a word, such as 'human', by anchoring its interpretation in zoological taxonomy, and we may even decide to make that interpretation 'a semantic marker', that is, an Archimedian point, in our assessment of the 'public' meanings of a set of other words. This may indeed seem plausible ' . . . after three hundred years of science and criticism of religion . . .' (Habermas, 1970, p. 137). But our doing so will not prevent religious people engaged in conversation or preaching from exploiting other 'lay' (or 'theological') potentialities of the word, such as those revealed in contrasts like human/divine, human/saintly, etc.

Archimedian points in assessment of human meaning are hence necessarily provisional and contingent upon some 'world view', never entirely 'neutral' with respect to competing ontologies. *And even a zoologically founded interpretation of 'human' is bound to contain some residual ambiguity*. This may indeed in principle be revealed in lack of referential consensus if we on some planet should happen to encounter entirely novel forms of living beings. Suppose, for instance, that some of them grow like plants. They are in possession of a sign system similar to our languages, however, and are clearly extremely intelligent according to earthly criteria. They also engage in a variety of creative and communicative activities. Some astronauts may maintain, therefore, that they are human, others may argue that they are not. And how could we, on the basis of *a taxonomy constrained by our earthly experiences* of *variants of life*, resolve that dispute?

The moral of this excursion into metaphysics and science fiction is very simple: the semantic system inherent in our everyday language is *orderly* and *borders on our knowledge of the world*, yet precisely for that reason it is *ambiguous* and *open*. And the notion of linguistic competence we encounter in early generative–transformational theories of language may, when viewed against this background, be conceived of as a heavenly version of our mastery of a common code, a version devoid of dialectical variations, stripped of all ambiguities, and dyed in pure Cartesian reason. Chomsky's postulation of unequivocal literal meanings and his evasion of the issue of negotiable residuals (Chomsky, 1972, p. 85) may hence be defended by reference to some of his own Cartesian, explicitly stated, metatheoretical assumptions: his ideal speaker–hearer's communication is a *monologue in disguise* because it is assumed to take place in a monistic semiotic universe, in a society characterized by *perfect commonality with respect to interpretation*.

The love child of this notion of linguistic competence and *individual* (as opposed to social) cognitive psychology was a *psycholinguistics of utterances 'in vacuo'*: we tried very hard and for many years to assess linguistic competence by having subjects respond to series of entirely unrelated written or tape-recorded sentences. Our subjects were thus put in a situation very similar to that of the Virgin Mary when she received words from the Lord about her pregnancy. It is said about the Virgin Mary that she did not understand what was meant by those words, but buried them in her heart. This, I think, was hardly the case with our experimental subjects. Their strategy was rather to engage in various mnemonic techniques such as, for instance, dreaming up plausible contexts and interpretative frames of their own (see Blakar and Rommetveit, 1975).

The 'Virgin Mary' paradigm of psycholinguistic experimentation is now *passé*. The practice of reading unequivocal 'literal' meaning into mere semantic potentialities and assigning propositional content to only partially determined message potentials, however, is not. It seems to pervade semantic analysis like a hereditary sin, in spite of recent concern with presuppositions and other definite symptoms of a pragmatic counter-revolution against Cartesian rationalism (see Rommetveit, 1974, pp. 79–101).

Sociolinguistics is by definition a study of human discourse under conditions of *linguistic, social,* and *cultural variation,* and for that reason, one should expect, precisely of *negotiable residuals in human communication.* It is very strange, therefore, to witness how its theoretical foundation nevertheless is being infiltrated by monistic assumptions very similar to those of the transformational–generative semanticists. A Trojan horse in this enterprise seems to be Searle's theory of speech acts and, more specifically, his basic 'principle of expressibility'.

Some of the consequences of this principle are explicated as follows (Searle, 1974, pp. 20–1):

... the principle that *whatever can be meant can be said* does not imply that whatever can be said can be understood by others; for that would exclude the possibility of a private language, a language that it was impossible for anyone but the speaker to understand ... It has the consequence that cases where the speaker does not say exactly what he means – the principal cases of which are *nonliteralness, vagueness, ambiguity,* and *incompleteness* – are not theoretically essential to linguistic communication. But most important ... it enables us to equate rules for performing speech acts with rules for uttering linguistic elements, since for any possible speech act there is a possible linguistic element, the meaning of which (given the context of the utterance) is sufficient to determine that *its literal* utterance is a performance of precisely that speech act.

(italics mine)

Notice, first of all, that the principle as such says nothing about *the hearer*. His interpretation of what is said is assumed to be identical to that of the speaker, however, provided that the latter '... is *speaking literally* and that the context is appropriate' (Searle, 1974, p. 18; italics mine). Searle (*ibid.*, p. 20) thus takes it to be an analytic truth about language, moreover, that '... for any speaker S whenever S means (intends to convey, wishes to communicate in an utterance, etc.) X then it is possible that there is some E such that E is an exact expression of or formulation of X'. And the communicated meanings are also, according to Habermas (1970, p. 143) identical for all members of a given speech community.

'What is meant' may be further explicated in terms of rules that connect *what is said* to *'actions being performed with words'*. These are rules of interpretation (and their *inverse*: rules of production). In addition, there are rules of sequencing which connect 'actions being performed with words' in everyday discourse. The major task of sociolinguistic discourse analysis is to analyse all such rules and '... thus to show that one sentence follows another in a coherent way'. And Labov's account of *incomplete expressions* in discourse is thus a formal explication of what happens *when shared propositional knowledge of the world merges with literal speech* (see Labov, 1972, pp. 121–3 and Rommetveit, 1978).

Current models of linguistic and communicative competence are thus based upon a very dubious assumption concerning unequivocal 'literal' meanings. And this monistic assumption has the important consequence – to quote Searle once more (1974, p. 21) '... that cases where the speaker does not say exactly what he means – the principal cases of which are nonliteralness, vagueness, ambiguity, and incompleteness – are not theoretically essential to linguistic communication'.

I have tried to show, however, that vagueness, ambiguity, and incompleteness – and hence also: versatility, flexibility, and negotiability – are inherent and essential characteristics of any natural language. This must be so simply because human discourse *takes place in* and *deals with* a pluralistic, only fragmentarily known, and only partially shared social world. There is accordingly no natural end, in the form either of a literal semantic interpretation or an ultimate knowledge of the world, to our explication of linguistically mediated meaning. As Garfinkel puts it (1972, p. 28): '... no matter how specific the terms of common understanding may be – a contract may be considered the prototype – they attain the status of an agreement for persons only insofar as the stipulated conditions carry along an unspoken but understood *et cetera* clause'. Whatever is meant and understood is thus contingent upon that something else (by both participants in that act of communication) is taken for granted.

What is conveyed by a word such as 'poor', for instance, may be different depending upon whether artistic skill or financial issues constitute the topic of discourse. What is intended and understood by 'poor' in a discourse about financial issues, moreover, may be unequivocally determined as the opposite of 'wealthy', yet, in a conversation about the Third World, specified as *living conditions below the subsistence level*, and in a chat about our neighbours in a welfare society as *dependency upon public financial support*. Full mastery of the *poverty–wealth* potentiality of 'poor' is thus revealed in contextually appropriate, though frequently negotiable, optional elaborations – and hence contingent upon a general capacity to adopt the perspective of different 'others' across a range of variant social situations. An expression such as 'a poor artist' is hence in itself necessarily ambiguous. It may in one case convey something about *artistic talents*, in another case something about *financial resources*, and in a third case simply convey *pity*. Which of these uses should be 'literal' and which 'parasitic', moreover, is not at all easy to decide. A developmental psychologist may argue that *pitying* is the ontogenetically primary use, whereas a Marxist philosopher may claim that all additional interpretations of the word 'poor' are contingent upon a hard and literal core of *economic poverty*.

The rejection of the notion of unequivocal literal meaning, however, implies an approach to semantic problems very different from that adopted by Chomsky, Habermas, Searle, and Labov. We have to assume that people within the same speech community may differ, not only with respect to what is taken for granted about the states of affairs they are talking about, but also with respect to what is meant by what is said. The basic problem of human intersubjectivity becomes then a question concerning *in what sense and under which conditions two persons who engage in a dialogue can transcend their different private worlds*. And the linguistic basis for this enterprise, I shall argue, is *not* a fixed repertory of shared 'literal' meanings, but very general and partly negotiable drafts of contracts concerning categorization and attribution inherent in ordinary language. Full semantic mastery of a word such as 'poor', for instance, thus entails the capacity to elaborate a very abstract draft into different and context-specific contracts. Institutionally, ritually, and situationally provided frames for social interaction and discourse, moreover, will determine which subsets of semantic potentialities are intended within different kinds of contexts. The entire set of basic semantic potentialities inherent in ordinary language may indeed be conceived of as a common code of such drafts of contracts, that is of *potentially* shared strategies of categorization and cognitive–emotive perspectives on whatever is being talked about. Intersubjectivity, I shall argue, is thus *a product of negotiation and elaboration of contracts*, and it comes into being in *a subtle interplay of presuppositions and semantic potentialities*.

There is, as Schutz (1951, p. 168) has put it, '. . . a selection of things and aspects of things relevant to me at any given moment whereas other things and other aspects are for the time being of no concern to me or even out of view'. Which aspects are focused upon by each of the two participants in any particular case of dyadic interaction are thus in part determined by the individual actor's engagement and perspective. How different *explicitly* introduced referential domains of discourse affect linguistic encoding and decoding has been cogently demonstrated in psycholinguistic experiments by Olson (1970) and Deutsch (1976): which of a set of possible verbal expressions will be used to refer to any particular object is clearly determined by *the range of objects from which the referent must be set apart*. And there is no reason to believe that such referential domains are of less significance when they are tacitly taken for granted, for instance in a case in which two people are talking about the 'same' state of affairs from different private perspectives, and hence *with different taken-for-granted referential domains in mind*. Which expression is the 'exact expression' may in such a case become a matter of *who is in control* of the temporarily established and potentially shared here-and-now of their dialogue.

3. The combinatorics of pluralism: an attempt at being precise about possible dyadic constellations of different private worlds

The order of simplification gained once we yield to the devil's seductive monism can only be fully appreciated if we venture to explore the alternative. Let us hence set out to construct a truly 'dialogical' truth table (see table 1) under the assumptions of *a pluralistic and only partially known social world*. The theoretical significance of such a table will hopefully be elucidated in terms of illustrative cases once the formal combinatorial scheme has been fully elaborated.

The initial basic unit to which we assign truth values is an individual state of belief concerning some fragment of the social world, that is an ordered pair consisting of one particular cognitive representation R_i of some given state of affairs S. The assertion A:

$$S \text{ is } R_i$$

may in one person p_1's private world w_1 either be held *true* (t), be rejected as *false* (f), or remain *undetermined* (u) with respect to truth value. (The latter case may be described as a state of agnosticism or ignorance, 'don't know'.) We are thus so far simply following Kleene and Kripke in their application of strong three-valued logic. Their term *'undefined'*

Table 1. *From a binary true/false in an unequivocal monistic world to 19,200 states of dyadic social reality*

Beliefs				Control		
I Actual		**II Assumed**		**III Actual**	**IV Assumed**	
p_1 in w_1	p_2 in w_2	$p_2{:}(p_1$ in $w_1)$	$p_1{:}(p_2$ in $w_2)$	p_1/p_2	$p_1{:}(p_1/p_2)$	$p_2{:}(p_1/p_2)$
(1) t	t	(1) t	t	(1) $p_1{>}p_2$	(1) $p_1{>}p_2$	$p_1{>}p_2$
(2) t	f_1	(2) t	f_1	(2) $P_1{=}p_2$	(2) $P_1{>}p_2$	$p_1{=}p_2$
(3) t	f_2	(3) t	f_2	(3) $p_1{<}p_2$	(3) $p_1{>}p_2$	$p_1{<}p_2$
(4) t	u	(4) t	u		(4) $p_1{>}p_2$	i
(5) f_1	t	(5) f_1	t		(5) $p_1{=}p_2$	$p_1{>}p_2$
(6) f_1	f_1	(6) f_1	f_1		(6) $p_1{=}p_2$	$p_1{=}p_2$
(7) f_1	f_2	(7) f_1	f_2		(7) $p_1{=}p_2$	$p_1{<}p_2$
(8) f_1	u	(8) f_1	u		(8) $p_1{=}p_2$	i
(9) f_2	t	(9) f_2	t		(9) $p_1{<}p_2$	$p_1{>}p_2$
(10) f_2	f_1	(10) f_2	f_1		(10) $p_1{<}p_2$	$p_1{=}p_2$
(11) f_2	f_2	(11) f_2	f_2		(11) $p_1{<}p_2$	$p_1{<}p_2$
(12) f_2	u	(12) f_2	u		(12) $p_1{<}p_2$	i
(13) u	t	(13) u	t		(13) i	$p_1{>}p_2$
(14) u	f_1	(14) u	f_1		(14) i	$p_1{=}p_2$
(15) u	f_2	(15) u	f_2		(15) i	$p_1{<}p_2$
(16) u	u	(16) u	u		(16) i	i
		(17) t	i			
		(18) f_1	i			
		(19) f_2	i			
		(20) u	i			
		(21) i	t			
		(22) i	f_1			
		(23) i	f_2			
		(24) i	u			
		(25) i	i			

corresponds to the term '*undetermined*' in the present scheme and is not to be interpreted as an extra truth value (see Kripke, 1975, p. 700).

The value '*false*' is, for reasons to be revealed later on, split into two separate variants, f_1 and f_2. This dichotomy may be briefly explained as follows: A person, p_1, may in one case reject A because he believes S to be some specified entity, R_j, other than R_1. Let us label such a rejection *falsity 1* (f_1). His private world, w_1 may in another case – apart from his rejection of A – be characterized by a state of ignorance with respect to S. He rejects A, yet does not entertain any particular alternative belief about S. This latter kind of rejection will be labelled *falsity 2* (f_2). Both f_1 and f_2 may at this stage simply be read as *false*, however, since each of them will behave precisely like their mother value f in our computation of the three truth values t, f and u of composite dyadic constellations.

Let us now, as a first step toward explication of very complex states of partially shared social reality, add another person (p_2 in w_2) and survey the resultant sixteen different dyadic constellations of individual states of belief (see the two left-hand columns under I in table 1). And we may ask: under which of these conditions can the representation R_i of S be said to constitute part of p_1's and p_2's shared social world?

This will be the case, we shall claim, if and only if the conjunction of (p_1 in w_1) and (p_2 in w_2) is true. We may accordingly examine every dyadic constellation as a conjunction of the two individual states. The truth values for (p_1 in w_1) and (p_2 in w_2) in table 1 are thus:

True for case (1).
False for cases (2), (3), (5), (6), (7), (8), (9), (10), (11), (12), (14), and (15).
Undetermined for cases (4), (13), and (16).

Notice that traditional two-valued logic reduces our number of dyadic combinations from *sixteen* to *four*. These will correspond to cases (1), (2), (5), and (6) in table 1, provided that we forget about our two variants of falsity and read f_1 simply as f. And *undertermined* states of social reality – our cases (4), (13), and (16) – are consequently not distinguished as constituting a separate set at all.

This loss of information is of no significance whatever *if our sole purpose is to single out only one perfect or idealized state of shared social reality (a postulated monistic world) from all other possible states.* A perfectly shared presupposition with respect to S (that S is R_i) may thus be defined as any conjunction of (p_1 in w_1) and (p_2 in w_2) that is *true*. And we end up with one and only one such conjunction, namely case I (1), regardless of whether we apply only the two values t and f, the three values t, f, and u, or our four values t, f_1, f_2, and u.

Our major purpose, however, is to explore the role of language in the transmission and creation of social representations. We are therefore neither primarily interested in perfect states of shared social reality, nor in a taxonomy of possible dyadic constellations for its own sake, but rather in *transformations* of possible states of social reality under real-life conditions of interaction and discourse. And *such transformations may be systematically described as transitions from one specific state to another.* We may thus examine the conditions under which particular dyadic constellations of individual beliefs other than perfect consensus are transformed into (temporary or enduring) states of perfectly shared social reality.

Which one of the two constellations I (2) and I (4) in table 1, for instance, is more likely to develop into an *enduring* fully shared social reality of type I (1), provided that p_1 and p_2 engage in sustained interaction and discourse? And what is required in order for a combination of actual beliefs such as I (4) to be transformed into a *temporarily* fully shared reality of type I (1) when p_1 and p_2 engage in their first conversation about S?

In order to pursue such questions, we have to expand our dialogical table far beyond the sixteen hypothetical dyadic constellations of beliefs. The fact that two individuals hold identical or conflicting beliefs is in fact of hardly any significance whatsoever if they do not happen to know about each other's existence. Each such combination represents indeed merely a potential state of social reality and is bound to remain so until p_1 and p_2 somehow are brought into contact with each other. It is only when p_2 constitutes part of p_1's social world and vice versa that some state of actual social reality can emerge.

This implies, more specifically, that *p_2 may entertain more or less veridical assumptions about p_1's outlook on the world and vice versa* [p_2: (p_1 in w_1) and p_1: (p_2 in w_2), see columns 3 and 4 in table 1]. Let us suppose that these assumptions both happen to be valid, that is, that p_2 assumes p_1 to believe precisely what p_1 actually believes *and* that p_1's assumption about p_2's state of belief is equally correct. This means for constellation I (4) of actual beliefs, for example, that p_2 assumes p_1 to believe that S is R_i (t in column 3), whereas p_1 assumes p_2 to be undertermined with respect to that issue (u in column 4). In the four left-hand columns of table 1 are thus listed, row by row, sixteen different cases of perfect correspondence between dyadic constellations of *actual* and *reciprocally assumed* beliefs.

An actual state of perfectly shared social reality may now be defined as a conjunction of (p_1 in w_1), (p_2 in w_2), p_2: (p_1 in w_1) and p_1: (p_2 in w_2) that is true:

Some representation R_i of S constitutes part of p_1's and p_2's perfectly shared actual reality if and only if both of them believe that S is R_i and each of them assumes the other to hold that belief.

The only conjunction of actual and reciprocally assumed states of belief that is true is constellation I (1), II (1) in table 1. This is a dyadic social reality of perfectly shared and reciprocally assumed *faith*, and only one out of sixteen cases of perfect correspondence between actual and reciprocally assumed states. But what, then, about perfectly shared and reciprocally assumed *agnosticism* (or ignorance)?

The most likely conditions for such a state are obviously constellations I (6), II (6); I (11), II (11); and I (16), II (16). Constellation I (6), II (6) is the case in which both p_1 and p_2 believe and assume the other to believe that S is something else than R_i. *What* else S is held to be, however, is not specified. It is possible, therefore, that their shared and mutually acknowledged rejection of the assertion that S is R_i actually entails conflicting outlooks: P_1 may for instance believe that S is R_j, whereas p_2 believes S to be R_k. But it may also be the case that they share *the same* alternative belief (that S is R_j, for instance).

Constellation I (16), II (16), on the other hand, is a case of fully shared and reciprocally acknowledged orientation of *complete agnosticism* toward S. We are accordingly in this case allowed to engage in assessment of intersecting parts of two different worlds by a procedure of elimination and claim that w_1 and w_2 intersect in an area of perfectly shared and reciprocally assumed ignorance. This implies, more specifically, that *for constellation I (16), II (16) we can eliminate conflicting presuppositions with respect to S as a possible source of misunderstanding in a dialogue betwen p_1 and p_2.*

Constellation I (11), II (11), finally, is a case of fully shared and reciprocally acknowledged orientation of *partial agnosticism* toward S. Both p_1 and p_2 believe and assume that the other believes that S is *not* R_i. Apart from that, however, they are both ignorant with respect to S and assume the other to be so too. We can therefore also in this case safely exclude the possibility that p_1 and p_2 misunderstand each other because they presuppose different things about S. And it should by now be clear why the single value *false* in the monistic, though only partially known, world of strong three-valued logic must be dichotomized in our dialogical table: our two variants f_1 and f_2 are indeed a *sine qua non* in a systematic analysis of shared social realities in terms of *agnosticism* as well as faith. Variant f_1 implies nothing about shared ignorance at all, whereas variant f_2 in case I (11), II (11) yields an intersection of the two individual worlds, w_1 and w_2 in terms of a perfectly shared and reciprocally acknowledged *partial agnosticism*.

Perfect correspondence is the case in only sixteen out of altogether 16 × 25 possible dyadic constellations of states of actual and reciprocally assumed belief in table 1, however. And let us now comment briefly upon some of the remaining 384 combinations.

The first thing we then have to do is to introduce a fifth state of *assumed belief*. This fifth value, *i*, may be defined as a state of *absence of assumptions* concerning the other person's state of belief with respect of S. An *i* in column p_2: (p_1 in w_1) means that p_2 is *ignorant* (or: undetermined) with respect to which of the four primary states t, f_1, f_2 or u exists in w_1. We might hence be tempted to define it as the disjunction of those four primary states, that is, as *either* t *or* f_1, *or* f_2 *or* u. This would lead us into serious difficulties, however, since such a disjunction is bound to be *true*. We would accordingly have to accept constellations I (1), II (17); I (1), II (21), and I (1), II (25) as actual states of perfectly shared social reality.

The value *i* must hence be defined as representing a second-order state with no counterpart in primary states of individual belief at all. An individual can be *undetermined* with respect to some state of affairs S in the sense that he does not know what S *is* or *is not*, but he cannot be fully *ignorant* of his own lack of determination. He may be said to be entirely ignorant (*i*) of *another person's state of belief* with respect to S, though, in the sense that he neither knows nor assumes to know anything about it. The value *u* in column p_2: (p_1 in w_1) thus means that p_2 assumes p_1 to be undetermined *with respect to S*, whereas *i* means that p_2 is undetermined *with respect to which one of the four previously defined primary states t, f_1, f_2 or u exists in w_1.*

The dyadic constellation of potentially shared faith I (1) yields therefore an actual state of perfectly shared social reality only in combination I (1), II (1), that is *when reciprocally taken for granted*, but not under conditions of false assumptions [combinations I (1), II (2) through I (1), II (24)] nor when nothing is assumed by either one of p_1 and p_2 about the other's state of belief [combination I (1) II (25)]. And the dyadic constellation of potentially shared agnosticism I (16) yields an actual orientation of perfectly shared agnosticism if and only if *reciprocally acknowledged*, that is, in [I (16) II (16)] as distinguished, for instance, from [I (16) II (25)].

A condition of *perfect pluralistic ignorance* may now be defined as a dyadic constellation of actual and reciprocally assumed states of belief such that *p_1 and p_2 privately believe the same, whereas both of them entertain the same false assumption concerning the other's state of belief*. The expression 'believe the same', moreover, must in view of our previous analysis of the state f_2 be specified as either shared faith (t, t) *or* shared complete agnosticism (u, u) *or* shared partial agnosticism (f_2, f_2). The entire set of constellations of perfect pluralistic ignorance in table 1 is hence:

I (1) II (11); I (1) II (16);
I (11) II (1); I (11) II (16); and
I (16) II (1); I (16) II (11).

Among these constellations are two cases of relatively 'mild' pluralistic ignorance: p_1 and p_2 may privately be only partially agnostic with respect to S, but assume the other person to be entirely undetermined [I (11) II (16)], or they may privately both be entirely undetermined, but take it for granted that the other person is only partially agnostic [I (16) II (11)]. The four remaining constellations are more severe cases of pluralistic ignorance in the sense that each of them yields a discrepancy between privately shared and reciprocally assumed states of belief in terms of *faith* versus *partial or complete agnosticism*.

Consider, for instance, constellation I (1) II (11) in table 1. This is the case in which p_1 and p_2 *privately* both believe that S is R_i, whereas both of them take it for granted that the other person, apart from *rejecting* that belief, is agnostic with respect to S. And such pluralistic ignorance was very clearly revealed in my early investigation of adolescent religious attitudes under cross-pressure from parents and peers in small Norwegian rural environments characterized by an ongoing process of urbanization and secularization (Rommetveit, 1953). Each adolescent was in this study first of all asked to express his own private belief with respect to particular Lutheran 'articles of faith'. He was subsequently asked what he thought 'the others' (e.g., his age-and-sex mates) believed about those same issues. Finally he joined another adolescent, and the two of them were asked to discuss the issues and work out a joint answer to each question.

The issues concerned God's omnipotence, whether the Holy Ghost can interfere directly in a person's life, etc. And the characteristic constellation of *privately held* and *reciprocally taken for granted belief* emerging from these inquiries was a state of private Lutheran faith combined with the assumption that 'the others' were non-believers. Thus, in a group of 26 adolescent boys it turned out that *every one of them conceived of himself as being more pro-religious than his comrades* (see *ibid.*, p. 120). What came out of the discussions in dyads of adolescent boys, moreover, was the reciprocally assumed agnosticism rather than the private faith of individuals. Two adolescent boys who *privately* believed that the Holy Ghost is a reality that can interfere in one's daily life, for instance, would *together* adopt a position of disbelief and agnosticism with respect to that issue. Such an outcome was in fact the rule in cohesive dyads, that is when each of them considered the other attractive and/or powerful and wanted to be accepted by him. What is taken for granted *in actual discourse* between p_1 and p_2 under such a condition of perfect pluralistic ignorance is thus clearly what both of them falsely assume that *the other* believes.

But what kind of shared social reality can temporarily be established in an encounter between two *different* private worlds? Are some of our dyadic constellations of individual and reciprocally assumed states of belief in table 1 perhaps such that it is impossible for p_1 and p_2 to transcend their pre-established private worlds and attain some mutual understanding? How – and in what sense – can some temporary state of shared social reality be achieved in communication between p_1 and p_2 about some state of affairs S if, for instance, they presuppose different things about that state of affairs? Is it possible that some state of intersubjectivity under certain such conditions can be achieved if, and only if, both p_1 and p_2 accept only one of two conflicting outlooks, *either* w_1 *or* w_2, as a temporarily shared social reality? And – if so – which one of the two different private worlds w_1 and w_2 will become *temporarily* shared?

These are questions about transformations of dyadic constellations of actual and reciprocally assumed states of belief into *temporarily established states of intersubjectivity*. And the moment we venture to examine encounters between different private worlds in actual communication, we are immediately faced with issues of *social control*. The case of our two believing adolescent boys who adopt a joint position of disbelief is thus, in a sense, a case of 'negative' social control. Neither p_1 nor p_2 wants to impose his own private world of religious faith upon the other. On the contrary: each of them tries in fact to conceal it by pretending to share what he falsely assumes to be the other's premises of disbelief and agnosticism. And neither can be said to possess any more power, expertise, or knowledge concerning issues of religious faith than the other.

They are peers and equals as far as actual resources and expertise are concerned [condition III (2), $p_1 = p_2$ in table 1]. However, each of them conceives of himself as inferior in that particular situation [condition IV (9), p_1: ($p_1 < p_2$) and p_2: ($p_1 > p_2$) table 1]. Thus, p_1 assumes that p_2 is 'tougher', less old-fashioned and religious, and more independent than he is himself. But *this is also precisely what p_2 assumes about p_1*, and each of them is seeking acceptance from the other. The resultant temporarily shared – though in some sense fictitious – social reality of their dialogue may accordingly now be distinguished from all remaining 19,199 possible combinations of 16 dyadic constellations of states of belief × 25 constellations of reciprocally assumed such states × 3 relationships of actual control × 16 variants of reciprocally assumed such relationships as *constellation I (1) II (11) III (2) IV (9)* in table 1.

Let us at this stage comment briefly upon some very basic mechanisms of control in p_1's communication with p_2. Notice, first of all, the reciprocal commitment of p_1 and p_2 the moment they engage in discourse. Initiating a dialogue is, in Merleau-Ponty's words (1962, p. 182) '... to transform a certain kind of silence into speech'. Once the other person accepts the invitation to engage in that dialogue, his life situation is temporarily transformed. The two participants leave behind them whatever their preoccupations were at the moment when silence was transformed into speech. From that moment on, they are jointly committed to a shared here-and-now, established and continually modified by their acts of communication.

Mutual understanding implies transcendence of pre-established private worlds, that is some state of temporary intersection of w_1 and w_2, *despite the differences between them*. And the basic mechanism of establishing intersubjectivity across different private worlds is that of *reciprocal role taking*: p_1 attempts to make known his w_1 to p_2 by addressing the latter on what he assumes to be p_2's premises, p_1: (p_2 in w_2), whereas p_2 tries to make sense of what p_1 is saying by adopting what he assumes to be p_1's private outlook p_2: (p_1 in w_1). There are thus in acts of human communication an inbuilt circularity and a component of self-fulfilling faith.

The anticipation that the other person *will* understand is, according to Garfinkel (1972, p. 6), a sanctional property of common discourse. We cannot establish any kind of mutual understanding unless we naively assume (Schutz, 1945, p. 534) that '... the world is from the outset ... an intersubjective world, common to all of us ...' This appears, in fact, to be *the basic pragmatic postulate of intersubjectivity*, firmly rooted in preverbal interaction between the infant and 'the significant other' and possibly even in inborn predispositions to respond in particular ways toward members of one's own species (see Bruner, 1978, and Trevarthen, 1974). And it is perhaps precisely this basic pragmatic postulate – that *intersubjectivity in some sense must be taken for granted* – that Royce (1962, p. 96) has in mind when he maintains: 'Minds I can understand, because I am myself a mind.' What happens when the component of self-fulfilling faith – and hence the inbuilt circularity – *fail* can perhaps only be fully understood when we examine particular cases of severe communications breakdowns under conditions of schizophrenia and autism (Rommetveit, 1974).

However, the circularity inherent in acts of communication does *not* imply that the two participants assume joint or equal responsibility for what is being meant by what is said. The speaker monitors what he says in accordance with what he assumes to be the listener's position, in order to make *his own private world* comprehensible to the other. What he says may still turn out to be an incomplete and very poor expression of what he means. But he cannot possibly be ignorant of his own state of belief concerning some state of affairs he himself introduced, nor can he misunderstand what he himself intends to make known about that state of affairs. He – *not* the listener – has hence the power to decide *what is being meant* and *whether it is being misunderstood*. Control of the temporarily shared social reality at any given stage of a dialogue is thus under conditions of perfect equality or symmetry between partners in principle unequivocally determined by *direction of communication*.

This means, more specifically, that reciprocal role taking under condition III (2) IV (6), $p_1 = p_2$; p_1: $(p_1 = p_2)$; and p_2: $(p_1 = p_2)$ in table 1 is combined with an unequivocal and reciprocally endorsed *primary contract* or *rule of control*: each of the two participants has *qua speaker* the privilege to impose his own private world upon the other and *qua listener* the commitment to try to grasp what the other person from within *his* private world is talking about. The speaker, or more generally, *the participant who introduced whatever is being talked about at that moment, is assumed to know what is being meant by what is said*. It is thus p_1's privilege, for instance, to decide whether some response from p_2 is an answer to *his* preceding question or not. In order to make sense of such a response as an *answer*, he must indeed take it for granted that p_2 actually is trying to answer that preceding question as *he*, p_1, intended or meant it.

A relation of actual equality or symmetry [condition III (2), $p_1 = p_2$ in table 1] implies therefore by no means *diffusion of* and/or *some vaguely defined status of equality with respect to* control, but merely *absence of actual constraints upon interchangeability of dialogue roles*. And Habermas who, like Searle and Labov, assumes that communicated meanings are identical for all members of the same speech community, maintains accordingly that 'pure intersubjectivity' is attained under conditions of unlimited interchangeability of dialogue roles, that is ' . . . when there is complete symmetry in the distribution of assertion and disputation, revelation and hiding, prescription and following, among the partners of communication' (Habermas, 1970, p. 143).

Notice, however, that such a notion of 'pure intersubjectivity' appears to fit the dialogue between our two believing adolescent boys under conditions of perfect pluralistic ignorance [constellation I (1) II (11) III (2) IV (9) in table 1] as well as, for example, a conversation between two persons under conditions of a perfectly shared social reality and perfect equality with respect to actual and reciprocally assumed power [constellation I (1) II (1) III (2) IV (6) in table 1]. Neither of our two boys has determined the topic of their discussion, and the latter may indeed be described as perfectly symmetric if they take equal turns at concealing their private faiths. The fact that p_1's false assumption about p_2's private state of belief, as well as p_2's equally false assumption about p_1's private state of belief, is sustained and in some sense even validated, is due however, to the fact that each of them takes it for granted that the other is revealing *his own private world* when he in fact is talking on what he assumes to be *the listener's private premises of disbelief*. And this *dynamic* aspect of pluralistic ignorance can only be assessed by a systematic analysis of particular combinations of actual and reciprocally assumed control of communication, that is as constellation III (2) IV (9) in table 1.

This particular pattern of control yields in the complete constellation I (16) II (1) III (2) IV (9) an entirely different varian. of pluralistic ignorance, namely the variant exposed by the naive child in H. C. Andersen's tale about the emperor's new clothes. The emperor is actually naked, yet treated and *talked about* by his shrewd tailors and obedient subjects as if he were dressed in a magnificent new suit. The latter is thus a firmly established social reality, despite the fact that every single obedient subject privately fails to see it.

Similar situations may arise even within respectable academic environments, for instance when notions from some particularly prestigious domain of scholarly research are assimilated into a neighbouring, though different and less prestigious, field of inquiry. Consider, for instance, what may happen when two post-doctorate fellows in psycholinguistics engage in a discussion of, for example, *deep structure of sentences*. Suppose that each of them is relatively ignorant in the field of linguistics, but impressed by the stringency and power of structural analysis. Suppose, furthermore, that each of them conceives of the other as more knowledgeable, more thoroughly trained, and hence more insightful in linguistic matters than he is himself. What p_1 says about deep sentence structure under such conditions will very likely be based upon the presupposition that it is something which he himself cannot yet 'see', but which p_2 has grasped because of his superior insight. P_2 is listening to him, though, on the assumption that *he*, p_2, is the one who has not yet experienced the light of revelation. Some kind of shared faith is hence established and sustained, and *a talked-about linguistic notion* is in such discourse assimilated as *a shared social reality* within the subculture of psycholinguistics.

My reason for these excursions into different variants of pluralistic ignorance is twofold. They indicate, first of all, that *issues of actual and reciprocally assumed control of communication* are as significant in the analysis of scientific discourse as in, for example, inquiries into ideological debate or case studies of conversations about religious faith. In addition, we have shown that very different patterns of control may be revealed under the disguise of a 'symmetric' dyadic relation of *actual control* once we venture to examine *reciprocally assumed control* as well. Absence of constraints upon interchangeability of dialogue roles may be said to yield a *genuine* dialogue if, and only if, a symmetric relationship is reciprocally assumed by the two partners, that is under condition III (2) IV (6). It may also yield a quasi-dialogue, however, *if both p_1 and p_2 take it for granted that only p_1 knows what is being talked about*, that is a situation in which some state of intersubjectivity is attained solely on the premises of p_1's private world w_1 [condition III (2) IV (1) in table 1]. And the pattern of control in our cases of pluralistic ignorance may acccordingly be described as '*a double quasi-dialogue*'.

The 48 possible constellations of actual and reciprocally assumed control in table 1 may thus be split into a number of different subsets. We have, first of all, three cases of perfect correspondence. These are the two versions of *the perfect quasi-dialogue* III (1) IV (1) and III (3) IV (11) and *the perfectly genuine dialogue* III (2) IV (6). There are, moreover, in addition to the perfectly genuine dialogue, three other constellations of *symmetric control patterns*. One of these is III (2) IV (3), the case in which p_1 is entirely engaged in imposing his private world w_1 upon p_2 and vice versa in the sense that each participant adopts the privilege of deciding what the other actually means by what he is saying. The second symmetric pattern is III (2) IV (9), our case of pluralistic ignorance. The third constellation is III (2) IV (16), a situation in which both partners are truly ignorant with respect to which one of them knows what is meant. Such a situation can hardly be sustained, yet attained as *a state of transition* when, for instance, control of communication changes from a pattern of *egocentric symmetry* such as III (2) IV (3) toward *the perfectly genuine dialogue* III (2) IV (6). All remaining constellations of actual and reciprocally assumed control are variants of an *asymmetric dyadic pattern*. And the variants characterized by a state of ignorance *i* in either one of columns p_1: (p_1/p_2) and p_2: (p_1/p_2) may all be conceived of as *transitory patterns of communication control*.

Let me finally add a few words about *actual control* (column III in table 1). Is not such a notion, after all, based upon the fundamental monistic assumption that we, in an otherwise pluralistic and only fragmentarily known world, are able to identify 'real' and unequivocal dyadic relations of power? What else can possibly be implied by the notion, and how can such 'real' control be disentangled from *reciprocally assumed* control of communication?

These are admittedly very difficult issues, and they will not be fully explored in this chapter. But let me attempt a partial explication.

Remember, first of all, that we defined equality with respect to actual control, $p_1 = p_2$, as *absence of constraints upon interchangeability of dialogue roles*. Conditions of asymmetry, $p_1 > p_2$ and $p_1 < p_2$, must accordingly be defined as *conditions of constraints*. And such conditions are in fact established in every social psychological experiment on dyadic interaction in which *the two participants are assigned fixed and different dialogue roles in their joint experimental task*. Let us now briefly comment upon two recent such experiments.

Ross, Amabile and Steinmetz (1978) conducted a series of experiments on dyadic communication in which the two participants were assigned different reciprocal roles. One of them, p_1, composed very difficult knowledge questions and the other, p_2, attempted to answer those questions. P_1 had thus the power to decide which states of affairs were going to be *talked about*, that is to make his own private world of (esoteric) knowledge w_1 the topic of discourse. He had also, for every single question, the power to decide what was *meant* by what was said while p_2 – as an obedient experimental subject – was committed to try to answer every question as 'meant' by p_1. The experimental assignment of roles in this study yields thus a situation of unequivocal asymmetry with respect to actual control, $p_1 > p_2$.

A main purpose of the experiment was to examine whether p_1 and p_2, by exposing themselves under such a condition of asymmetry, would modify their self-perceptions and images of the partner. It turned out that p_1, the 'questioner', was consistently rated as more intelligent and knowledgeable than p_2, the 'answerer', both by uninvolved observers and by p_1 and p_2 themselves. It is possible, therefore, that p_1's and p_2's participation in a quiz game under those particular conditions might affect their reciprocally assumed control of communication in subsequent 'free' discourse between them. The main finding of Ross, Amabile and Steinmetz indicates that, when interpreted within the framework of table 1, a condition of asymmetry with respect to actual control, III (1), $p_1 > p_2$, imposed upon a symmetric relationship of reciprocally assumed control IV (6), $p_1: (p_1 = p_2)$ and $p_2: (p_1 = p_2)$ may modify the latter in the direction of asymmetry IV (1), $p_1: (p > p_2)$ and $p_2:$ $(p_1 > p_2)$.

Consider, next, an experiment by Blakar and Pedersen (1978). The two participants in their experiment, p_1 and p_2, are each given a map of a complicated network of roads and streets in a town centre. On p_1's map a specific route from one particular location to another is marked by arrows. On p_2's map there is no such route. And p_1 is assigned the role as *'explainer'*. His task is to inform p_2 about the route step by step, and in such a way that p_2, the *'follower'*, can find his way to the pre-determined destination. The route is thus by the very visual display (the arrows) made part of p_1's private world, w_1, but has to be made known to p_2 by verbal communication. P_1 is thus at every stage in control of the talked-about 'here' of the guided tour in the sense that he – and only he – can define it in terms of a specific location along the sequence of arrows. And p_2's questions about the route as they are wandering along make sense if, and only if, he takes it for granted that p_1 knows the entire route *and* precisely where on the map they are located when the question is asked.

We have thus again a case of unequivocal and experimentally induced asymmetry with respect of actual control, $p_1 > p_2$. The role of the 'explainer' in Blakar and Pedersen's experiment is similar to that of the 'questioner' in the study by Ross, Amabile and Steinmetz in that *it assigns to p_1 the privilege of having the final word concerning what is meant by what is said*. P_1's exploitation of such a privilege in the role as an *'explainer'*, however, may very likely be contingent upon personal self-confidence in that particular role as affected by, for example, her/his familiarity with city traffic, skill in map reading, and experience in guidance of other people. And Blakar and Pedersen observed in their population of experimental subjects a definite sex-bound difference in that respect: male undergraduate students were clearly more self-confident than female undergraduates.

This means, more specifically, that we should expect, *in a free conversation* between a male and a female subject about explanation of routes with reference to a city map, a pattern of reciprocally assumed asymmetry: the male is the one who is assumed to 'know what is being talked about', the female the one who has to take for granted *his* competence to explain what is meant. A mixed-sex dyad composed of a *male* 'explainer' and a *female* 'follower' in the experiment by Blakar and Pedersen represents accordingly a situation of perfect *correspondence* between actual and reciprocally assumed control, namely condition III (1) IV (1) in table 1. If, on the other hand, the 'explainer' is *female* and the follower *male*, we get constellation III (1) IV (11) in table 1, that is a condition of *discrepancy* between experimentally induced and reciprocally assumed control of communication. We would accordingly expect that the first couple (the female 'follower' guided by the male 'explainer') would arrive quickly and elegantly at their destination, whereas the second couple (the male 'follower' guided by the female 'explainer') might run into considerably more difficulties along that same route. And this is precisely what happens in the experiment by Blakar and Pedersen when the two maps are identical and the problem can be solved. *Communication efficiency appears to be maximal under conditions of perfect correspondence between actual and reciprocally assumed control and very poor under conditions of discrepancy.*

The notion of *actual control* may thus be partially explicated in terms of externally (in the cases above experimentally) induced constraints upon communication. The two experimental studies we have referred to provide us, in addition, with evidence suggesting a subtle interplay of externally induced constraints and 'internal' mechanisms of control. An externally induced asymmetry $p_1 > p_2$ can apparently easily be imposed upon a dyad in which that asymmetry already is reciprocally assumed (male 'explainer' and female 'follower'), but not so easily upon a dyad with a pre-established opposite pattern of reciprocally assumed control (female 'explainer' and male 'follower' in the experiment by Blakar and Pedersen). And an externally provided asymmetry with respect to actual control may also, as suggested by Ross, Amabile and Steinmetz, quickly become 'internalized' and reciprocally taken for granted. The notion of actual control may also be explicated in terms of *institutionally provided constraints* upon communication in particular real-life settings. Every formal educational system, for instance, may be said to possess a definite and unequivocal pattern of asymmetry: topics of discourse are pre-determined by curricula, and the teacher is, by virtue of his superior knowledge and his role as an educator, the one who is supposed to have the final word concerning what is meant by what is said. The progressive teacher may hence define his own trade as the art of creating an internal symmetric pattern of reciprocally assumed control within an actual, institutionally given, frame of asymmetry [constellation III (1) IV (6) in table 1].

4. Social representations and transformation of dyadic states of social reality

Let us now – at least for a while – withdraw from tedious combinatorics and return to some of the issues I raised in my critical comments on mainstream psycho-, socio-, and 'linguo'-linguistics. The synthesis of mainstream linguistics and sociolinguistics, I argued, yields an analysis of human discourse in terms of 'literal meanings', shared propositional knowledge of the world, and 'actions performed with words'. What is easily overlooked in such an analysis, however, is the *innocence of silence* (Ducrot, 1972) and *the subtle transformation of knowledge which at times seems to be part and parcel of the very act of verbalization.* An old lady I knew used to talk about 'the mercy to be able to keep silent'. What she had in mind, I think, was that quite a few things may as well remain unspoken because putting them into words will somehow alter the status of the potential topic from that of possibly shared, yet so far not socially confirmed, intuitions to that of 'public', embarrassing knowledge. This subtle transformation – or *construction* – of knowledge is considered to be, by Merleau-Ponty, the distinctive features of *authentic acts of speech*, yet disregarded in current psycho- and socio-linguistic theory. What is being meant the moment an authentic act of speech is completed is thus, in some sense, a product of that very act.

What is 'performed with words' under such conditions is thus apparently a transformation of an individual state u to either state t, f_1 or f_2 in column I of table 1: some individual pre-verbal state of ignorance or innocent agnosticism is transformed into reflective belief or even 'public knowledge' by the very act of verbalization. The latter may for instance be an answer to some specific question. And let us now ponder how *what is meant* in such a case may in part be determined by *the person who asked that question.* Imagine, for instance, a situation in which you are asked *what kind of a person one of your friends is,* and let us assume that you have never tried to find words for your impression of that particular friend of yours until the very moment you are asked about it. Suppose, moreover, that the person asking you about him does so because he is considering your friend as an applicant for some job. Being aware of that and knowing that the job is neither well paid nor particularly interesting, you may perhaps answer: (1) *Oh, he is easy to please.*

Imagine, on the other hand, a situation in which you know that your friend has decided to start out on a long and solitary expedition which in all likelihood will be very monotonous and not exciting at all. Assuming, on this occasion, that the person asking you about your friend is worried whether he will endure the monotony, you may very well answer: (2) *Oh, he can gain pleasure from small things.*

Your answer is thus on each occasion clearly something more than hitting upon the exact verbal expression of some ready-made cognitive representation of your friend's personal characteristics. It is a genuinely social activity in the sense that you spontaneously monitor what you say in accordance with tacit assumptions concerning what both of you already know and, what is more, your listener wants to know. What is being *meant* by you and *understood* by your listener, moreover, is on each of the two different occasions in part determined by the question you are attempting to answer. And let us now return to table 1 and try to account in detail for what happens on each occasion.

The questions are asked by two persons who *differ with respect to their private concern for your friend*. The first person wants to know: (1) Is he easy to please? (S is R_i?); whereas the other wants to know: (2) Is he the kind of person who can endure monotony? (S is R_j?).

Let us label *you* p_1 and *your interrogator* p_2. The state of dyadic social reality at the moment you are asked what kind of a person your friend is will then by *I (16) II (25) III (2) IV 6)*. You (p_1) are *undetermined* with respect to your friend's personal attributes in the specific sense that *you have so far never verbalized your impression of him*, and p_2 *does not know* what kind of a person your friend is. Moreover, each of you is at this stage ignorant about the other's state of belief. There are no externally provided constraints upon your conversation and, let us assume, a perfectly symmetric pattern of reciprocally assumed control. This means, we remember, that control at each stage of the dialogue is to be determined by direction of communication or – more generally – by *dialogue role*.

What happens the moment p_2 asks the question is that the value *i* in column p_2: (p_1 in w_1) is replaced by a specific request for information, either (1) *S is R_i?* or (2) *S is R_j?*. And your commitment to answer on p_2's premises implies simply that the temporary pattern of reciprocally assumed control at that moment is IV (11). This means, more specifically, that you in response to question (1) are committed to make known your not-yet-verbalized impression of your friend *by talking about him as a potential manipulandum*. The state of dyadic social reality attained the moment your answer is understood, moreover, is the perfectly shared social reality I (1) II (1) III (2) IV (6). What has become 'public knowledge' about your friend has thus, whether it is true or false, in part been determined by p_2's private interest in him as a potential employee. And it may possibly be embarrassing knowledge. The fact that you have *reflected upon* and *talked about* your friend in such a particular way may even make you blush the next time you see him.

Question (2), on the other hand, represents an invitation to engage in *a temporarily shared strategy of attributing some talent or capacity to your friend.* The content of the perfectly shared social reality generated by your answer is hence the 'public knowledge' that *He can* . . . (gain pleasure from small things). And expressions such as *'He is easy to please'* and *'He can gain pleasure from small things'* are linguistically mediated options with respect to the social representation of personal attributes. Either one of them – or some entirely different expression – may thus be the one you end up with when immersed in solitary reflections about your friend without any commitment to an interrogator.

The situations we have described above, however, are such that it is your partner in the conversation who, from his private concern, proposes *which* contract concerning categorization or attribution shall be endorsed by the two of you. This implies, in the terminology of Wittgenstein (1968, pp. 104–5 and pp. 210–13) that the talked-about *aspect* of your friend on each occasion is salient because he is viewed temporarily by *both of you* from the perspective of p_2's private world, w_2. *What is meant by you* when you answer p_2 may thus in each case be an 'exact verbal expression' of what you already intuitively 'knew', yet on each occasion is contingent upon p_2's particular request for information – and for that reason is *a genuinely social enterprise.* And this will be the case also if your answer has the form of a negation, for instance, (1) that he is *not* easy to please or (2) that he *cannot* gain pleasure from small things. The resultant state of dyadic social reality will then, provided that you are honest and p_2 trusts you, be constellation I (11) II (11) III (2) IV (6) in table 1, that is *a state of perfectly shared partial agnosticism* (see p. 338 and p. 341).

I have dealt with this hypothetical case at such length for two main reasons. I have tried to show, first of all, that Searle's 'principle of expressibility' is itself very likely an 'incomplete expression'. Nothing is ever *said* in a social vacuum, and *what is meant by what is said* can for that reason hardly be fully explicated in terms of the 'literal utterance of an expression'. What is required is a thorough analysis of the pattern of reciprocally assumed control of what is being meant at the moment it is said.

Our hypothetical case may also possibly serve to de-mystify the very notion of different private worlds. The difference between your two interrogators is by no means of a mystical or profoundly ontological nature. Nor are they imprisoned in peculiar idiosyncracies. They differ simply with respect to personal perspective on what is going to be talked about, that is with respect to which aspect (R_i or R_j) of your friend's total constellation of personal attributes they want you to make known to them. You have the capacity to adopt either perspective, but you may also refuse to engage in a conversation with either one of them.

The issue of reciprocally assumed control in a dialogue may thus often be a matter of which *aspect* of some composite state of affairs, the aspect that is salient in w_1 or that which is salient in w_2, will be jointly attended to by p_1 and p_2. What is meant and understood in a discourse between them becomes a question of whose private world is to be accepted as the foundation of a temporarily shared social reality. Communication will then, if the pattern of reciprocally assumed control is one of egocentric symmetry [III (2) IV (3) in table 1], be locked in a conflict between competing alternative premises for intersubjectivity. This is the dyadic manifestation of a frozen ideological conflict.

A different kind of conflict may arise in society at large when some new and entirely unfamiliar state of affairs has to be coped with and assimilated into a traditional pattern of social institutions. The identity of the previously unknown entity may then be determined in a competition between different institutionally founded social representations. A new variant of deviant behaviour, for instance, may, from different ideological positions within our pluralistic society, be baptized respectively as *crime*, *illness*, or *cultural innovation*. What will become 'public knowledge' about the initially unfamiliar and controversial phenomenon, moreover, will be contingent upon *which questions are raised about it at a very early stage*. An active minority with a consistent perspective may therefore have considerable impact upon the course of cultural assimilation, as pointed out by Moscovici (1976: 273). What happens in society at large under such conditions is thus a transformation of pre-verbal agnosticism into 'public knowledge', with patterns of communication control analogous to those revealed in our analysis of transformation of dyadic states of social reality.

Let us now return to our dyad, however, and examine the role of *presuppositions* under relatively simple conditions of discourse. Consider, for instance, the following situation:

Two friends, p_1 and p_2, are driving together in a car. P_1 is the driver, p_2 his passenger and guest, and the drive is in fact a guided tour in the neighbourhood of p_1's home. As they are driving along, they pass a big, shabby, derelict-looking building. It is obvious to any observer that the building has been left to decay, but its appearance is otherwise such that it leaves the observer with no clue whatsoever with respect to its previous identity. It may be a forlorn apartment house, an empty office building, a closed-down factory, or something else. As they are passing that building, however, p_1 says to p_2: *there wasn't enough profit from the production*.

Let us assume that p_2 was truly ignorant with respect to the identity of the building until this very moment. He may later on, though, inform his wife that there is a closed-down *factory* in the neighbourhood of their friend p_1's home. And he will in that case do so in perfect confidence that he is telling the truth. *His state of agnosticism has thus been transformed into a state of belief the moment he understood what p_1 told him as they were passing that building.*

This transformation must in part be explained in terms of 'shared propositional knowledge of the world' as proposed by Labov in his theory of discourse (Labov, 1972): what is meant by p_1 as they are passing the building can hardly be understood by p_2 at all unless both of them take it for granted that production takes place in factories rather than, for example, apartment buildings. But *this would also be the case if p_1 were, for example, a fellow passenger in a tourist bus passing that same building*. But would p_2 in such a case later on confidently tell his wife about the factory? If not, why not? Under which particular conditions will p_1's *presupposition* that the building is a factory automatically become p_2's *belief*?

The case of the two friends, I shall argue, is a simple case of what I in previous casuistic analysis have labelled *prolepsis* (Rommetveit, 1974, p. 87). P_1's presupposition that the building is a factory is of the form S is R_i, and the state of dyadic social reality at the moment when he starts talking about insufficient profit is constellation I (4) II (21) III (1) IV (6). A truly proleptic feature of the situation is that p_1 talks *on the assumption that or as if* p_2 already knows what he himself knows about the building [*t* in column p_1: (p_2 in w_2)]. Another essential feature of the situation is the constellation of *p_2's ignorance concerning p_1's state of belief* and the actual constraints upon their conversation due to the fact that *p_1 lives in that area whereas p_2 is a stranger* [*i* in column p_2: (p_1 in w_1) and $p_1 > p_2$ in column III]. The state of dyadic reality at *the moment p_2 understand what p_1 is saying*, I (4) II (21) III (1) IV (1), is under these conditions immediately transformed into the perfectly shared social reality I (1) II (1) III (1) IV (6): p_1's unwarranted assumption that p_2 knows that the building is a factory has *become* true.

The case of the two tourists is, as already indicated, identical as far as *shared abstract propositional knowledge of the world* is concerned. The state of dyadic social reality prior to p_1's utterance, however, is in this latter case

I (4) II (13) III (2) IV (6); I (4) II (16) III (2) IV (6); or I (4) II (20) III (2) IV (6). Notice that the constellation of actual constraints upon the situation *and* p_2's assumption concerning p_1's state of belief now is an entirely different one: *p_1 and p_2 are both unfamiliar with that particular neighbourhood* ($p_1 = p_2$ in column III) *and p_2 will in all likelihood take it for granted that p_1 is as ignorant concerning the identity of the building as he is himself*. He will, even if p_2 speaks on the false assumption that p_1 too has identified it as a factory, necessarily *become aware of* and probably also *question* that pre-supposition.

Presuppositions concerning the identity of derelict-looking buildings are, indeed, very trivial ingredients of our pluralistic social world. They are of the general form S is R_i, though. Our analysis of very simple and trivial cases, such as those above, may hence *in principle* help us understand *how* and *under which conditions of actual and reciprocally assumed control of communication* other people's presuppositions of an ideological or even ontological nature become our private beliefs.

It is, of course, impossible within the scope of the present chapter to pursue more than a few implications of a consistently pluralistic outlook on language and social representations. Let me finally, however, comment briefly upon some problems we encounter if we venture to pursue some of Wittgenstein's reflections on *private experience and public knowledge* (Wittgenstein, 1968) in a systematic analysis of patterns of control in dyadic constellations of different private worlds. We have shown that a state of intersubjectivity *other than that of a perfectly shared social reality* under certain conditions may be attained if both p_1 and p_2 accept *either* p_1's *or* p_2's private world as the foundation. The issue of communication control becomes then a matter of *whose* private world is accepted as *intersubjectively*, and therefore in some sense, *publicly, valid*. And we may now add: what is implied by such a validation?

Berger and Luckmann (1967, p. 38) maintain: 'It can ... be said that language makes "more real" my subjectivity not only to my conversation partner but also to myself.' This is very important to keep in mind in any serious analysis of encounters between different private worlds. The nature and significance of such a social validation of one's own subjectivity, however, can only be fully appreciated in the light of some additional pluralistic assumptions.

The first of these is the assumption that *linguistically mediated social representations to some extent are negotiable and border on our imperfect knowledge of the world*. What is *made known* by what is said in particular contexts of human discourse is thus to a considerable degree contingent upon negotiated specification of linguistically mediated general drafts of contract concerning categorization. Negotiated specification, moreover, allows for adjustment of categorizations in accordance with *private and contextually determined perspectives*. And mutual understanding will always entail a residual of *presupposed commonality with respect of interpretation* or *faith in a common world*.

Inherent in this residual is also a component of truly *private, subjective experience*. This component is, of course, neither a legitimate object of inquiry in formal semantic analysis nor of any practical concern in our everyday discourse about publicly familiar states of affairs. It may be brought to the foreground, though, in situations in which we struggle to make known to other people particularly idiosyncratic fragments of our private worlds. And Kelly (1955) reports in his study of people's 'personal constructs' an interesting case of semantic productivity in such a situation: when one of his clients was asked to name a very salient attribute in her assessment of similarities and differences between people she knew well, she ended up with the word '*Mary-ness*'. What was meant by that word was entirely bound to the client's subjective experience of a particular friend of hers, Mary. This subjective experience, though, seemed to serve as an Archimedian point in her entire private world of personal attributes and interpersonal relations.

The novel word 'Mary-ness' is in this case the means by which a personally significant and truly subjective experience can be *talked about* and therefore – possibly – made 'more real'. The very composition of the word, moreover, brings out very clearly the bi-polar nature of language as a bridge between different private worlds: the component '*Mary*' is intelligible only in terms of truly subjective experience, whereas the component '-*ness*' is comprehensible to everybody, yet nearly devoid of experiential content. And it is precisely in the interplay of such residuals of subjective experience and a common linguistic code that one's subjectivity can be made 'more real'.

The position of Kelly's client is therefore in a sense, a caricature of *the minority position in a language game*. It resembles, for example, the position of an African fiction writer who attempts to convey his uniquely African cultural background in a world language (English) with an inbuilt '*et cetera*' of shared experiential residuals different from that of his own culture. Another variant of such a position is, of course, that of the heretic pluralist who tries to convey his ideas about human communication to a scientific community pervaded by seductive monistic assumptions about our language and the world. What Berger and Luckmann maintain about making one's subjectivity 'more real' to *oneself* must therefore be further specified in terms of patterns of actual and reciprocally assumed control of what is meant and understood. And we may ask, under which conditions of therapeutic discourse will 'Mary-ness' become 'more real' to Kelly's client? What is required on the part of *the listener*? Must Kelly, in order for some social validation to take place, perhaps have to *learn more about Mary* and – possibly – even arrange to meet her? And – if so – does he not then attempt to validate 'Mary-ness' *in principle* in the same way as we are making Shakespeare's *initially* private world of Hamlet and Fallstaffian characters 'more real' by reading and/or watching his plays?

We may accordingly return to our 48 possible patterns of actual and reciprocally assumed control of communication in table 1 and examine *necessary and optimal conditions for validation of one's subjectivity*. What, for instance, is the opportunity of p_2 in constellation III (1) IV (1) for such validation? Will his lip-service to p_1 in that constellation serve to make p_2's *publicly endorsed subjectivity* 'more real' at all? If so, in what sense? And what about the minority position in a scientific dispute about competing paradigms (Kuhn, 1962)? Is such a position essentially that of p_2 in constellation III (1) IV (3), that is a situation of 'internal' egocentric symmetry within an asymmetric frame of actual control?

These are some of the many issues that have to be left unexplored. And I leave them to my reader in the hope that I *by doing so* may engage him as an ally in an attempt to rescue the written-about combinatorics of pluralism from imprisonment in my own private world.

15. Representation and mentalization: from the represented group to the group process*

RENÉ KAËS

In psychology, the concept of representation means both the process of mentally constructing psychic reality and a series of effects which can be classified together under the general heading of *mentalization*. By mentalization we mean the very activity whereby the human psyche is constituted, that is the transformation of quantities of physiological energy into psychic quantities. It is none the less a good idea to make clear that these qualities are structured by man himself – a talking and highly social animal – and that they are subject to the laws governing speech and the formation of groups.

One part only of the definition of mentalization is in fact given when one speaks of this qualitative transformation which accounts for the physical anaclisis of mentalization. The complement is to be found in its group anaclisis. In this paper I remind the reader of the role of groups in supplying models and functions of mentalization through their social contents, procedures and form.

The concept of social representation remains within the field of psychology when it assumes the task of explaining this double anaclisis. However, it indicates more precisely how the representation is structured and how it functions in inter-personal and group communication and, more widely, within society. But it also takes into account those aspects of the work of mentalization which are strictly psychic. In this study my intention will be to go deeper into these relationships between representation and mentalization. After that I will show both the direct and the indirect effects of the representation of the group upon the group process.

The theoretical frame of reference I am using is principally that of psychoanalysis, and the clinical field in which I work is that of small training or therapy groups. I shall aim to achieve a tie-up, both

*Translated by Dr John L. Carr

361

theoretical and practical, between the process of group formation, how the human psyche is structured and the formation of micro-mentalities (Kaës, 1976, 1980).

1.   Mentalization, absence-work and linking-work

By mentalization I mean, first and foremost, a psychic work, that is work concerned with the *formation and transformation of psychic qualities*: e.g. hallucinations, images, fantasies, dream-thoughts, ideas, secondary thinking.

It is possible to distinguish between two sorts of transformation: (*a*) that which occurs in transitions *between* levels, for example in moving from physiological energies to psychic qualities or from cultural artifacts or aspects of the social structure to their psychic cathexis and reconstructions, and (*b*) that which occurs *within* the same level, for example the intra-psychic level as when one passes from one psychic structure to another. In psychoanalytic theory, the idea of *Durcharbeitung*, translated as 'a complete working through', shows how the process of transformation, which can affect the structure of the psyche, has repercussions on other structures, *through which* the transformation takes place.

The idea of work, by virtue of its etymology, brings us back to two other terms. In French villages a *travail* is a sling or jack for shoeing horses, a device for holding them up when being shod or administered to by a vet; it is a support or framework. But it is also a process, because, as English has it, it is a journey ('travel'), the business of going across, of traversing. And these two meanings can help us to characterize the psychic work of mentalization; it depends upon a frame or support, but it is also a journey across, a crossing or even a meandering.

Once this dimension of work has been emphasized, what is mentalization? To what is this work directed? It seems to me possible to isolate a single proposition which is common to all the studies undertaken on this matter: *to mentalize is to establish or re-establish a link*. So I shall declare that mentalization is the business of linking. This can be done in three ways: (i) by establishing a transformation-link between an energy-surge and a psychic structure which is closely allied both to this instinctual tension and to its release under conditions in which the energy-surge does not find *direct* satisfaction. Here a new way opens up, by experiencing the absence or loss of the object, which comes to supercede the direct way (ii) by establishing, through the experience of loss, a link or bond between something that was present and no longer is and something that is absent but represented and (iii) by associating an intra-psychic (i.e. subjective) representation and a code or code-system which is external (i.e. social). This link will confer upon each of them a status and a future in inter- and intra-subjective communication.

W. Bion gives an example of these three aspects of linking in what he calls the *alpha* capability of the mother; it is here a matter of a reaction by the psychic apparatus of the mother, which transforms painful impulses which the child is unable to transform into psychic representations. But the power of this alpha function is not limited to a transforming of the contents to which the mother is sensitive and which she can control; it extends also to the very processes and modes of the transformation itself. And these processes are, to an important extent, linked to local, group and social codes.

Sufficient attention has probably not been paid to the fact that the classification of psychic contents is as important as their transformation and that both depend on structure and group process. They depend, in the first instance, on that group which itself contains the mother, that is the primary group, and on the totality, both in social reality and in fantasy, of the links organized therein between mother, father and child, at the intersection between the sexes and the generations within a given culture and society. The work of mentalization establishes itself (or does not) as the linking-work between psychic representations, in so far as they are representations of absent objects and the classifications of groups which are a medley of procedures and contents, ready-made and potentially usable for creating representations. What I call group-anaclisis provides not only a support but also a form and, even more, an accreditation for an intra-psychic representation and a 're-run' in speech-form which gives it meaning within the context of interpersonal, group and societal relationships. My point of view is, therefore, that the work of mentalization establishes a link between these three orders: between the body and the psyche, and between the structures of the psyche and of the group. The work of mentalization is a psychic work of the intermediate process, the twin extremes of which are probably body and code, presence and absence, fantasy and myth. To make a finer point, I must say a word about what I mean by anaclisis for mentalization.

The multiple anaclisis for mentalization

The concept of anaclisis is central to the problem of psychoanalytic explanation. But its fortunes in the literature and in clinical practice are quite amazing: dilution, distortion and complete misunderstanding characterize its usage and its history. A critical re-evaluation is called for, the fruitfulness of which becomes clear when we make use of the result in analysis.

Referring back to the elaboration and history of this concept in Freud's work, its scaling down (in customary use) to the single dimension of anaclitism becomes immediately apparent. Now, it is easy to demonstrate that, for Freud, the concept of anaclisis is organized, in accordance with the semantic richness of the German word, around three aspects: (a) support, from an origin or even from the foundation of the structure of the psyche based on the exercise of bodily functions, (b) modelling (in the sense of the German expression *sich lehnen an etwas*, that is to model oneself on, to take something as one's exemplar). Anaclisis is here closely linked with identifications; and (c) the 're-run' or 'return', or a half-openness, or opportunity, in the sense in which two wholes communicate with each other through a space specially arranged for that purpose, which allows for the transition from one order, or one level, to another.

Among the consequences of this conception of anaclisis I should like to point to two: first, besides the bodily anaclisis of impulse and its expression (affect, representation), and besides the cathexis upon the object or object-relation (maternal) two other types of anaclisis appear in the full meaning of the support, of the model and of the 're-run': the dependence of the psyche upon the group, on the one hand, and its dependence on endopsychic structures on the other. One can call this latter self-anaclisis, for example its dependence on certain psychic structures, such as the Ego-ideal or the Ideal Self in the experience of depression, or on certain thought contents, as in anxiety neurosis.

Among the consequences of criticisms of the notion of anaclisis it appears that mentalization cannot occur divorced from its relationship with the body, with the mother, with the group and with the social and cultural structures. To be precise: the multiple anaclisis of psychism (and of mentalization) implies that the relationship between that which is supported and that which supports it is one of mutual support, of mutual modelling and of self-reflection. The father–mother–child relationship, at the point of severance, supplies a good example of this: that which ceases to be anaclitic at that point concerns the object-relationship between the mother, the nursling and the father. That which the child *mentalizes*, starting from the experience of separation (of severance), is directly related to the nature of the relationship between the mother and the father. That which, at that moment, from the mother's standpoint becomes more complex concerns also her own experience of separation and of the upsurge of her desire. In this perspective it is important to ensure that research is brought to bear on this interstice of anaclisis; this is probably the space within which mind is born, for it is in the vacuum created by absence and discontinuity that the articulation between different levels and different orders – bodily, mental, group and societal – may be achieved on the mental mode of representation (or 're-run').

This notion of multiple anaclisis as a mutual support may explain the articulation between individual mind and group process and structures. We have at our disposal a handy tool for figuring out situations of break-up and of crisis. For them we can give an account of facts of a like nature which we meet in clinical practice: the experience of a *loss of support*, and the search for a new support; that of a *split* experienced as a break-up and as violence in the transition from one source of support to another. From mother to group, from bodily need to fantasy, from fantasy to myth and to speech there is always the solution of continuity.

Since we have shed light upon these notions of mentalization and of anaclisis the moment has come to put them to the test in respect of representation. I shall discuss the values of it in psychoanalytic theory, for this notion offers a notable advantage: it possesses a double aspect, the one made up of *things*, the other of *words*: it is, therefore, with some justification that we can speak of a double anaclisis for representations.

It is known that, in the Freudian psychoanalytic perspective, *Vorstellung* denotes the inscription of an object in the memory system: the object is represented through its inscription in the memory system. The distinction which Freud drew in 1915 between the representation of things and the representation of words involved his initial topographical model of the mind. The representation of things results from the very perception of the thing and this representation characterizes the unconscious system: from the point of view of psychic economy it comprises a cathexis of the memory traces which are more or less derived from the thing itself. The representation of the words, for its part, derives from the utilization of the organized systems of speech and language. The thing is thus linked to the word used to express it and is, therefore, linked to the group anaclisis. This type of representation characterizes the preconscious/conscious system. This distinction raises the question as to how the transition between the representation of things and that of words comes about. Here I do not wish to enter into a theoretical and over-specialized discussion which would bring to the fore the role of the Ego and of the Preconscious in this transition, that is the authorities to which appeals are principally made in the creation of intermediate structures (Kaës, 1980).

Besides psychoanalytic research certain ethnological work is extremely valuable: it helps us to understand how the experiences of the thing, those of its absence and those of its representation come together in a code and a group organization. The anaclisis of the Ego based upon the group and upon the code is not without its structural effect on the work of mentalization and upon the psychic processes which are triggered off within the mentalities that result therefrom. The 'group Ego' of the Dogons does not perceive 'things' in the same way as does the Ego of an Anglo-Saxon. The words used to express it imply reference to a code (which is linguistic and mythical) and to group organization: the studies of M. Leenhart (1947) have shown us how the form of the code structures the perception of the object and how the designation of persons structures interpersonal and intra-psychic relationships. The indications of the name, for example, among the Melanesians, orients us towards a quite different system of relationships obtaining between objects and interpersonal relationships.

Piaget had this intuition regarding the dependence of mental activity upon the group; to be in a group and to group mental activities together go hand in hand: 'without the exchange of thought and co-operation with others, the individual would not succeed in grouping together his activities into a coherent whole' (Piaget and Inhelder, 1967, p. 174); and later: 'The individual achieves logic only by virtue of co-operation' (*ibid.*, p. 176). For the psychoanalyst, mentalization originates and forms within the primary group, first of all, in the group-mother, that is within that which, in the early days, becomes reality for the child as far as the links are concerned which obtain between mother, father and child at the meeting-point of the sexes and of the generations.

2. Psychic and socio-cultural organisers of the representation of the group

In the studies I have undertaken concerning the group as an object both of representations and of cathexis, I was led to make a distinction between two anaclitic systems, by means of which the representation of the group is built up: on the one hand, the psychic system, in which the group functions as a representative object – the representation of impulsivity – and, on the other, a *socio-cultural* system in which the group figures as a prescribed model for interpersonal relationships and the expression of feelings. Both systems involve specific organizers, that is to say, adjacent schemas which form the composition of the group, in so far as it is an object of representation.

The organizers I call 'psychic' correspond to an unconscious structure which is close to the vivid nucleus of the dream: they comprise the more or less 'scripted' objects of infantile desire: they can be common to several individuals and assume a typical character, in the sense in which Freud and Abraham spoke of typical dreams. They borrow, from everyday experience and from the social models for representing the group, the day-time material necessary for working them out. My studies have led me to single out from these psychic organizers symbolic properties which are well scripted and pro-active and to distinguish from amongst them: the image of the body; original fantasy; family images and complexes; the image of the psyche (with its topographical systems and proceedings). Thus the group is represented as a body or as part of a body – the vocabulary of the group testifies to this: head, member, cell, nucleus – or, starting from a fantasy of the primitive science, or from the image of brotherhood or as an ensemble representing the Ego, the That, the Super-Ego and the Ideal.

I have been able to show that the chief characteristic of these organizers is their being endowed with a *group structure*, that is the power to compose specific combinations out of the relationships between objects directed to an objective in accordance with a more or less coherent dramatic scenario symbolizing alliance-relationships or processes of exclusion, for example.

The *socio-cultural organizers* are the end-product of the transformation of this unconscious nucleus through the social work common to members, initially, or a given socio-cultural ambiance and then, eventually, of several cultures. They function as codes recording, in the same way as a myth does, the different orders of reality: bodily, psychic, social, political, philosophical. They make possible the symbolic elaboration of the unconscious nucleus of the representation and of the communication between members of a society. They thus operate in the transition from the dream to the myth. This is equivalent to saying that the socio-cultural organizers of the representation result from the social elaboration of the experience of different forms of group life. For this reason they are infiltrated by the psychic organizers. The study of the *social representations* of the group in its different modalities of expression (myth, ideologies, romances, iconographics and verbal expressions etc.) concerns the transformation of group experience and of intra-psychic group experience in a social system of a more or less coherent representation, established by means of language, and of which one of the major functions is to make intelligible an order of relationship to an object, and to establish, in this connection, an inter-subjective communication.

Such a system defines culture – that is the code common to all members of an organized structure; this code comprises social practices and systems of representations such as rites, myths, ideologies, conceptions of the universe, philosophical doctrines, scientific theories etc. Such a code implies two essential characteristics:

(*a*) It records the representations of various orders of reality: psychic, social, religious, cosmic, physical etc. Thus it permits the establishment of links between the peculiar representations of things which are not yet expressed in words and representations of words which are governed by common sense and socially accepted. It links the unconscious to the 'already known'.

(*b*) Its constituent parts tolerate more or less ample variations as a function of the state of social relationships and of the psychological needs of the different members of this social structure. The study of the contents of representations is, for this very reason, of less interest that that of the processes of their own organization and of their psychic and social make-up.

I should like to venture an illustration of the part played by this second series of organizers of representations. I have studied the group as a heroic symbol in numerous myths, tales, romances and movie representations. The analysis of the heroic saga of the group was carried out in accordance with the two ways of looking at things which I recommend: that of the psychic organizers, and I have pointed out the structuring role of the entreaties of the Ego-Ideal, of the Oedipus Complex, of fantasies of being consumed and of being saved: these internal psychic groups control the arrangement of positions and of the relationships between the protagonists and those of the heroic group as a whole. The hypotheses formulated by Otto Rank (1909) about the myth of the hero's birth find their validation here. Endo-psychic structures have none-the-less a support or a *social anchorage*, as Serge Moscovici (1961) has it, in what I call socio-cultural organizers. In one of Grimms' fairy tales *The seven Swabians*, the socio-cultural organizer is the Celtic myth of the Grail cycle and, more precisely, the model for the Knights of the Round Table. In fact this reference model puts forward a homosexual organization of the group which is egalitarian and circular, and which takes its direction from the quest for a common phallus. The principle of *organization* (i.e. the socio-cultural organizer) is also a principle of *identification* and of *expression*: it is one of the terms necessary to the work of mentalization.

In our culture the commonest socio-cultural organizers of the representation of the group are the *Judeo-Christian* models (the group of the twelve apostles of Christ and the mystical body, the gathering of God's people (the kibbutz)); *Celtic* models (Knights of the Round Table) and *Greek* models (the Argonauts). Certain more or less subversive variants of these are maintained in a sort of quiescent condition – whether it is a matter of female groups (Bacchantes) or of political groups (plotters; co-religionists) or of sexual utopias (Sade's group in *The 120 days of Sodom*).

3. The analysis of a representation of the group: the image of the body and the body-group

Amongst the four psychic organizers of the representation of the group, the body image occupies a special place. Organic or cybernetic theories concerning the group have their origin in this common representation of the group, according to which the group is an organism or a part thereof, a cell. This *organism*, an ordered aggregate of individuals maintained within the body-envelope, is endowed with a head (*chef*), members, a bosom and a spirit (*esprit de corps*) dwelling within this body: present-day terminology gives proof of this and so does etymology. D. Anzieu (1964) has traced the origin and evolution of the word 'group', the French use of which is quite recent. It came from the Italian (*groppo, gruppo*) which makes use of it in the technical terminology of fine art to designate several individuals painted or sculpted and forming one subject. Introduced into France towards the middle of the seventeenth century, it remains a studio word – it is also used to denote a collection of elements, a category, a class or a collection of beings or objects. 'Group' means a 'collection of people' only towards the middle of the eighteenth century in France (*groupe*) in Germany (*gruppe*) as well as in England. If one questions the origin of the word, it is possible to discover within it some clarification of its latent meanings. The sense of the first Italian word *groppo* is a *knot*; then it refers to a meeting or a gathering of people.

Linguists find a parallel with the Old Provençal word *grop* (knot) and assume that it comes from the West German word *kruppa* (a rounded mass): the idea of roundness appears to be at the base of 'group' and 'rump' (in French *groupe* and *croupe*). Thus etymology supplies two fields of force that one discovers again in the life of groups: the *knot*, and by metanomic derivation, the *link*, denoting a degree of cohesion, and *roundness* symbolizing the spatial enclosure of which the bodily envelope is the metaphor.

The semantic field of this term implies some notable characteristics: beyond the idea of assembly, of meeting and of collection, we find there the representation of the male and female sex organs: *rounded mass*, rump, roundness, circle and *knot*, which is at the same time one of the metaphors of the circle, the slang term used in France to describe the male seminal glands and, in the language of Racine, it is equivalent to sexual union. This image of the group as a closed cell, knotted in upon itself as a totality, is countered and completed by that of the group as an open and limitless body, fragmented and protoplasmic.

Certain contemporary painters have given to the group as a body an image of the body as a group[1]: a painting by Niki de Saint-Phalle, *L'Accouchement Rose* (1964), depicts an immense mother's body open to reveal its contents: celluloid babies, aeroplanes, wild animals, spiders, octopuses, masks, flowers, a glutinous collection of sea-shells and young animals in a mass of hair and incongruous objects. This representation of the body-group confirms the viewpoints suggested by Melanie Klein regarding infantile fantasies concerning the contents of the mother's body: children–penis or children–excreta which tear each other apart or form a compact and undifferentiated mass.

Another contemporary painter, Jacques van den Bussche, depicts amoeba-like groups, the elements of which fuse into an immense body: a few heads, a few limbs are, like those of the Hydra, appendages which are common to all. The bodies, molten and confused, larva-like and protean, illustrate the primeval organic unity constantly threatened with morcellation or binary fission that only the unity of the picture and the frame holds together within a limited area.

4.   To be and to make a body: group embryology

The representation of the group as a body wavers between an attempt to be a body, an initial safeguard against the unthinkable feeling of non-existence and a plan to reconstitute a unity that is constantly threatened

L'Accouchement Rose. Reproduced by kind permission of Niki de Saint-Phalle and the Nationalmuseum, Stockholm

by the internal and external dangers that lie concealed within the early stages of psychic existence: to make a body is to give form to a body threatened with fragmentation, in order to give it unity.

To be a body is to incorporate and to be incorporated: it is to achieve an aggregation, internalized and incorporated, of an uncertain early body, whose internal and external boundaries are still in a state of flux and whose differentiations in the structure of space is barely outlined. Some drawings by lads of nine or ten spontaneously provide this symbolization of the group as being-body or making-body: one of them rather humorously shows an army general, whose decorations and the adornments on his uniform, as well as the whole of his chest, are made up of a multitude of soldiers; the word associations which he provides relate to the plan of an imaginary underground city and the life of babies prior to their birth. He does this drawing whilst his mother is expecting a child.

To incorporate and be incorporated depends upon eating and drinking: by way of proof see, for example, the paintings of the Last Supper, those of Civic Guard banquets, photographs of pensioners' meals,[2] the prevalence in advertising of edible objects associated with the group. To be a body within a group is already to make a body over against the anguish of separation and of attack, against the fear of not being given a place within an assembly which must start from feeding, protecting and looking after. Photographs of old-age pensioners represent future 'disembodied' people gathered in a circle or the arc of a circle around a table loaded with food and gifts and joined together by their physical proximity. Such a souvenir print guarantees ultimate incorporation, it provides, as it were, a last sacrament and a relic to leave behind before quitting one's working life.

The analysis of group photographs, of paintings, of advertisements, discloses the fundamental dimension of mirror identification in this attempt at being, at making and remaining a body. One discovers above all that in the struggle against the *psychotic anxieties* of fragmentation, of persecution and of depression the social representation *offers* a remarkable tool: photography and the group-portrait take on functions analogous to those of the *mirror* during those identifications which resolve the anxiety of fragmentation and those tensions which are destructive in fantasy of self and other. To calm this anxiety, photography and the group-portrait convey a visual *Gestalt* with which each member of the group can identify narcissistically at the very moment when the commemoration of the striking triggers off, as a reaction, the fear of rejection or of becoming remote from the collective ideal. Photography, exactly like the civic portrait in Dutch painting, allows us to counter anxiety about dismemberment by an ideal unity 'a salutary imago' (J. Lacan), in the image of a cohesive group form, the fruitful aspects of which are the extreme conformity of each single person to the group norm and the reflecting surface of unblemished unity.

The visual representation of the group as a body, in which each person is a coordinated part of a unit that is coherent, accredited, idealized, overvalued, is the narcissistic component in identification with the object-group. The present/absent aspect of the image, the possibility of losing and recovering this group-image constitute the very anaclisis of the mentalization of the group as an object and a system of internalised objects.

5. Corporate feeling (*l'esprit de corps*)

This imaginary incarnation which is the basis for the social linkage – to make a body, to be a body within a group, via the group and its mirror-games – calls for a supposed subject of this body which the 'spirit of the group', its 'word', its 'speech', its 'thinking', its 'emotions' must assume: 'the group thinks, says, descries, decides', not yet like a 'we', but initially like a fantastic 'one'.

It is not surprising that one of the conditions for joining the group stated during the discussions is that the group should be an organic whole united together in cohesion and unity, in which each individual takes second place, so that the group can act against individual limitations and weaknesses 'like one man', 'a single mind' opposed to dispersal and internal struggles. These representations confirm certain aspects of the religious image of Whitsuntide – the decisive and unifying answer to chaos and the confusion of Babel: the boy's drawing of the army general would also serve as an illustration of this idea.

To make of the group a body is to give it what it lacks by locating in an *imaginary unity* that which for every subject is recorded as weakness and privation, division and dissociation.

Organicist or cybernetic theories of the group and of society operate on the basis of such a belief, which indicates the status which the object-group is capable of assuming in the unconscious.

The group is a biological totality, or a biological analogy, whose elements are linked by a vital solidarity and by regulatory systems which transcend subjective individualities and which are henceforth manipulated by the system directing them. The paranoid nature of the most important fears experienced in such organizations stems fairly directly from this representation, like the defence mechanisms most commonly employed against anxieties. Every deviation, or impediment to regulation, every weakness is a threat directed against the bio-groupal unity and its capacity for survival or developments: every dangerous member is expelled, cut off and replaced by another who is better adapted; every loss of an object jeopardizes the whole; every internal quarrel is fatal, as in the fable about the limbs and the stomach.[3] It comes about in Freud's description, in *Group psychology and the analysis of the ego*, of the subject of Holopherne who was beheaded by Judith: 'that the "leader" lacks and the "members" lose their head'.

Let us sum up our point of view about the psychic and social components of the representation.

The *psychic organizers* of the representation of the group are the original structures set up in the progressive development of the psyche; in their unvarying structure they owe nothing to any given social model of the group and nothing to such-and-such a system of collective representations, whose elaboration depends upon specific principles and processes. *Group* properties of these organizers define their ability to mobilize (energy, cathexis), to distribute and to permute (both places and relationships) for group members and for intergroup relations.

Since the work of Serge Moscovici (1961) we know that the social character of a representation is defined not only by a quantitative yardstick, as when one considers its diffusion throughout a collectivity, or solely by a production criterion, as when one analyses it as the expression of a particular social structure, but also by a functional criterion, if one tries to grasp its own contribution in shaping behaviour and communication within a social gathering. I have called *social organizers* of the representations models of grouping and of relationships suggested by cultural studies and which function as socio-cultural codes appropriate to a given society: they maintain social functions to the extent that they organize the collective internalization of reference group models which maintain and regulate social and interpersonal exchanges. The point of view which I elaborated in my study of 1968 made me emphasize the function of social representations as a point of reference for the purposes of identification; the validity of this viewpoint was confirmed by the analysis of group representations in advertising, photography and portraiture. Not merely is each and every group founded upon an emblematic representation of its object of identification, but also the common representation maintains common identifications to the same object, through a shared representation (or idea) which performs a similar function to that of leadership. This within-group trans-narcissistic emblem identifies the frontiers of group belonging and of intergroup relations. The representation is called 'social' in that it guarantees the possibility of communication and exchange. It is a nucleus of identification for members of the group which distinguishes it from the non-group.

The psychic functions of the representation are not therefore separable from its social functions. From this viewpoint social representations constitute one element in a progression towards the symbolization of unconscious psychic representations. Therefore, they provide access to these latter by way of their functions relating to anaclisis and defence. Concerning social representations we could say that they are potentially capable of functioning, either as fetishes or as transitional objects, the range of which (according to Winnicott) defines exactly the ambiance of the culture. They are ready-made objects which leave room for communication, mediation and creativity. In this space a more or less free play is established between the unconscious and the social representations. The highest degree of constraint could be achieved by the invasion of this representational space by ideology which is conducive to symbolic reductionism and the creation of an illusion of a one-way determinism. Social representations, by reason of their collective nature and their status of temporal priority which locates them within cultural experience, constitute a framework, a code and a ready-made content, which is both available and necessary for developing internal psychic reality. Thus social representations constitute, at one and the same time, reference models and fracture points for the symbolization of unconscious representations and, like their psychic equivalents, are subject to cathexes.

6.   From representation to group process

I have endeavoured to show how the process and products (mentalities) of mentalization constitute a psychic activity which is subject to a double anaclisis, and how representation is a necessary factor in mentalization, which is defined as work concerned with absence and bonding. From this standpoint, every representation is social, and this includes its individualizing function, to the extent to which it takes shape and becomes mobilized when the bond weakens.

Within the limits of this chapter, I can only sketch out the transition from the representation of the group (its mentalization as absence and bonding organizing intra-psychic group structures, e.g. the 'in-groups') to the group process itself. My thesis is that the group is formed and constructed as a specific entity that begins from the effects of the representation which members mutually bestow on each other in relation to this object-process.

Group clinics have led me to think that the way to construct a group is through the elaboration of a psychic group apparatus, which provides the mutually supporting metaphorical illusion of being an immortal, indivisible, all-powerful body, that is a pure spirit. When the psychic organizers of the participants set sail on the bodily *imago*, the group comprises artificial devices and spare parts which are subject to dismemberment and to death. The metaphor or fantasy concerning the group-body calms the subject's anxiety of excision and the even greater anxiety about his having no place, no existence, within another's desire. Such a fantasy is clearly a denial of what differentiates the group from the personal system, a suture in the anaclitic space of mentalization.

To be a body is to strengthen the weld preventing an internal break which the group seals over: to be a body is to set in motion a process of resistance against the anti-body, the enemy banished to the outside and against whom the coming together again (the reunion) organized under the aegis and guardianship of an Ideal, gives some insurance that each can take his place within such a group-body.

Taken *in toto* my analysis insists upon the specific means of mentalization we call representation, absence-work (the represented) and bonding (the present shared). Dependent upon both the body and the group, and upon already articulated speech, somewhere between fantasy and myth, the double series of the organizers of the representation are, in the fullest meaning of the term, an organization-process of psycho-social relationships and not the reproduction of a mental or social state.

Notes

1. Certain theorists writing about the body have represented it as a group: 'the body', writes G. Groddeck (1923), 'is a society of organs'. Examples are plentiful in painting and the literature of representations of the body as a group. This reversibility of the metaphor sets up a field of forces where one passes from the body to the group and from the group to the body: a tension which might well define the paradoxical space within which are created together the anaclitic support for psychism and the group.

2. These form part of a corporate tradition which has always been honoured in certain professions e.g. those of railway officials, administrators etc. They play a key social psychological role in the elaboration of work, of the group and in the maintenance of social cohesion; the shared meal at the point of retirement is a traditional rite whose aim is to maintain ties of identification, despite the separation.

3. Around 500 BC the Roman Consul Menenius Agrippa quelled a popular revolt by proposing to the people the metaphor of the limbs and the stomach. He explained that just as the members of the body cannot live without the work of the stomach, and vice versa, so members of the social body are united in an organic whole of which they form part. Six centuries later St Paul proposed a similar metaphor in order to reduce internal quarrels within the Christian assemblies by highlighting the unity and solidarity of the members of the body of Christ.

References

Abelson, R. P. (1972). Are attitudes necessary? In B. T. King and E. McGinnies (eds.). *Attitudes, conflict and social change.* New York: Academic Press.

Abric, J.-C. (1971). Experimental study of group creativity: task representation, group structure and performance. *European Journal of Social Psychology,* **1** (3), 311–26.

Abric, J.-C. (1976). Jeux, conflits et représentations sociales. Thèse de Doctorat ès Lettres, Université de Provence, Aix-en-Provence.

Abric, J.-C., Faucheux, C., Moscovici, S. and Plon, M. (1967). Approche et évitement dans des jeux à motivation mixte. *Psychologie Française,* **12** (4), 277–86.

Abric, J.-C. and Kahan, J. P. (1972). The effects of representations and behaviour in experimental games. *European Journal of Social Psychology,* **2,** 129–44.

Abric, J.-C. and Mardellat, R. (1974). Etude expérimentale des représentations dans une situation conflictuelle: rôle du contexte de la tâche, de la place et de la pratique des sujets dans la formation sociale. *Bulletin de Psychologie,* **27** (1–4), 146–52.

Abric, J.-C. and Vacherot, G. (1975). Méthodologie et étude expérimentale des représentations sociales: tâche, partenaire et comportement en situation de jeu. *Bulletin de Psychologie,* **29** (14–15), 735–46.

Ackermann, W. and Zygouris, R. (1974). Représentation et assimilation de la connaissance scientifique. *Bulletin de CERP,* **22** (1–2).

Adair, J. G. (1973). *The human subject: the social psychology of the psychological experiment.* Boston, Mass.: Little, Brown & Co.

Ajzen, I. *et al.* (1970). Looking backward revisited: a reply to Deutscher. *American Sociologist,* **5,** 267–72.

Alexander, J. (1978). Formal and substantive voluntarism in the work of Talcott Parsons: a theoretical and ideological reinterpretation. *American Sociological Review,* **43,** 177–98.

Allport, F. H. (1924). *Social psychology.* Boston: Houghton Mifflin.

Allport, F. H. (1937). Towards a science of public opinion. *Public Opinion Quarterly,* **1,** 7–23.

Aloisio, R. (1970). Image des relations amicales dans une entreprise hierarchisée. Mémoire de Maîtrise, Université de Provence.

American Child Health Association (1934). *Physical defects: pathways to correction.* New York.

Anderson, N. H. (1974). Cognitive algebra: integration theory applied to social attribution. In L. Berkowitz (ed.). *Advances in Experimental Social Psychology*, vol. 7. New York: Academic Press.

Anonymous (1951). Paris, une enquête psychosociale. *Sondages: Revue Française de l'Opinion Publique*, **2**, 1–41.

Anzieu, D. (1974). Le Moi-pecui. *Nouvelle Revue de Psychanalyse*, **9**, 195–208.

Asch, S. (1946). Forming impressions of personality. *Journal of Abnormal and Social Psychology*, **41**, 258–90.

Asch, S. (1952). *Social psychology*. Englewood Cliffs, N. J.: Prentice-Hall, Inc.

Audierne, J.-F. (1973). Nature et place du biais d'équilibre dans les représentations de structures sociales. Mémoire de Maîtrise, Université de Provence.

Bannister, D. (1960). Conceptual structure in thought-disordered schizophrenics. *Journal of Mental Science*, **106**, 1230–49.

Bannister, D. (1962). The nature and measurement of schizophrenic thought disorder. *Journal of Mental Science*, **108**, 825–42.

Bannister, D. (1963). The genesis of schizophrenic thought disorder: a serial invalidation hypothesis. *British Journal of Psychiatry*, **109**, 680–6.

Bannister, D. (1965). The genesis of schizophrenic thought disorder: re-test of the serial invalidation hypothesis. *British Journal of Psychiatry*, **111**, 377–82.

Bannister, D. (ed.). (1970). *Perspectives in personal construct theory*. London: Academic Press.

Bannister, D. (ed.). (1977). *New perspectives in personal construct theory*. London: Academic Press.

Bannister, D. and Fransella, F. (1980). *Inquiring man* (2nd ed). Harmondsworth, Middlesex: Penguin Books.

Barbichon, G. and Moscovici, S. (1965). Diffusion des connaissances scientifiques. *Social Science Information*, **4**, (1), 7–22.

Bartlett, F. C. (1932). *Remembering: a study in experimental and social psychology*. Cambridge: Cambridge University Press. Quotations in the text are taken from the 1961 edition.

Baubion-Broye, A., Lapeyre, M. and Malrieu, Ph. (1977). Remarques sur la notion de représentation sociale. *Psychologie et Education*, no. 3, May 1977, 37–56.

Beck, B. (1970). Cooking welfare stew. In R. W. Habenstein (ed.). *Pathways to data: field methods for studying ongoing social organisations*. Chicago: Aldine Publishing Co.

Berger, P. and Luckmann, T. (1967). *The social construction of reality: a treatise in the sociology of knowledge*. London: Allen Lane.

Bernard, M. (1978). *Quelles pratiques corporelles maintenant?* Paris: J. P. Delarge.

Besin, A. and Pollack, M. (1977). La Rationalisation de la sexualité. *Cahiers Internationaux de Sociologie*, **LXII**.

Billig, M. (1976). *Social psychology and intergroup relations*. London: Academic Press.

Blacking, J. (1977). *The anthropology of the body*. London: Academic Press.

Blakar, R. M. and Rommetveit, R. (1975). Utterances in vacuo and in contexts. *International Journal of Psycholinguistics*, **4**, 5–32.

Blakar, R. M. and Pedersen, T. B. (1978). Control and self-confidence as reflected in sex-bound patterns in communication: an experimental approach.

I-Informasjons-bulletin fra Psykopatologie og Kommunikasjonsprojektet, **7**, 3–35. University of Oslo.

Blancheteau, M. (1969). *L'Orientation spatiale chez l'animal, ses indices et ses repères*. Paris: Ed. du CNRS.

Blumer, H. (1947). Sociological theory in industrial relations. *American Sociological Review*, **12**, 271–8.

Blumer, H. (1948). Public opinion and public opinion polling. *American Sociological Review*, **13**, 542–9.

Blumer, H. (1956). Sociological analysis and the variable. *American Sociological Review*, **21**, 683–90.

Blumer, H. (1966). Sociological implications of the thought of George Herbert Mead. *American Journal of Sociology*, **71**, 535–44.

Blumer, H. (1969a). *Symbolic interactionism: perspective and method*. Englewood Cliffs, N. J.: Prentice-Hall, Inc.

Blumer, H. (1969b). Fashion: from class differentiation to collection selection. *Sociological Quarterly*, **10**, 275–91.

Blumer, H. (1980). Mead and Blumer: the convergent methodological perspectives of social behaviourism and symbolic interactionism. *American Sociological Review*, **45**, 409–19.

Bogdan, R. and Taylor, S. J. (1975). *Introduction to qualitative research methods*. New York: John Wiley.

Bourdieu, P. (1980). *Le Sens pratique*. Paris: Ed. de Minuit.

Bower, T. (1977). *The perceptual world of the child*. London: Fontana.

Bramel, D. (1963). Selection of a target for defensive projection. *Journal of Abnormal and Social Psychology*, **66**, 318–24.

Branthwaite, A. and Jones, J. E. (1975). Fairness and discrimination: English versus Welsh. *European Journal of Social Psychology*, **5**, 323–38.

Bresson, F. (1965). Des décisions. In Fraisse, P. and Piaget, J. *Traité de psychologie expérimentale*, vol. 8. Paris: Presses Universitaires de France.

Brohn, J. M. (1975). *Corps et politique*. Paris: J. P. Delarge.

Brown, R. (1965). *Social psychology*. New York: The Free Press.

Brown, R. (1978). Divided we fall: an analysis of the relations between sections of a factory workforce. In H. Tajfel (ed.). *Differentiation between social groups: studies in the social psychology of intergroup relations*. London: Academic Press.

Bruner, J. S. (1978). From communication to language: a psychological perspective. In I. Markova (ed.). *The social context of language*. Chichester: Wiley.

Bruner, J. S. and Perlmutter, H. V. (1957). Compatriot and foreigner: a study of impression formation in three countries. *Journal of Abnormal and Social Psychology*, **55**, 253–60.

Bullinger, A. (1973). Comparaison, mesure et transitivité. Monographie no. 1 des *Archives de Psychologie*.

Campbell, D. T. (1957). Factors relevant to the validity of experiments in social settings. *Psychological Bulletin*, **54**, 297–312.

Campbell, D. T. (1963). Social attitudes and other acquired behavioural dispositions. In S. Koch (ed.). *Psychology: a study of a science*. Vol. 6. New York: McGraw-Hill.

Campbell, D. T. and Stanley, J. C. (1966). *Experimental and quasi-experimental designs for research*. Chicago: Rand McNally.

Carroll, J. S. and Paine, J. W. (1976). *Cognition and social behaviour*. Hillsdale, N. J.: Lawrence Erlbaum.

Chombart de Lauwe, M.-J. (1971/78). *Un monde autre: l'enfance, de ses représentations à son mythe*. Paris: Payot.

Chombart de Lauwe, M.-J. (1972). Les Catégories sociales sans pouvoir. Réflexion sur la marginalisation particulière des femmes et des enfants dans la société globale. Sixth Congrès international de l'Institut de Sociologie, Caracas: Mimeo.

Chombart de Lauwe, M.-J. (1975/76). L'Interaction de l'enfant et de l'environnement. Objet de recherche et révélateur social. *Bulletin de Psychologie*, **XXIX**, 954–69.

Chombart de Lauwe, M.-J. (1977). Un intérêt ambigu, des discours piégés. *Autrement*, no. 10. *Dans la ville, des enfants*, pp. 6–13.

Chombart de Lauwe, M.-J., Bonnin, Ph., Mayeur, M., Perrot, M., de la Soudière, M. (1976). *Enfants en-jeu: les pratiques des enfants durant leurs temps libre en fonction des types d'environnement et des idéologies*. Paris: Ed. du CNRS.

Chombart de Lauwe, M.-J., Bonnin, Ph., Mayeur, M., Perrot, M., Rieunier, C. and de la Soudière, M. (1979). *Espaces d'enfants: la relation enfant-environnement et ses conflits*. Switzerland: St Saphorin.

Chombart de Lauwe, M.-J. and Bellan, C. (1979). *Enfant de l'image: enfants-personnages des médias/enfants-réels*. Paris: Payot.

Chombart de Lauwe, M.-J. (ed.). (1980). Intériorisation des modèles sociaux. Congrès international de psychologie de l'enfant, Paris, 4 July 1979; *Enfance*, special issue no. 4–5. (summary), 160–9.

Chombart de Lauwe, P. H., *et al.* (1963/67). *La Femme dans la société. Son image dans différents milieux sociaux*. Paris: Ed. du CNRS.

Chombart de Lauwe, P. H. (1971). *Pour une sociologie des aspirations*. 2nd edn. Paris: Denoël-Gonthier.

Chombart de Lauwe, P. H. (1975). *La Culture et le pouvoir*. Paris: Stock.

Chomsky, N. (1972). *Studies on semantics in generative grammar*. The Hague: Mouton.

Codol, J. P. (1968). Représentation de la tâche et comportements dans une situation sociale. *Psychologie Française*, **13**, 241–64.

Codol, J. P. (1969a). Représentations de soi, d'autrui et de la tâche dans une situation sociale. *Psychologie Française*, **14**, 217–28.

Codol, J. P. (1969b). Notre terminologique sur l'emploi de quelques expressions concernant les activités et processus cognitifs en psychologie sociale. *Bulletin de Psychologie*, **23**, 63–71.

Codol, J. P. (1970b). Influence de la représentation d'autrui sur l'activité des membres d'un groupe expérimental. *L'Année Psychologique*, **70**, 131–50.

Codol, J. P. (1970b). La Représentation du groupe: son impact sur les comportements des membres d'un groupe et sur leurs représentations de la tâche, d'autrui, et de soi. *Bulletin de Psychologie*, **24**, 111–22.

Codol, J. P. (1971). Perception des relations de bienveillance, d'individualisme, et d'égalitarisme entre les membres d'un groupe fictif. *Bulletin de Psychologie*, **24**, 1048–63.

Codol, J. P. (1972). Représentations et comportements dans les groupes restreints. (Pour une approche cognitive des phénomènes de groupe:

contribution expérimentale). Mimeo. Aix-en-Provence: Université de Provence.

Codol, J. P. (1974). On the system of representations in a group situation. *European Journal of Social Psychology*, **4**, 343–65.

Codol, J. P. (1975). On the so-called 'Superior conformity of the self' behaviour: twenty experimental investigations. *European Journal of Social Psychology*, **5**, 457–501.

Codol, J. P. (1979). Semblables et différents. Recherches sur la quête de la similitude et de la différentiation sociale. Thèse d'Etat, Université de Provence.

Codol, J. P. and Flament, C. (1969). Note sur une tâche à usages multiples. *Le Travail Humain*, **32**, 169–76.

Codol, J. P. and Flament, C. (1971). Représentation de structures sociales simples dans lesquelles le sujet est impliqué. *Cahiers de Psychologie*, **14** (3), 203–18.

Cooley, C. H. (1909). *Social organisation*. New York: C. Scribner & Sons.

Coombs, C. H. (1964). *A theory of data*. New York: Wiley.

Coser, L. A. (1960). Durkheim's conservatism and its implications for his sociological theory. In K. H. Wolff (ed.). *Emile Durkheim, 1858–1917*. Columbus: The Ohio State University Press.

Coser, L. A. (1971). *Masters of sociological thought*. New York: Harcourt Brace Jovanovich.

Coser, L. A. (1976). Sociological theory from the Chicago dominance to 1965. *Annual Review of Sociology*, **2**, 145–60.

Cottrell, L. S. (jun.) (1977). George Herbert Mead and Harry Stack Sullivan: an unfinished synthesis. Unpublished Xerox.

Crane, D. (1972). *Invisible colleges: diffusion of knowledge in scientific communities*. Chicago: University of Chicago Press.

Crockett, W. H. (1965). Cognitive complexity and impression formation. In B. A. Maher (ed.). *Progress in experimental personality research*. Vol. 2. New York: Academic Press.

Danziger, K. (1979). The positivist repudiation of Wundt. *Journal of the History of the Behavioural Sciences*, **15**, 205–30.

Darwin, C. (1872). *The expression of the emotions in man and animals*. London: Appleton.

Davis, J. A. (1967). Clustering and structural balance in graphs. *Human Relations*, **20**, 181–7.

Deschamps, J. C. and Doise, W. (1975). Evolution des représentations intersexes entre 7 et 13 ans. *Revue Suisse de Sociologie*, **1**, 107–28.

Deschamps, J. C., Doise, W., Meyer, G. and Sinclair, A. (1976). Le Sociocentrisme selon Piaget et la différenciation catégorielle. *Archives de Psychologie*, **44**, 31–44.

Deutsch, M. (1962). Cooperation and trust: some theoretical notes. In M. R. Jones (ed.). *Nebraska Symposium on Motivation*. Lincoln, Neb.: University of Nebraska Press.

Deutsch, W. (1976). *Sprachliche Redundanz und Objectidentifikation*. Marburg: Lahn.

Deutscher, I. (1973). *What we say/what we do: sentiments and acts*. Glenview, Ill.: Scott, Foresman & Co.

Deutscher, I. and Gold, M. (1979). Traditions and rules as obstructions to useful program evaluation. In N. Denzin (ed.). *Studies in symbolic interaction: an annual compilation of research.* Vol. 2. JAI Press.

Doise, W. (1969). Stratégies de jeu à l'intérieur et entre des groupes de nationalités différentes. *Bulletin du CERP,* **18,** 13–26.

Doise, W. (1972). Rencontres et représentations intergroupes. *Archives de Psychologie,* **41,** 303–20.

Doise, W. (1976). *L'Articulation psychosociologique et les relations entre groupes.* Brussels: de Boeck.

Doise, W. (1978). Images, représentations, idéologies et expérimentation psychosociologique. *Social Science Information,* **17,** 41–69.

Doise, W. (forthcoming). *L'Explication en psychologie sociale.*

Doise, W. and Weinberger, M. (1972/73). Représentations masculines dans différentes situations de rencontres mixtes. *Bulletin de Psychologie,* **26,** 649–57.

Douglas, J. D. (1967). *The social meaning of suicide.* Princeton: Princeton University Press.

Douglas, M. (1975). *Natural symbols.* Harmondsworth, Middlesex: Penguin Books.

Downs, R. and Stea, D. (1973). *Image and environment: cognitive mappings and spatial behaviour.* Chicago: Aldine Publishing Co.

Droba, P. D. (1933). The nature of attitude. *Journal of Social Psychology,* **4,** 444–63.

Ducrot, O. (1972). *Dire et ne pas dire. Principes de sémantique linguistique.* Paris: Hermann.

Dumont, R. (1980). *Homo hierarchicus: the caste system and its implications.* Complete revised English edition. Chicago: University of Chicago Press.

Durkheim, E. (1893/1947). *De la division du travail social.* 8th edition. Paris: Presses Universitaires de France (1967). Translated into English by G. Simpson as *The division of labour in society.* New York: The Free Press.

Durkheim, E. (1898). Représentations individuelles et représentations collectives. *Revue de Métaphysique et de Morale,* **VI,** 273–302.

Durkheim, E. (1898/1950). *Leçons de sociologie: physique des moeurs et du droit.* Paris: Presses Universitaires de France.

Durkheim, E. (1912/15; 1961a). *The elementary forms of the religious life.* New York: Macmillan. Translated by J. W. Swain. Reprinted New York: Collier Books.

Durkheim, E. (1897/1951). *Suicide: a study in sociology.* Translated by J. A. Spaulding and G. Simpson. New York: The Free Press.

Durkheim, E. (1961b). *Moral education.* Translated by E. K. Wilson and H. Scjnurer. New York: The Free Press.

Durkheim, E. (1895/1963). *Les Règles de la méthode sociologique.* Paris: Presses Universitaires de France.

Durkheim, E. (1924/53). *Sociology and philosophy.* New York: The Free Press.

Durkheim, E. (1974). *Sociology and philosophy.* New York: The Free Press. Reprinted with additions by arrangement with Routledge and Kegan Paul.

Edlow, D. and Kiesler, C. (1966). Ease of denial and defensive projection. *Journal of Experimental Social Psychology,* **2,** 56–69,

Eiser, J. R. and Stroebe, W. (1972). *Categorisation and social judgment.* London: Academic Press.

Ellison, R. (1965). *Invisible man.* Harmondsworth, Middlesex: Penguin Books.

Enard, C. (1968). Analyse et aménagement d'un langage technique: 'Chronique' d'un avion pour le contrôleur de la navigation aérienne. *Bulletin de CERP*, **XVII**, 3.

Evans-Pritchard, E. (1937). *Witchcraft, oracles and magic among the Azande*. Oxford: Oxford University Press.

Farr, R. M. (1976). Experimentation: a social psychological perspective. *British Journal of Social & Clinical Psychology*, **15**, 225–38.

Farr, R. M. (1977). Heider, Harré and Herzlich on health and illness: some observations on the structure of 'représentations collectives'. *European Journal of Social Psychology*, **7**, (4), 491–504.

Farr, R. M. (1978*a*). On the social significance of artifacts in experimenting. *British Journal of Social & Clinical Psychology*, **17**, 299–306.

Farr, R. M. (1978*b*). On the varieties of social psychology: an essay on the relationships between psychology and other social sciences. *Social Science Information*, **17**, (4/5), 503–25.

Farr, R. M. (1981). On the nature of human nature and the science of behaviour. In P. Heelas and A. Lock (eds.). *Indigenous psychologies: the anthropology of the self*. London: Academic Press.

Fassina, A. (1962). L'entretien: méthode de recherche des pannes et apprentissage. *Bulletin du CERP*, **11**, 269–85.

Fassina, A. (1969). Un intermédiaire dans le système homme-travail: le dessin technique. Thèse de 3ème cycle, Paris: Université René Descartes.

Faucheux, C. and Moscovici, S. (1968). Self-esteem and exploitative behaviour in a game against chance and nature. *Journal of Personality & Social Psychology*, **8**, (1), 83–8.

Feeger, H. (1974). Die Erfassung individueller Einstellung structkuren. *Zeitschrift fur Social Psychologie*, **5**, 242–54.

Festinger, L. (1957). *A theory of cognitive dissonance*. Stanford: Stanford University Press.

Feuerhahn, N. (1978). L'Enfant, objet publicitaire. Analyse psychosociologique de ses représentations et des systèmes de valeurs qui lui sont sous-jacent. Thèse de 3ème cycle, Université de Paris V.

Feuerhahn, N. (1980). La Représentation de l'enfant et sa manipulation par la publicité. *Bulletin de Psychologie*, **XXXIII**, (18), 949–55.

Fishbein, M. and Ajzen, I. (1972). Attitudes and opinions. *Annual Review of Psychology*, **23**, 487–544.

Fishbein, M. and Ajzen, I. (1975). *Belief, attitude, intention and behaviour*. Reading, Mass.: Addison-Wesley.

Flament, C. (1968). Theories in structural balance. In *Algebraic models in psychology*. Leiden: University of Leiden.

Flament, C. (1970). Equilibre d'un graphe: quelques résultats algébriques. *Mathématiques et Sciences Humaines*, **8**, 5–10.

Flament, C. (1971). Image des relations amicales dans des groupes hiérarchisés. *Année Psychologique*, **71**, 117–25.

Flament, C. (1979). Independent generalisations of balance. In P. W. Holland and S. Leinhardt (eds.). *Perspectives on social network research*. New York: Academic Press.

Flament, C. (1981). L'Analyse de similitude: une technique pour les recherches sur les représentations sociales. *Cahiers de Psychologie Cognitive*, **1**, 375–96.

Flament, C. and Monnier, C. (1971*a*). Schèmes d'équilibre et de congruence dans la représentation de structures sociales multirelationnelles. *Archives de Psychologie,* **41,** 71–88.

Flament, C. and Monnier, C. (1971*b*). Rapports entre amitié et hiérarchie dans la représentation du groupe. *Cahiers de Psychologie,* **14,** 209–18.

Flament, C. and Bullinger, A. (1977). Représentation de l'amitié et équivalence formelle. *Bulletin de Psychologie,* **30** (issue in honour of J. Piaget), pp. 198–205.

Fodor, J. A. (1975). *The language of thought.* New York: Thomas Crowell Co.

Fransella, F. and Bannister, D. (1967). A validation of repertory grid technique as a measure of political construing. *Acta Psychologica,* **26,** 97–106.

Fransella, F. and Joyston-Bechal, M. P. (1971). An investigation of conceptual process and pattern change in a psychotherapy group. *British Journal of Psychiatry,* **119,** 199–206.

Fransella, F. and Bannister, D. (1977). *A manual for repertory grid technique.* London: Academic Press.

Frege, G. (1977). The thought: a logical inquiry. In P. F. Strawson (ed.). *Philosophical logic.* Oxford: Oxford University Press.

Galperine, P. (1966). Essais sur la formation par étapes des actions et des concepts. In *Recherches psychologiques en U.R.S.S.* Moscow: Ed. du Progrès.

Gantheret, F. (1961). Historique et position actuelle de la notion de schéma corporel. *Bulletin de Psychologie,* **15,** 41–4.

Garfinkel, H. (1964/72). Studies of the routine grounds of everyday activities. *Social Problems,* **11,** 225–50. Also in D. Sudnow (ed.). *Studies in social interaction.* New York: The Free Press.

Garfinkel, H. (1967). *Studies in ethnomethodology.* Englewood Cliffs, N. J.: Prentice-Hall, Inc.

Gergen, K. J. (1973). Social psychology as history. *Journal of Personality & Social Psychology,* **26,** (2), 309–20.

Giddens, A. (1978). *Durkheim.* Fontana Modern Masters Series. London: Fontana.

Glaser, B. and Strauss, A. (1965). *Awareness of dying.* Chicago: Aldine.

Glaser, B. and Strauss, A. (1967). *The discovery of grounded theory: strategies for qualitative research.* Chicago: Aldine.

Goffman, E. (1961). *Asylums.* New York: Doubleday Anchor.

Gombrich, E. H. (1972). *Symbolic images.* London: Phaidon.

Gonos, G. (1977). 'Situation' versus 'frame': The 'interactionist' and the 'structuralist' analyses of everyday life. *American Sociological Review,* **42,** 854–67.

Gorin, M. (1980). *A l'école du groupe: heurs et malheurs d'une innovation éducative.* Paris: Dunod.

Gould, P. (1967). Structuring information on spacio-temporal preferences. *Journal of Regional Science,* **7,** (2), (supplement).

Gould, P. and White, R. (1974). *Mental maps.* Baltimore: Penguin Books.

Griffin, D. (1948). Topographical orientation. *Foundations of psychology.* New York: Wiley.

Grize, J. B. (1964). Remarques sur la structure de la geométrie élémentaire. In Piaget, J. (ed.). *L'Epistémologie de l'espace.* Paris: Presses Universitaires de France.

Groddeck, G. (1923/73). *Das Buch von Es*. Wiesbaden: Limes Verlag. French trans: *Le Livre du ça*. Paris: Gallimard.

Guttman, L. A. (1944). A basis for scaling qualitative data. *American Social Review*, **9**, 139–50.

Habermas, J. (1970). Toward a theory of communicative competence. In P. E. Dreitzel (ed.). *Recent Sociology*, no. 2. London: Macmillan.

Hagendoorn, L. (1976). Conceptuele systemen. Doctoral thesis Katholieke Universiteit: Nijmegen.

Halbwachs, M. (1930). *Les Causes du suicide*. Paris: Félix Alcan.

Handel, W. (1979). Normative expectations and the emergence of meaning as solutions to problems: convergence of structural and interactionist views. *American Journal of Sociology*, **84**, 855–81.

Harary, F. (1953). On the notion of balance of a signed graph. *Michigan Mathematical Journal*, **2**, 143–6.

Hare, A. P., Borgatta, E. F. and Bales, R. F. (eds.) (1955). *Small groups: studies in social interaction*. New York: Knopf.

Harré, R. and Secord, P. F. (1972). *The explanation of social behaviour*. Oxford: Blackwell.

Harvey, O. J., Hunt, D. E. and Schroder, H. M. (1961). *Conceptual systems and personality organisation*. New York: Wiley.

Heider, F. (1944). Social perception and phenomenal causality. *Psychological Review*, **51**, 358–74.

Heider, F. (1946). Attitude and cognitive organisation. *Journal of Psychology*, **21**, 107–12.

Heider, F. (1958). *The psychology of interpersonal relations*. New York: Wiley.

Heider, F. (1979). On balance and attribution. In P. W. Holland and S. Leinhardt (eds.). *Perspectives on social network research*. New York: Academic Press.

Herzlich, C. (1969). *Santé et maladie: analyse d'une représentation sociale*. Paris: Mouton.

Herzlich, C. (1972). La Représentation sociale. In S. Moscovici (ed.). *Introduction à la psychologie sociale*. Vol. 1. Paris: Librairie Larousse.

Herzlich, C. (1973). *Health and illness: a social psychological analysis*. London: Academic Press.

Hewstone, M. and Jaspars, J. (1982). Intergroup relations and attribution processes. In H. Tajfel (ed.). *Social identity and intergroup relations*. Cambridge: Cambridge University Press.

Hillairet, J. (1964). *Dictionnaire historique des rues de Paris*. Paris: Ed. de Minuit.

Hinkle, D. N. (1965). The change of personal constructs from a viewpoint of a theory of implications. Unpublished doctoral dissertation: Ohio State University.

Hinkle, R. C. (jun.) (1960). Durkheim in American sociology. In K. H. Wolff (ed.). *Emile Durkheim 1858–1917*. Columbus: Ohio State University Press.

Hoy, R. M. (1977). Some findings concerning beliefs about alcoholism. *British Journal of Medical Psychology*, **50**, 227–35.

Ichheiser, G. (1949). Misunderstandings in human relations: a study in false social perception. Supplement to the September 1949 issue of the *American Journal of Sociology*. Chicago: University of Chicago Press.

Inhelder, B. (1954). Les Attitudes expérimentales de l'enfant et de l'adolescent. *Bulletin de Psychologie*, **VII**, 272–82.

International Herald Tribune (1978). Goodbye neurosis. 11 September.

Jahoda, G. (1970). A psychologist's perspective. In P. Mayer (ed.). *Socialisation: the approach from social psychology*. London: Tavistock.

Jahoda, G. (1979). The construction of economic reality by some Glaswegian children. *European Journal of Social Psychology*, **9**, 115–27.

James, W. (1890). *The principles of psychology*. Quotations in the text are taken from the 1980 edition. New York: Dover.

Jaspars, J. (1965). On social perception. Unpublished Ph.D. thesis. Leiden: University of Leiden.

Jaspars, J. (1973). The case against attitudes. Paper presented at the Social Psychology Section Conference of the British Psychological Society.

Jaspars, J. (1978). The nature and measurement of attitudes. In H. Tajfel and C. Fraser (eds.). *Introducing social psychology*. Harmondsworth: Penguin Books.

Jaspars, J., Van de Geer, J. P., Tajfel, H. and Johnson, N. (1972). The development of nationalism in children. *European Journal of Social Psychology*. **2/4**, 348–69.

Jaulin, R. (1973). *Gens du soi, gens de l'autre*. Paris: Union générale d'édition.

Jodelet, D. (1983). Civils et bredins: représentation de la maladie mentale et rapport à la folie en milieu rural. Unpublished Thèse de Doctorat d'Etat. Paris: EHESS.

Jodelet, D. and Moscovici, S. (1975). La Représentation sociale du corps. Mimeo, laboratoire de psychologie sociale. Ecole des Hautes Etudes en Sciences Sociales, Paris.

Jodelet, D. and Milgram, S. (1977). Cartes mentales et images sociales de Paris. Mimeo, laboratoire de psychologie sociale, Ecole des Hautes Etudes en Sciences Sociales, Paris.

Jodelet, D., Ohana, J., Bessis-Monino, C., Dannenmuller, E. (1980). *Systemes de représentation du corps et groupes sociaux*. Paris: CORDES.

Jordan, N. (1953). Behavioural forces that are a function of attitudes and of cognitive organisations. *Human Relations*, **6**, 273–87.

Jordan, N. (1968). *Themes in speculative psychology*. London: Tavistock Publication.

Kaës, R. (1968). *Images de la culture chez les ouvriers français*. Paris: Ed. Cujas.

Kaës, R. (1976). *L'Appareil psychique groupal: constructions du groupe*. Paris: Dunod.

Kaës, R. (1980). *L'Idéologie, études psychanalytiques. Mentalité de l'idéal et esprit de corps*. Paris: Dunod.

Katz, I., Glass, D. C. and Cohen, S. (1973). Ambivalence, guilt and scapegoating of minority group victims. *Journal of Experimental Social Psychology*, **9**, 423–36.

Kelly, G. A. (1955). *The psychology of personal constructs*. Vol. 1. New York: Norton.

Kelly, G. A. (1965). The strategy of psychological research. *Bulletin of the British Psychological Society*, **18**, 1–13.

Kelly, G. A. (1970). Behaviour is an experiment. In D. Bannister (ed.). *Perspectives in personal construct theory*. London: Academic Press.

Kendall, M. and Stuart, A. (1963). *The advanced theory of statistics*. London: Griffin.

Kohlberg, L. (1966). A cognitive-developmental analysis of children's sex-role concepts and attitudes. In E. E. Maccoby (ed.). *The development of sex differences*. Stanford, Calif.: Stanford University Press.

Kohlberg, L. and Ullian, D. Z. (1974). Stages in the development of psychosexual concepts and attitudes. In R. C. Friedman, R. M. Richart and R. L. Van de Wiele (eds.). *Sex differences in behavior*. New York: Wiley.

Kripke, S. (1975). Outline of a theory of truth. *Journal of Philosophy*, **72,** 690–716.

Kuhn, T. (1962). *The structure of scientific revolutions*. Chicago: The University of Chicago Press.

Labov, W. (1972). Rules for ritual insults. In D. Sudnow (ed.). *Studies in social interaction*. New York: Free Press.

Lamberigts, R. (1980). Van opvoedingsconflict naar interactie problemen. Doctoral dissertation, Katholieke Universiteit: Nijmegen.

Landa, L. N. (1959). De la formation chez les élèves d'une méthode générale d'activité intellectuelle leur permettant de résoudre les problèmes. Trad. Lab. Psychol., *Travail*, 1971.

Laplanche, J. and Pontalis, J. B. (1967). *Vocabulaire de la psychanalyse*. Paris: Presses Universitaires de France.

Latour, B. and Woolgar, S. (1979). *Laboratory life: the social construction of scientific facts*. Beverly Hills/London: Sage Publications.

Le Bon, G. (1896). *Psychologie des Foules*, 2nd edn. Paris: Alcan.

Leenhart, M. (1947). *Do Kamo, la personne et le mythe dans le monde mélanésien*. Paris: Gallimard.

Lemaine, G., Clémençon, M., Gombis, A., Pollin, B. and Salvo, B. (1977). *Strategies et choix dans la recherche: à propos des travaux sur le sommeil*. Paris: Mouton.

Léonard, F. (1972). Un modèle du sujet: l'équilibre de Heider. In S. Moscovici (ed.). *Introduction à la psychologie sociale*. Vol. 1. Paris: Larousse.

Lerner, M. J. (1971). Justice, guilt and veridical perception. *Journal of Personality & Social Psychology*, **20,** 127–35.

Lerner, M. J. (1980). *The belief in a just world: a fundamental delusion*. New York: Plenum Press.

Levine, R. A. and Campbell, D. T. (1972). *Ethnocentrism: theories of conflict, ethnic attitudes, and group behaviour*. New York: Wiley.

Lévi-Strauss, C. (1950). Introduction à l'oeuvre de Marcel Mauss. In M. Mauss, *Sociologie et anthropologie*. Paris: Presses Universitaires de France.

Lewin, K. (1948). *Resolving social conflicts*. New York: Harper & Row.

Lichtman, R. (1970). Symbolic interactionism and social reality: some Marxist queries. *Berkeley Journal of Sociology*, **15,** 75–94.

Loux, F. (1978). *Saggesse du corps: la santé et la maladie dans les proverbes français*. Paris: G. P. Maissoneuve et Larose.

Loux, F. (1979). *Pratiques et savoirs populaires: le corps dans la société traditionnelle*. Paris: Berger-Levrault.

Loux, F. and Peter, J. P. (eds.) (1976). Langages et images du corps. *Ethnologie Française*, **6** (3–4).

Lukes, S. (1973a). *Emile Durkheim: his life and work. An historical and critical study*. London: Allen Lane.

Lukes, S. (1973b). *Individualism*. Oxford: Blackwell.

Lynch, K. (1960). *The image of the city*. Cambridge, Mass.: MIT and Harvard University Press.

McCoy, M. (1977). A reconstruction of emotion. In D. Bannister (ed.). *New perspectives in personal construct theory*. London: Academic Press.

McDougall, W. (1908). *Introduction to social psychology.* London: Methuen.

McDougall, W. (1920). *The group mind: a sketch of the principles of collective psychology with some attempt to apply them to the interpretation of national life and character.* Cambridge: Cambridge University Press.

McDougall, W. (1933). *The energies of men.* New York: Scribner.

McGuire, W. J. (1969). The nature of attitudes and attitude change. In G. Lindzey and E. Aronson (eds.). *Handbook of social psychology.* Vol. 3. Reading, Mass.: Addison-Wesley.

MacIver, R. M. (1943). *Social causation.* New York: Harper.

McPhail, C. and Rexroat, C. (1979). Mead vs. Blumer. *American Sociological Review*, **44**, 449–67.

Maines, D. R. (1977). Social organisation and social structure in symbolic interactionist thought. *Annual Review of Sociology*, **3**, 235–59.

Maines, D. and Denzin, D. (1977). *Work and problematic situations: the structuring of occupational negotiations.* New York: Crowell.

Manis, J. G. and Meltzer, B. N. (eds.) (1967). *Symbolic interaction: a reader in social psychology.* Boston: Allyn & Bacon.

Marx, G. T. and Wood, J. R. (1975). Strands of theory and research in collective behaviour. *Annual Review of Sociology*, **1**, 1975.

Mauss, M. (1906). Essai sur les variations saisonnières des sociétés eskimos. *Année Sociologique*, **9**, 39–132.

Mauss, M. (1950/79). *Sociology and psychology: essays by Marcel Mauss.* Translated by Ben Brewstèr. London: Routledge & Kegan Paul.

Mead, G. H. (1934). *Mind, self and society: from the standpoint of a social behaviourist.* Edited with an introduction by C. W. Morris. Chicago: University of Chicago Press.

Meltzer, B. N. and Petras, J. W. (1970). The Chicago and Iowa Schools of symbolic interactionism. In T. Shibutani (ed.). *Human nature and collective behaviour: papers in honor of Herbert Blumer.* Englewood Cliffs, N.J.: Prentice-Hall Inc.

Merleau-Ponty, M. (1962). *Phenomenology of perception.* London: Routledge & Kegan Paul.

Meyer, M. F. (1921). *The psychology of the other one: an introductory text book.* Columbia, Miss.: The Missouri Book Co.

Milgram, S. (1977). *The individual in a social world: essays and experiments.* Reading, Mass.: Addison-Wesley.

Milgram, S. and Jodelet, D. (1976). Psychological maps of Paris. In H. Proshansky, W. H. Ittelson and L. G. Rivlin (eds.). *Environmental psychology: people and their physical settings.* 2nd ed. New York: Holt, Rinehart & Winston.

Morin, E. (1977). *La Méthode, Vol. I, la nature de la nature.* Paris: Ed. du Seuil.

Moscovici, S. (1961/76). *La psychanalyse: son image et son public.* Paris: Presses Universitaires de France.

Moscovici, S. (1963). Attitudes and opinions. *Annual Review of Psychology*, **14**, 231–60.

Moscovici, S. (1967). Communication processes and the properties of language. In L. Berkowitz (ed.). *Advances in Experimental Social Psychology.* Vol. 3. New York: Academic Press.

Moscovici, S. (1973). Foreword. In C. Herzlich, *Health and illness: a social psychological analysis.* London: Academic Press.

Moscovici, S. (1976a). *Social influence and social change*. London: Academic Press.

Moscovici, S. (1976b). La Psychologie des représentations sociales. *Cahiers Vilfredo Pareto*. Vol. 14.

Moscovici, S. (1979). Communication présentée au colloque sur les représentations sociales. Paris.

Moscovici, S. and Farr, R. M. (1978). Colloquium on social representations. Mimeographed invitation to participants.

Murchison, C. (ed.) (1935). *Handbook of social psychology*. Worcester, Mass.: Clark University Press.

Nelson, J. (1974). Towards a theory of infant understanding. *Bulletin of the British Psychological Society*, **27**, 251.

Newcomb, T. (1958). Attitude development as a function of reference groups: the Bennington study. In E. Maccoby, T. M. Newcomb and E. Hartley (eds). *Readings in social psychology*. 3rd edn.

Newell, A. & Simon, H. A. (1972). *Human problem solving*. Englewood Cliffs, N.J.: Prentice-Hall Inc.

Newman, G. R. (1977). Social institutions and the control of deviance: a cross-national opinion survey. *European Journal of Social Psychology*, **7** (1), 39–61.

Nisbet, R. A. (1974). *The sociology of Emile Durkheim*. New York: Oxford University Press.

Nisbett, R. and Ross, L. (1980). *Human inference: strategies and shortcomings of social judgment*. Englewood Cliffs, N. J.: Prentice-Hall Inc.

Norman, D. A. (1976), *Memory and attention*. 2nd edn. New York: Wiley.

Norris, M. (1977). Construing in a detention centre. In D. Bannister (ed.). *New perspectives in personal construct theory*. London: Academic Press.

Ochanine, D. (1978). Rôle des images opératives dans la régulation des activités de travail. *Psychologie et Education*, **2**, 63–72.

Olson, D. (1970). Language and thought: aspects of a cognitive theory of semantics. *Psychological Review*, **77**, 257–73.

Orley, J. (1976). The use of grid technique in social anthropology. In P. Slater (ed). *Explorations of intrapersonal space: the measurement of intrapersonal space by grid technique*. London: Wiley.

Orne, M. (1962). On the social psychology of the psychological experiment: with particular reference to demand characteristics and their implications. *American Psychologist*, **17**, 776–83.

Osgood, C. E., Suci, G. S. and Tannenbaum, P. H. (1957). *The measurement of meaning*. Urbana: University of Illinois Press.

Pailhous, J. (1970). *La Représentation de l'espace urbain: l'exemple du chauffeur de taxi*. Paris: Presses Universitaires de France.

Pailhous, J. (1971). Elaboration d'images spatiales et de règles de déplacement: une étude sur l'espace urbain. *Le Travail Humain*, **34**, 299–324.

Pailhous, J. (1972). Influence de l'ordre de présentation des données sur la constitution de l'image spatiale: une étude sur l'espace urbain. *Le Travail Humain*, **35**, 69–84.

Palmonari, A. and Ricci Bitti, P. E. (eds.) (1978). *Aspetti cognitivi della socializzazione in età evolutiva*. Bologne: Il Mulino.

Parsons, T. (1937). *The structure of social action: a study in social theory with special reference to a group of recent European writers*. New York: The Free Press.

Parsons, T. (1951). *The social system*. New York: The Free Press.

Peabody, D. (1968). Group judgments in the Philippines: evaluative and descriptive aspects. *Journal of Personality and Social Psychology*, **10**, 290–300.

Pettigrew, T. F., Allport, G. W. and Barnett, E. O. (1958). Binocular resolution and perception of race in South Africa. *British Journal of Psychology*, **49**, 265–78.

Peyre, H. (1960). Durkheim: the man, his time, and his intellectual background. In K. H. Wolff (ed.). *Emile Durkheim: 1858–1917*. Columbus: The Ohio State University Press.

Phillips, D. L. (1973). *Abandoning method: sociological studies in methodology*. San Francisco: Jossey-Bass.

Piaget, J. (1945). *La Formation du symbole chez l'enfant*. Neuchatel and Paris: Delachaux & Niestlé.

Piaget, J. (1963). *La Construction du réel chez l'enfant*. 3rd edn. Neuchatel: Delachaux & Niestlé.

Piaget, J. (1964). Remarques sur la structure de la géométrie élémentaire. In *L'Epistémologie de l'espace*. Paris: Presses Universitaires de France.

Piaget, J. and Inhelder, B. (1946). *La Représentation de l'espace chez l'enfant*. Paris: Presses Universitaires de France.

Piaget, J. and Szeminska, A. (1948). *La Géométrie spontanée de l'enfant*. Paris: Presses Universitaires de France.

Piaget, J. and Inhelder, B. (1966). *L'Image mentale chez l'enfant*. Paris: Presses Universitaires de France.

Piaget, J. and Inhelder, B. (1967). Genèse des structures logiques élémentaires. Lausanne: Delachaux et Niestlé.

Pichevin, M.-F. and Poitou, J. P. (1974). Le 'Biais' d'équilibre: un exemple de consigne implicite. *Cahiers de Psychologie*, **17**, 111–18.

Pichevin, M.-F. and Rossignol, C. (1976). Représentation du groupe, structure du sujet et équilibre structural. *Bulletin de Psychologie*, **29**, 724–34.

Poitou, J.-P. (1978). *La Dynamique des groupes: une idéologie au travail*. Marseille–Paris: Ed. du CNRS. English translation *Group dynamics: an ideology at work*. London: Academic Press (forthcoming).

Pruitt, D. (1967). Reward structure and cooperation: the decomposed prisoners' dilemma game. *Journal of Personality and Social Psychology*, **7**, 21–7.

Quaglino, G. P. (1979). Relazioni tra gruppi e percezione sociale. *Studi di ricerche di psicologia*. Turin.

Rabbie, J. M. (1974). Effecten van een competitieve en cooperatieve intergroeps orientatie op verhoudingen binnen en tussen groepen. *Nederlands Tijdschrift voor de Psychologie*, **29**, 239–57.

Rabbie, J. M. and Horwitz, M. (1969). The arousal of ingroup–outgroup bias by a chance win or loss. *Journal of Personality and Social Psychology*, **13**, 269–77.

Rank, O. (1909). *Der Mythus von den Geburt des Helden*. Leipzig und Wien: F. Deutrike.

Riley, S. and Palmer, J. (1976). Of attitudes and latitudes: a repertory grid study of perceptions of seaside resorts. In P. Slater (ed.). *Explorations of intrapersonal space: the measurement of intrapersonal space by grid technique*. London: Wiley.

Rogers, E. M. and Shoemaker F. F. (1971). *Communication of innovations: a cross-cultural approach*. 2nd edn. New York: The Free Press.

Rommetveit, R. (1953). *Social norms and roles*. Oslo: Universitetsforlaget.

Rommetveit, R. (1974). *On message structure: a framework for the study of language and communication*. London: Wiley.

Rommetveit, R. (1978). On negative rationalism in scholarly studies of verbal communication and dynamic residuals in the construction of human inter-subjectivity. In M. Brenner, P. Marsh and M. Brenner (eds.). *The social contexts of method*. London: Croom Helm.

Roqueplo, P. (1974). *Le Partage du savoir*. Paris: Ed. du Seuil.

Rosch, E. (1977). Human categorisation. In N. Warren (ed.). *Studies in cross-cultural psychology*. Vol. 1. London: Academic Press.

Rose, A. M. (ed.) (1962). *Human behavior and social processes*. Boston: Houghton Mifflin.

Rosenberg, M. H. (1969). The conditions and consequences of evaluation apprehension. In R. Rosenthal and R. L. Rosnow (eds.). *Artifacts in behavioural research*. New York: Academic Press.

Ross, L. D., Amabile, T. M. and Steinmetz, J. L. (1978). Social roles, social control, and bias in social-perception processes. *Journal of Personality & Social Psychology*, **35**, 485–94.

Rossignol, C. (1975). Approche expérimentale de la dynamique du champ de représentation lié à la notion du groupe. *Bulletin du CERP*, **XXIII** (1), 31–41.

Rossignol, C. and Flament, C. (1975). Décomposition de l'équilibre structurel: aspects de la représentation du groupe. *Année Psychologique*, **75**, 417–25.

Rossignol, C. and Houel, C. (1976). Analyse des composantes imaginaires de la représentation du groupe. *Cahiers de Psychologie*, **19**, 55–69.

Royce, J. (1962). Reality and idealism: the inner world and its meaning. In W. Barrett and H. E. Aitken (eds.). *Philosophy in the twentieth century*. Vol. 1. New York: Random House.

Runkel, P. J. (1956). Cognitive similarity in facilitating communication. *Sociometry*, **19**, 178–91.

Saarinen, T. (1971). The use of projective techniques in geographic research. Mimeo.

Salomon, A. (1960). Some aspects of the legacy of Durkheim. In K. Wolff (ed.). *Emile Durkheim, 1858–1917*. Columbus: Ohio State University Press.

Schank, R. C. and Abelson, R. P. (1977). *Scripts, plans, goals and understanding: an enquiry into human knowledge structures*. Hillsdale, N.J.: Erlbaum.

Schilder, P. (1971). *L'Image du corps*. Paris: Gallimard.

Schultz, D. P. (1969). The human subject in psychological research. *Psychological Bulletin*, **72**, 214–28.

Schutz, A. (1945). On multiple realities. *Philosophical & Phenomenological Research*, **5**, 533–76.

Schutz, A. (1951). Choosing among projects of action. *Philosophical & Phenomenological Research*, **12**, 161–84.

Searle, J. (1974). *On speech acts*. Cambridge: Cambridge University Press.

Secord, P. F., Bevan, W. and Katz, B. (1956). The negro stereotype and perceptual accentuation. *Journal of Abnormal & Social Psychology*, **53**, 78–83.

Shaver, K. G. (1975). *An introduction to attribution processes*. Cambridge, Mass.: Winthrop Publishers Inc.

Shemyakin, (1963). In B. Lomov (ed.). *Man and technology: outlines of engineering psychology*. Technical translation NASA.

Sherif, M., Harvey, O. J., White, B. J., Hood, W. R. and Sherif, C. W. (1961).

Intergroup conflict and co-operation: the robbers' cave experiment. Norman, Oklahoma: University Book Exchange.

Simpson, G. (ed.) (1963). *Emile Durkheim.* New York: Thomas Crowell.

Slovic, P. and Lichtenstein, S. C. (1971). Comparison of Bayesian and regression approaches to the study of information processing in judgment. *Organisational Behaviour and Human Performance*, **6**, 649–744.

Stea, D. (1969a). Environment perception and cognition: toward a model for mental maps. Student publication of the North Carolina State University School of Design.

Stea, D. (1969b). The measurement of mental maps: an experimental model for studying conceptual spaces. Studies in Geography No. 17: Behavioural Problems in Geography: A symposium. Northwestern University.

Stone, G. P. and Farberman, H. A. (1970). On the edge of rapprochement: was Durkheim moving toward the perspective of symbolic interaction? In G. P. Stone and H. A. Farberman (eds.). *Social psychology through symbolic interaction.* Waltham, Mass.: Ginn-Blaisdell.

Stryker, S. (1962). Conditions of accurate role taking: a test of Mead's theory. In A. M. Rose (ed.). *Human behaviour and social processes.* Boston: Houghton Mifflin.

Suttles, G. (1972). *The social construction of communities.* Chicago: University of Chicago Press.

Tajfel, H. (1959a). Quantitative judgment in social perception. *British Journal of Psychology*, **50**, 16–29.

Tajfel, H. (1959b). A note on Lambert's evaluational reactions to spoken languages. *Canadian Journal of Psychology*, **13**, 86–92.

Tajfel, H. (1969). Social and cultural factors in perception. In G. Lindzey and E. Aronson (eds.). *The handbook of social psychology.* Vol. 3. Reading, Mass.: Addison-Wesley.

Tajfel, H. (ed.). (1978). *Differentiation between social groups: studies in the social psychology of intergroup relations.* London: Academic Press.

Tajfel, H. (ed.) (1982). *Social identity and intergroup relations.* Cambridge: Cambridge University Press.

Tajfel, H. and Wilkes, A. L. (1963). Classification and quantitative judgement. *British Journal of Psychology*, **54**, 101–14.

Tajfel, H., Sheikh, A. A., and Gardner, R. C. (1964). Content of stereotypes and the inference of similarity between members of sterotyped groups. *Acta Psychologica*, **22**, 191–201.

Tarde, G. (1910). *L'Opinion et la foule.* 3rd edn. Paris: Alcan.

Thomas, W. I. (1917). The persistence of primary-group norms in present-day society and their influence in our educational system. In H. S. Jennings *et al.* (eds.). *Suggestions of modern science concerning education.* New York: Macmillan.

Thomas, W. I. (1927). The behavior pattern and the situation. *Publications of the American Sociological Society*, **22**, 1–13.

Thomas, W. I. (1931). *The unadjusted girl.* Boston: Little, Brown & Co., pp. 41–50.

Thomas, W. I. and Znaniecki, F. (1918–20). *The Polish peasant in Europe and America.* 5 volumes. Boston: Badger.

Thurstone, L. L. (1928). Attitudes can be measured. *American Journal of Sociology*, **33**, 529–54.

Trahtenbrot, B. A. (1964). *Algorithmes et machines à calculer*. Paris: Dunod.

Trevarthen, C. (1974). Conversation with a two-month-old. *New Scientist*, **2**, (May), 229–35.

Trowbridge, C. C. (1913). On fundamental methods of orientation and imaginary maps. *Science*, **38**.

Turner, J. C. (1975). Social comparison and social identity: some prospects for inter-group behaviour. *European Journal of Social Psychology*, **5**, 5–34.

Turner, J. C. (1978). Social comparison, similarity and in-group favouritism. In H. Tajfel (ed.). *Differentiation between social groups: studies in the social psychology of inter group relations*. London: Academic Press.

Turner, J. C. and Brown, R. J. (1978). Social status, cognitive alternatives and intergroup relations. In H. Tajfel (ed.). *Differentiation between social groups: studies in the social psychology of intergroup relations*. London: Academic Press.

Tversky, A. and Kahneman, D. (1974). Judgment under uncertainty: heuristics and biases. *Science*, **185**, 1124–31.

Van Knippenberg, A. (1978). Status differences, comparative relevance and intergroup differentiation. In H. Tajfel (ed.). *Differentiation between social groups: studies in the social psychology of intergroup relations*. London: Academic Press.

Vaughan, G. M. (1978). Social categorisation and intergroup behaviour in children. In H. Tajfel (ed.). *Differentiation between social groups: studies in the social psychology of intergroup relations*. London: Academic Press.

Vergnaud, G. (1968). La Réponse instrumentale comme solution de problème: contribution. Thèse de Troisième Cycle, Paris: Université René Descartes.

Verhagen, E. J. (1975). Koörientatie in machtsverhoudingen. Doctoral dissertation. Katholieke Universiteit: Nijmegen.

Vigotsky, L. S. (1977). *Thought and language*. Cambridge, Mass.: MIT Press.

Volkart, E. H. (ed). (1951). *Social behavior and personality: contribution of W.I. Thomas to theory and social research*. New York: Social Science Research Council.

Volton, D. (1974). *Le Nouvel ordre sexuel*. Paris: Ed. du Seuil.

Warner, L. G. and de Fleur, M. L. (1969). Attitude as an interactional concept: some constraint and social distance as intervening variables between attitudes and action. *American Sociological Review*, **34**, 153–69.

Warren, H. C. (1922). *Elements of human psychology*. Boston: Houghton.

Warren, N. (1966). Social class and construct systems: an examination of the cognitive structure of two social class groups. *British Journal of Social & Clinical Psychology*, **5**, 254–63.

Warshay, L. H. (1975). *The current state of sociological theory: a critical interpretation*. New York: David McKay.

Wason, P. C. and Johnson-Laird, P. N. (1972). *Psychology of reasoning*. Cambridge, Mass.: Harvard University Press.

Weinreich, P. (1979). Ethnicity and adolescent identity conflicts. In V. S. Kahn (ed.). *Minority families in Britain*. London: Macmillan.

Wicklund, R. A. and Brehm, J. W. (1976). *Perspectives on cognitive dissonance*. Hillsdale, N.J.: Erlbaum.

Wiley, N. (1979*a*). Recent journal sociology: the substitution of method for theory. *Contemporary Sociology*, **8**, 793–99.

Wiley, N. (1979*b*). The rise and fall of dominating theories in American sociology. In W. E. Snizek *et al.* (eds.). *Contemporary issues in theory and research*. New York: Greenwood Press.

Willis, R. H. (1960). Stimulus pooling and social perception. *Journal of Abnormal & Social Psychology*, **60**, 365–73.

Wishner, J. (1960). Reanalysis of 'impressions of personality'. *Psychological Review*, **67**, 96–112.

Wittgenstein, L. (1968). *Philosophische Untersuchungen: Philosophical Investigations*. Ed. by G. E. Anscombe. Oxford: Basil Blackwell.

Wolff, K. H. (ed.) (1960). *Emile Durkheim. 1858–1917*. Columbus: Ohio State University Press.

Wyer, R. S. (1975). *Cognitive organisation and change: an information processing approach*. New York: Wiley.

Zajonc, R. B. (1969). Cognitive theories in social psychology. In G. Lindzey and E. Aronson (eds.). *Handbook of social psychology*. Reading, Mass.: Addison-Wesley. Vol. 1.

Bibliography of social representations

The following is a selective listing of research on social representations. It is arranged, for convenience, in the following categories: (A) book-length studies, (B) doctoral theses and research reports, (C) theoretical and review articles, and (D) empirical studies. Works are listed within each category in order of appearance.

(A) Book-length studies

Moscovici, S. *La psychanalyse, son image et son public*. Paris: Presses Universitaires de France, 1961 (2nd edition, 1976).

Chombart de Lauwe, M.-J., P. H. *et al. La femme dans la société. Son image dans différents milieux sociaux*. Paris: Editions du CNRS, 1963 (2nd edition, 1967).

Kaës, R. *Images de la culture chez les ouvriers français*. Paris: Editions Cujas, 1968.

Herzlich, C. *Santé et maladie. Analyse d'une représentation sociale*. Paris: Mouton, 1969.

Pailhous, J. *La représentation de l'espace urbain*. Paris: Presses Universitaires de France, 1970.

Chombart de Lauwe, M.-J. *Un monde autre: l'enfance. De ses représentations à son mythe*. Paris: Payot, 1971 (2nd edition, 1979).

Huguet, M. *Les femmes dans les grand ensembles: De la représentation à la mise en scène*. Paris: Editions du CNRS, 1971.

Guillaumin, C. *L'idéologie raciste: Genèse et langage actuel*. Paris, La Haye: Mouton, 1972.

Herzlich, C. *Health and illness: A social psychological analysis*. European Monographs in Social Psychology, no. 5. London: Academic Press, 1973.

Ledrut, R. *Les images de la ville*. Paris: Anthropos, 1973.

Vadee, M. *L'idéologie*. Paris: Presses Universitaires de France, 1973.

Auge, M. (ed.). *La construction du monde: religion, représentations, idéologie*. Paris: François Maspero, 1974.

Maho, J. *L'image de l'autre chez les paysans*. Paris: Le champ du possible, 1974.

Roqueplo, P. *Le partage du savoir*. Paris: Le Seuil, 1974.

Kaës, R. *L'appareil psychique groupal. Construction du groupe*. Paris: Dunod, 1976.

Doise, W. *L'articulation psychosociologique et les relations entre groupes*. Bruxelles: Editions de Boeck, 1976.

Robert, P. and Faugeron, C. *Image du viol collectif et reconstruction d'objet*. Paris: Masson, 1976.

Baechler, J. *Qu'est-ce que l'idéologie?* Saint-Amand: Gallimard, 1976.

Windisch, U., Jaeggi, J. M., de Rham, G. *Xénophobie, logique de la pensée populaire*. L'Age d'Homme, 1978.

Robert, P. and Faugeron, C. *La justice et son public. Les représentations sociales du système pénal*. Paris: Masson, 1978.

Doise, W. *Groups and individuals: Explanations in social psychology*. Cambridge University Press: 1978.

Percheron, A., Bonnal, F., Boy, D., Dehan, N. Grunberg, G. and Subileau, F. *Les 10–16 ans et la politique*. Paris: Presses de la Fondation Nationale des Sciences Politiques, 1978.

Lipiansky, E. *L'âme française ou le national libéralisme*. Paris: Anthropos, 1979.

Chombart, de Lauwe, M.-J. and Bellan, C. *Enfants de l'image, enfants personnages des medias, enfants réels*. Paris: Payot, 1979.

Gorin, M. *A l'école du groupe: Heurs et malheurs d'une innovation éducative*. Paris: Dunod, 1980.

Lefebvre, H. *La présence et l'absence: Contribution à la théorie des représentations*. Tournai (Belgique): Casterman, 1980.

Deconchy, J.-P. *Orthodoxie religieuse et sciences humaines*. La Haye: Mouton Editeur, 1980.

Gilly, M. *Maitres-élèves: Roles institutionnels et représentations*. Paris: Presses Universitaires de France, 1980.

Kaës, R. *L'idéologie, études psychanalytiques. Mentalité de l'idéal et esprit de corps*. Paris: Dunod, 1980.

Gourevitch, J.-P. *L'Imagerie politique*. Paris: Flammarion, 1980.

Moscovici, S. *L'âge des foules: Un traité historique de psychologie des masses*. Paris: Fayard, 1981.

Windisch, U. *Pensée sociale, langage en usage et logiques autres*. Lausanne: L'Age d'Homme, 1982.

(B)   Doctoral theses and research reports

Ackermann, W. and Rialan, B. Transmission et assimilation des notions scientifiques: Une étude de la représentation de quelques faits scientifiques chez des ouvriers de l'industrie chimique. *Bulletin du CERP*, 1963.

Kaës, R. La culture, son image chez les ouvriers français. *Thèse de Troisième Cycle*. Université de Paris X – Nanterre, 1966.

Apfelbaum, E. Interdépendence, renforcement social et réactivité: Analyse de la dynamique des interactions dans le cadre des jeux experimentaux. *Thèse de Doctorat d'Etat*, Université de Paris, 1969.

Codol, J. P. Représentations et comportements dans les groupes restreints. *Thèse de Doctorat de Troisième Cycle*, Université de Provence, Aix-en-Provence, 1971.

Kaës, R. Processus groupal et représentations sociales. Etudes psychanalytiques sur les groupes de formation. *Thèse de Doctorat d'Etat*. Université de Paris, X – Nanterre.

Ramognino, N. *Les images de l'automobile et du train à travers 'France-Soir' (1972–1974)*. Etudes et Recherches du Groupe pour l'Intervention, la Formation et la Recherche en Sciences Humaines (GIFRESH), No. 5, juin 1975.

Morin, M. *Le voyage professionnel en train: Analyse psychosociologique des strategies et des représentations du déplacement.* Etudes et Recherches du GIFRESH, No. 7, 1975.

Jodelet, D. *La représentation sociale du corps.* Laboratoire de psychologie sociale, Ecole des Hautes Etudes en Sciences Sociales Paris, 1976.

Abric, J.-C. Jeux, conflits et représentations sociales. *Thèse de Doctorat d'Etat*, Université de Provence, Aix-en-Provence, 1976.

Groupe de Recherche et d'Education pour la Promotion GREP. L'acquisition et la transmission des connaissances: L'utilisation des représentations en formation d'adultes. *POUR*, 1976, 49.

Pegurier, Josette. La vie relationnelle des femmes en milieux rural égyptien. *Thèse de 3ème cycle.* Paris: EHESS, 1977.

Jodelet, D. and Milgram, S. *Cartes mentales et images sociales de Paris.* Laboratoire de psychologie sociale, Ecole des Hautes Etudes en Sciences Sociales, Paris, juin 1977.

Marie, M., Masson, G., Mathieu, S., Oliver, B., Ricard, J. F. and Weis, P. Les représentations sociales de l'informatique. Rapport de recherche. Paris: Centre ESTA, 1977.

Gilly, M. Enseignant, enseigné: Roles institutionnels et représentations. *Thèse de Doctorat d'Etat.* Université de Paris V, 1978.

Massonat, J. Evolution de la représentation de l'avenir professionnel sous influence éducative controlée. *Thèse de Troisième Cycle.* Université de Provence, Aix-en-Provence, 1978.

Feuerhahn, N. L'enfant, objet publicitaire: Analyse psychosociologique de ses représentations et des systèmes de valeurs qui lui sont sous-jacent. *Thèse de Troisième Cycle.* Université de Paris V, 1978.

Lew, Fai P. Transformations matérielles, changement culturel et acculturation: Etude des représentations, modèles et systèmes de valeurs dans la socialisation de l'enfant à l'Ile Maurice. *Thèse de Troisième Cycle.* Université de Paris V, 1978.

Aebischer, V. Les femmes et le bavardage: Observations en psychologie sociale. *Thèse de Troisième Cycle.* Paris: EHESS, 1979.

Banchs, M. Changements des représentations sociales des étudiants Vénézueliens en France. *Thèse de Troisième Cycle.* Paris: EHESS, 1979.

Codol, J. P. Semblables et différents. Recherches sur la quête de la similitude et de la différentiation sociale. *Thèse de Doctorat d'Etat*, Université de Provence, 1979.

Coudin, G. La maladie mentale au Congo: Contribution à l'étude d'une représentation sociale en situation d'acculturation. *Thèse de Troisième Cycle.* Université de Paris V, 1979.

Drory, S. Relations médecin-malade. *Thèse de Troisième Cycle.* Paris: EHESS, 1979.

Gaudin, A. Sociopédagogie des publications destinées à la jeunesse. Contribution à la psychosociologie des 9–16 ans. *Thèse de 3ème cycle.* Paris: EHESS, 1979.

Le Bouedec, G. Contribution à la méthodologie d'étude des représentations sociales: Etude de la participation. *Thèse de doctorat en psychologie.* Université de Louvain, 1979.

Sanchez, Margarita. Le phénomène des fractionnements populaires à la ville de Guadalajara Jalisco, Mexique. *Thèse de 3ème cycle*, Paris: EHESS, 1979.

Mardellat, R. Rôle des représentations, du contexte, de la place et du niveau d'implication en situation d'inter-action conflictuelle. *Thèse de 3ème cycle*, Université de Provence, 1980.

Mucchi Faina, Angelica. Les rôles des psychologues dans les structures publiques: Aspects psychosociologiques. *Thèse de 3ème cycle*. Paris: EHESS, 1980.

Boize, P. Sur l'imaginaire de 'l'habité individuel': Elaboration des représentations sociales d'un vécu à travers la rhétorique publicitaire. *Thèse de 3ème cycle*, Paris: EHESS, 1981.

Yapo Yapi. Modèles culturels et représentations sociales: Les représentations sociales de la ruralité en Côte d'Ivoire. *Thèse de 3ème cycle*. Université de Provence, 1981.

Andriamifidisoa, I. La transformation d'une représentation sociale: Exemple des relations sociales à Madagascar. *Thèse de 3ème cycle*. Université de Provence, 1982.

Dufour, G. Valeurs et représentation sociale: Etude du role des valeurs dans la formation de la représentation sociale d'un mass-media, la Télévision. *Thèse de 3ème cycle*, Université de Provence, 1982.

Perrinjaquet, R. La projettation architecturale relative à l'espace-univers de l'enfant d'âge scolaire. *Thèse de 3ème cycle*, Paris: EHESS, 1982.

Jodelet, D., Ohana, J., Bessis-Moñino, C., Dannemuller, E. *Systèmes de représentation du corps et groupes sociaux*. Rapport CORDES. Paris: EHESS, 1982.

Tayebi, S. Les changements sociaux et culturels dans les villages socialistes d'Algérie: Etude d' une représentation sociale. *Thèse de 3ème cycle*. Université de Provence, 1982.

Aebischer, V., Thommen, B., von Cranach, M. and Moscovici, S. *Représentations sociales et organisation de l'action orientée vers un but* (à partir de l'exemple de l'hypnose et de la sophrologie). Rapport DGRST. Paris: Laboratoire Européen de Psychologie Sociale, 1983.

Barjonet, P. Les acteurs de la circulation et la sécurité: Etude des représentations sociales de l'action routière. *Thèse de 3ème cycle*, Paris: EHESS, 1983.

Jodelet, D. Civils et bredins: Représentation de la maladie mentale et rapport à la folie en milieu rural. *Thèse présentée pour le Doctorat d'Etat*. Paris: EHESS, 1983.

(C) Theoretical and review articles

Moscovici, S. Attitudes and opinions. *Annual Review of Psychology*, 1963, 231–60.

Durkheim, E. Représentations individuelles et représentations collectives. *Revue de Métaphysique et de Morale*, 1898. In: *Sociologie et philosophie*. Paris: PUF, 1967.

Kaës, R. Processus et fonctions de l'idéologie dans les groupes. *Perspectives Psychiatriques*, 1971, **33**, 27–48.

Herzlich, C. La représentation sociale. Chapter 9 in Moscovici (ed.): *Introduction à la psychologie sociale*. Vol. 1, Paris: Librairie Larousse, 1972.

Plon, M. 'Jeux' et conflits. Chapter 7 in Moscovici (ed.): *Introduction à la psychologie sociale*. Vol. 1, Paris: Librairie Larousse, 1972.

Doise, W. Relations et représentations intergroupes. Chapter 7 in Moscovici (ed.). *Introduction à la psychologie sociale.* Vol. 2, Paris: Librairie Larousse, 1973, 194–213.

Chebat, J. C. Social representation and symbol. *International Journal of Symbology,* 1975, **6** (1), 38–45.

Farr, R. M. Heider, Harré & Herzlich on health and illness. Some observations on the structure of 'représentations collectives'. *European Journal of Social Psychology,* 1977, **7** (4), 98–111.

Kaës, R. L'utopie dans l'espace paradoxal: entre jeu et folie raisonneuse. *Bulletin de Psychologie,* 1978, **12** (17), 853–80.

Jodelet, D. Changement culturel et représentation du corps. Actes du colloque *'Le corps dans les sciences de l'homme: De la biologie à la culture'.* Centre d'Ethnologie Française. Marseilles 1979. Forthcoming.

Kaës, R. Eléments pour une psychanalyse des mentalités. *Bulletin de Psychologie,* 1980/81, **XXXIV** (350), 451–63.

Di Giacomo, J. P. Aspects méthodologiques de l'analyse des représentations sociales. *Cahiers de Psychologie Cognitive,* 1981, **1,** 397–422.

Farr, R. M. On the nature of human nature and the science of behaviour. In P. Heelas and A. Lock (eds.): *Indigenous psychologies: The anthropology of the self.* London: Academic Press, 1981, 303–17.

Flament, C. L'analyse de similitude: Une technique pour les recherches sur les représentations sociales. *Cahiers de Psychologie Cognitive,* 1981, **1,** 375–96.

Moscovici, S. On social representations. In J. P. Forgas (ed.). *Social cognition: Perspectives on everyday understanding.* London: Academic Press, 1981, 181–209.

Jodelet, D. Représentations, expériences, pratiques corporelles et modèles culturels. In *Conceptions, mesures et actions en santé publique.* Paris: Editions INSERM, 1982.

Jodelet, D. Les représentations socio-spatiales de la ville. In P. H. Derycke (ed.). *Conceptions de l'espace.* Paris: Université de Paris X, 1982.

Moscovici, S. The coming era of social representations. In J. P. Codol and J. P. Leyens (eds.): *Cognitive approaches to social behaviour.* The Hague: Nijhoff, 1982.

Houdebine, A. M. Sur les traces de l'imaginaire linguistique. In V. Aebischer and C. Forel (eds.). *Parlers masculins, parlers féminins?* Lausanne: Delachaux and Niestlé, 1983.

Coudin, G. Un exemple d'adaptation au changement social: La transformation des croyances et pratiques relations à la folie en milieu africain. *Cahiers d'Anthropologie,* **4.**

(D) Empirical studies

Abric, J.-C., Faucheux, C., Moscovici, S., Plon, M. Rôle de l'image du partenaire sur la coopération en situation de jeu. *Psychologie Française,* 1967, **12,** (4), 267–75.

Andrieux, C. Association de quelques variables socioculturelles avec la représentation du rôle de la mère. *Psychologie Française.* 1967, **12.**

Apfelbaum, E. Représentation du partenaire et interactions à propos d'un dilemme du prisonnier. *Psychologie Française,* 1967, **12.**

Flament, C. Représentation dans une situation conflictuelle. *Psychologie*

Française, 1967, **12**, 297–304.

Codol, J. P. Représentation de la tâche et comportements dans une situation sociale. *Psychologie Française*, 1968, **13**, 241–64.

Faucheux, C. and Moscovici, S. Self-esteem and exploitative behaviour in a game against chance and nature. *J. Personality & Social Psychology*, 1968, **8**, (1), 83–8.

Codol, J. P. Représentation de soi, d'autrui et de la tâche dans une situation sociale. *Psychologie Française*, 1969a, **14**, 217–28.

Codol, J. P. Notre terminologique sur l'emploi de quelques expressions concernant les activités et processus cognitifs en psychologie sociale. *Bulletin de Psychologie*, 1969b, **23**, 63–71.

Abric, J.-C. Image de la tâche, image du partenaire et coopération en situation de jeu. *Cahiers de Psychologie*. 1970, **13**, 71–82.

Codol, J. P. Influence de la représentation d'autrui sur l'activité des membres d'un groupe expérimental. *L'Année Psychologique*, 1970a, **70**, 131–50.

Codol, J. P. La représentation du groupe: Son impact sur le comportement des membres d'un groupe, et sur leurs représentations de la tâche, d'autrui, et de soi. *Bulletin de Psychologie*, 1970b, **24**, 111–22.

Abric, J.-C. Experimental study of group creativity: Task representation, group structure, and performance. *European J. Social Psychology*, 1971, **1**, (3), 311–26.

Codol, J. P. and Flament, C. Représentation de structures sociales simples dans lesquelles le sujet est impliqué. *Cahiers de Psychologie*, 1971, **14**, (3), 203–18.

Flament, C. Image des relations amicales dans les groupes hiérarchisés. *Année Psychologique*, 1971.

Abric, J.-C. and Kahan, J. The effects of representations and behaviour in experimental games. *European J. Social Psychology*, 1972, **2** (2), 129–44.

Abric, J.-C. and Mardellat, R. Etude expérimentale des représentations dans une situation conflictuelle: Rôle du contexte de la tâche, de la place et de la pratique des sujets dans la formation sociale. *Bulletin de Psychologie*, 309, **XXVII**, 1–4, 1973–4, 146–52.

Kaës, R. Représentations du groupe. La geste du groupe héroïque. *Les Etudes Philosophiques*, 1974, **1**, 45–58.

Codol, J. P. On the system of representations in a group situation. *European J. Social Psychology*, 1974, **4** (3), 343–65.

Codol, J. P. On the so-called 'superior conformity of the self' behaviour: Twenty experimental investigations. *European J. Social Psychology*, 1975, **5** (3), 457–501.

Rossignol, C. Approche expérimentale de la dynamique du champ de représentation lié à la notion de groupe. *Bulletin du CERP*, 1975, **XXIII** (1), 31–41.

Rossignol, C. and Flament, C. Décomposition de l'équilibre structural (aspects de la représentation du groupe), *L'Année Psychologique*, 1975, **75**, 417–25.

Abric, J.-C., and Vacherot, G. Méthodologie et étude expérimentale des représentations sociales: tâche, partenaire et comportement en situation de jeu. *Bulletin de Psychologie*, 323, **XXIX**, 14–14, 1975–6, 735–46.

Faugeron, C. and Robert, P. Les représentations sociales de la justice pénale. *Cahiers Internationaux de Sociologie*, 1976, **61**, 341–66.

Rossignol, C. and Houel, C. Analyse des composantes imaginaires de la représentation du groupe. *Cahiers de Psychologie*, 1976, **19,** 55–69.

Mollo, S. Les représentations réciproques des agents du processus éducatif: parents, enfants et maîtres. In Debesse and Mailaret (eds.). *Traité des Sciences Pédagogiques*, Vol. V, chapter XIV. Paris: Presses Universitaires de France, 1977.

Chombart de Lauwe, M.-J. La rappresentazione del bambino nel film. In *Infanzia nel cinema*. Universita di Ferrara, 1979.

Perrinjaquet, R. La genèse de la chambre d'enfant dans la pensée architecturale. *Architecture d'Aujourd'hui*, juin 1979.

Barjonet, P. E. L'influence sociale et les représentations des causes de l'accident de la route. *Le Travail Humain*, 1980, **43,** 243–53.

Chombart de Lauwe, M.-J. L'interaction enfant/télévision. *Neuropsychiatrie de l'Enfance*, 1981, **29,** (3), 157–68.

Lew Fai, P. Modèles culturels dominants et socialisation des enfants à l'Ile Maurice. In P. H. Chombart de Lauwe (ed.). *Transformation sociales et dynamique culturelle*. Paris: Editions du CNRS, 1981, 167–83.

Abric, J.-C. Cognitive processes underlying co-operation: The theory of social representation. In Derlega and Grzelak (eds.). *Co-operation and helping behavior*. New York: Academic Press, 1982, 73–94.

Chombart de Lauwe, M.-J. El niño icónico: el niño personaje de los media frente al niño real. *Infancia aprendizaze* (revista trimestral de estudues e investigacion), Madrid, 1982, **17,** 105–14.

Gaudin, A. Sociopédagogie des publications destinées à la jeunesse. Contribution à la psychosociologie des 9–16 ans. *Bulletin de Psychologie*, 1982, **XXXV,** 1–5, 266–71.

Chombart de Lauwe, M.-J. Il bambino nelle città, rivelatore sociale o mito. In OIKOS, *La rinascita della città*. Bologne: OIKOS, 1983.

Index

405

Index of names